Th⋯ ⋯rned on or before

STUDIES IN MODERN KENTISH HISTORY

(Photo.: B. Thomas, Kent Archives Office)

FELIX HULL AND ELIZABETH MELLING

STUDIES IN MODERN KENTISH HISTORY

PRESENTED TO
FELIX HULL AND ELIZABETH MELLING

on the occasion of the fiftieth anniversary of the Kent Archives Office

Edited by
ALEC DETSICAS AND NIGEL YATES

KENT ARCHAEOLOGICAL SOCIETY
MAIDSTONE
1983

Produced by Alan Sutton Publishing Limited, Gloucester
Printed in Great Britain by Redwood Burn Limited, Trowbridge

ISBN 0 906746 05 1

CONTENTS

List of Contributors, vii; List of Figures, ix; List of Plates, xi.

LIST OF CONTRIBUTORS

PETER BLOOMFIELD, B.A., Senior Assistant County Archivist, Gloucestershire County Council.

EILEEN BOWLER, B.A., B.Sc. (Econ.), Ph.D., Principal Lecturer in Geography, Thames Polytechnic.

CHRISTOPHER CHALKLIN, M.A., B.Litt., Reader in History, University of Reading.

JENNIFER CLARK, B.A., University Archivist, University of Loughborough.

PETER CLARK, M.A., F.R.Hist.S., Reader in Social History, University of Leicester.

BRYAN KEITH-LUCAS, M.A., D.Litt., Emeritus Professor of Government, University of Kent at Canterbury.

H.C.F. LANSBERRY, M.A., Ph.D., Lecturer in History, School of Continuing Education, University of Kent at Canterbury.

ANNE M. OAKLEY, M.A., F.S.A., A.L.A., Cathedral, City and Diocesan Archivist, Canterbury.

PAUL OLDHAM, M.A., Secretary, Kent Archives Fellowship.

DAVID ORMROD, B.Sc. (Econ.), Ph.D., Lecturer in Economic and Social History, University of Kent at Canterbury

KATHLEEN TOPPING, B.A., Assistant County Archivist, Kent County Council.

PETER WALNE, M.A., F.S.A., F.R.Hist.S., County Archivist, Hertfordshire County Council.

JOHN WHYMAN, B.Sc. (Econ.), Ph.D., Lecturer in Economic and Social History, University of Kent at Canterbury

NIGEL YATES, M.A., F.R.Hist.S., County Archivist, Kent County Council.

MICHAEL L. ZELL, M.A., Ph.D., Senior Lecturer in History, Thames Polytechnic.

LIST OF FIGURES

LIST OF PLATES

EDITORIAL PREFACE

When the Kent County Council decided, in no great blaze of publicity, but quietly and thoughtfully, to set up an Archives Office in 1933, it can have little dreamed of the prestige in which that office would be held, both nationally and indeed internationally, fifty years later. That such should be the case has been largely the result of the labours of the two co-recipients of this present volume, Felix Hull and Elizabeth Melling, who between them created the office as it is today. The individual appreciations by Peter Walne and Paul Oldham set their contributions to the office in a wider perspective, but there can be no doubt about the esteem in which they were, and are still, held by the County Council, by historians of Kent, both amateur and professional, and by the many users of the archives office, past and present. It is therefore highly appropriate and fitting that a volume published to mark the fiftieth anniversary of the Archives Office should be a series of essays in their honour, which also make a significant contribution to the historiography of Kent. It is also particularly appropriate that this volume should be published jointly by the Archives Office and the Kent Archaeological Society, since the two institutions have enjoyed a close relationship with one another for many years, and as both Felix Hull and Elizabeth Melling have served on the Council and various Committees of the latter body.

The early development of the Kent Archives Office was admirably rehearsed on the occasion of its silver jubilee[1] and requires only the briefest summary here, though one can afford some more detailed reflections on developments over the past two decades. The foundation of the Kent Archives Office resulted from the appointment of W.L. Platts as Clerk to the County Council in 1929. Platts took a personal interest in the archives of the county, far greater than was actually required by the duties attached to his office, and the first archivist – not *County Archivist* for Platts believed that that title was reserved to himself – Miss N. Dermot Harding was appointed in 1933. During her brief tenure of office, until 1936 when she became the first County Archivist of Somerset, Miss Harding was able to put in order the older records of the County Council and those of its predecessor (in administrative terms) the Quarter Sessions. Her successor, Richard Holworthy (1936–52), was able to negotiate the deposit or transfer of the records of the various Boards of Guardians and Commissioners of Sewers, and in 1946 the probate records for the dioceses of Canterbury and Rochester. Miss Harding was also able to design the purpose-built records block, completed in 1938. Despite the achievement of both early archivists, however, the impact of the Archives Office before 1952 was exceptionally limited. Platts himself still considered it to be essentially the County Clerk's private repository and was very unwilling to accept any records which did not belong to the County Council. This explains why a large number of the family collections acquired before 1952 were acquired as outright gifts, and why a number of those that were not were subject to a legal contract

1. *Twenty-Five Years: A Report on the Work of the Kent County Archives Office, 1933–1958;* see also F. Hull, The Kent Archives Office, *Arch. Cant.,* lxvi (1953), 64–71.

between the owner and the County Council governing their conditions of deposit.

It was with the appointment of Felix Hull (1952–80) as third archivist, and effectively first *County Archivist*, that the Kent Archives Office began to make the progress that has resulted in its present reputation in the archival world. It is always difficult to write with adequate perspective about recent events, but it is probably fair to say that this reputation has been achieved largely as a result of three particular policies that were each, in their way, trend-setters: publication, records management and the educational use of archives. But in addition to that the Archives Office was also able to extend greatly both its records holdings and its service to users.

The publications policy of the period between roughly 1955 and 1975 was geared in two particular directions. The first was, modelled on the example of Essex, the publication of comprehensive guides to records holdings. The core of this policy was the publication of the *Guide to the Kent Archives Office* in 1958, followed by the *First Supplement* in 1971 and *Second Supplement* in 1983. These were supplemented by the individual catalogues to important collections, still in progress, and the *Catalogue of Estate Maps,* reflecting Felix Hull's own particular interests. The second, and much more trend-setting, group of publications was the original six volumes in the *Kentish Sources* series, the brainchild of Elizabeth Melling. These local publications provided an ideal mixture of selected documents and commentary, which inspired a whole range of similar national publications in the 1970s. It is planned to continue this series, in a slightly different format, in the 1980s.

In the field of records management it was the pioneering work on the modern records of the Kent County Council in the 1960s which has inspired many other local government archivists to tackle the modern records of their own authorities in the years since then. Although some have been able to make advances on what has been done in Kent, particularly in respect of computerised techniques, it is the Kent Archives Office which is still turned to regularly by archivists and administrators, both in Britain and overseas, to give advice, from the depths of its experience, on the problems involved and the ways in which they can be overcome.

The educational use of archives, in which the Kent Archives Office played a pioneering role, has had a much more chequered development both locally and nationally. Whilst there is no doubting the validity of the principle whereby archives are used widely as a teaching source at all levels of education, there has been less of a concensus between archivists and educationists on the ways in which this can be best achieved. The early pioneers saw the answer in the secondment of teachers with an interest in the raw material of history. More recently there has been a strongly held view, at least among archivists, that the appointment of archivists with teaching ability might be more effective. There is no doubt that the educational activities of the Kent Archives Office since the mid-1960s have resulted in the improved use of primary sources in history teaching in some schools. But the benefits have perhaps been less wide-spread than was originally hoped, and the County Council is now going through a major period of reassessment of the objective and the best methods of its achievement.

In addition to what they have given to the care and administration of Kent's archives, Felix Hull and Elizabeth Melling have both made major contributions to the county's historio-graphy, as the bibliography of their published writings shows. It is therefore particularly fitting that they should be honoured with a volume of essays on aspects of Kentish history. It is, however, pleasurable, too, that some of these contributions should be from former colleagues: Peter Walne, Anne Oakley, Jennifer Clark, Peter Bloomfield and Christopher Chalklin.

Others are from present or former members of staff of the University of Kent – David Ormrod, Frederick Lansberry, Bryan Keith-Lucas and John Whyman – or recent regular users or close friends of the archives office – Paul Oldham, Eileen Bowler, Peter Clark and Michael Zell. We are grateful, as editors, for the quality, and punctuality of submission, of all these excellent contributions. We are also grateful to Kathleen Topping for her general help with the volume, and her preparation of the bibliography of Felix Hull's and Elizabeth Melling's publications, to the Council of the Kent Archaeological Society for agreeing to include it within the publications programme of the Society, and to those subscribers who have made its publication possible.

ALEC DETSICAS
NIGEL YATES

STUDIES IN MODERN KENTISH HISTORY

PRESENTED TO

FELIX HULL AND ELIZABETH MELLING

on the occasion of the fiftieth anniversary of the Kent Archives Office

FELIX HULL – AN APPRECIATION

PETER WALNE

That Felix Hull's retirement as County Archivist of Kent should be marked by the publication of this volume of essays is entirely appropriate. His services to the cause of the archives and history of the county since 1952 are amply attested to by the papers herein printed by his friends and colleagues. Of his services to the history of Kent others are better qualified to speak; this note concerns his archival career.

Trained originally as a teacher at Borough Road College before World War II, he entered the service of Essex County Council in 1938 as an Assistant Archivist under the then County Archivist, F.G. Emmison. He was one of the small band who entered the archival profession at a time when there was neither qualification required nor available and like his Essex colleagues of the time – Hilda Grieve, Edward Erith, Irvine Gray and the late Francis Steer – he learnt his job the hard way and learnt it well by experience and apprenticeship.

During World War II, Felix's career was interrupted by service in the Friends Ambulance Unit mainly in London where he endured and saw far more of the sufferings of his fellow men than many of us who saw active service in other theatres of war.

Peace restored, he returned to the Record Office in Chelmsford to take part in the heady developments of the archive service of the county, which marked the immediate post-war period and, at the same time, threw himself into the research on Essex agricultural and rural society between 1560 and 1640, under the tutelage of R.H. Tawney, which gained him his external Ph.D. in 1950 from the University of London.

In 1948 he secured appointment as first County Archivist of Berkshire, setting up office in one small room in the basement of the old Shire Hall in Reading and, in two years, as a one-man and half a tea-girl operation laid the secure foundations of the Berkshire Record Office. In 1950, the writer joined him – and the half tea-girl – as Assistant Archivist.

In December 1952, Felix left Berkshire for Kent and its already well-established, well-developed Record Office which he promptly and rightly renamed the Kent Archives Office. Aware before he left Berkshire that the traditional pattern of the archivist's task was on the brink of drastic change in content, course and comprehensiveness, he was amongst the pioneer local archivists to tackle the daunting challenge of records management as applied to the authority's own records. So much so that Kent was and still remains in many ways a model for the rest of us.

It was his commitment to records management which led, in time, to a part-time lectureship at the School of Library, Archive and Information Studies, University College, London, in the subject and to special lectureships and external examinerships in the subject and generally in archive studies at the archive training schools at Liverpool University and at the University College of North Wales in Bangor. So respected was his expertise that when the British Council, in collaboration with the International Council on Archives and Unesco held an international seminar on records management at Easthampstead Park, in his old, familiar Berkshire, in September 1980, Felix was appointed course director, a role he will repeat at a similar seminar in 1983. Though a late-comer to the international archive scene, Felix has participated in a number of international meetings and has undertaken tasks for Unesco and ICA, most notably a magisterial study of the archivally vexed question of the techniques and methods to be adopted in the selection of samples for permanent preservation of large bodies of records of common form, type or subject matter.

His involvement in the wider aspects of the archive profession in the United Kingdom dates from the foundation in 1947 of the Society of (Local) Archivists, of which he was a founder member. Ever since then as a member of its Council Committees (especially its Training Committee, of which he was for some years Chairman) and working groups, as Chairman of the Society from 1960 to 1963 and as President since 1976, his knowledge, experience, wisdom and common sense have always been at the disposal of his colleagues, who have never ceased to benefit from them to the great advantage of the profession he chose to follow more than forty years ago.

ELIZABETH MELLING – AN APPRECIATION

PAUL OLDHAM

Elizabeth Melling prepared for her career by obtaining a B.A. in history at Durham University in 1949 and a Diploma in Archives Administration at Liverpool University in 1950 before joining the Archives Office of the Kent County Council as Assistant Archivist. She was appointed Assistant Archivist (Education) in 1958, and Assistant County Archivist in 1966, though in fact she had been the senior assistant from 1953. Having prepared for her career in the bracing North, Elizabeth Melling clearly found the softer southern clime to her liking as the Kent Archives Office absorbed her professional energies and interest until her retirement in 1980. At a time when several changes of employer are recommended by personnel experts as a way of 'getting on', the devotion and loyalty to Kentish records and local history must be particularly commended.

As a result, her knowledge of the records collection and of the users of the archives service, their needs as well as their eccentricities, is marked. Her knowledge of the local history of Kent is wide and deep. Few researchers could not benefit from her advice on documentary sources, as anyone with a genuine interest in historical research could look for encouragement, guidance and painstaking help. This was so important as demands on the Archives Office increased with the expansion of public interest, and public participation, in the study of the past. In addition to the rising number of professional researchers, increasing numbers of people participate in local history and archaeology through societies, groups and adult education classes. Interest in family history flourishes as never before. Amateur researchers have appreciated the help and encouragement promoting the existing smooth working relationship between professional and amateurs. The contrast with the state of practical archaeology in Kent, where the absence of a guiding institution has significantly contributed to the atmosphere of bitterness and resentment, could not be more striking.

Her lectures throughout Kent have done much to promote interest while the value of her work as Assistant Archivist (Education), as the contact between schools and the Archives Office, started the excellent reputation of the office in this field. Her work to bring documentary sources to the attention of a wider audience owes much to her own combination of professional interest and participation in voluntary activities. For example, she has served as a President of the Maidstone Scientific and Antiquarian Society and has been a member of the Council of the Kent Archaeological Society for some years. These interests have enabled her to avoid the danger of seeing an archives office as an isolated and inward looking backwater, where users are resented as a disturbance to a peaceful, ordered way of life; not all archivists (let alone museum curators!) can say the same. However, as with her published work, Elizabeth Melling has made no concession on academic standards in the cause of popularisation.

The authorship of the *Kentish Sources* series of books remains the most important aspect of her pioneering work in spreading knowledge of records. Using documents from the Kent Archives Office, this series shows the contribution that the study of original manuscript sources can make to the study of history. The common theme is the effect of national events, changes and themes on particular localities, and the influence of local affairs on the nation. The first volume *Some Roads and Bridges* appeared in 1959 to coincide with an interesting exhibition of documents, in Maidstone Museum, entitled 'Transport in Kent'. The succeeding volumes were II *Kent and the Civil War* (1960), III *Aspects of Agriculture and Industry* (1961), IV *The Poor* (1964), V *Some Kentish Houses* (1965) and VI *Crime and Punishment* (1969). No one document can give a complete picture as single, unrelated documents can only illustrate particular instances of known trends and perhaps supply some additional information. Therefore it is difficult to draw general conclusions from the books. For example, volume II gives examples of how individual royalists suffered in Kent during the Civil War but a general picture cannot emerge from the individual cases. The documents were selected with the intention of making some local sources more widely known and, as the books were planned for the general reader, each book contains an introduction to the subject. For example, the introduction to Volume VI gives a history of courts and the working of the law, describing the types of records available and changing attitudes to crime and punishment. There have been many expressions of regret that the first *Kentish Sources* series ended in 1969, and there cannot be a better testimonial to the success of the series than that.

However, Elizabeth Melling was soon engaged on the *History of the Kent County Council*, a major work which was published in 1975 as a monument to the former county council that disappeared in the reorganisation of local government. The book describes, in narrative form, the development of the services of the county council and the way in which events shaped this development. It is a chronicle that does not attempt a historical evaluation of the county council's achievements. The main sources are formal documents recording decisions made, such as the Quarterly Volumes of Committee Reports, together with the annual and other reports of committees and chief officers. There is little information on the process leading up to the making of decisions or the role of individual Members or officers. This is a pity as interviews with former Members and officers, and reference to their personal papers, could have produced a more vivid account. A whiff of gossip or scandal will always focus attention. However, the thorough mastery of the sources used is most impressive.

Whilst the scale of the problems faced by the county council has changed, Members to-day will recognise the perennial arguments about road maintenance or standards in education, not to mention the stop-go financial policies of successive central governments that the county council had to pretend to comply with under protest. Elizabeth Melling recognised the decade of the 1930s as the climax with all major services finally brought under the control of all purpose authorities whilst new functions, such as planning were developing. The Reports produced were not equalled before or subsequently. Only a dedicated archivist could unconsciously judge an authority by the quality of records produced as a sign of efficiency and care (but perhaps this is as good an indicator as any!).

Whilst her career was based in Kent, her standing in her profession nationally is attested by her election to the Council of the Society of Archivists, becoming Vice-Chairman of the Society in 1976–77. In addition, she served as Chairman of the South-East Region of the Society. She brought to her profession the same high standards, dedication and integrity that she shows in her private life. Although Elizabeth Melling had to retire due to ill health in 1980, it is to be hoped that she will continue her work and interest in records and local history – she has so much to offer.

A SELECTED BIBLIOGRAPHY OF THE PUBLICATIONS OF FELIX HULL, B.A., Ph.D., D.Litt., F.R.Hist.S.

'Court Rolls of the manor of Great Dunmow, 1382–1507', *Essex Review* (July 1940), 152–7.

'Early Friends in central and northern Essex', *Essex Review* (April 1946), 64–72.

Illustrated Handbook to Exhibition of Essex Estate, County and Official Maps [with F.W. Steer], Chelmsford, 1947.

'More Essex Friends of the Restoration period', *Essex Review* (April 1948), 60–71.

'Billericay market in the days of Queen Anne', *Essex Review* (July 1949), 122–6.

Guide to the Berkshire Record Office, Reading, 1952.

'The Work of the Berkshire Record Office', *Berkshire Archaeological Journal,* li (1952), 10–16.

'The Kent Archives Office', *Arch. Cant.,* lxvi (1953), 64–71.

'The Lathe in the Early Sixteenth Century', *Arch. Cant.,* lxviii (1954), 97–100.

'An early Kentish militia roll', *Arch. Cant.,* lxviii (1954), 159–66.

'Local Archives of Great Britain. II. The Kent Archives Office', *Archives,* ii (1955), 237–46.

'A tour into Kent, 1759', *Arch. Cant.,* lxix (1955), 171–8.

'Kentish Historiography', *Arch. Cant.,* lxx (1956), 221–30.

'English Politics and the Sheriff of Kent, 1378', *Arch. Cant.,* lxxi (1957), 206–13 [with Rosemary A. Keen].

Guide to the Kent County Archives Office [editor], Maidstone, 1958.

'Melcombe Mill: a fourteenth century building account', *Arch. Cant.,* lxxii (1958), 54–9.

'The Custumal of Kent', *Arch. Cant.,* lxxii (1958), 148–59.

'Archives services and smaller repositories. II. The county's case', *Archives,* iv (1960), 191–3.

A Calendar of the White and Black Books of the Cinque Ports, 1432–1955, H.M.S.O., 1967.

'The spittlehouse of Key Street', *Arch. Cant.,* lxxxii (1967), 179–83.

'John Marsham, a forgotten antiquary', *Arch. Cant.,* lxxxiii (1968), 49–54.

'The management of modern records', *Society of Archivists Journal,* iv (April 1970), 45–50.

Guide to the Kent County Archives Office, First Supplement, 1957–1968 [editor], Maidstone, 1972.

Handlist of Kent County Council Records, 1889–1945, Maidstone, 1972.

'The Coming of the Barons, 1403', *Arch. Cant.,* lxxxvii (1972), 1–8.

'"Modern Records" then and now', *Society of Archivists Journal,* iv (April 1972), 395–9.

Kentish Maps and Map-Makers, 1590–1840, Maidstone, 1973.

Catalogue of Estate Maps, 1590–1840, in the Kent County Archives Office, Maidstone, 1974.

'"Momento Mori" or Dr. Cliff's diary: An unusual demographic document', *Arch. Cant.,* lxxxix (1974), 11–23.

'Qualification or ?', *Society of Archivists Journal,* v (October 1976), 369–72.

A History of Bearsted and Thurnham [editor] [with M. Bourner and R. Tate], Bearsted and Thurnham History Book Committee, 1978.

'The archivist and society', *Society of Archivists Journal,* vi (April 1979), 125–30.

'The archivist and the genealogist', *Genealogists Magazine*, xix (June 1979), 339–45.

'Memoranda from the Queenborough Statute Book, 1452–1556', *A Kentish Miscellany* [editor], 79–101, Kent Archaeological Society, 1979.

'The appraisal of documents: problems and pitfalls', *Society of Archivists Journal,* vi (April 1980), 287–91.

'The archivist should not be an historian', *Society of Archivists Journal,* vi (April 1980), 253–9.

The use of sampling techniques in the retention of records: A RAMP study with guidelines, Paris: UNESCO, 1981.

A BIBLIOGRAPHY OF THE PUBLICATIONS OF ELIZABETH MELLING, B.A.

'Kentish Tradesmen in the early nineteenth century', *Arch. Cant.*, lxvi (1953), 98–102.

Some Roads and Bridges, Kentish Sources I [editor], Maidstone, 1959.

Kent and the Civil War, Kentish Sources II [editor], Maidstone, 1960.

Aspects of Agriculture and Industry, Kentish Sources III [editor], Maidstone, 1962.

The Poor, Kentish Sources IV [editor], Maidstone, 1964.

Some Kentish Houses, Kentish Sources V [editor], Maidstone, 1965.

Crime and Punishment, Kentish Sources VI [editor], Maidstone, 1969.

History of the Kent County Council, 1889–1974, Maidstone, 1975.

Guide to the Kent Archives Office, Second Supplement, 1969–1980, [editor], Maidstone, 1983.

THE CROMWELLIAN COMMISSION IN KENT, 1655–57

PETER BLOOMFIELD

On 26 October, 1655, Oliver Cromwell wrote to Thomas Kelsey to convey his 'Orders and Instructions . . . for securing the Peace of this Commonwealth.'[1] The peace, shaken by the rising of 1655 and threatened by continued Royalist plotting, was to be maintained by military government. The country had been divided into eleven districts, each under a major-general.[2] Kelsey, who already held the key post of Lieutenant of Dover Castle,[3] had been appointed in August to command the militia in Kent and Surrey,[4] and was now in receipt of orders which provided him with a blueprint for action and set out the names of commissioners who were to assist him in Kent.

This Commission, dominated by Cromwellian colonels and captains, was a very different affair from the County Committee of the 1640s. Local interests were now firmly subordinated to the requirements of central government. The appointment of the Commission, its terms of reference, and its activities during the period November 1655 to January 1657 are recorded in a minute book which the Kent Archives Office purchased in 1980.[5]

Some twenty-nine commissioners[6] are named in the orders, with four more added later. The numbers attending varied from meeting to meeting, but those principally present apart from Kelsey were: Sir Michael Livesey (the Regicide), Colonels Crompton and Needler, and Captains Bowles, Browne, Kadwell, Monins and Pyke, together with Alexander Roberts, John Rabson, and William Palmer.

Thomas Kelsey had, in some ways, the most challenging job of Cromwell's major-generals because the Royalists in Kent were most readily and easily in touch with the exiled Court, and the proximity of the county to the Continent of Europe has always made its shores the most likely place for an invading force to land. Kelsey had, at the beginning of 1655, been highly successful in unearthing the Kentish element of that great national conspiracy which most dramatically manifested itself in Penruddock's rising in March. He had seized the magazine of the Kentish Royalists and arrested leaders like Sir John Boys and Edward Hales the Younger.[7] His soldiers and spies maintained a firm hold on the county and he was able to keep Secretary of State John Thurloe fully informed of developments in his area.

Although there are several different strands to the Royalist conspiracies of the 1650s the most serious threat to the Cromwellian regime came from the Sealed Knot. Formed late in 1653, the Knot had the endorsement of King Charles II. It consisted, by May 1654 of six

---

1. Kent Archives Office U2341, Minutes of the Commissioners for Kent, 1655–1657.
2. *CSPD 1655*, 232–233.
3. *DNB*.
4. *CSPD 1655*, 275.
5. U2341 *op. cit.* The volume, of 92 pages in the hand of John Thatcher, Clerk to the Commissioners, may be incomplete in respect of its last few leaves.
6. See Appendix I
7. A.M. Everitt, *The Community of Kent and the Great Rebellion, 1640–1660*, 284.

prominent Royalists,[8] and through secret correspondence and the use of agents worked towards the organization of an armed uprising. Yet, to many Royalists, the Knot was over-cautious and, in 1655, more vigorous elements had joined together to promote action. This 'Action Party' was composed of Royalists less prominent in status than the leaders of the Knot and lacking close connections with Sir Edward Hyde. Its high command included two Kentish men, Sir Thomas Peyton and Richard Thornhill.[9]

Whatever the failings of these Royalist groups, their activities and the rising of 1655 combined to maintain pressure upon the Government and caused it to regard all Royalists with suspicion. In the unsettled atmosphere of the time it is not surprising that the main concern of the Government was security and the preservation of the peace.

To secure the peace in Kent, Kelsey and his Commission were provided with a nine-point plan. These 'Orders and Instructions' were, in summary:

(1)   to imprison or banish, and to sequester the estates of those involved in designs against the Protector;
(2)   to imprison or banish any who 'appear by their words or actions to adhere to the interest of the late King or of Charles Stuart his son';
(3)   to levy a Decimation Tax;
(4)   to transport those Royalists who did not possess a taxable estate and 'who live loosely and without labour';
(5)   to prevent Royalist families from employing sequestered or ejected ministers and teachers;
(6)   to curtail the activities of such ministers and teachers;
(7)   to stop members of 'the late King's Party' from holding arms;
(8)   to provide for the sequestration of those sent overseas who returned without licence;
(9)   to empower the Commissioners to take oaths, send for persons, papers and records, and to imprison anyone for contempt of their orders.[10]

The principal burden of work of the Commission is revealed by the title on the cover of its minute book: 'Decimations'. It was the commissioners' duty to assess, levy and enforce payment of an extraordinary tax. The basis of this impost was a tax of £10 on every £100 of real estate, although it also covered personalty.

It was designed to fall upon those who had been sequestered for delinquency or who had served under arms for the King in the Civil Wars. Undoubtedly, there was a punitive element in this taxation, to which the essential background are the events of 1648 and 1655. Indeed, Cromwell justified its wide application by an accusation of general complicity, in thought if not in deed: 'The late King's Party have notoriously shown that they adhere to their old principles and have been all along hatching disturbance by secret assassination or open force. Therefore, it will not be thought strange that we have seized many who were not in open arms in the late insurrection, nor that we have laid a burden on the estates of the rest, to defray the charge that they have occasioned.'[11] And again: 'It may seem great severity to tax the whole party, when

8.   The six were: John, Lord Belasyse; Sir William Compton; Henry Hastings, Lord Loughborough; Colonel John Russell; Colonel Edward Villiers; Sir Richard Willys.
9.   D. Underdown, *Royalist Conspiracy in England, 1649–1660*.
10.   U2341, 1–6.
11.   *CSPD 1655*, 406.

few have been convicted or detected, in which case their whole estates had been confiscated, but we appeal to all indifferent men whether the Party was not generally involved in this business.'[12]

Whatever the justifications, however, the aim remained to secure the maximum yield rather than to punish. To meet the financial burden of military rule the net was spread widely, and it is significant that top of the list of those summoned was the richest man in the county, John Tufton, Earl of Thanet.

Thanet had been an active Royalist from the outset of the Civil War, joining King Charles I at Nottingham with a hundred horse in August 1642.[13] His estate sequestered, he compounded for £9000[14] in December 1644, paying dearly for his loyalty with the devastation of his woods and parks, and by loss of deer and other animals. Fear of such consequences may well have been in his mind in 1648 when his sudden change of direction struck a major blow against the Royalist cause in Kent.

At first, Thanet appeared as enthusiastic as ever, raising 4000 men from his Kentish estates. Then he had second thoughts, attempted a compromise with the Parliament, and accepted their offer of indemnity.[15]

Yet, neither this desertion, nor his appointment as Sheriff in 1654,[16] were to count in his favour in 1655. His great wealth made him a prime target for decimation, and Thanet was assessed for payment of £314 15s., and further ordered, on 9 March 1656, to bring in particulars of his estates outside of Kent.[17] When he was slow to pay an order was drawn up for the sequestration of his estates in Sussex and his rents secured to satisfy a sum of £40 outstanding.[18] Thanet protested and demurred, and was eventually granted a reduction. Yet, Parliament made no allowance for his good service in 1648, and he was regarded as a 'suspected person', his movements monitored by a system of registration.

Under this system lists of Royalists were compiled by local registrars and the names forwarded to London for entry in volumes of Returns, arranged by county. When a suspect travelled he had to notify the local registrar, who would send details of the intended place of residence to the central office in London. A similar notification had to be made of arrival and departure. In this way, the major-generals both kept the Government informed, and were themselves notified, of all movements of suspected persons. Thus, on 1 May 1656, it is recorded that 'John, Earl of Thanet, of the parish of Buttolphs Aldersgate, on the 1st present certified his L[ordshi]pphs intention the same day to remove from his said dwelling to Hothfield in the Countie of Kent.'[19]

If Thanet, by virtue of his estates both inside and outside of Kent, was the wealthiest of those summoned for assessment, the most highly rated in Kent was Edward Hales the Younger of Tunstall.

12. *Ibid.,* 410.
13. H.F. Abell, *Kent and the Great Civil War,* 66.
14. Kent Archives Office U455 04, Tufton MSS. Ordinance Discharging the Earl of Thanet from his Delinquency, 21 December, 1644.
15. Abell, *op. cit.,* 138, 203.
16. Kent Archives Office Qb/C 1/39, Letter from John, Earl of Thanet as 'Sheriffe' to the Mayor of Queenborough, 1654.
17. U2341, 12, 20, 49, 86. His charge was eventually settled at £261.
18. U455 04, Order for the Sequestration of the Earl of Thanet, 10 April 1656.
19. A. Rhodes, 'Suspected persons in Kent', *Arch. Cant.,* xxiii (1898), 76.

Hales, grandson and heir of the committeeman Sir Edward Hales (who died in 1654) contributed nearly 25 per cent of the total yield of the Kentish decimation. Involved in the Kentish rising of 1643, he had really come to the fore in 1648 when, under the influence of Roger L'Estrange, he agreed to lead the insurgents and placed £80,000 at their disposal.[20] Although superseded as general by George Goring, Earl of Norwich, Hales' role in the Second Civil War marked him down for special attention.

Summoned by the commissioners to attend on 4 December, 1655, he was assessed for £773 17s. Affirming in April 1656, that he had no estates outside of Kent, he subsequently petitioned for a reduction – and allowances were, in fact, made in respect of a number of payments issuing out of his estate.[21] Like Thanet, Hales was a 'suspected person', a watch kept on his movements by the authorities.[22]

Thanet and Hales were certainly the most prominent, in terms of wealth, of those summoned to appear before the Commission. Over 380 names are featured in the minute book in this connection, the volume constituting something of a directory of Kentish Royalists.[23] Many Royalists escaped the tax, though, because their estates fell below the £100 minimum laid down, a clear indication that the aim was fiscal rather than punitive. The minutess reveal a marked concentration of Royalists in the north-west of the county, especially in the area of Bromley, Dartford and the Crays.[24] This was an area of great activity in the early days of the Kentish Rising of 1648, as the petitioners gathered to march on the rendez-vous point of Blackheath. Rochester, where Hales sought to muster his forces and which later defied Fairfax, also yields a significant number of names. In east Kent the main concentration is in and around Canterbury, scene of revolt at Christmas, 1647.

Several of those summoned by the commissioners, it is specifically noted, had been involved in the 'Insurrection' of 1648. Among those so named are William Steed and Arnold King.

Dr. William Steed of Harrietsham was ordered to appear, in December 1655, having confessed that 'he was at Maidstone in the time of the Insurrection of 1648'.[25] He had been informed against in 1650, accused of supplying arms, money, horses, and men to the Royalist party, and with harbouring fugitives in his house.[26] Steed was a man of some wealth, as his assessment at £107 9s. 4d. shows, and a considerable debate was generated on his case. The doctor claimed a reduction, later allowed, on account of £400 being paid as an annuity to Lady Peyton, granted to her by her late husband, Cromer Steed.[27]

Arnold King of Bromley was likewise the subject of much discussion. He was accused of aiding the Cavaliers 'with Horse and Armes' and Jackson, the minister of Harrietsham, was summoned to testify against him. King was regarded with considerable suspicion and, apart from bringing in particulars of his estates, was ordered to provide 'sureties for his Peaceable demeanour'.[28] His name appears on the list of 'suspected persons'.[29] The commissioners

20. Abell, op. cit., 181.
21. U2341 12, 20, 52, 74, 79.
22. Rhodes, loc. cit.
23. See Appendix II.
24. Fig. 1
25. U2341, 18
26. Abell, op. cit., 241
27. U2341, 48, 56.
28. Ibid., 36.
29. Arch. Cant., xxiii (1898), 71.

assessed King at £40 and sent a messenger to deliver the demand for payment, but he was absent, and it was left with his maid-servant. When King proved recalcitrant, he was threatened with sequestration. Further investigation showed that he had not declared all his lands in Kent, while he refused to give particulars of his estates in other counties. For a second time, in July 1656, he was threatened with sequestration, and this, finally, led to a settlement.[30]

While the Royalism of Steed, King and many others was quite evident, it soon became apparent that certain of those named by the commissioners had been included in error. Thus, Nicholas Ruffine of Sheppey, it was admitted, had been 'sent for by a mistake'; while Edmund Waller of Paul's Cray 'was summoned upon a misinformacion'.[31]

The inclusion of Waller, a poet of Royalist sympathies, but cousin to John Hampden, is particularly interesting. A plot, in 1643, to secure London for Charles I and to force Parliament to make peace, bears his name. Imprisoned and banished, he returned in 1651, and by December 1655, had managed to ingratiate himself sufficiently with Cromwell to be appointed a commissioner for trade.[32]

While some individuals were mistakenly summoned, others were able to obtain a discharge by claiming good service to the Parliamentary cause in the past. Sir Thomas Peirs, for example, satisfied the commissioners 'of his good affecion to the State . . . by being in Armes for the late Parliament and many other wayes. And that he did in compliance with ye Insurrection in 1648: he did act under a force as appears by the order of Indemnity of the Committee of Kent.'[33]

Very different was the case of those identified by the commissioners as 'dangerous persons', and summoned to give security for 'their peaceable demeanour'. Such were Thomas Bateman, Thomas Kadwell and Willcock Knight, all of Lydd, Robert Spice of Old Romney, and Thomas Dixon of Canterbury.[34]

In a similar category were two Yalding victuallers, Nicholas Bar(e)foot and William Brooke. Accused of 'aydeing assisting or abetting the late King or his party' and refusing to give security, they were committed to Maidstone Gaol on 19 March, 1656. The commissioners continued to keep these two under scrutiny and, on 10 September, they were ordered to appear by 2.00 p.m. with their beer licences 'if they have any at their perills'.[35] Yalding, it might be noted, had been a centre of Royalist revolt in 1643.[36]

Those summoned to provide particulars of their estates cover a wide range of political persuasion. At one end are uncompromisingly Royalist figures, men who had suffered for their cause in the first Civil War and were involved in the various conspiracies of the 1650s. Such were Sir Thomas Peyton, Richard Thornhill, Sir John Boys and Sir John Mayne. Next, there were those who had fought for the King in 1648, but whose previous inclination had been for the Parliament. The prime example of these is Sir Richard Hardres. Then, there were those who had tried to steer a middle course, moderates like Sir Roger Twisden and Sir George

30. U2341, 63, 72, 76.
31. *Ibid.*, 18, 30.
32. *DNB.*
33. U2341, 17.
34. *Ibid.*, 49.
35. *Ibid.*, 48, 85.
36. Kent Archives Office Q/SO21, Quarter Sessions Order (Easter 1644) for a pension to be paid to Henry Clerke, who had suffered in 'the late rebellion and risinge at Yalding and Tunbridge.'

Sondes. At the other end of the scale were those, albeit few in number, who had inclined to the Parliament side and who, indeed, were quickly able to prove their service. Such were Sir William Mann, Sir Edward Scott, and Sir John Sedley.

Sir Thomas Peyton of Knowlton, though not presenting the popular image of a Cavalier, was nevertheless a Royalist of tenacity and endurance. Expelled from the House of Commons in 1644, his estates sequestered, he compounded for £1000[37] but emerged to take a leading role, with Hales, in the events of 1648. Then, in spite of frequent and lengthy imprisonments, Peyton continued to work for the Cause in the 1650s. Knowlton Court became a centre of conspiracy, and he emerged as leader of the Kentish Royalists, a member of the high command of the 'Action Party' and, in 1659, of the 'Great Trust'.[38] Peyton's inclusion in the Decimation list is not the least surprising; nor is his procrastination, with threats of sequestration for non-payment in March and June 1656.[39]

Richard Thornhill of Olantigh, Peyton's principal co-conspirator in the 1650s, was a Royalist cast in a very different mould from the cool, sober owner of Knowlton Court. An inscription on his wife's monument in Wye Church recalls 'a gentleman, whose loyalty and sufferings, steady adherence, and large contributions to the Royal Cause were not inferior to the greatest examples.'[40] In stark contrast, Peyton's sister-in-law, Dorothy Osborne, describes him as 'the veriest beast that ever was', damning him as a drunken debauchee.[41] Yet, one cannot fault Thornhill's activity on behalf of the Stuarts, from the moment that he raised, at his own expense, a body of horse for the King at Nottingham in 1642, through sequestration and war to conspiracy. He was described as the 'Chief Agent' in Kent for the abortive rising of 1655,[42] and he was arrested on Kelsey's orders in January. Like Peyton, he was a member of the 'Action Party's' high command.[43]

Thornhill's decimation, therefore, was thoroughly deserved, and he was amongst the first summoned to bring in particulars of their estates. Rated at £128, he did his best to be obstructive, and by September 1656 he was behind in his payments. The commissioners ordered his tenants to withold payment of rent to force his compliance, but this had no effect. In December, therefore, it was decided that orders should be sent 'unto two or three of his chiefe tenants to keepe soe much rent in their handes as is due to ye State for payment of his decimation.'[44]

Sir John Boys of Bonnington, who had been knighted by King Charles I for his gallant defence of Donnington Castle during the first Civil War,[45] was another Royalist who suffered for his loyalty yet never wavered in his determination to see Charles II back on his rightful throne. He had taken up arms anew in 1648, fighting with a desperate valour in east Kent when there was little hope left of success. Wounded in an unsuccessful attack upon Roundhead

37. Abell, *op. cit.,* 98n.
38. Underdown, *op. cit.*, 109, 235–236, 267.
39. U2341, 48, 61.
40. Thornhill was married to Joanna, daughter of the Cornish Royalist Sir Beville Grenvile who was slain at the Battle of Lansdown in 1643.
41. G.C. Moore-Smith (ed.), *Letters of Dorothy Osborne to William Temple* (1928), 177.
42. Everitt, *op. cit.*, 283.
43. Underdown, *op. cit.*, 109.
44. U2341, 12, 20, 86, 89.
45. H.C.B. Rogers, *Battles and Generals of the Civil Wars, 1642–1651*, 87.

troops near Sandown Castle, his pessimistic utterance, 'Poor Prince, what will he do now? All is lost, all is lost', belied his indomitable spirit. He was soon involved in the conspiracies of the 1650s. As one of the subordinate officers named as party to Gerard's Plot in 1651, he was arrested on the confession of the Royalist agent Thomas Coke, and only released on heavy security. Seized again in February 1655, in consequence of his involvement in the scheme for a general uprising,[46] Boys was summoned by the commissioners in December and assessed to pay £25 6s., although the charge was reduced on appeal to £22 6s.[47]

The Decimation tax had no more of a deterrent effect upon Boys than it did upon Peyton. He continued to be associated with Royalist conspiracy, was a member of the 'Great Trust', and instigated the Kentish Petition of 1660 which formed part of the final movement to Restoration.

Sir John Mayne[48] of Linton Place was another Kentishman whose devotion to the Stuart Cause was maintained through great adversity. He had been active in securing support for the famous Kentish Petition of March 1642,[49] and was numbered among the 'divers young gentlemen' who drew up the Petition and Instructions of July,[50] and carried them to the King at York. With the onset of hostilities he raised troops from amongst his tenants, was sequestered, and later compounded for a very large sum. In 1648, Mayne was one of the most active leaders in the Royalist rising in Kent, and featured prominently in the Battle of Maidstone, in which he was at first believed to have been slain.[51]

Mayne was involved in the conspiracy of 1655, but although summoned by the commissioners and assessed at £64 18s., it was found upon investigation 'that his whole estate is in the handes of the several persons to whom the same are engaged', and proceedings against him had to be suspended.[52]

Sir Richard Hardres[53] of Upper Hardres was prominent amongst those who had supported the Parliamentary cause in the first Civil War yet exerted themselves for the King in 1648. He is believed to have opposed Dering's Petition in the Spring of 1642,[54] and he served on the County Committee in the early 1640s.[55] In 1648, by contrast, he appeared under arms with the Regiment of the Lathe of St. Augustine in support of Hales, Peyton and the petitioners, and subsequently took a leading role in the fighting in east Kent, at the Siege of Dover Castle and in the action around the fortresses of Deal, Walmer and Sandown. Following his surrender to Fairfax he was imprisoned and sequestered, and had to compound.[56] Summoned by the commissioners in 1655, Hardres was assessed at £45, although this was reduced on appeal.[57] In

46. Abell, *op. cit.,* 117; Everitt, *op. cit.,* 270, 282, 287.
47. U2341, 16, 20, 84.
48. Variously spelt Mayne, Mayney, Mainy, Manny.
49. T.P.S. Woods, *Prelude to Civil War, 1642: Mr. Justice Malet and the Kentish Petitions,* 65.
50. Kent Archives Office U47/47 01, Diary of Sir Roger Twisden, 1635–1672; J.M. Russell, *History of Maidstone,* 250. Woods, *op. cit.,* 105–106.
51. Fairfax reported in his dispatch, dated at Rochester 4 June 1648: 'Sir John Mainy and divers others of quality were slain.'
52. U2341, 12, 20, 35, 46.
53. Variously spelt Hardres, Hardress, Hardred.
54. Woods, *op. cit.,* 42, 63.
55. Abell, *op. cit.,* 97, 101.
56. John Bavington-Jones, *Annals of Dover,* 29; Everitt, *op. cit.,* 243–244, 249–250; Abell, *op. cit.,* 188, 202.
57. U2341, 12, 37, 45.

spite of his actions in 1648, and even though he was looked upon as a 'suspected person',[58] Hardres was essentially a moderate.

Sir Roger Twisden of Roydon Hall, East Peckham, appears on the Decimation list as the arch-type neutral. His very prominence in Kentish society in 1642 had made it anathema to Parliament that he should decline to take sides.

Twisden had been opposed to Ship Money and had disliked Laud's methods of church reform. Yet, although opposed to the extreme claims of the Royalist Party, he had become seriously concerned at the activities of Pym and his associates in the Commons. In Kent, he had resented the presumption of Sir Michael Livesey (under Kelsey, the leading commissioner in Kent, 1655–57) in promoting a Puritan petition as representative of the feelings of the county. The result was Twisden's involvement in the great events at the Maidstone Assizes in March.

Although not responsible for drawing up the Kentish Petition of March 1642, Twisden encouraged its distribution, and was arrested along with its architects, Sir Edward Dering, Sir George Strode, and Richard Spencer.[59] Thus began a most unhappy period for the Knight of Roydon Hall, in and out of custody, his estates under sequestration, and his timber felled.

The House of Commons wanted Twisden to declare his opposition to the Royalist Party, 'to promise I would defend the liberties of the subject',[60] but, as he told Sir Francis Barnham, his conscience forbade such. Conversely, he would not join the King at Oxford. 'He would commit himself unreservedly to neither party, and thus, perhaps, incurred the enmity of both.'[61]

In June 1643, Twisden attempted to flee the country in disguise, but was arrested at Bromley, where the Kentish Committee was sitting, and he was recognised by Sir Anthony Weldon. It is known that Weldon (whose son, Ralph, was appointed a commissioner in 1655) bore a grudge against Twisden, who noted in his Journal that 'there had beene former differences betwixt our two families'.[62]

Returned to custody, Twisden found that he had been under sequestration since May. Try as he might to establish the reasons for this and to obtain justice, he was faced at every turn by the hostility of the Kent Committee. Apart from Weldon, Twisden had another vindictive opponent in Sir John Sedley of St. Clere, whom he considered was out to ruin him. There is a touch of irony that when the commissioners drew up the Decimation list in 1655, Sedley and Twisden were named on the same page. Twisden's case was respited in January 1656, and there is no evidence from the Minutes that he was actually required to pay.

Sir George Sondes of Lees Court had, like Twisden, been imprisoned and sequestered during the first Civil War. His refusal to support the County Committee coupled with his considerable wealth marked him down for special attention although, as Twisden noted in his Journal, 'they could not charge him with any delinquency.'[63] Sondes himself outlined his dilemma, one which faced so many in 1642, of loyalty to the King on the one hand, sympathy with the just claims of Parliament on the other: 'I was bound by many several oaths to my King

58. Rhodes, *loc. cit.*
59. Woods, *op. cit.,* 41–46.
60. U47/47 01; *Arch. Cant.,* ii (1859), 196.
61. *Arch. Cant.,* i (1858), 185.
62. U47/47 01; *Arch. Cant.,* iii (1860), 146.
63. U47/47 01; *Arch. Cant.,* ii (1859), 204–205.

which I did not so readily know how to dispense with. Yet I was never so great a royalist as to forget I was a freeborn subject.'[64]

Sondes was eventually forced to compound for £3500. Like Twisden, his neutrality proved even more expensive due to the mismanagement of his estates under sequestration, and the destruction of his woodlands. Further, it rendered him liable to the Decimation tax, for which he was initially assessed at £200. He complained, in June 1656, that he was over-rated, and the charge was later reduced by half.[65]

The inclusion of Sir John Sedley of St. Clere in the Decimation list is little more than an ironic joke, a reflection of his irascible nature. A staunch Parliamentarian, he had been appointed a Deputy Lieutenant for Kent in April 1642, at the very moment that he was providing the Lords with evidence against the Royalist Sir George Strode over the latter's responsibility for the Kentish Petition.[66] A member of the County Committee under Sir Anthony Weldon, Sedley had been active in the suppression of the Royalist Rising of 1643. He was an implacable enemy of Sir Roger Twisden[67] while, on the Committee he quarrelled with his fellow members. In December 1646, he fell out with Weldon himself and was arrested and removed from his military command. His subsequent sequestration and the false charge that he had assisted the Royalists in 1648, account for his inclusion in the list in 1655.

Sir William Mann of Canterbury had served on the County Committee in the 1640s. His assessment for payment of the Decimation tax in 1655, when he was charged to find £40 4s.,[68] stems from his stance at Christmas 1647 when he offered indemnity and mediation to those involved in the Canterbury Revolt. Sir Anthony Weldon had been enraged by Mann's soft line, and when Colonel Hewson restored Parliament's authority over the city, Mann was arrested and imprisoned for a time in Leeds Castle.[69]

In 1655, Mann was quick to petition Cromwell against his decimation. The Protector referred the matter to the Commission, together with a certificate subscribed by 'persons of knowne Integrity', and it was decided, in February 1656, that 'there will noe damage accrue to the Commonwealth by his discharge.'[70]

Sir Edward Scott of Scott's Hall had also served on the County Committee in the 1640s, and been head of the local Committee for the Lathe of Shepway. Increasingly unhappy at the attitude of committeemen like Livesey, he eventually withdrew his suppport. Scott was essentially a moderate Parliamentarian and, although summoned by the commissioners on 16 December, 1655, it was ordered only two days later that he should not be assessed. They were, it was noted, 'satisfied of his good affecion to the state showed by his being in Armes for the late Parliament and other wayes.'[71]

If the maintenance of law and order, and the suppression of plots and riots, was the prime duty of the major-generals, and the enforcement of the Decimation tax formed the main burden of business of the Commission, then their next principal concern was to see that godli-

64. Everitt, *op. cit.,* 122.
65. U2341, 37, 67, 81.
66. Woods, *op. cit.,* 65–66.
67. *Arch. Cant.,* iii (1960), 167.
68. U2341, 15.
69. Everitt, *op. cit.,* 234–236.
70. U2341, 37.
71. *Ibid.,* 16, 18.

ness and virtue prevailed. This led them to actions against Anglican ministers and Royalist schoolmasters,[72] and to the suppression of 'unlawful sports'. Such measures, whatever their attraction to the Puritan minority, only served to make the regime unpopular in many eyes.

Aside from considerations of virtue and efficiency, the Commission was anxious to proceed against suspect ministers and teachers because these individuals were in a position to influence others to violent action against the Government. Thus, Richard Coppin of Rochester was ordered to come before the commissioners because, it was said, 'he doth hold forth and vent Doctrines derogatory to the glory of God and endangering the peace of the Commonwealth.'[73] And John Woodcock, minister of Borden, being 'under scandall' was duly informed that 'if he offend against His Highnes Proclamation that ye Penaltyes therein mencioned [would] be inflicted on him.'[74]

Petitions to Cromwell were often referred to the Commission. Such was the case with Dr. Philip Satterthwayte, schoolmaster. The commissioners examined him in June 1656, and found him to be 'very superstitious' and, they concluded, quite unfit to have children in his care. Accordingly, they recommended to the Council that he should not be allowed to teach.[75]

Others were more fortunate than Coppin, Woodcock and Satterthwayte. John Clerke, schoolmaster of East Greenwich, had also petitioned Cromwell, and the commissioners, upon investigation, found that he had 'demeaned himselfe Religiously diligently and quietly in his imployment for severall yeares last past.' They recommended that he be allowed to continue to teach.[76]

William Belke, minister of Wootton, was similarly commended to the Council following an investigation by the Commission. Examination of their records showed that, by an order of the Committee for Plundered Ministers (6 August, 1644) he had been sequestered from the rectory, but 'for what cause is not therein expressed'. A second order (6 December, 1645), it transpired, had permitted Belke to 'exercise and perform his Pastorall functions'. He could produce testimonials in his favour from several deputy lieutenants and from ministers 'of known integrity'. These, together with recommendations from 'divers of the Assembly of Divines of his conformity to ye Parliament soundnes and orthodoxnes in Doctrine and unblameable conversation' resulted in his speedy exoneration.[77]

Another aspect of the Commission's work, which combined the Puritan desire for a strongly enforced morality with the need to prevent dangerous and disorderly gatherings, was the suppression of what were broadly termed 'unlawful sports'. Whitsun-ales, the setting up of maypoles, help-ales, and the treading of barn floors, it was adjudged, 'produced no other fruits but drunkenes, swearing and all other kindes of lowness and debauchery.' Accordingly, it was resolved to 'Inhibitt and forbidd all such meetings for the future' and orders were sent to parish officers to ensure obedience, while High Sheriffs were to have the orders read in public meeting places.[78]

Horse racing was another object of suspicion. Such meetings, with their attendant crowds,

72. See Appendix III.
73. U2341, 17, 18.
74. *Ibid.*, 60.
75. *Ibid.*, 65.
76. *Ibid.*, 27.
77. *Ibid.*, 78.
78. *Ibid.*, 82–83.

provided an excellent venue for Cavalier gatherings, and might even serve as a launching point for another uprising. Cock-fighting and bear-baiting were also frowned upon and prohibited.[79]

A number of minor matters came before the Commission for action. Two examples may suffice to illustrate the sort of incident or problem with which they had to deal.

Nicholas Wydlowe of Swanscombe complained that on 1 June, 1656, he had been stopped on his way to a church meeting by one John Barker, servant to Captain John Ware of Stone. Ware was one of those summoned by the Commission to be assessed for the Decimation tax, and had been ordered to pay £10. On his master's orders Barker had Wydlowe put in the stocks. The commissioners duly instructed Ware and his servants to appear before them to answer Wydlowe's complaint.[80]

In 1643, a serious insurrection had broken out in the neighbourhood of Tonbridge and amongst those fined for taking part had been Esay Simmons of East Peckham. In June 1656 it was found that he was some £20 in arrears and he was ordered to pay the whole sum to William Polhill within 14 days or face sequestration. Simmons petitioned the commissioners that part of his fine be abated 'in consideration of his great age'. They relented and agreed that £5 should be paid and the rest remitted.[81]

Such, then, was the range of problems with which the Commission in Kent had to deal. The Commission itself was organized, as in other counties, so that any three or more commissioners could meet to administer oaths. Between November 1655 and January 1657 the Kent Commission met 23 times. All the meetings were held in Maidstone, save for the last two recorded where the venue was Rochester. Some of the gatherings are styled 'General Meetings', such as the first, on Tuesday, 20th November.

To record their meetings and otherwise act as clerk, the commissioners appointed John Thatcher at an annual salary of £60. Two messengers, David Steere and Richard Cole, were chosen, each to be paid £40. Thomas Hewes was appointed Door Keeper at £10. Collection of 'the Extraordinary tax upon malignants' was entrusted to William Polhill of Maidstone, whom it was resolved should receive 'threepence in ye pound for his Paines'.[82]

It was vital that the commissioners could prove that those summoned for assessment were, in fact, guilty of delinquency. Much evidence had been accumulated by the old County Committee under Sir Anthony Weldon so, on 19 December, Thatcher was instructed to write to Colonel Ralph Weldon to ask him to send in 'such papers touching Delinquents as are in his Custody of his late fathers.' Lt.-Colonel Seyliard received a similar request in January, and the following March Mr. Heyward of Chatham, who had been clerk to the Committee of Accounts, was ordered to bring in the records of that body.[83]

By March 1656, sufficient money had come in to enable considerable sums to be paid out to Captains Browne, Kadwell and Monins for the pay and maintenance of their troops. Browne and Kadwell each received £539 16s. 6d., Monins £501 16s. 6d.[84]

Yet, by 1657, it was clear that the major-generals could not provide a permanent solution to the problem of stable government. Their rule had proven unpopular and its financial basis was

79. G.M. Trevelyan, *England Under the Stuarts*, 294.
80. U2341, 73–74.
81. *Ibid.*, 62, 72.
82. *Ibid.*, 9, 11.
83. *Ibid.*, 13.
84. *Ibid.*, 41.

unsound. The Decimation tax, though simple in theory, was difficult to administer in practice. The minutes of the Kentish commissioners are full of references to cases being respited, suspended or discharged.

There were many reasons for this. Some individuals were summoned in error, while others had to be excused for lack of evidence. Some, it was found, were dead or gone away, and lands had been sold or leased or, upon investigation, were under value. Others were able to obtain discharge by provision of testimonials of good service to the Parliament in the past. The more stalwart spirits resisted payment and had to be threatened with sequestration. The tax served only to antagonise those who had been quiescent since 1648. The landowning classes in general were uneasy at what they saw as a dangerous and unparliamentary expedient. Nor did it succeed as a punitive measure.

By this time, Cromwell had found it necessary to turn again to Parliament. It met in September 1656, and before the session ended in June 1657, judgement had been passed on both major-generals and Decimation tax. The Militia Bill was rejected and Parliament refused to continue the policy of an extraordinary tax upon the Royalists.[85]

Kelsey and his fellow commissioners had laboured hard, but time was running out for the Commonwealth. The very make-up of the Commission shows how the mass of Kentish gentry had been alienated, or were at best indifferent. The Decimation tax served only to irritate, without bringing in the expected revenue. The limit below which the impost was not applied meant that many of the most ardent and active Cavaliers were not penalized at all. Nor were Royalist plots to cease. In retrospect, the work of the Cromwellian Commission in Kent may be said to have helped to pave the way for the Restoration.

APPENDIX I

List of Commissioners for Kent, with number of appearances at meetings to January 1657

Beale, Colonel Richard	0	Mascall, Robert (of Canterbury)	6
Bowles, Captain Charles	21	Monins, Captain Thomas	19
Broughton, Andrew	3	Needler, Lt.-Colonel Henry	20
Browne, Captain John	23	Oxinden, Henry	0
Crompton, Lt.-Colonel	19	Palmer, William	23
Cullen, William	1	Parker, John (Serjeant-at-Law)	2
Eltonhead	5	Pyke, Captain Martin	23
Foche, Major Thomas	1	Rabson, John	22
Garland, Augustine	1	Rabson, Richard	3
Gibbon, Colonel Robert	5	Roberts, Alexander	22
Godfrey, Lamberde	0	Skynner, Captain Augustine	14
Harrison, Captain Thomas	20	Skynner, Captain William	8
Hayles, Robert	2	Twisleton, Colonel John	2
Kadwell, Captain	20	Watson	6
Kelsey, Thomas (The Major-General)	19	Weldon, Colonel Ralph	0
Livesey, Sir Michael	15	Wilson, Captain Thomas	6

85. C. Hill, *The Century of Revolution, 1603–1714*, 138; Trevelyan, *op. cit.*, 295.

APPENDIX II

List of those required to bring in particulars of their estates or security for their peaceable demeanour.

Abbott, Richard	Orpington	Blissett, Michael	Chislehurst
Ady, John		Bode, John	Maidstone
Allen, John	Rochester	Bourne, Daniel	Ashford
Allington, Henry	Bromley	Boys, Christopher	Uffington
Andrewes, Captain	Bromley	Boys, Lt.-Colonel Sir John	Bonnington
Andrewes	Crayford	Braems, Arnold	Bridge
Appleton, Sir Henry		Braems, Walter	
Argoll, Thomas		Brazier, John	Leaves Green
Artnope, William	Shoreham	Brazier, John (junior)	Chelsfield
Aucher, Sir Anthony	Bourne	Brett, John	Hawkhurst
Austen, John[86]	Tenterden	Brett, Thomas	Brenchley
Austen, Robert	Bexley	Brett, Thomas	Snave
Babbage, William	Brenchley	Brett, William	Wye
Back, Kenneth	Hinxhill	Brewer, William	Ditton
Back, Thomas	Hinxhill	Brickman, Daniel	Maidstone
Barefoote, Nicholas	Yalding	Brockman, Zouch	Cheriton
Bargrave, Captain Robert	Patrixbourne	Bromesell, Captain	Bromley
Barham, Robert	Sittingbourne	Brooke, William	Yalding
Barham, Major	Farleigh	Buggins, William	North Cray
Barnham, Robert	Boughton	Bunes, Mathew	Throwley
Bashpoole, John	Haddiscoe, Norfolk	Burre, Nathaniel	Bethersden
		Burroughs, Thomas	Longfield
Bassage, William	Brenchley	Carey, John	
Bateman, John	Wormshill	Carpenter, Thomas	Farningham
Bateman, Thomas	Lydd	Champnes	Greenwich
Bathurst, Sir Edward	Horton Kirby	Chase, Mathew	Stone
Beeching, John	Ebony	Chase, Ralph	Stone
Bennett, Richard		Chase, Thomas	Dartford
Best, John	Canterbury	Chase, Thomas	Stone near Dartford
Bettenham, Anthony	Bromley		
Bettenham, John	Chislet	Child, Major John	Northfleet or Southfleet
Bettenham, Stephen	Bromley		
Beveridge, Myles	Orpington	Childrens, George (the Elder)	Leigh
Bill, John			
Bird, Dr. Thomas	Biddenden	Clarke, Francis	Ulcombe
Bird, Captain	Biddenden	Clarke, Captain	Key Street
Bishopp, John	Hunton	Clerke, Sir Thomas	Plumstead
Bix, Thomas	Fordwich	Cock, John	Chelsfield
Blinckthorne	Chislet	Codd, George	Ash or Kemsing

86. John Austen 'dead'.

Collins	Frindsbury or Gravesend	Fibbenden, John	Brenchley
		Fidgett, William	Bexley
Compton, Sir Charles		Finch, John: Lord Finch	
Cooke, George	Bexley	Finch, Thomas	Kingsdown
Cooke, Henry	Kingsdown	Firrell, John	Brenchley
Cooke, Captain	Bromley	Fissenden, John	Brenchley
Couper, William	Bexley	Fletcher, James	East Malling
Court, Mathew[87]	Elham	Fludd, Thomas[90]	Otham
Courthopp, Alexander	Horsmonden	Francis, John	Harrietsham
Courthopp, Thomas	Hackington	French, Martin	Bromley
Crispe, Sir Nicholas	Thanet	Fryer, Henry	Rainham
Croucher, John	Bexley	Gaddes, Richard	Sittingbourne
Croucher, William	Crayford	Gardner, Nicholas	Bromley
Culpeper, Thomas	Bedgebury	Gay, Jeremy	Nonington
Culpeper, Sir Thomas	Hollingbourne	Geale, Richard	Paul's Cray
Culpeper, William	Bedgebury	Gibbon, Thomas (Senior)	
Darell, Edward	Calehill	Gibbon, Thomas (Junior)	
Darell, Sir John	Calehill	Gibbs	Newington near Dover
Darey, Edward			
Davidge, William	Bromley	Gilbourne, Henry	Bromley
Dawson, John	Westenhanger	Gilpin, John	Orpington
Deereing, Anthony	Egerton	Ginder, Stephen	Benenden
Digges, Edward[88]	Chilham	Glover, Richard	Cudham
Dixon, Thomas	Canterbury	Gobbeere, William	Maidstone
Dorman, Nicholas (Senior)	St. Mary Cray	Goddin	Trottiscliffe
Dorman	Wrotham	Godfrey, Sir Thomas	Nackington
Dorman, Captain[89]	Wrotham	Goodyeare (als. Goodhue), Robert	Tunbridge
Duke, Richard	Maidstone		
Ellis, Anthony	Foot's Cray	Gookin, John	Ripple
Engeham, Thomas	Canterbury	Grattwick, Richard	Bromley
Everard, Major Thomas	Beckenham	Graunt, Paul	Sittingbourne
Everist, Edward	Shoreham	Greenestreete, Edward	Lynsted
Fane, Mildmay: Earl of Westmorland		Greenestreete, John	Borden
		Greenestreete, Peter	Ospringe
Fane, Robert	Sundridge	Greenestreete, Symond	Lynsted
Fanes, Bonham	Cliffe	Grimes, Colonel	
Fanes, Bonham	Westerham	Gyles, John	Challock
Farby, Sir Leonard	Paul's Cray	Haffenden, Richard	Tenterden
Farnaby, John	Sevenoaks	Haffenden, Thomas	Tenterden
Farrard, Anthony	Linsted	Hales, Sir Edward	Tunstall
Fearne, Thomas	Bredgar	Hales, Sir James	

87. Mathew Court 'dead'.
88. Edward Digges 'beyound ye Seas'.
89. Captain Dorman, 'Son of Dorman of Wrotham', himself 'dead'.
90. Thomas Fludd 'Entred by a mistake'.

Halfepenny	Greenwich	King, Arnold	Paul's Cray
Hall, Henry	Farnborough	King, Henry	Bromley
Hall, John	Stone-in-Oxney	Kingsland, John	Eynsford
Hall, Nevill	Ashford	Kingsley, William	St. Stephen's
Hammon, Thomas	Hockenden	Knatchbull, Thomas	Hollingbourne
Hammond, Anthony	Nonington	Knight, Thomas	Ashford
Hamond, Mainwaring		Knight, Willcock	Lydd
Hardres, Colonel Sir		Know, Roger	Cudham
Richard	Hardres	Knowler, Stephen	Chislehurst
Hardres, Thomas	Canterbury	Knowles, John	Faversham
Harfleete, Sir Christopher	St. Stephen's	Lake	Borden
Harlackendane, Thomas	Bearsted	Lake, John (Senior)	Stone
Harlackendane, Silvester	Sittingbourne	Lake, John	Stone
Harrison, Edward	Dymchurch	Lake, Richard	Stone
Harvey, John	Erith	Lambarde, Thomas	Sevenoaks
Harvey, William	North Cray	Lee, Henry	Hadlow
Haslyn, Henry	Meopham	Lee, Richard	Rochester
Hawker, Gibbon	Challock	Leigh, John	Cranbrook
Heath, Francis	Brasted	Leigh, Thomas	East Wickham
Heppard, Richard	Wittersham	Leonard, Sir Stephen	West Wickham
Hills, Francis (Senior)	Sevenoaks	Lewin, Thomas	Shoreham
Hills, Robert	Shoreham	Longsen, James	Bredgar
Hobbs, William	Erith	Mainwaring, William	Canterbury
Hobert, Christopher	Hunton	Maning, Edward	St. Mary Cray
Hogbin, John	Elham	Maning, Thomas	Westerham
Hollenby (als. Nicholas),		Mann, Sir William	Canterbury
John	Chiddingstone	Manning, Robert	St. Mary Cray
Horsmonden, John	Goudhurst	Mantle, Thomas	Horton
Hoy, John	Doddington	Maplisden, John	Boxley
Hubbard, Christopher	Hunton	Marsh, Thomas	Northbourne
Huffam, Edward	Chislet	Marshall, Robert	Foot's Cray
Hugesson, William	Lynsted	Marshall, Thomas	Foot's Cray
Hules, Richard	Bethersden	Marsham, John	Cuxton
Hurleston, John	Fordwich	Masters, Edward	Canterbury
Ibbitt, John	Orpington	Masters, Humfrey	Kingsnorth
Ibbitt, William	Gilton Hill[91]	Masters, Richard	East Langdon
Jackson, Anthony	Westerham	Masters, Samuel	Seal
Jeffery, Edward	Tonbridge	May, George	Rochester
Jeffery, Ralph	Sheppey	May, Robert	Brookland
Kadwell, Thomas	Lydd	Mayne, Sir John	Linton
Kennard, John	Yalding	Meriwether, Captain	
Kennard, Robert	Sandhurst	William	Shepherdswell
King, Arnold	Bromley	Milles, John	Biddenden

91. Gilton Hill in Sutton at Hone.

Mills, George	Canterbury	Post, William	Pluckley
Monger, John		Powell, Joseph	Farnborough
Monins, Sir Edward	Waldershare	Rayner, Captain	Borden
Moore, John	Foot's Cray	Reynolds, William	Hollingbourne
Morris, Robert	Benenden	Richards, Thomas	Lynsted
Mountayne, John	Milton	Richards, Gabriel	Rowling
Munn, Thomas	Cranbrook	Rigden, William	Hardres
Nash, Joseph	Shoreham	Rigden, William	Lyminge
Nepean, Peter	Hougham	Robbins, Henry	Hawkhurst
Nevill, John: Lord		Robbins, Mathew	Hawkhurst
Abergavenny		Roberts, Edward	Canterbury
Newman, Colonel George	Rochester	Rogers, Thomas	Sevenoaks
Newman, James	Thanet	Rogers, Thomas	Sundridge
Newton, Sir Henry[92]	Charlton	Round, John	Shoreham
Norton, William	Eastwell	Ruffine, Henry	Sheppey
Oliver, Robert	St. Mary Cray	Ruffine, Nicholas	Sheppey
Osbourne, Captain Thomas		Sabb	Eltham
Owre, Robert	Faversham	Sabine, Walter	Canterbury
Oxinden, Captain Henry	West Langdon	Sackville, Thomas[94]	Boxley
Palmer, Sir Roger		Sandwell, Captain Jeffery	Thanet
Palmer, Sir Thomas[93]	Wingham	Saxby, William	Leigh
Payne, Thomas	Hayes	Scott, Sir Edward	Scott's Hall
Peirs, Sir Thomas	Ightham	Scudder, Henry	North Cray
Peke, Thomas	Ash	Scudder, John	North Cray
Penshurst, George	Yalding	Scudder, Thomas	North Cray
Petley, Richard	Shoreham	Sedley, Sir Isaac	St. Clere
Petley, Robert	Chelsfield	Sedley, Sir John	St. Clere
Petley, Thomas	Pilsen-in-	Sheafe, Edmund	Willesborough
	Shoreham	Short, Peter	Tenterden
Pettit, Henry	Thanet	Shorte, William	Tenterden
Pettit	Otford	Shott, James	Bromley
Peyton, Sir Thomas	Knowlton Court	Simmons, Esay	East Peckham
Phillip, William	Bromley	Simonds, John	Swingfield
Phillpott, Ralph	Worth	Skynner, George	Monkton
Pix, William (the Elder)	Hawkhurst	Smale, George	Dartford
Poines, Sir Roger		Small, William	Shoreham
Polhill, Daniel	Otford	Smyth, John (Senior)	
Polhill, David	Otford	Smyth, Leonard	Lynsted
Pordage, John	Ospringe	Smyth, Thomas	Greenwich
Pordage, Thomas	Ospringe	Smyth, William	Stanford
Porter, George		Smyth	Westerham

92.　Sir Henry Newton *alias* Puckering.
93.　Sir Thomas Palmer died in 1656, and a sum of £42 8s. was charged on the estate of his son, Sir Henry who, after an appeal, won a discharge.
94.　Thomas Sackville's estate, it transpired, lay in Sussex.

Smythson, John	Wickham	Tomlyn, George	Newington
Solley, John	Trapham	Tong, James	Bredgar
Sondes, Sir George	Sholden	Tray, Richard	Bredhurst
Southland, Thomas	Littlebourne	Tucker, William	Elham or
Spaine, Richard	Sturry		Bekesbourne
Spencer, Richard	Orpington		
Spice, Robert	Old Romney	Tufton, John: Earl of	
Stanley, Captain Thomas	Plaxtol	Thanet	
Staple, Joseph	Orpington	Turney, John[95]	Postling
Staple, Richard	Bexley	Twisden, Sir Roger	East Peckham
Staples, Henry	Orpington	Upton, John	Faversham
Stapleton, Sir Robert		Wade, Nicholas	Faversham
Start, John	St. Mary Cray	Wakerley, Ralph	Lynsted
Steed, Dr. William	Harrietsham	Waller, Edmund	Paul's Cray
Stephens, Captain	Olantigh	Walter, Captain Thomas	Appledore
Strouggles		Ware, Clement	Dartford
Styles, John	Lewisham	Ware, Captain John	Stone
Summers, William	Rochester	Warner, Dr. John[96]	Rochester
Swan, George	Eastchurch	Warwick, Phillip'	Chislehurst
Swanne, William	Knowlton	Wells, Richard	Wittersham
Swift, Thomas	Smarden	Wentworth, Sir George[97]	Cleeve
Taylor, Edward	Leeds or	Whiffin, Richard (Junior)	West Wickham
	Hollingbourne	Whitfeild, Francis	Bethersden
Taylor, James	Aylesford	Wilsford, Captain John	Barham Downs
Terry, Augustine		Wood, John	East Farleigh
Thatcher, Thomas	Frinsted	Wood, Richard	Bexley
Thinne, Sir Thomas		Wood, Richard	Tonbridge
Thomas, Edmund	Chevening	Woodgreene, John	Frindsbury
Thomas, Edmund	Westerham	Woodgreene, John	Greenwich
Thomas, Robert	Selling	Woodin, Edward	Stansted
Thompson, Anthony	Kingston	Woodward, Major	Challock
Thompson, Henry	Peckham	Wybourne, Allen	Bexley
Thornhill, Richard	Olantigh	Zouch, Sir Allan	Banham,
Till	Sevenoaks		Norfolk

95. John Turney 'dead'.
96. Dr. John Warner, Bishop of Rochester.
97. The Commissioners had confused Sir George Wentworth with his namesake in Yorkshire. As he was not the Sir George who had been sequestered, the charge was taken off.

APPENDIX III

List of Ministers and Schoolmasters subject to enquiry by the Kent Commission

Belke, William	Wootton
Clerke, John	East Greenwich
Coppin, Richard	Rochester
Cosby	Milsted
Gibbs	Canterbury
Gibson, William	Meopham
Satterthwayte, Dr. Phillip	
Scarlett, William	Bobbing
Slater	Frinsted
Woodcock, John	Borden

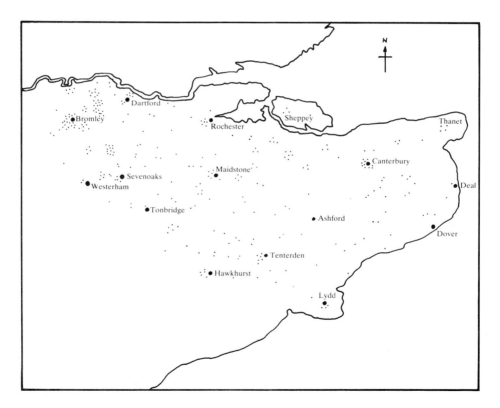

Fig. 1.   Distribution of those named to appear before the commission to bring in particulars of their estates or to provide security for their peaceable demeanour, 1655–57.

'FOR THE BETTER DEFENCE OF LOW AND MARSHY GROUNDS': A SURVEY OF THE WORK OF THE SEWER COMMISSIONS FOR NORTH AND EAST KENT, 1531–1930

EILEEN BOWLER

'considering daily great damages and losses which have happened in many and diverse parts . . . by reason of the outrageous flowing surges and course of the sea in and upon marsh grounds and other low places . . . as also by occasion of land waters . . . (it is) enacted that Commissions of Sewers shall be directed in all parts. . . .'
23 HVIII C15 (1531) A General Act concerning Commissions of Sewers.

The marshy and low grounds of Kent (excluding Romney Marsh) came largely under the jurisdiction of three such Commissions: two covered north Kent, running from Lombards Wall to Gravesend Bridge and from Gravesend Bridge to Sheerness; a third covered most of the extensive low grounds east of the Swale, including the river meadows bordering the Great Stour as far as Ashford.[1] Some lands remained outside their control if the landowners wished to undertake their own sea defences, but even they had to obey the edicts of the Commissioners if their defaults threatened Commission lands.

The problems they had to tackle were by no means new: tempests and floods which 'consume the works of men' had been the subject of comment at least since the eleventh century, and individuals and communities had fought a long, arduous and often unrewarding battle to preserve their lands from inundation, and to win some of the extensive saltings which fringed much of the coast. These efforts had been supplemented since the early thirteenth century by Commissions *de walliis et fossatiis* appointed by the Crown on an *ad hoc* basis. The time had now come for these Commissions to be placed on a permanent footing and to be made responsible for the main burden of coastal defence work. The new Commissioners would be supported by the strength of long established customs relating to the upkeep of the marsh and could call upon a wealth of experience in the problems of embanking and draining. Their duties and powers were set out very clearly: (i) to survey and remedy annoyances; (ii) to

---

1. A considerable number of documents relating to the work of the Commissions are preserved in the Kent Archives Office and are catalogued under the title of the Commission Area. For this paper the records of the Commission for East Kent (S/EK) and for North Kent (S/NK) have been extensively used. The documents are subdivided according to content, the most important classes being those covering the Minutes of Sessions and the Order Books, and the Expenditors Accounts. These are all in chronological order using the administrative year which runs from Easter to Easter. Legal, administrative and estate documents throw further light on matters referred to in the Minutes, e.g. Report of Surveys.

    For the North Kent area 'Lombards Wall to Gravesend Bridge' there is abundant evidence from 1629–1712 but nothing thereafter until the end of the eighteenth century: for the North Kent area 'Gravesend Bridge to Sheerness' there are few records before 1690, but they are detailed after that date though in practice they refer only to the area west of the Medway. The records of the East Kent Commission begin in the sixteenth century and are detailed from the early seventeenth century. The area between the Medway and Graveney is unfortunately sparsely documented, as is Sheppey.

    Events referred to in the paper are drawn from the Minute or Order books unless separately referenced in the notes.

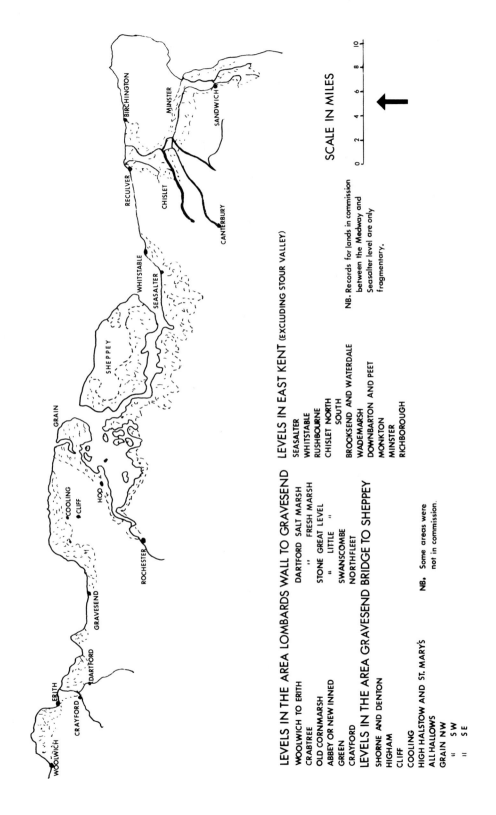

LEVELS IN THE AREA LOMBARDS WALL TO GRAVESEND

WOOLWICH TO ERITH
CRABTREE
OLD CORNMARSH
ABBEY OR NEW INNED
GREEN
CRAYFORD

DARTFORD SALT MARSH
    "   FRESH MARSH
STONE GREAT LEVEL
   "   LITTLE   "
SWANSCOMBE
NORTHFLEET

LEVELS IN THE AREA GRAVESEND BRIDGE TO SHEPPEY

SHORNE AND DENTON
HIGHAM
CLIFF
COOLING
HIGH HALSTOW AND ST. MARY'S
ALL HALLOWS
GRAIN NW
   "   SW
   "   SE

NB. Some areas were
not in commission.

LEVELS IN EAST KENT (EXCLUDING STOUR VALLEY)

SEASALTER
WHITSTABLE
RUSHBOURNE
CHISLET NORTH
        SOUTH
BROCKSEND AND WATERDALE
WADEMARSH
DOWNBARTON AND PEET
MONKTON
MINSTER
RICHBOROUGH

NB. Records for lands in commission
between the Medway and
Seasalter level are only
fragmentary.

SCALE IN MILES

Fig. 2.   Map of the coastal Area of north Kent

enquire by whose defaults the annoyances came about; (iii) to assess the persons to be contributors to the charge; (iv) to repair walls, cleanse sewers, throw down or amend mills, weirs, etc., as necessary; (v) to appoint bailiffs, collectors and other officers who shall render an account to them; (vi) to distrain for arrears of scot; (vii) to take workmen and retain them at a proper wage and to take carriages, timber and other necessaries from areas nearby and pay for them at a reasonable price; (viii) to make statutes, etc., after the Laws and Customs of Romney Marsh, or otherwise by their discretion; (ix) to serve writs and follow their orders through the courts as necessary.

Under the Act, which stood until replaced by the Land Drainage Act of 1930, small groups of able and public-spirited men gave generously of their time and energy in trying to keep back the ever-encroaching sea and in promoting efficient land drainage, so that maximum advantage might be obtained from the inned land.

Throughout the four centuries physical conditions worsened: normal high tide levels in the twentieth century are at least four feet above those of the sixteenth, and storm surges reach higher still; the erosion of protective areas of foreland has exposed the walls to increasingly severe wave attack and rising sea level has made the efficient discharge of land waters more and more difficult. As a result, the present day 'natural' coast would lie somewhere close to the landward margin of the area shown on Fig. 1 as being below the level of mean-high water, though its precise location would depend upon the local balance of erosional and depositional forces. The successes of the Commissions are therefore plain to see – the thousands of acres of productive marshland stretching away behind the sea walls – their failures are hidden from view, for much that was land in 1531 now lies beneath the sea, 'eaten' as one eighteenth-century lease mournfully puts it 'by the Thames'.

The area controlled by each Commission was subdivided into a number of levels which varied enormously both in acreage, from under 20 acres to over 3,000, and in the length of river wall that had to be maintained. Some levels, like Cooling or Minster, were in the relatively happy position of having no front sea wall and were responsible only for internal drainage; others, like Cliffe or Green level in Erith, had huge exposed sweeps of river frontage to defend. The scot the lands were called upon to pay depended on the number of acres over which the costs were spread, and on the extent and vulnerability of the defences and other works; in a run of bad years the scot could exceed the annual income derived from the land, but so highly was inned marshland prized that defences were only abandoned with great reluctance.

The Commissions met at least twice a year for routine business, and otherwise as frequently as the pressure of work demanded; when emergencies arose they could be in session several times in one or two months. The Expenditor for each level organised the day-to-day work, sometimes with the assistance of a foreman or bailiff. Both direct and contract labour was used, and specialists were called on as required, often from outside the district. In the early days a jury of local men perambulated the level and presented the work to be done, but doubts were sometimes expressed about their competence, and in 1627 the Dartford jury received the services of a paid foreman to advice them. The system gradually fell into disuse as the professional skills of surveyors and engineers were increasingly recognised; in the eighteenth and nineteenth centuries the expenditors themselves often belonged to one of these professions.

Although only fragmentary records remain of their work before the end of the sixteenth century, it seems unlikely that the new Commissioners could have viewed their tasks with enthusiasm or the future with optimism; indeed gloomy foreboding might well have prevailed at those early sessions, for already the whole of Erith and Plumstead marshes were drowned by the succession of storms of 1527–30, and walls elsewhere along the Thames were in serious danger. Within a few years worse was to befall, for the period 1550–70 witnessed an unusual number of severe gales and tempestuous seas against which few defences remained standing. By 1570 much land around Hoo and Grain was under water, some having been drowned for so long as to be virtually useless, and the situation elsewhere was little better; fishing vessels were said to sail at will through the breaches and fish on the one-time land. The Plumstead marshes were subject to several Acts of Parliament,[2] and the Privy Council was active in promoting their reclamation, yet after many years of effort Camden could say: 'Below Greenwich, the Thames throwing down its banks, has laid several acres of ground under water: and some, for many years endeavouring to keep it out at vast expense, scarce find their works and walls able to defend the neighbouring fields against the incursions of the tide'.[3] It was not until the early seventeenth century that the area was won and placed under the jurisdiction of the Commission.

Despite this unpropitious beginning, the various Commissions seem to have promoted the work of reclamation with considerable vigour: a new wall was built at Whitstable in 1583 'for the better defence of certain houses and grounds lying in the level . . . from being further damaged by the sea' ('Middle Wall' is the remaining part of this new wall) and in 1578 it was suggested that a new wall should be built from Wademarsh to Reculver (Fig. 1) but it was not undertaken immediately for in 1591 owners and occupiers of lands in the contributory levels of Rushbourne and Chislet were required to show reason why such a wall should not be built. This they failed to do, for a wall was built forthwith. Such works were expensive and necessitated heavy scots for some years; in the case of the Rushbourne wall a complicated system of whole, half and quarter scots was devised on the basis of the degree of benefit the contributory lands were held to enjoy. The costs of the Whitstable wall were partly defrayed by the tolls on goods carried across the wall to and from the vessels beached on the shore.

Unqualified approval was not given to all reclamation schemes, however, for when Corpus Christi College, Oxford, whose lands were not in commission, undertook the inning of some of their land in Seasalter level in 1608–9 the Commission was exceedingly critical, for 'this new wall would likely cause loss in shutting up the sea in such a strait lying open to the north-west and north winds' (i.e. between the College lands and the Commission's wall) and they ordered that the new wall 'was to be quite thrown down, on pain of £20, unless the College will bring over the said wall . . . 40 rods at least northwards over the salt sewer . . . and lay a good sluice to sew the valleys . . . and land the wall on Seasalter wall', to which work the Commission would contribute £30, and if it proved beneficial, it would contribute henceforth to the maintenance costs of the sewer, sluice and wall. The College complied and the wall was built by 1611.

To facilitate construction and to minimise maintenance costs the new walls were generally set some distance back from the shore, leaving an area of salting and reed beds to take the brunt of the breaking waves. The wisdom of this procedure may be gauged from a report concerning Rushbourne level in 1636, where it was stated that a new inset was needed 'to

2.   22 H VIII; 5, 8, 14, 23, 27, Eliz; 4 Jac I.
3.   W. Camden, *Camden's Britannia*, facsimile of 1595 ed. (1951), 189.

replace 33 rods set too near the sea (in 1591–92) and much broken'.

This period of active reclamation probably restored the defences to more or less the position they had occupied in the early sixteenth century. It is not possible to say how much, if at all, they had retreated from the late medieval position, but it appears that there was no substantial advance except along the Stour channels where some new ground was taken in.

The disastrously stormy conditions, which plagued the coastlands during much of the sixteenth century, were happily rare in the seventeenth until its last decade, and once the main thrust of reclamation was over, the Commissions could settle down to develop a regular pattern of maintenance and to evolve an organisation and management system designed to promote the security and efficiency of their works. This involved a whole series of orders concerning the upkeep of marshlands, watercourses and walls, for the thoughtless or selfish action of individuals could easily expose everyone to needless expense and danger.

The height and strength of the embankments could be impaired in a number of ways, particularly by overgrazing and by their use as drove and carriageways. Since the herbage on the walls was valuable pasture, the Commissions sought to regulate its use either by making decrees concerning the type and number of animals permitted, or by leasing and supervising the pasture rights. In Shorne, for example, from the early eighteenth century, no horses or cattle were permitted on new made walls between Michaelmas and 1 April following the new making, and from 1627 no cattle or hogs were allowed on any wall in Erith or Plumstead. In these levels it appears that the pasture rights were granted to the foremen as part of their wages, for in 1641 it was decreed that anyone infringing these rights with their cattle would be fined £5 per offence with distraint for non-payment. The wall at Richborough seems to have been regularly used as a way: in 1602 three persons were fined £5 each for passing over it with carriages, the fine to be levied by distress of cattle, but in 1613 its use for this purpose between 1 May and the Feast of St. Luke was acknowledged. By 1629 the passage of heavy carts had become such a nuisance that gates had been put up – for men were fined that year for breaking them. In other levels, too, locked gates or bars were used to discourage traffic.

Nevertheless, some walls were acknowledged roads, and in these cases tolls could be levied to help pay the extra costs of upkeep. Everyone using Sarre wall to and from Thanet with cart loads of wood or corn had to pay 2d. per load from 1592, whilst anyone using Pope's wall to Wademarsh was required, from 1639, to lay a load of bushes on the wall on every third passage made between Michaelmas and Lady Day.

Where they lay close to the shore, walls made good wharves, but the effect of such use was disastrous and was usually prohibited. An order made to Messrs. Bowtell, Browne and Smales in 1654 indicated an alternative to prohibition: they were told to plank and pile the sides of Dartford Creek – which was being much damaged by their lighters and hoys – or stop using the creek. They complied with the order and the Commission helped by apportioning the costs between them.

The Commissioners were very sharp with offenders whatever their social status and the threat of distraint was not an idle one; few ignored or disobeyed their edicts after a warning. Important as these orders were in maintaining the walls in good repair, their security was seen to depend, first and foremost, on the soundness of a good depth of foreland, and strenuous efforts were made to preserve these as much from the depredations of men as from the ravages of the sea. In the upper part of the estuary this was a particularly serious concern, for the forelands were inevitably narrower here, and the ebbing tide exposed a long mud slope to the river channel. Reeds were often sown on the banks as they were thought helpful in breaking the force of the waves, but they were also a valuable commodity and were cut from the early part of the year when winter storms were still to be expected. To prevent this it was decreed in 1639 that no cutting should take place until after 1 March; a number of equinoctial gales caused this to be amended to 1 April in 1660. Despite heavy penalties the practice continued, so in 1689 cutting was limited to the month of April only in order to make supervision easier.

Even worse, some dug the banks themselves and carried the mud and gravel away in boats. In 1656 the expenditors and foremen of the levels above Dartford Creek complained that they were powerless to stop this practice because 'the lewd persons called low watermen' came from London, and being of no repute their names were not known, and if they were approached they either ignored the Commission's officers or threatened them. The Water Bailiff of the Lord Mayor of London was asked to assist in the matter, and was given 40s. for his trouble. A few years later the same complaint was made and the same course of action followed. Some digging of the salts was allowed for mending the walls but only under the authority of the expenditor for the level concerned.

Lower down the estuary, by Cliffe, Grain and Seasalter, the fringing saltings were wider but were being eroded at an alarming rate, and from at least the middle of the seventeenth century attempts were being made to preserve them, but these efforts were very low-key compared with the almost frenzied activity of the next century. Eastwards again most of the shoreline was fringed by shingle banks and beach which drifted westwards from Thanet. The vagaries of tides and currents frequently removed this from some stretches and piled it elsewhere, but it was also moved, sometimes in considerable quantities, by men. Since it was seen to provide a natural defence, its removal was deplored and miscreants were firmly dealt with. More difficult to control were the offences committed by other public officials, notably the Highway Surveyors, who saw beach as the cheapest, most easily accessible road repairing material; they were curtly requested to desist from their depredations and usually complied. The problem was a recurrent one however, and as late as 1878 several men were prosecuted in Margate County Court for carrying away beach after they had been warned that this was illegal.

By these various decrees, largely promulgated in the seventeenth century and reiterated at intervals thereafter, and by the vigorous prosecution of offenders – including its own officials if need be – the Commission sought to secure the levels from marine inundation. This was of little avail however, if the marshes were drowned as the result of overflowing creeks, as happened in Plumstead in 1633 when it was recorded that much land had been under water all winter because 190 rods of the common sewer in the New Inned marsh (Abbey level) had not been scoured. This complaint highlights one of the major difficulties facing the Commissions, that of divided responsibility. In this case two levels were concerned and the matter was quickly settled by an order made at the next sessions. In other cases the question concerned the respective liabilities of owners/occupiers and the Commission in the matter of ditch scouring. Main watercourses were the responsibility of the level, minor ones were maintained by the farmers, though under some direction from the expenditor, but it was not always clear which was which, especially after alterations had been made to the drainage layout. The dyke in question might also turn out to be the responsibility of several people who ought to co-operate on maintenance but seldon did, e.g. in Seasalter in 1641 it was declared that a certain sewer was half the responsibility of Dr Spenser, one quarter that of the heirs of William Pordage, and one quarter pertained to the valley (i.e. the Commission); seven years later Sir

William Pordage and Corpus Christi College were required to show why they should not pay a proportion of the costs of widening and deepening a commision sewer to the sea since they also benefited from it.

The maintenance of miles of sewer system could pose all sorts of problems: the ditches were useful rubbish dumps – or so it seems from a strongly worded order concerning the levels in Plumstead marsh in 1662, which prohibited the chucking of weed, wood or rubbish into the ditches on pain of 20s. per offence, with a rider which suggests some previous offenders thought they had found a way to avoid the penalty, for it states that if a wife or servant was guilty of the offence then the husband or master was liable. Overflowing ditches in Dartford in 1634 were said to be 'the cause of losses in orchards and land and to be a peril to health'; to improve the situation an order was made that all watercourses should be amended by 1 June and again by 1 October, with a penalty of 2s. per rod left uncleaned with a further 5s. for every month the work remained undone, and 10s. for dumping rubbish. Men were frequently brought before the session to explain their defaults, and if they persisted then the fines were levied. Wood cutting, shoring, siding, bottoming were all jobs which had to be done regularly, and the scope for doing them badly or causing inconvenience to all and sundry was almost endless as the order books show. Workmen, it appears, were not always devoted to their jobs even in the 'good old days', nor were they backward in requesting more money for their labours – which was seldom granted. The Commissioners were, however, sensible of good work and devotion to duty and not infrequently gave some honorarium to men who had 'shown exceptional diligence in and about the level' – usually at a time of emergency.

Main rivers posed yet another set of problems, not least that they tended to split up and then get choked with weeds, a process accelerated by the rising sea level which checked their flow and hastened aggradation. This problem was never solved successfully, but not for want of trying; in 1576 it was ordered that all lighters plying between Fordwich and Sandwich in summer should drag an iron harrow at the stern to break up woods and abate shallows; this was reiterated several times, but by 1670 it was said to be ineffective. The Commissioners were prepared to try new methods, for in 1617 the expenditor for the General Vallies (Stour) was told to employ one Stephen Gibbes and to report whether 'his device for draining the valleys will be more beneficial than the present method' – it was not, but he was given £6 towards his costs; twenty years later a 'new engine' was tried to see if it was better than several labourers, but after four years it broke and was not replaced.

Another important way of improving the flow of land water was by shortening the course of the sewers or rivers and by planning a more efficient drainage layout. The Stour was straightened in several places and the Wantsum given a new channel, and a jury in Wademarsh in 1618 was set to view the inconvenience of the crookedness of the sewers and to pronounce on the making of straighter ones. So flat were many of the levels, and so numerous and tortuous the channels, which frequently followed the lines of old creeks, that it was not always clear which way the water was flowing, and an order had to be made for a view and survey to find out – the area around Sarre was particularly bad in this respect. In addition to this, in the Chislet valleys, the old inned land, next to the upland, was generally lower than the new inned salts nearer the river which had received increments of silt throughout the medieval period when they lay open to the tides (Fig. 2). Since water control not only served to sew the land but also had to provide them with adequate fresh water for stock in summer, this difference in level could be crucial, for at the water level required for stock on the higher lands, the lower,

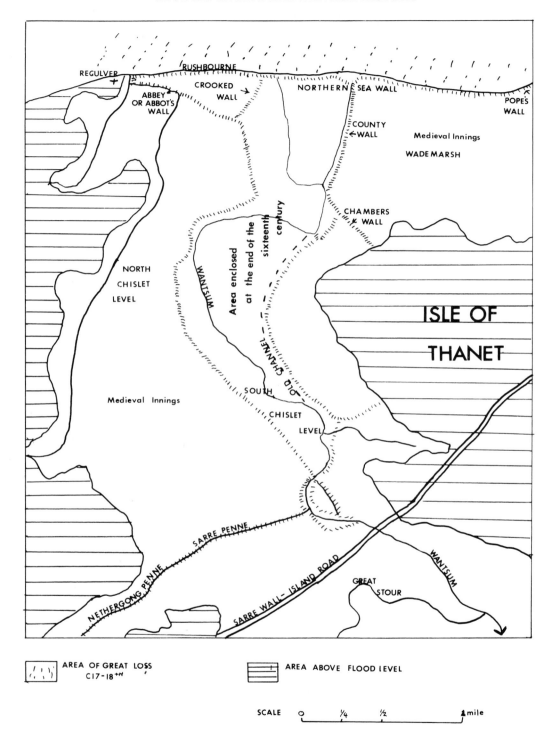

AREA OF GREAT LOSS C17-18 +H

AREA ABOVE FLOOD LEVEL

SCALE   0   ¼   ½   1 mile

Fig. 3.   Map of the Chislet Valleys

inner marshes could be flooded. The area around Nethergong in Chislet suffered in this way and a system of pens and summer dams was needed to satisfy everyone. In the Lydden Valley the whole internal drainage system was never satisfactory, partly because Sandwich drew its fresh water from streams in the valley and was not always responsible in its attitude towards the proper maintenance of outfalls, and partly because the inner lands of the valley were the lowest. Here new cuts, diversions, pens and gutts were for ever being tried out, but success was very limited. The maintenance of sluices was one of the most expensive drainage works, and was made increasingly difficult as sea level rose. The Chislet levels and those draining to the Stour were particularly affected, and it was not until the Stonar cut and sluice were made in 1766 that there was much improvement.

Despite all the difficulties the lands seemed relatively secure and efficiently sewed through-out most of the seventeenth century and most levels coped well with the emergencies which did arise, such as the 'greatest tide remembered in England' (according to Pepys) which occurred on 7 December, 1663; it was only the exposed Rushbourne wall which seemed to be in imminent danger from every storm and spring tide. The first breaks occurred in 1600 only nine years after the wall was built, and a new, stronger wall, 24 ft. in the seat and 8 ft. high was made. Yet, by 1608 the sea was 'working forcibly along the wall' and an inset soon followed.

The sea was gaining ground rapidly here and a petition to the Justices of the Peace by the inhabitants of Reculver and Chislet, dated 14 January, 1657, recited that 'the sea has since Michaelmas last encroached on the land 6 rods', i.e. 100 ft. in 15 weeks. More inset walls followed; in the 1660s they were being made 40 ft. in the seat and 10–12 ft. high. Despite these efforts the whole front wall from Reculver to the Crooked Wall was abandoned in 1682; the land between it and Abbot's Wall was freed from scot and owners were told to take what measures they would to protect their grounds.

It seems possible that sea level had been rising rather faster from the middle of the century, but it had not been particularly remarked because of the infrequency of storms coinciding with high tides, but in 1690 this dreaded conjunction happened and resulted in disastrous floods not only along the Kent coast but along the low-lying shores all round the southern North Sea, where 'all (walls) are broken down, destroyed, consumed, wasted and washed away by reason of the late innundation and overflowing by the late extraordinary, unheard of and unusual high tide'; these words referred specifically to Grain North West level, but similar language was used to describe the disaster in most other levels. This marked the onset of a number of bad years in which tempestuous seas caused numerous breaches even in new inset walls, and the erosion of forelands proceeded apace. In north-west Grain there were new insets in 1690, 1699, 1702, 1704 and 1711 as a result of which 33 acres of inned land were 'flung to sea' – and the new walls occupied several acres more. The series of storms ended with a fearful gale and high tide on 13 March, 1713, which created havoc all along the coast. The report from Grain South West level was not untypical: 'by reason of the late extraordinary high tides flowing over the walls of the said level in the southernmost part thereof, there has happened a very large breach and the whole level has been drowned . . . and several other parts of the wall are decayed and worne away by the extraordinary violence and beating of the sea . . . shutting the breach will be impracticable by reason of its great width, depth and largeness . . . and the scarcity of earth or clay to shut the same with, . . . and the forelands are so much worne away that they are not sufficient to preserve the marshlands'. In this case the Commission decreed that a new inset wall should be built 'to begin from the East sluice next to the salt pans (the limit of the level) and go in a straight line directly across the first creek and from thence in a circular line across the other two creeks . . . about 40 rods beyond the said breach . . .' this alone excluded 16 acres outside the new wall (Fig. 4).

The walls along much of the Thames frontage had retreated during these stormy years and many acres were lost. The 'Russell' map of 1697 of Cliffe (Fig. 5) shows that the new inset of 1690 had shut out 19 acres at Hope Point, and this now formed part of the 60 acres of salt forelands. Similarly, several named salt marshes shown on a map of North West Grain of about the same date (Fig. 6) had been at least partially fresh a century earlier; in another century they would have vanished altogether.

Once again these calamitous years were followed by several decades punctuated by just one or two bad years, like 1735 or 1763, and over most of the river frontage the main focus of attention in the eighteenth century was on the preservation of the shrinking forelands. Chalk was already being used in west Kent to strengthen the walls, now it was to be used in prodigious quantities to load the forelands, e.g. 2280 tons were used on a narrow frontage in St. Mary's and High Halstow between 1742 and 1745, and from about this date increasing quantities of the more durable ragstone were used, too, despite the extra cost (in 1760 chalk could be delivered to Cliffe level for 1s. 6d. per ton, ragstone for 4s.). Vast numbers of oak piles were cut and driven, and the chalk rammed between them; in 1773 – not an exceptionally bad year – Cliffe level used 1090 oak spears and 20 loads of bushes, and spent £74 11s. 8d. on chalk and £10 10s. on stone, virtually all for Hope Point where the wall was again under attack although the new inset of 1690 had been supplemented by another in 1714. At almost every high tide along this frontage from Gravesend to Grain chalk was being washed out and the piles 'blowed' and men were constantly employed re-driving the piles and re-stowing the chalk. By the end of the century Cliffe was taking 4–6,000 piles annually and 500–1,000 tons each of chalk and stone, virtually all for foreland work.

The map of North West Grain (Fig. 6) shows that the various salts were divided by creeks, of which Pope's creek was the largest. By the late eighteenth century much of the salting had gone, and Pope's creek was scouring the bottom of the wall and seriously diminishing its stability. To prevent this the creek was dammed by bushes, and when this proved ineffective, was filled with chalk near the wall. This, too, provided no solution, so in 1790 a new channel was cut to turn the creek farther from the wall, and the old one was again blocked. But it was to no avail, for the same job was done all over again in 1793, 1794 and 1795, and the adjacent wall at Shell End was greatly strengthened. Despite the sharply rising costs, consequent on the Napoleonic wars, similar work was done annually over the next decade, yet in 1805 it was noted that Pope's creek was dammed and 'blowed within a week', and this was in June! In 1807 another substantial channel was cut 17¼ rods long, 12 ft. wide and 7 ft. deep, and the wall at Shell End was thickened by 3 ft. to increase its strength. Seven years later it was almost reconstructed and 500 cu. yds. of earth and 2327 tons of block stone were used to create a heavy wall with a seaward slope of 1:4 or 1:5, and siding was done 34 ft. deep and 3 ft. thick to the tenuous strip of salts which remained. Pope's creek and the Thames had won, many acres of fresh marsh had been gradually given up to become salt, and then had been lost altogether.

There was retreat, too, in the Whitstable area; for in 1779 it was decided that the old wall could no longer be repaired. Attention had been given all century to groynes or jetties built to break the force of the waves and to collect beach, and they had had some success. As the grassy banks were eaten away and the shoreline advanced inland, the wall came under increas-

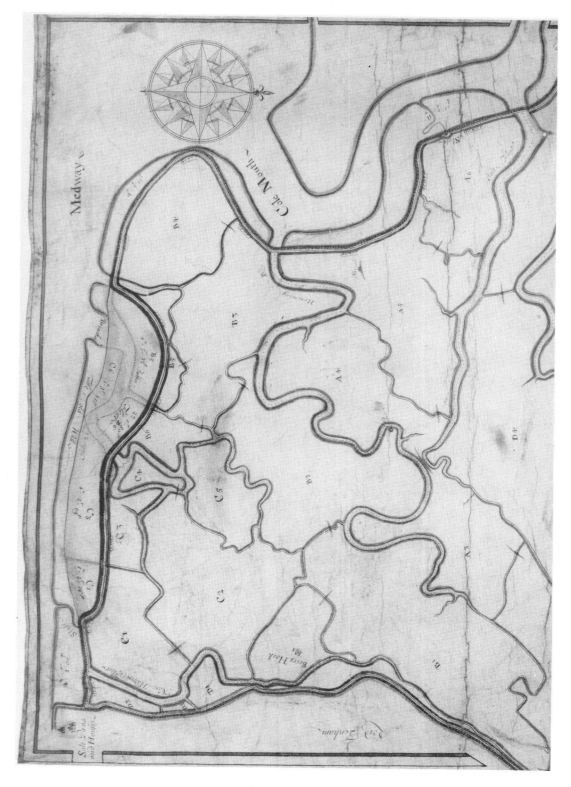

Fig. 4.   An Extract of the 'Russell' Map of Grain south-west Level

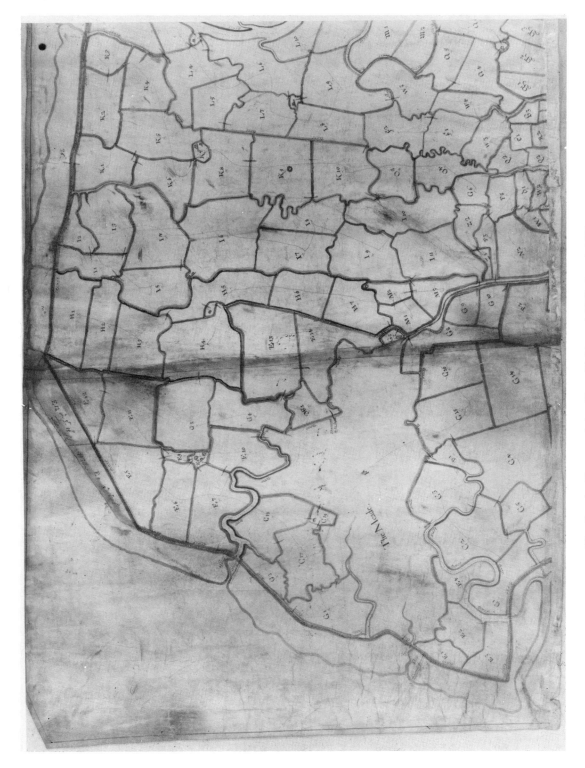

Fig. 5. An Extract of the 'Russell' Map of Cliffe Level 1697

Fig. 6.   An Extract of the 'Russell' Map of Grain north-west Level

ing attack and from the 1760s could only just be maintained in 'normal' years. It could in no way withstand the onslaught which came with the New Year storm in 1779, reported thus by the *Kentish Gazette*, 'on January 1st at Whitstable is a most dreadful sight, the high tide flowed through the street to such a height that . . . ground floors were entirely under water some feet deep'. An emergency view suggested that it would be more costly to repair the old wall than build a new one, a view with which Mr. James Jordan of Dymchurch, who had been called in to advise, wholly concurred. He gave his opinion that the new inset wall should be set back no less than 40 rods at the east end next Tankerton cliff – a retreat of 220 yards, requiring the exclusion of 16 acres of land known as 'The Outletts'. This marsh had, in the sixteenth century, been accounted 28 acres, 12 acres had already gone, and much of the 16 acres would be covered by beach in the next fifty years.

Not all was loss here, for in the area lying west of the Horsebridge, and known as 'The Salts', by estimation 97 acres, there was some reclamation in the 1780s by which approximately 50 acres were inned within the 'Island Wall'. This was completed none too soon, for Edward Hasted remarked in 1797 that 'it was observed by the inhabitants that the sea gains greatly on this shore every year'.[4]

The inhabitants of Reculver would have had even greater cause for such an observation, for along this strip of coast there were no successes to report, only dismal tales of damage, loss and retreat. The first major defeat had been the abandonment of the wall from Reculver to Crooked Wall in 1682; only twenty years later Abbot's Wall, which stood well back behind this, was said to be inadequate to withstand any severe strain, and was made 20 ft. broad in the seat, 2 ft. higher, and widened at the top to a minimum of 7 ft., and thenceforth no cattle or horses were allowed to graze on it. This work required over 5 acres, which were bought by the Commission for the purpose. Subsequently, the owners of Rushbourne salts, in front of Abbot's Wall, asked for help from the Commission in maintaining their own low bank along the shore, which held back some of the beach, and broke the force of the waves before they reached Abbot's. This request was made on several occasions and was generally viewed sympathetically by the Commission who had no wish to see their own wall further exposed.

By 1727 the adjoining stretch of wall, eastwards from Crooked Wall to Cold Harbour sluice, was in great decay. This was particularly serious for it defended the whole area of marsh along the Wantsum channel (i.e. between the medieval innings which lay behind Abbot's and Chambers walls) and if it were to be breached the salt water could run back to Sarre wall and flood a great part of South Chislet, and possibly even break through these old counter walls which were not made to front wall standards. For this reason strenuous efforts were made to keep this wall intact, and Capt. Wm. Markwick of the Royal Engineers was engaged to advise the Commission. His report was significant in that he suggested that in addition to the substantial repair of the old wall 40–45 ft. in the seat and 10 or 11 ft. high, an inner wall should be built behind this 'for in case of a very high tide and swell of the sea, and violence of a strong wind an overflow may happen, in such a case an insett wall will prevent any great break in the sea wall for as soon as the cavity or place between the sea wall and the insett wall is full of water, the sea has no more power to make any further break to the sea wall'.

By the 1740s much was again in decay and more new insets were required, and the groynes were all substantially repaired – but to no avail, for in 1750 the whole length of the 'new wall'

---

4. E. Hasted, *Historical and Topographical Survey of the County of Kent*, 1797–1801.

(Capt. Markwick's inner wall) and Abbot's wall to Reculver were heightened and strengthened.

The storm at New Year 1779 caused great damage along the whole frontage to Birchington, and here, too, it was James Jordan who was consulted. Again there was some retreat, but by 1788 yet more had to be given up in new insets against Wademarsh and at Cold Harbour, and now the wall had to be made 50 ft. at the base and 13 ft. high, with a width at the top of 9 ft. in order that waggons could pass over it, and be backed by a foreland of 12 ft. and a ditch 10 ft. wide and 5 ft. deep to collect the fresh water and keep it from sapping the land toe of the wall. This represented a much larger structure and a more integrated total defence system than ever before, especially as the groynes were overhauled and given strong footings of clite (chalk).

Heavy maintenance work continued, but by 1800 there was a new fear – that the Commission walls would be endangered by the erosion of the cliffs at each end which would allow the sea to enter the marshes from the side. The severity of the encroachment can be judged from Hasted's comment that in Leland's time (1540s) the village of Reculver was a quarter of a mile from the sea, 'whereas now (1797) what is left, is so close to the sea, as to be washed by the waves, and the church itself is only a few rods from it'.[4] In fact, the sea was close under the wall of the Roman fort by 1685, and the wall began to fall in 1691; the sea was within 60 yds. of the church after the gale of 1735, and within 30 yds. of it by 1792; by 1805 it was 'as close as the width of a highway passable by a carriage'.

Since the uplands were not in commission, the co-operation of owners and occupiers was sought in order that safety measures could be taken. Several engineers were asked for their opinions, and Trinity House, which had taken over the defence of the church in order to safeguard the towers which were an important navigational aid, was approached about taking part in a coherent defence scheme. They were exceedingly unco-operative, but the landowners did all in their power to assist the Commission, for in so doing they were also protecting their own good arable fields on the cliff from being washed away. The defences crept further and further along the cliff foot and got larger and stronger almost annually, especially under the care of James Rennie, an engineer noted for his marine and river works, who was retained as consultant from 1804 to 1820.

By the early nineteenth century the relative benefit received by Rushbourne and the Chislet valleys from the sea walls was felt by some owners to have changed radically since 1591 when the differential scotting system was established. In 1814 they expressed their view that however fair it was 'in those days' that the back lands should pay less when the village (of Reculver) stood some distance from the sea, now the said lands were in quite as much danger because of the encroachment of the tide and should be scotted equally. A jury found that the complaint had some substance and the rating was revised such that the half scotted lands were henceforth to pay three-quarters scots, and some one-quarter scots were increased to half.

Soon after this, in 1821, a proposal was made that yet another counter wall should be built in the Chislet valleys from Abbot's wall to the upland so that if a breach occurred in or at the side of the front wall the tidal water should be kept in the northern 383 acres rather than spread across the whole 1453 acres in the levels. The owners and occupiers of the 383 acres were, understandably, very upset. They argued that their land had already depreciated through the change in the rating system which had doubled their scots, that under the new proposal the water would linger on their marshes, perhaps for days if a contrary wind blocked North Chislet sluice and the fret of such a flood might even breach the counter wall and the whole level be flooded anyway. Their argument was accepted and the front wall was strengthened and turned back to run into the upland to limit the possibility of floods getting in from the side.

Thus the outlook in the early nineteenth century was uniformly bleak: the saltings were almost gone; it required heavy outlay to maintain a full of beach where this was available, and the inexorable rise in sea level necessitated higher, broader and heavier walls which in themselves increased maintenance problems since the marsh clay on which they were founded was not strong. Few would have predicted that the shoreline could be held, even with great expense, yet this is what happened and the line of the walls was substantially maintained except where sharp angles were set back to limit the fret of the sea. This was the result of the adoption (under professional advice) of the latest techniques of wall building and of the judicious use of the best materials. During the century there were several reports by consultants on one or other stretch of wall and the study of these allows a picture of changing methods and techniques to be built up, as the following examples will serve to show.

The Commission for the area from Lombard's wall to Gravesend Bridge called in James Easton to report on their defences in 1847. He was asked to comment on a number of specific points concerning construction, materials and workmanship, and to give details on the work needing to be done in each level.

The main points of this report may be summarised as follows: (i) the total disuse of piles was to be recommended since they were not currently used by men of eminence in engineering for sea wall work; (he said that they had not been much used by the Commission of late years, but this was certainly not true of the adjoining area where they were being used in large numbers at Higham, Shorne, Cliffe and High Halstow, but it seems that the practice was soon after discontinued there too); (ii) chalk should be replaced by stone, even above high water mark, as chalk was soft and easily worn away or dissolved, whilst stone remained fixed and thereby encouraged the growth of weed which made it immune to erosion; (Easton remarked that the stone pitching had not been well done in the past but was now much improved); (iii) construction was generally on scientific principles as surveyors had copied the slope which had best resisted the wash of boats (he noted that the increase of steam boat traffic would certainly cause increased erosion); (iv) some angles should be set back and the walls raised to a uniform height; (v) saltings should be maintained although this would be costly and uneconomic in terms of the value of the saltings themselves, but was essential if the line of the walls was to be maintained (e.g. 880 yards of narrow salts outside Abbey level in Plumstead and Erith marsh would cost £1316 6s. 8d. to protect, yet the acreage was 'too negligible to state').

On individual levels Easton noted in particular the variable cross sections and recommended that many banks should be broadened and given a flatter slope. Discussing the internal drainage he commented unfavourably on the different levels to which sluices were laid, pointing out that this made it impossible to develop a coherent drainage system. The Plumstead marshes were notoriously badly drained at this period, causing severe attacks of ague and poor health locally. After Easton's recommendations had been carried out the situation was said to be rendered much more healthy, and good crops were being grown on marshland recently the haunt of a host of wild fowl.

The Commission followed the advice given and the walls were improved, but the high tides of 1897 showed just how much the situation had deteriorated in the half century since Easton's report. A report was made by Mr. Hurtzig following the storm, in which he noted that 83 breaches had occurred, many extending below the stone pitching, and in some places the banks were level with the saltings. At Swanscombe the sluice had been ripped out along with 130 ft. of embankment to a depth of 16 ft. below the base of the wall, and many sewers were completely choked by sea wall débris. He recommended a considerable expanse of sheet piling extending to the firm bottom, however deep this might be, backed by a line of timber piling, the cavity between being filled with puddled clay to the depth of low water, in order to provide a watertight foundation. He added a rider to his report to the effect that so called 'extra-ordinary' high tides seemed to be recurring with greater frequency and reaching ever greater heights; he therefore advocated that walls should be built high enough to take account of this and be made 18 ft. 6 in. high. In this respect his advice was not followed and most walls were some inches lower.

Similar reports exist for other areas and show that the Commissioners generally sought the best solutions available, but on occasions they were not so sensible and tried to save money by building to lower standards than those advocated. This happened in Seasalter in the 1840s when the dilapidated condition of the wall was endangering the whole level. The surveyor suggested using the high ridges of shingle which had accumulated in front of the old wall, as the basis of a new defence recommending that the ridges should be opened and a good core of puddled clay inserted. Utilising a natural bulwark appealed to the Commissioners, but they chose to avoid the cost of the clay core and allowed substantial additional defences to be built directly on the unconsolidated shingle. The same practice was followed in Whitstable and has been the cause of considerable trouble and great additional expense in the twentieth century.

Throughout the century continuing emphasis was placed on the retention of beach by groynes. Everyone agreed on their usefulness but there was no consensus about how they should be used: they were too long, too short, too high, too low, or incorrectly made. One problem was that the system used in one place might not work elsewhere, and minor shifts in tide or current action could render costly works ineffective. There were many experiments, and most worked well for a time, but with rising sea level the beach is inevitably drawn down at the toe and flung back at the top under stormy conditions, thus migrating inland. Even walls did not stop this, and beach was frequently barrowed back to the sea side and cast out of the delph ditches at Wademarsh and Reculver. The problem was felt acutely near the sewer out-falls which were difficult to keep free from shingle, and several types of 'knocks', jetties and walls were tried to shield the sluice and gutt.

Inside the walls there was no let up in the age-old problem of internal drainage: the Fordsbourne valley in Seasalter was frequently flooded in winter, and in 1844 the surveyor was told to draw up plans to improve matters; this he did by shortening the main sewer by nearly half to achieve a better flow. At the same time Faversham Union complained that the poor drainage of the adjoining Graveney and Hernhill marshes resulted in high mortality among the local communities and requested that the system be improved. Whilst this was an old, recurrent problem, the rapidly changing society of the nineteenth century brought a whole host of new ones, some of which proved exceedingly intractable.

The quickening pace of economic activity and the interest in improved transport which this engendered affected even this rural county, and proposals were afoot for a canal from Canterbury to St. Nicholas Bay in 1810, and for a 'navigation' to Sandown Castle in 1824, either of which would have had serious repercussions on the drainage system. The Stour navigation project dragged on for years and the Commission was put to some expense in retaining professional advisers. A plan for a new harbour off the Downs threatened the whole of the Stour Valley lands, but was dropped in the face of stiff opposition. The Commissioners undertook some improvements of their own, notably on Dartford Creek which was straightened and provided with a lock below the town, and in improved cleansing of the Stour by means of a 'blow boat'.

The increase in road traffic frequently necessitated bridge repairs across the main sewers, a responsibility of the Commission who not unnaturally felt that the Highway Authorities should shoulder part of the financial burden: several agreements were reached which allowed for wider and more substantial bridges to be made at shared cost, and to their mutual advantage.

The coming of the railways also caused some anxiety, for not only did the companies want to build numerous bridges, but also their embankments would cut right across established drainage lines, making the reorientation of the ditches an absolute necessity, and this in turn affected penstocks and sluices. For these reasons the Commissioners concerned themselves closely with the passage of each Railway Bill which affected their jurisdiction, requesting their MPs to promote certain clauses which would ensure that the railway engineers had to comply with specifications made by the Sewer Commissioners. Generally, the companies were co-operative, but some sharp words were exchanged, for example over interference with drains in the Lydden valley in the 1860s where drainage was poor at the best of times and the Commissioners were in no mood to have their task made more difficult.

In the 1870s there was great consternation over a grand plan to reclaim the whole of Pegwell Bay which, it was feared, would entail a complete change of the outfall in the Stour, which would affect adversely the drainage of all the contributory levels as far up as Canterbury. There was much acrimonious discussion for nearly twenty years before the plan was finally abandoned.

Urban growth and the increased use of rivers and sewers for effluent disposal posed serious problems, especially acute in the case of Canterbury, for the city's sewage was emptied direct into the Stour polluting it heavily for some miles downstream and promoting weed growth which rendered clearance more costly. Since the wholesome state of the water as well as the maintenance of the channel were Commission concerns, they regarded this practice with mounting indignation. By 1869 they were complaining about the effect on the health of their workmen and on the riverside communities, and in 1871 the expenditor reported that he had removed 1900 cu. yds. of town drainage deposit from the main river; by 1875 the deposit was heavier than ever and stinking mud fouled all the banks for miles downstream. The city authority took some steps to alleviate the nuisance, but was so dilatory that the Commission sought legal advice regarding action against them. This seems to have spurred the Corporation into more energetic action and steps were taken to improve the situation, but it was not until the early 1900s that the nuisance was abated.

Meanwhile other local authorities were coming to grips with their sewerage problems – and aggravating those of the Commissioners: Eastry erected a new sewage works in 1892 in the Upper Wingham valley, but it did not work and the valley was fouled and filled with an unbearable stench; Eastry accepted liability and contributed to the greatly increased costs of cleansing the valley.

Mills had caused difficulties since medieval times, because of the way in which they penned their water which caused flooding elsewhere. Increasingly now the problem became one of effluent disposal as more and more works sought riverside locations. In 1865 the Canterbury Gas Company and local firms of dyers were told that it was 'contrary to the law to allow filthy or unwholesome water or washings of manufactories or other foul or poisonous liquids to flow into the river' and they were requested to comply with the law. In 1888 Ash brewery was said to be fouling the water, but that this was not serious because no solid matter was involved and the effluent did not promote weed growth.

An entirely new problem connected with land use affected the Commissioners in west Kent in 1864 when, on October 1st, gun-powder exploded in the magazines of William Hall near the sea wall in Erith. This apparently set off more explosions in other magazines nearby which resulted in a 26-yd. breach in the wall and severe damage to the adjoining sections. By great good fortune the tide was low at the time and the expenditor rapidly assembled a large work-force including 400 navvies from the new sewage outfall works at Crossness and 200 soldiers from Woolwich. The local paper printed a graphic account of the race between the labourers and the tide, noting with macabre relish, the possibility present throughout the operation, that the wall would give way and several hundred men be drowned. The firms concerned were not bound by any tenure or covenant to defray the cost of repairs so this fell on all local scot payers, to their intense chagrin.

Less than twenty years later the walls had to be repaired again for in 1881 'an extraordinary high wind and an extraordinary and violent storm from the east occurred in the Thames . . . the said storm caused extraordinary heavy waves resembling the waves of the ocean to break on and over the wall' (the reporter's vocabulary seems to have been extraordinarily limited!). This event, following the disaster of 1864, and the flooding of factories on Dartford Creek in 1875, convinced the Commission that the method of rating for wall work should be changed as factories clearly derived more benefit and avoided danger to a greater degree than agricultural lands, yet on the acreage basis they paid very little scot. The change to assessment on the basis of rateable value was made first in the western area and followed by the Commission from Gravesend Bridge to Sheerness in 1909, though not without opposition.

The high tides of 1874, 1875 and 1881 were little more than a foretaste of what might ensue when high water was backed by strong gales, for on November 29th, 1897, persistent gales raised waves well above the high tide level, and water flowed freely over walls all along the Thames. The lands highest up the estuary suffered most, breaches totalling one-tenth of the wall length occurred above Gravesend; below this there were fewer breaks but everywhere marshes were inundated and walls greatly weakened. The next few years were occupied with the total overhaul of defences, and the next 'unusual' high tide, in 1906, was less devastating in its effect.

From now on general maintenance work was carried out, but during the war and the depression which followed no substantial improvements took place as the Commissions tried to keep the scots to their pre-war levels. The damage caused by the storms of 1928 and 1929 showed that the strength and reliability of many walls had been impaired by this policy, and it was fortunate that the worst weather did not coincide with Spring tides. A report on the walls in 1929 suggested that it was folly to allow the defences to be impaired in an effort to keep scots down. However, the cost of modern engineering work was really too great to be funded in the old way and in the following year the Land Drainage Act brought the Commissions of Sewers to an end.

The Commissioners for North and East Kent had fought a long, hard battle; given the conditions under which they operated and the problems with which they were faced, it is not surprising that they, like Canute, failed to stop the tide from coming in: that they stopped it from coming further and greedily devouring yet more good farmland, is a tribute to their responsible attitudes and hard work 'in and about the levels'.

BRIDGE BUILDING IN KENT, 1700–1830: THE WORK OF THE JUSTICES OF THE PEACE

CHRISTOPHER CHALKLIN

Introduction

In the seventeenth and eighteenth centuries numerous bridges all over England of varying size and importance were being looked after by county justices, paying for repairs and rebuilding out of county rates. This was not true of the majority of the largest English bridges, such as many over the big rivers like the Thames and the Severn, which were maintained or rebuilt by corporations, trusts or companies using the income from tolls on passengers or from property given for their repair. Innumerable small bridges, often just foot and horse bridges or intended merely for local use, were the responsibility of a particular parish or municipality or other jurisdiction by prescription (that is, because it had always been accustomed to do so), or of a landowner *ratione tenurae* (that is, as an incident of his tenure of the land). Nevertheless, by 1700 probably between 800 and 1200 foot, horse and carriage bridges were dealt with by the justices, and they were making occasional grants towards the cost of rebuilding or repairing several hundred more bridges in the care of a parish or private owner. Common law held that all bridges forming part of the public highway should be kept repaired and that in default of any special liability, the county was responsible for the maintenance of public bridges within the area. An act of 1531 stated that where no other liability could be proved definitely, the burden of maintenance should fall on the county or corporate town within which the bridge lay. The act gave the justices in general sessions the authority to deal with bridges needing repair (including the approach roads 300 feet from each end), to appoint two surveyors to act on their behalf, and to levy rates. Before an act of 1739, it was usual to raise bridge rates; thereafter, payments were made out of the general county rates. These levies were collected from the parishes by the constables of the hundreds and passed to the county treasurer. In some counties many of the less important bridges for which the justices had charge were treated as 'hundred bridges', the rates for the bridges being levied just on the hundred in which the bridge lay, and the expenditure being administered by the justices of the division or the constable of the hundred.[1]

The number of bridges for which a county was responsible varied very sharply. In at least a dozen counties in the Midlands and southern England the justices only had charge of a handful of bridges. In the early eighteenth century Berkshire was only repairing two bridges, and both of them were shared with other counties.[2] The large county of Shropshire only handled six bridges at the beginning of the eighteenth century.[3] On the other hand in about half the English counties quarter sessions dealt with at least 15 or 20 bridges, and in some cases many more. Between 1630 and 1733 the Dorset justices paid for work on 22 stone county bridges.[4] In

1. S. and B. Webb *The Story of the King's Highway* (*English Local Government,* 5), 1963, 88–9.
2. Berkshire R.O. Q/SO 1, 2.
3. (Ed.) G.C. Baugh *A History of Shropshire,* III, 1979, 101.
4. E. Boswell *The Civil Division of the County of Dorset,* Sherborne, 1795, 76–86.

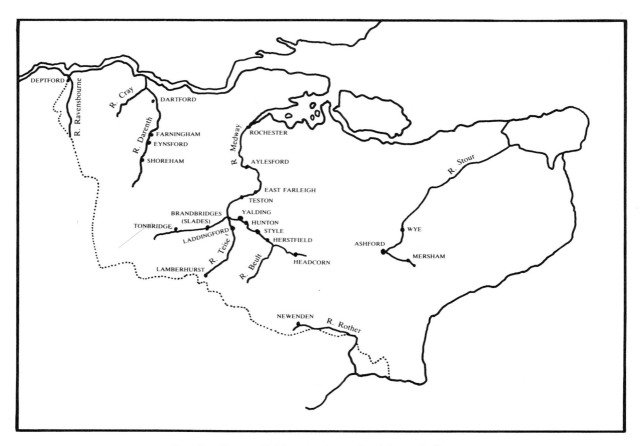

Fig. 7. County Bridges in the early eighteenth Century

the years 1681 to 1710 the justices of the North Riding dealt with about 75 county bridges, and gave gratuities for about 50 bridges for which parishes or private individuals were responsible.[5] The expenditure on bridges in the later seventeenth and early eighteenth centuries naturally varied according to the number in the care of the county. The counties with a large number of bridges spent an average of perhaps no more than £20 or £30. Essex raised £10,550 in 'bridge levies' between 1671 and 1700, or an average of £352 a year.[6] On the other hand, in the neighbouring county of Hertfordshire where there were ten county bridges but none of them large, the treasurer of the bridge money paid out £340 12s. 6½d. on county bridge works between Christmas 1690 and Easter 1703, an average of about £26 a year.[7] Expenditure on individual bridgeworks in the counties with many bridges in their care, whether involving major repairs and alterations or entire new bridges, was not outstanding. While bridge works

5. (Ed.) J.C. Atkinson *North Riding Record Society Publications*, VII, *Quarter Sessions Records*, 1889.
6. Essex R.O. Q/FAc 1.
7. (Ed.) W. le Hardy *Hertfordshire County Records: Calendar to the Sessions Books and Sessions Minute Books, 1658–1700*, VI, Hertford 1930, 39–40, 163.

costing £200 or £300 were common in the early eighteenth century, only a handful of new bridges in the whole of England cost more than £1000 before the 1770s.

From the 1770s and 1780s many counties were beginning to increase their outlay on bridges. This is revealed in the increase in the number of bridges for which the county assumed responsibility, and in the appearance of bigger bridge undertakings. For example, Shropshire added two bridges in the later 1760s to the six county bridges of the early eighteenth century; then, between 1768 and 1777, Atcham bridge was rebuilt for £8674 6s. 8½d., one of the biggest county bridge undertakings of the 1770s and 1780s, followed by Tern bridge, 1778–81 at a cost of £4676 6s. 6d.[8] The number of Shropshire county bridges grew sharply from 1788; by 1808, there were 38 and, by 1825, at least 81.[9] The principal reason for the greater county expenditure was the sustained growth of wheeled transport in the late eighteenth and early nineteenth centuries. The courts were favouring the increasing liability of the counties for bridge maintenance after the famous Glasburne decision against the West Riding Sessions in 1780 that 'if a man build a bridge, and it becomes useful to the county in general, the county shall repair it'. Larger outlays on some of the more important bridges reflect the erection of wider bridges with better approaches and (probably) a higher standard of construction.

The Kent County Bridges

In Kent, the justices' care of bridges is documented from the time of the earliest surviving sessions records at the beginning of the seventeenth century. During the next hundred years major bridge works were fewer than in the eighteenth and early nineteenth centuries. This probably reflects the smaller amount of carriage and waggon traffic than in the later period, and possibly the fact that the raising of money for bridge works by the justices was still relatively unfamiliar in the county. Outlay was considerable on the building of Wye bridge in 1638, on major repairs to Tonbridge Great Bridge, Lamberhurst and Slades bridges in the early 1660s, and the repair of Ashford and Newenden bridges in the 1680s, both costing Kent about £110, but no similar works are recorded for the 1650s and 1670s.[10] In this century the means by which the bridge works were paid was still fluid. At the beginning of the century bridges were not repaired out of a county stock raised by a rate on all or a large part of the county, but by *ad hoc* levies on the hundreds nearest the respective bridges.[11] Later in the case of county bridges, the lathe or lathes nearer the bridge were expected to pay more than the rest of the county.[12] In the 1680s, some bridge works were paid for on the basis of two-thirds by the part of the county (west or east) in which the bridge lay, and one-third from the other part.[13] County bridge rates were being levied in connexion with particular bridge works in the 1660s and earlier, when collection was often very slow on account of the relative unfamiliarity of a bridge rate.[14] In the 1670s and 1680s payments were being made for bridges out of the general county stock for the east and west divisions of the county.[15] Bridge rates for the whole county

8. Baugh, *Shropshire*, 125–27; Shropshire R.O. county treasurer's accounts, 1764–77, 1778–88.
9. Baugh, *Shropshire*, 127.
10. Kent Archives Office U352 010, Q/SOw 2, 3 *passim*, Q/SOw 4, 24/4/88, 2/10/88.
11. E. Melling, *Some Roads and Bridges*, Maidstone 1959, 46–8.
12. K.A.O. U386 0/3; Q/SOw 1 ff. 161, 162, 178, Q/SOw 2 f. 26.
13. K.A.O. Q/SOw 4, eg. 24/4/88.
14. K.A.O. Q/SOw 2 ff. 83, 106, 128, 136.
15. K.A.O. Q/SOw 3 f. 49, Q/SOw 4, eg. 2/10/88.

were levied in 1692 and 1701, the money being collected by officials for the east and west respectively.[16] At least by the early 1710s the two divisions of the county were paying for their own bridges by rates levied independently, a method which was to continue until 1814, when expenditure became a matter for the whole county. As in other counties, the money was levied as bridge rates until the bridge act of 1739, after which the bridge expenditure came out of the general rate.

During the eighteenth century about 22 or 23 bridges were repaired or rebuilt by one of the two divisions of the county. They did not include Rochester bridge, the largest in Kent, which was the responsibility of bridge wardens appointed from amongst the owners of certain lands, or Maidstone bridge, which was repaired by the Corporation. Otherwise they were the more important bridges in the county, as follows:

Deptford, River Ravensbourne;
Dartford, Eynsford, Farningham, Shoreham, River Darenth;
Aylesford, East Farleigh, Teston, Yalding (including Twyford), Slades, Brandbridges, Tonbridge, River Medway;
Hunton, Style, Herstfield, Headcorn, River Beult;
Laddingford, Lamberhurst, River Teise;
Newenden, River Rother;
Wye, Ashford, Mersham, River Stour.[17]

All except the last three on the River Stour lay in the west division of the county. In the early nineteenth century the number of county bridges increased, including two bridges on the Cray (Gad's, Bexley and Foot's Cray), and others on the Ravensbourne, Darenth, Stour and tributaries of the upper Medway.

Among the more important eighteenth-century county bridges Deptford and Dartford lay on Watling Street, the most important road crossing the county from London to the coast, with an extensive carriage and waggon traffic linking London to the most thickly-populated and prosperous part of the county, including the Medway towns, Canterbury and Dover. Deptford bridge also carried much suburban traffic and it is thus understandable that its rebuilding in 1810–11 was the largest county bridge undertaking. Farningham lay on the useful though relatively less important thoroughfare between London and Maidstone. Tonbridge and Lamberhurst lay on the busy route across the county which linked London to the Channel coast at Hastings. The other bridges helped the local collection and distribution of goods, some of which were received from, or destined for, London or the north Kent ports. Thus, the bridges in the Weald on the tributaries of the Medway were essential for local traffic; they helped the export of timber, hops and agricultural produce down the navigable River Medway, and the import of coal and other goods in the area.

Many of the smaller bridges, which far outnumbered the county bridges, were the responsibility of the hundreds. The work of the constables in handling repairs or rebuilding and raising a hundred rate was supervised by the justices. They lay particularly on the tributaries of the Medway; for example, there was a group of little bridges in the hundreds of Washlingstone and

16. K.A.O. Q/SOw 5, 5/4/92, 29/4/01.
17. Based on lists of county bridges in K.A.O. Q/AB 71, and the eighteenth century order books (Q/SOe and Q/SOw).

Somerden to the south-west of Tonbridge town. In the early nineteenth century some of these hundred bridges became a county responsibility, though at least a few of the new county bridges had previously been built or maintained by turnpike trustees, individuals or parishes.

Bridge Expenditure, 1700–1830

Throughout the whole period 1700–1830 the west Kent justices were active over bridge works. In east Kent any sizeable expenditure was infrequent on account of the few bridges in the justices' care. In the western division outlay on major repairs or rebuilding occurred in every decade, with bridge works becoming more numerous from the 1760s. If one takes account of the inflation of the later eighteenth century and 1800s and 1810s, when building costs more than doubled, and adopts constant prices from 1771, there were about 60 bridge works involving an outlay of more than £100 (see Tables I and II).

Many of these undertakings involved considerable repairs without (probably) the rebuilding of a substantial part of the bridge. The typical Kentish bridge in the care of the justices was of several arches of sandstone or ragstone, occasionally partly wooden, wide enough for one carriage to cross, probably built between the fourteenth and seventeenth centuries, such as the surviving examples of East Farleigh on the Medway or Eynsford on the Darenth. Brick was also being used from the seventeenth century. A general weakness of this type of bridge was the fact that the arches were not wide enough to take flood waters in rainy seasons, and it flowed out onto the approach roads or even over the parapets. Among repair works undertaken were the restoration of the stone work of the buttresses or the body of the arches. Typically, the stones decayed or were washed out by the water, flood water in particular being likely to weaken the stone work. The foundations, too, might need strengthening or a wharf required at a particular point of the structure to break the force of the water. For example, in July 1768, the justices Samuel Boys and Robert Monypenny reported to the Court that they had viewed Newenden bridge; they found that the east and west buttresses and the north cove were greatly decayed so that had repairs been deferred the arches would shortly have given way. It was necessary to build a wharf at the north arch to break the force of the water there; the south cove was settled and it was necessary to erect a wing of stone work to prevent it going further. No estimate could be made because the condition of the stone work under water was unknown. They had employed a stone mason on the repairs and asked for £100 from the treasurer.[18]

Other repairs were done to the paving or parapets of bridges damaged by the increasing number of carriages or carts. In 1770 William Meredith was paid £221 6s. 4d. for paving Dartford bridge, mainly consisting of 965 yards of new pebble paving at 4s. per yard at £193.[19] Approach roads needed making up, and occasionally fencing which protected the adjoining land. In 1790, John Parks was paid £117 1s. 8d. for 'paving and repairing the road, 100 yards in length and five yards wide, from the county bridge at Aylesford, finding the stones, gravel, workmanship and all materials'.[20]

The supply and carriage of building or road materials (in most cases mainly stone) were the major cost of repairs, with payments to masons and bricklayers being also considerable. The

18. K.A.O. Q/AB 42/4.
19. K.A.O. Q/AB 13/35.
20. Melling, op. cit., 49.

precise nature of the repairs is often not stated. For example, in 1762 £178 14s. 2½d. was spent on work on Herstfield bridge, a medieval stone bridge with some more recent brick work. The bricklayer was paid £42 17s. 1½d., which included payments to workmen at a daily rate, £14 16s. 7d. to the carpenter, and a large bill for 263 loads of rocks and stones supplied by a mason, presumably to repair the roadway, at £98 12s. 6d.[21] In 1770–71 the three neighbouring bridges of Yalding and Laddingford and a horse bridge at the end of Yalding Lees and their approach roads were repaired. The total of £411 14s. included two large bills of £110 11s. 10d. for 577 tons of stone delivered and £98 2s. 2½d. for 'work and stones' (mainly in fact the cost of stones and freightage payments); there were two other bills of £49 10s. and £27 0s. 2d. for the carriage of stone and some bricks and earth; a bricklayer was paid £77 18s. 4d., and there were two tiny bills for posts and plank, and gravel, respectively.[22]

In a minority of instances during the eighteenth century, but in a majority of cases between 1800 and 1830 the new building of part or all the bridge is said to have been undertaken. This sometimes comprised the replacement of one or several arches, or of one side of the bridge, widening to provide footways or allow two carriages to pass, or to convert a horse bridge into a carriage bridge. A better road surface was also an improvement. The rebuilding of one side of a bridge took place at Deptford bridge in the 1710s. In 1708 and 1709, £200 was ordered by Quarter Sessions to be given to the justices of Blackheath hundred for payment to craftsmen; in 1712 and 1713, a carpenter, William Baker, was paid £191 9s. 9½d. for timber work. Then, in the winter of 1715–16, the north side of the bridge collapsed under the rapid pressure of the current and, in January, the Sessions was told in a petition that the whole bridge would probably collapse when it thawed unless immediate action was taken: 'the crowns of the arches being in a falling condition the parapett walls and the very foundations of the peers undermined and totally ruined by the rapid course of the River Ravensbourne which in all great raines and sudden thaws brings downe great inundations of land waters and which in ye first charge of weather will inevitably happen and in all probability raze up the whole bridge if not immediately sustained and prevented . . .'. As usual the local justices were ordered to view and repair it. Over £400 was spent in 1716, the mason, Samuel Edge of Deptford receiving £203 19s. 5d., two smiths for various ironwork £138 6s. 3½d., and William Baker £76 5s. 3d.[25] A partial rebuilding, involving several arches, was done at Herstfield bridges over the River Beult between Boughton Monchelsea and Staplehurst. At Easter Sessions 1726, the local justices were ordered to carry out repairs with an expenditure limit of £100. At Michaelmas Sessions, three justices reported that they had ordered the double arch to be rebuilt for £49 13s., and had had the level of the ground between the arches raised by spreading 15 waggon loads of small stones, had paved the footway, erected a parapet wall and posts and a rail to support the banks, all for £23 19s. They recommended that two more arches be rebuilt, and

---

21. K.A.O. Q/AB 53/10–12.
22. K.A.O. Q/AB 64/67–70.
23. Comprising all bridge works costing more than £100.
24. All bridge works costing more than £100 in the constant prices of the 1760s. The inclusion of constant prices reveals the great rise of building costs in money terms between the 1790s and the 1810s. The constant prices, which must of course be regarded as approximate, are based on surviving wage data, prices of imported softwoods, and prices paid by Greenwich Hospital and the Office of Works for bricks: C.H. Feinstein 'Capital Formation in Great Britain', *Cambridge Economic History of Europe,* vii, Cambridge, 1978, 38.
25. K.A.O. Q/SOw 6, 13/4/08, 3/5/09; Q/AB 15/3–11.

two more repaired for £120, and other minor works done. These tasks were probably done in 1730 and 1731, when a stonemason of Boughton Monchelsea, Joseph Simmonds, received £269 9s.[26] As an example of the enlargement of an existing bridge, Dartford bridge was widened in 1790–91 for £342. At Epiphany Sessions 1790, it was said to be 'not only out of repair but so narrow as to be incommodious and unsafe'; a plan was produced and approved for widening and repairing it; the approach road was also widened which involved a further £150 bill for altering the wall of Dartford church.[27]

Alternatively bridges were entirely or largely rebuilt. Among the smaller bridges rebuilt by the county were Newenden in the 1710s (£475 14s. 6d.), a wider bridge at Dartford in 1754–55 accompanying road improvements (£474 12s. 4d.), although by 1790 this was in turn considered too narrow, a stone bridge at Lamberhurst in 1753–55, a four-arched brick bridge at Farningham in 1772–73 for £499 2s. (again a wider bridge), and eight bridges between 1810 and 1828, all among those for which the county was newly responsible. These included tiny bridges such as Little Chart (costing £173 14s. 6d. in 1813), and Bridge (£190 14s. in 1821). In the majority of cases the motive was the decay or collapse of the old bridge, but the need for a wider bridge was also a contributory factor in several instances. Thus Farningham bridge was rebuilt in 1772–73 for £499 2s. because the existing structure was 'very narrow and inconvenient for carriages and in great decay'.[28] Lamberhurst bridge was rebuilt in 1754 purely on account of the decay of the previous bridge. On 10 July, 1753, the local justice and landowner William Morland wrote to the Clerk that 'our bridge at Lamberhurst is so much out of repair that it really is dangerous to pass over especially for heavy carriages, and if something is not verry speedily done to it to keep it where it is, for ye rem.ʳ of the sumer and next winter, till a thoro' repair or a stone arch can be prepared for and made ye next spring and sumer, it will not I verily believe be capable of carrying any wheel carriages, nor is there any ford . . . near it or near the turnpike . . .' Estimates were obtained of a timber and stone bridge, the Clerk of Sussex hoped that Kent would want a stone bridge on account of its durability 'and then it may be made a very handsome noble little bridge and last for ever'. For this reason a stone bridge was erected.[29]

The four largest undertakings also deserve special mention. By far the most costly project in the eighteenth century was the rebuilding of Tonbridge Great Bridge in 1775–76. Minor sums had been spent on its repair several times earlier in the century, but there is no evidence to explain the decision to rebuild in 1775. A stone bridge of three arches, it was designed and its construction superintended by the London surveyor Robert Mylne, who was responsible for the building of the great Blackfriars bridge (1760–69), and several smaller but important bridges in the provinces.[30] The total cost was £1104 5s. 1½d. including Mylne's commission and expenses (£67 7s. 8d.); the work comprised (according to Mylne's bill) 'pulling down, rebuilding and finishing the county bridge at Tunbridge; making, erecting, and removing a temporary bridge, taking up the pavements of the road and streets adjoining, altering the houses near the bridge; and the purposes connected with the said work'. The largest outlay was the payment to the mason, Daniel Pinder, according to his contract and bill of extras (£581

26. K.A.O. Q/AB 53/6, 7, Q/SOw 7 pp. 277, 372.
27. K.A.O. Q/SOw 12, pp. 200, 453.
28. K.A.O. Q/SOw 10, p. 523.
29. K.A.O. Q/AB 35/27–29.
30. H. Colvin A Biographical Dictionary of British Architects 1600–1840, 1978, 574–75.

10s.), but the purchase, cutting and carriage of stone for the bridge from the local quarries within a distance of two miles, which the two justices paid for separately, cost at least £250.[31] The use of Mylne suggests the willingness to pay for a strong and durable bridge designed by a bridge engineer of national reputation, as the Hampshire justices were to do in the early 1780s in the case of the much more expensive Romsey bridge.[32]

The Lower Bridge at Tonbridge was rebuilt in 1814 following its collapse early in 1811. It was a one arch brick bridge (apart from the wooden piles) with the road 20 feet wide and a 5-foot footpath. The road on the north side where the soil was marshy originally intended to be built up on low arches supported by piles and provided by a wooden fence was placed instead on a raised causeway.[33] The designer was the well-known architect Daniel Alexander, who was responsible for other important bridges in west Kent rebuilt at the time; the total cost £2195 11s. 10d. was comparable with that of the Great Bridge in 1775–76, taking into account the fact that the cost of building materials had more than doubled since the 1770s.

Ashurst bridge was rebuilt by Kent and Sussex jointly. The immediate cause was the damage it suffered in the severe winter of 1813–14. It was built principally in the summer of 1814 and finished in the following building season as (in the words of Alexander, the designer) 'a wooden bridge rising from brick abutments' at a total cost of £2332.[34]

Lastly, the greatest county bridge undertaking was Deptford bridge in 1810–11. Part of the existing structure, consisting of a brick widening to a stone bridge built in the first quarter of the seventeenth century was washed away by flood water in February 1809. Plans for rebuilding were obtained from three local firms (two being stonemasons, and the other bricklayers and builders) and Alexander was asked to make a further examination and decide the final details. It was decided to build a wider bridge of brick 42 feet 10¼ inches wide comprising a roadway 29 feet 10¼ inches, paths 5 and 8 feet as cheaper than stone, incorporating the remaining old structure about 33 feet wide, with granite carriage way and footpaths and floor of cast iron plates. Its cost was £5522, with property for the approaches being purchased for £1255 6s. 4d.[35]

The Organization of Bridge Building

The decay of a bridge was formally brought to the notice of quarter sessions by a presentment by the grand jury or one or two justices. A group of justices in the area were ordered to have the work undertaken after they had examined the defects. They were either granted a sum of money out of which to pay the workmen, or quarter sessions ordered the treasurer to pay the craftsmen's bills after the work had been completed and certified as such by two or three of the justices. Thus at Epiphany Sessions 1739, Yalding, Teston, Brandbridges and Huntonford bridges were reported to be out of repair, and the justices of the division were appointed to view and contract for their repair. A year later five people were paid a total of £98 16s. 1d. for repairing Teston bridge, and Thomas Martin £43 17s. 10d. for repairing Huntonford bridge and clappers.[36] In the case of Tonbridge Great bridge in 1775–76 the three local justices

31.   K.A.O. Q/AB 58/31.
32.   Hampshire R.O. bridge committee minute books, 1782–1817, f. 29.
33.   Melling. *op.cit.,* 45 (photograph); K.A.O. Q/SOw 15 p. 256.
34.   K.A.O. Q/SOw 15 p. 213; Q/GO 1, p. 71.
35.   K.A.O. Q/AB 1, 15/20, 26–29; Q/SOw 15, pp. 274–76.
36.   K.A.O. Q/SOw 8, pp. 158, 194.

Thomas Hooker, Thomas Harvey and George Children were allocated money to pay the mason contractor and to buy the materials. In 1775 £700 was voted to them to pay the summer season's bills, the treasurer to pay £500 by 10 October and £200 by Christmas.[37]

During the eighteenth century there was no regular county surveyor for the west division, and the local justices usually employed a neighbouring craftsman to view the bridge and estimate the cost of repairs or rebuilding. In the case of Lamberhurst bridge which was out of repair in 1753 a mason and carpenter were employed to make estimates of a stone and wooden bridge respectively; the cost of a stone and brick bridge was put at £331 3s. 10d., the major items being 7342 feet of stonework at 6d. per foot (£183 11s.) and 6¼ rods of brickwork 'if the arches be turned with brick' at £8 8s. per rod (£52 6s.); this compared with an estimate of £193 17s. 8d. for a timber bridge. Five justices (three from Kent, two from Sussex) viewed it on 28 September, having received the estimates, and recommended to the respective Courts that a stone bridge should be erected.[38] When a single craftsman was used, the work may not have been superintended by a skilled workman or surveyor; when several craftsmen were employed one may have been given general responsibility and asked to certify it for the justices' benefit on completion, or a surveyor or workman not involved in the work may have been used. When Dartford bridge was repaired in 1718 a mason, carpenter, smith and plumber were all used, and the carpenter (John Paine), who received £44 6s. 2d. for timber and labour (by himself at 3s. per day and several men at 2s.) also certified the work.[39] When the bridge was rebuilt in 1754 a surveyor, Charles Sloane of Gravesend (who also designed the new county gaol in Maidstone), was asked to prepare a plan; he appears to have supervised the construction, being entrusted by the county with money to pay the contracting workmen.[40] The work done by a typical surveyor of a bridge is summed up in the account of Samuel Nicholson of Rochester who handled the widening of the same bridge in 1790–91, for £300. 'To surveying the bridge at Dartford for the purpose of ascertaining the propriety of altering it, making designs, attending the magistrates at the Quarter Sessions at Maidstone, and also at Dartford, inspecting the execution of the works, and examining and checking the charges of the different bills, journies and all expenses included from Sep.[r] 1790 to Sep.[r] 1791, £42.'[41]

From 1796, west Kent employed a regular surveyor to deal with its bridges and public buildings. At Michaelmas Sessions, John Boys of Teston was appointed to survey and value all county works done by carpenters and bricklayers; he was to be paid a guinea per day for work done within ten miles, and 1s. for each extra mile.[42] In 1810, John Smith of Maidstone was appointed County Surveyor of Bridges and Public Works at £75 a year, to include all business done within five miles of Maidstone, and 1s. per mile whenever required by two justices to attend to county business at more than five miles distance.[43] Not all the work was handled by him. In the following years Daniel Alexander, a well-known architect who was responsible for the great new Maidstone county gaol, handled the three important bridges, Deptford,

37. K.A.O. Q/SOw 11, p. 81.
38. K.A.O. Q/AB 5/27–31.
39. K.A.O. Q/AB 13/3, 7.
40. K.A.O. Q/AB 13/28–29; Q/SB 1755, 1756.
41. K.A.O. Q/AB 13/40.
42. K.A.O. Q/SOw 13, p. 69.
43. K.A.O. Q/SOw 15, p. 336.

Tonbridge Lower Bridge and Ashurst, and smaller bridge works such as the new Catford bridge and the alterations to Style bridge.[44]

In the eighteenth century bridge works in west Kent were not put out to tender by advertisement. Dartford bridge (1754) was the exception. In this case, the Clerk of the Peace was required to advertise for proposals according to the plan deposited with him for inspection by workmen.[45] This was becoming normal practice in most counties in the 1740s and 1750s, as a result of the act of 1739 requiring justices engaged on brick works to accept 'the most reasonable price or prices' after public notice had been given at Quarter Sessions. Instead the Kent justices contracted with craftsmen whom they had employed previously or whose work was well-known in the locality; whether they made any informal efforts to ensure that their prices were reasonable or indeed among the lowest that might be obtained is not clear from the surviving documents. An example may be given to illustrate the tendency to use the same craftsman if he was available. In 1779, a bricklayer named Henry Town received £84 4s. 10d. for work on Style bridge, and in 1783–84 a further £154 11s. 3½d.; next year he received £126 4s. 8d. for work on Herstfield bridge.[46]

Some craftsmen fulfilled the role of county workmen. Apart from being allocated work on the prisons at Maidstone as a matter of course, they often dealt with bridges in the Medway valley. In April 1745, Thomas Martin, bricklayer was appointed mason to the gaol and house of correction at Maidstone in place of John Pollard who had died. In the previous five years Pollard had repaired Yalding and Brandbridges bridges in 1740 (for £96 10s. 4d. and £37 2s. 8d. respectively), Twyford bridge in 1743 (£30 4s.) and East Farleigh bridge in 1774 (£48 2s. 9d.). He also repaired the Maidstone gaol or house of correction in 1740 (twice), 1741, 1743 and 1744.[47] Martin did little or no bridge work, but the bricklayer for the county gaol and house of correction from 1764 (Samuel Giles) not only did the brickwork on the gaol and house of correction until 1782 (including that of the new bridewell in 1774–77), but also on the repairs to the bridges above Maidstone; his largest receipt was £231 0s. 6d. for the brickwork involved in the rebuilding of Brandbridges in 1781. In July 1782, it was ordered that 'Samuel Giles the bricklayer at present usually employed in the county works . . . be no longer employed therein', and Benjamin Ruck of Maidstone was appointed in his place.[48] In the first ten years Ruck was paid £935 7s. 3d. for bridge works, and at least £1500 for works on the gaol and house of correction. He was paid £151 15s. 10½d. for Teston bridge in 1784, £208 18s. 11½d. at Michaelmas 1785 for Yalding and Twyford bridges, and £182 17s. 7d. in 1786 for work on Aylesford bridge.[49] The firm continued to be employed by the county, receiving similar sums during the 1790s and 1800s, during which time other members of the family took over the business.

The payments to the craftsmen were either for measured work (consisting of materials and the labour of fitting or laying them), or, probably more usually, for materials supplied and for labour on a daily basis. Thus in the work on Deptford bridge in the 1700s, William Baker,

44. K.A.O. Q/AB 1.
45. K.A.O. Q/SOw 9, p. 103.
46. K.A.O. Q/AB 40/21, 23; Q/AB 53/13.
47. K.A.O. Q/SOw 8, pp. 330, 342, 384, 428.
48. K.A.O. Q/SOw 10 p. 81; Q/SOw 11 pp. 330, 334, 342, 377.
49. K.A.O. Q/SOw 11 pp. 488, 557, 609.

house carpenter, was paid £81 4s. 2d. for carpenters' work and timber planks. This included '271 dayes works done by carpenters and labourers 33 02 00', and '162 piles used for makeing of foot wharf under the arches of the bridge . . . 10 feet long at 2s. 6d. per pile'. In 1716, the mason's work of Samuel Edge, which included materials, was measured by John Andrews at £203 19s. 5d.[50]

In the 1810s and 1820s, advertising for tenders became common. For the largest undertaking contracted in this way, Tonbridge Lower Bridge in 1814, five tenders were received at £4575, £2381 6s., £2365, £2350, and £1811; two of these tenders were submitted by Tonbridge builders, but the lowest proposal (which was accepted) came from a Maidstone partnership, that of William Cutbush, carpenter and Benjamin Ruck, bricklayer.[51] Nevertheless important work was still being contracted informally in the 1810s, the notable instance being the contract at prices (to be settled by measuring) for the new Deptford bridge with John and Henry Lee, bricklayers of Chiswell Street, London, in 1810.[52]

Bridge Building by the County Justices in South-East England

Altogether in Kent in the eighteenth century expenditure on bridges was steady without any outstanding outlay on a single bridge (or two or three bridges) at any one point of time. This may be seen by comparing the work of the Kent justices with that by other county justices in south-east England. Expenditure on the biggest Kent undertaking in the century, Tonbridge Great Bridge (£1104) was much exceeded by that on a number of bridges in counties elsewhere in south-east England. Chertsey bridge over the River Thames, for which responsibility was shared by Middlesex and Surrey, was a major problem for the two counties during part of the period. Repairs to the wooden bridge cost Surrey £1507 in 1744, and repairs, campshotting and road widening £1787 3s. 5d. in 1767.[53] Its outlay on the new stone bridge in 1779–85 was £6813 4s. 11d.[54] Almost simultaneously, between 1782 and 1787, the county spent £6600 on four other bridges.[55] The county also had several other smaller bridges to maintain, on which repairs of varying expenditure were carried out, usually quite small. Middlesex only had three bridges in its care, but occasionally the outlay was outstanding compared with that in Kent. A new bridge at Brentford in 1741–42 cost £3350, and in 1744 £1354 was spent on repairs to Chertsey bridge.[56] The county's share of the new stone bridge at Chertsey in 1779–85 was £6700.[57] Previously, between 1767 and 1770, over £4500 was paid out on repairs and alterations to Brentford and Chertsey bridges, of which at least £3500 may have been spent on Chertsey bridge.[58] Essex was similar to Kent in that there were a considerable number of bridges in the care of the justices; bridge undertakings costing over £100 occurred throughout the eighteenth century and the largest was probably the rebuilding of Moulsham bridge in 1785–86 for about £1600.[59]

50. K.A.O. Q/AB 15/3, 6.
51. K.A.O. Q/SOw 15, p. 258.
52. K.A.O. Q/AB 1, p. 1.
53. Surrey R.O. QS 2/1/16 (7/11/44, 21/2/45); QS 5/7/2 pp. 25–26; QS 2/1/21 p. 398, 2/1/22 p. 57.
54. Surrey R.O. QS 2/1/26 p. 377.
55. Surrey R.O. QS 2/1/25 pp. 495, 667–71, QS 2/1/26 pp. 10, 12, 596.
56. G.L.R.O. MF 1.
57. G.L.R.O. MA/C 1–2; MF 1.
58. G.L.R.O. MF 1.
59. Essex R.O. Q/FAa 4/2.

In the first three decades of the nineteenth century annual figures of outlay on bridges available for most counties reveal the fluctuations in expenditure in Kent in comparison with other counties in south-east England (Table III).[60] Kent spent an average of about £3500 a year in 1810–12 (three years) when Deptford bridge and several smaller bridges were being rebuilt. Outlay totalled about £5500 in 1814 and 1815 when Tonbridge Lower Bridge and Ashurst bridge were being rebuilt. In other years an expenditure of between £200 and £300 and £1000 was usual, and in the 1820s the figure was only three times between £1000 and £1200. In the few years of considerable bridge works the cost represented a significant proportion of all county expenditure. In some years in the 1820s the cost of bridge works was no more than 1 or 2 per cent of total county outlay. On the other hand in 1810 and 1811 outlay on bridge works was between 18 and 20 per cent of county expenditure; in 1814–15, taken together, it was about 9 per cent. Outlay in Kent dwarfed that in Sussex, where the county's responsibilities were insignificant, most bridge works being paid for by the individual rape or hundred; it was also greater than in Surrey, where expenditure only reached £1000 three times, and also than in Essex (except in the 1820s). Only in Middlesex in the 1820s (but not in earlier years) was expenditure much higher than in Kent, principally because of the erection of Brentford bridge, contracted at £7277 in April 1824.[61] With the exception of Brentford bridge, Deptford bridge in 1810 was by far the largest bridge undertaking in these five counties. Bridge expenditure in Kent in the eighteenth and early nineteenth centuries was not outstanding in comparison with some other counties; but the fact that the justices were active in this field throughout the period, and that a large number of bridge works were undertaken make the Kent bridges a study of considerable interest.

60. *Parliamentary Papers,* 1825, vi; 1833, xxxii.
61. G.L.R.O. MA/D/Br 10; for Middlesex bridge expenditure before the 1820s, MJ/OC 15–19.

TABLE I

Major Bridge Undertakings, 1700–1770[23]

Date	Bridge	Cost	Type of Work	Source (Kent Archives Office)
1706–07	Newenden	£230	'repair'	Q/SOw6 22/4/07
1716	Newenden	£475 14 6	'rebuilding'	Q/SOw7 p. 53
1708–09	Deptford	c. £200	'repair'	Q/SOw6 13/4/08, 3/5/09
1713–14	Deptford	£191 9 9½	woodwork including making foot wharf	Q/AB 15/3, 7
1716–17	Deptford	£430 8 6½	rebuilding north side of bridge	Q/AB 15/5–11
1716–17	Brandbridges	£208 10	'repair'	Q/SOw7 pp. 53, 78
1717–18	Dartford	£364 14 11	extensive repairs	Q/AB 13/3
1720–22	Style	£272 12 6	'repair'	Q/SOw7 pp. 200–1
1721	Twyford	£126 5 3	'repair'	Q/SOw7 pp. 200–1
1721	East Farleigh	£150 5 0	'repair'	Q/SOw7 p. 182
1725–26	Aylesford	£112 17 11	'repair'	Q/SOw7 pp. 261, 271, 292
1730–31	Herstfield	£269 9 0 (also £73 2 0 in 1726)	rebuilding and repair of five arches	Q/AB 53/7; Q/SOw p. 372
(1739, 1740	Teston, Yalding and Shoreham	£98 16 1, £96 10 4 and £70 respectively		Q/SOw8 pp. 194, 209, 242)
1749	Style, Huntonford, Laddingford, Twyford, Yalding	£472 10 8	'repairs'	Q/SOw8 p. 682
1750	Brandbridges	£172 13 1	'repair	Q/SOw8 p. 709
1753–55	Lamberhurst	£500	rebuilding	Q/AB 35/27–33; Q/SB 1755, 1756; East Sussex R.O. QO/EW 20
1754–55	Dartford	£474 12 4	rebuilding of wider bridge	Q/AB 13/28, Q/SB 1755, 1756, 1758
1761–62	Style	c. £150	'repair'	Q/AB 40/12
1762	Herstfield	£178 14 2½	repair	Q/AB 53/10–12, Q/SOw10 p. 53
1764	Shoreham	£144 16 0	repair or rebuilding	Q/SOw10 p. 132, Q/AB 51/11–12
1765	Brandbridges	£228 19 3	repairs	Q/SB 1766
1765	Wye	£105 0 2	repair	Q/SOe8 p. 47
1766	Gaffords (hundred bridge)	£119 7 7	repair	Q/SOw10 p. 225
1768	Style	£198 9 7½	repair	Q/SOw10 p. 314
1768	Newenden	c. £100	repairs	Q/AB 42/4
1770	Twyford	£103 12 6½	repairs	Q/SOw10 p. 450
1770	Dartford	£254 10 4	new paving	Q/AB 13/34
1770–71	Yalding and Laddingford	£411 14 0	repairs	Q/AB 64/67–70

TABLE II

Major Bridge Undertakings, 1771–1830[24]

Date	Bridge	Cost (1) (current prices)	Cost (2) (constant prices of 1760s)	Type of Work	Source
1772–73	Farningham	£499 2	£474	rebuilding of a wider bridge	Q/SOw11 p. 35, Hasted II, p. 510
1775–76	Tonbridge (Great bridge)	£1104 5 1½	£1049	rebuilding of a wider bridge	Q/AB 58/30
1778	Kent Ditch	£215 16 0½ (shared with Sussex)	£205	rebuilding	Q/SOw11 p. 214
1781	Brandbridges	£516 7 7	£464	rebuilding	Q/SOw11 pp. 330, 342, 380
1783–84	Style	£201 15 2	£182	repairs	Q/SOw11 p. 488
1784	Teston	£297 18 10½	£268	repairs	Q/SOw11 p. 488
1785	Yalding (and Twyford)	£208 18 11½	£188	repairs	Q/AB 64/84
1785	Herstfield	£135 0 11	£121	repairs	Q/SOw11 p. 546
1786	Aylesford	£182 17 7	£172	'work at'	Q/SOw11 p. 609
1790	Aylesford	£130 19 11	£117	paving	Melling pp. 49–50
1790–91	Dartford	£342	£308	widening	Q/SOw12 pp. 268, 465
1793	Dartford	£150	£105	road widening	Q/SOw12 p. 453
1794–95	Teston	£284 18 0	£200	'work at'	Q/SOw12 pp. 529, 616
1794–95	Yalding	£185 5 0	£130	'work at'	Q/SOw12 p. 604
1795–96	Twyford	£170 2 2	£119	repair	Q/SOw12 p. 634, Q/SOw13 p. 69
1796–97	Brandbridges	£150 10 7	£105	'work at'	Q/SOw13 pp. 151, 258
1799	Hunton	£174 19 5	£122	clappers repaired	Q/SOw13 p. 437
1802	Ashurst	£265 17 1	£117	'work at'	Q/SOw14 p. 235
1802	Ashford	£321 5 4	£141	'work at'	Q/FAe5 pp. 131, 167
1806	Yalding	£297 12 3½	£131	repair	Q/SOw14 pp. 622, 665
1810	Dartford (Mill Pond = Phoenix bridge)	£334 6	£152	rebuilding	Q/FAw1 pp. 242, 280
1810–11	Catford	£1164 3 3	£498	rebuilding	Q/FAw1 pp. 242, 261
1810–11	Deptford	£6777 5 6 (including property £1255 6 4)	£2866	rebuilding	Q/FAw1 pp. 242, 261
1811	Style	£691 3 5	£282	alteration	Q/FAw1 pp. 261, 280, 343
1813	Penshurst (Colliers Lane)	£826 6 9	£338	building	Q/FAw1 p. 343, Q/AB 48/2
1814–15	Ashurst	£2332 (shared with Sussex)	£951	rebuilding	Q/GFa1 pp. 55–6, 130–3
1814	Tonbridge (Lower)	£2195 11 10	£895	rebuilding	Q/GFa1 pp. 55, 57, 131
1814	Foot's Cray	£328 14 10	£134	rebuilding	Q/GFa1 pp. 57, 130
1817–18	Deptford	£338 7 10	£138	pavement repairs	Q/GFa1 pp. 303, 404
1820	Deptford (Grove Street)	£250	£102	rebuilding	Q/GFa2 p. 154
1821	Marden (Old Mill)	£221 5 (shared with Surrey)	£103	rebuilding	Q/GFa2 p. 248
1824	Lee	£226	£105	repairs	Q/GFa3 p. 165

Date	Bridge	Cost (1) (current prices)	Cost (2) (constant prices of 1760s)	Type of Work	Source
1824	Bexley (Gad's Hill)	£347 9 9	£161	rebuilding	Q/GFa3 p. 166
1827–28	Twyford	£538 8 2	£250	repairs	Q/GFa3 p. 454; Q/GFa4 p. 54
1828	Sutton-at-Hone (New bridge)	£369 17 6	£172	rebuilding	Q/GFa4 pp. 54–55
1830	Teston	£318 6 4	£148	'work'	Q/GFa4 p. 230

TABLE III

Bridge Expenditure in South-East England, 1806–1830 (to nearest pound)

	Kent		Surrey		Sussex		Essex		Middlesex	
	(A)	(B)	(A)	(B)	(A)	(B)	(A)	(B)	(A)	(B)
1806	£256		£1065				£48			
1807	£269		£847				–			
1808	£153		£447				£105			
1809	£398		£150				£215			
1810	£2101		£2199				–			
1811	£6359		£659				£30			
1812	£2024		£908				£274			
1813	£675		£680				£94			
1814	£3946		£850		£464		£55			
1815	£1592		£479		£720		£112			
1816	£454		£265		£217		£913			
1817	£719		£520		£328		£249			
1818	£876		£795		£394		£455			
1819	£415		£501		£384		£740			
1820	£646		£1410		£109		£1181			
1821	£848	£911	£510	£1410	£137		£251	£621		
1822	£206	£486	£1070	£510	£250		£441	£957		£2522
1823	£585	£279	£323	£1070	£155		£407	£800		£1950
1824		£356		£323				£960		£4266
1825		£1134		£193				£2664		£7725
1826		£220		£616				£2436		£5886
1827		£457		£770				£986		£1956
1828		£1075		£664				£1336		£1010
1829		£1193		£268				£1572		£2208
1830		£592		£532				£918		£2513

(A) *Parliamentary Papers*, 1825, vi;   (B) *P.P.*, 1833, xxxii

THE SOCIAL ECONOMY OF THE CANTERBURY SUBURBS: THE EVIDENCE OF THE CENSUS OF 1563*

PETER and JENNIFER CLARK

In the century before the Civil War virtually all English towns increased in population. The growth was most spectacular in the case of London (rising nearly eight-fold over the period), but the larger provincial cities also recorded advances of between 50 and 100 per cent, much of this stemming from immigration. Part of the new population was absorbed by the central parishes of towns, where there was often vacant land or spare housing in the early Tudor period. But growing streams of people took up residence in the more peripheral urban districts, frequently outside the walls, in suburbs stretching into the adjoining countryside. Unlike many of their continental counterparts most English cities had acquired suburbs in the Middle Ages, but they grew substantially from the late sixteenth century onwards: in London the new East and West Ends came to overshadow the old city itself.[1]

Corporations were increasingly worried about the expansion of the suburbs and the kinds of people who lived there. As early as 1518 Coventry magistrates denounced 'these big beggars that will not work to get their living' but lie in the city outskirts. A century later Oxford council spoke of 'the great multitude of poor people increased in this city and suburbs, wandering, walking and going idly up and down the streets and other places begging and often times pilfering'; such folk lived in 'cottages and squabd (sic) houses' built about the town. Poor people drifted into the suburbs not only in hope of cheap, squatter accommodation, but because administrative controls were frequently lax there (with city authorities engaged in jurisdictional clashes with county justices and local landowners). As well as begging, some immigrants, it was said, tried to set up in business and compete with city freemen, challenging the established urban economy. At Leicester in the 1620s we hear the complaint that 'foreign (outside) tailors like drone bees to the hive paying neither scot nor lot live lurking in the suburbs and other secret places' robbing the citizens of work.[2]

Recent studies have shown how the demographic profile of the outer, mainly suburban

---

* The data for this paper was mainly collected and collated by Jenny Clark; the writing was undertaken by Peter Clark. We are indebted to the late William Urry, cathedral archivist at Canterbury, Anne Oakley, the present archivist, and Felix Hull and Elizabeth Melling of the Kent Archives Office, Maidstone, for their help with the documentation. David Souden and Nicholas Davidson read the paper in draft and we are grateful for their comments.

1. D.J. Keene, 'Suburban growth' in M.W. Barley (ed.), *The Plans and Topography of Medieval Towns in England and Wales*, 1976, 71–82; P. Clark and P. Slack, *English Towns in Transition 1500–1700*, 1976, 63–4, 83, 87, 94–5; also M.J. Power, 'The East and West in Early Modern London', in E.W. Ives *et al.* (eds.), *Wealth and Power in Tudor England* 1978, 167–85.
2. M.D. Harris (ed.), *The Coventry Leet Book* (Early English Text Soc., cxxxiv, cxxv, cxxviii, cxlvi, 1907–13), 658; Oxford Central Library, City MSS., 0.5.9., pp. 201–2; H. Stocks (ed.), *Records of the Borough of Leicester: IV*, 1923, 238; also R.H. Morris, *Chester during the Plantagenet and Tudor Periods*, n.d., 108–10; P. Clark 'The Migrant in Kentish Towns, 1580–1640', in P. Clark and P. Slack (eds.), *Crisis and Order in English Towns 1500–1700*, 1972, 150.

parishes of pre-industrial towns might vary markedly from that of the inner districts, with a bias towards small families and few servants compared with the bloated households crowded with apprentices, journeymen and maids found in the wealthier core areas.[3] But as yet the economic and social organization of the urban periphery has attracted little attention in its own right. How far were the suburbs overwhelmed by a sea of poverty as civic authorities regularly claimed? In what measure did such areas constitute a real threat to the established economic and social order of the city? The aim of the present paper is to shed light on these questions by making use of a partial survey of four outer parishes of Canterbury in 1563. The basic evidence of the survey, in the city archives in the Cathedral Library, Canterbury,[4] has been supplemented by a wide range of material from other city records, cathedral rentals, tax rolls, diocesan deposition books, and also from the splendid series of probate volumes in the Kent Archives Office.

In common with other provincial centres, the population of Canterbury, a medium-sized cathedral city, was growing steadily during the period before the English Revolution. It may have had 3,000 inhabitants in the 1520s and 3,500–3,600 in the 1560s, rising to over 6,000 by the mid-seventeenth century.[5] If the parish registers are any guide, almost none of the expansion occurred as a result of natural increase. A selection of registers from both wealthy and poorer parishes points to a chronic demographic deficit for most of Elizabeth's reign with burials far exceeding baptisms, notably in the suburbs.[6] Expansion was fuelled by large-scale immigration: roughly four out of five Canterbury men giving evidence before the church courts between 1580 and 1640 had come to the city from elsewhere; 28.5 per cent were born outside Kent. Quite a number of the new arrivals were poor subsistence migrants who had been driven on to the road by deteriorating economic conditions.[7] The problem of absorbing this influx was aggravated by the instability of Canterbury's economy. Already in the doldrums before the Reformation as industry drifted away to the countryside, the city was inevitably affected by the dissolution of its many religious houses and the suppression of what remained of its pilgrimage traffic. There were numerous complaints of the town's penury. In 1561, for example,

3. N. Goose, 'Household size and structure in early Stuart Cambridge', *Social History*, v (1980), 347–85; D. Souden, 'Migrants and the Population Structure of Later Seventeenth Century English Provincial Cities and Market Towns' in P. Clark (ed.), *Innovation and Tradition in English Provincial Towns, 1600–1800 (forthcoming)*. For an excellent detailed analysis of urban/suburban contrasts see E. Helin, *La Démographie de Liège au XVIIe et XVIIIe siècles*, Brussels, 1963, 77 *passim*.

4. Canterbury Cathedral Library (hereafter CCL), City MSS., E/Q/1 (hereafter referred to as the Census). The document was found in a decayed condition and rescued by William Urry after the Second World War; it was restored under his direction.

5. P. Clark, *English Provincial Society from the Reformation to the Revolution: Religion, Politics and Society in Kent 1500–1640*, 1977, 8–9; demographic estimates for the 1560s based on parochial returns in 1563 (British Library [hereafter BL], Harleian MS. 594, fol. 63–5v); in 1565 (CCL, Z.3.8, fol. 136); and in 1569 (CCL, Visitation Returns 1569, fol. 33–5). C.W. Chalklin, *Seventeenth Century Kent*, 1965, 31.

6. In the suburbs, St. Dunstan's 1570–1600 had a cumulative deficit of 137 (burials exceeding baptisms); and St. Paul's 1561–1600 a deficit of 48. In the inner parishes St. Peter's 1561–1600 had a surplus of 4 (baptisms exceeding burials) and St. George's 1560–1600 a deficit of 34. Sources: J.M. Cowper (ed.), *The Register Booke of Christeninges, Mariages and Burialls in St. Dunstan's, Canterbury 1559–1880*, 1887; idem, *The Register Book . . . in the Parishe of St. Paule . . . Canterburie*, 1893; idem, *The Booke of Regester of the Parish of St. Peter in Canterbury . . . 1560–1800*, 1884; idem, *The Register Booke of the Parish of St. George the Martyr within the Citie of Canterburie*, 1891.

7. Clark and Slack, *Crisis and Order*, 122.

magistrates noted the 'great poverty of the most part of the commons of the city'.[8]

By the early 1560s the plight of the lower orders had become a principal concern of civic government. In 1561 the council ordered the aldermen to make a survey of all the poor and impotent people and children that went begging, and there was a purge of vagrants; the next year part of the fines levied on newly elected councillors was devoted to poor relief.[9] But the situation became acute in 1563. The harvest the previous autumn had been meagre and by the summer food shortages were widespread. In late July Archbishop Parker wrote to William Cecil of 'famine' at Canterbury; the magistracy set up a corn stock to help those in need; and the dean and chapter distributed special money for the relief of the poor.[10] By September there was the additional, frightening problem of infectious disease. At nearby Sandwich the chronicler observed for 1562–63 'a threefold plague – pestilence, want of money, dearth of victuals'. Plague was endemic in London in 1563 and during the summer advanced along the north Kent coast. The city fathers did their best to isolate Canterbury. During August townsmen were banned from visiting St. Bartholomew's fair in the capital and in September and December Londoners and other strangers were forbidden to lodge in the city; even the usually busy winter fair was closed to metropolitan merchants.[11] The bans were ineffectual. In November and December a succession of people were buried in St. Mary Northgate parish, allegedly dying of plague; in St. Dunstan's, the suburb on the London side of town, burials in the half year September 1563/March 1564 reached five or six times the normal rate. When warm weather returned in 1564 the infection took a savage toll, with St. Mildred's parish and later St. George's worst affected (a hundred people died in St. Mildred's during the year). Nationally, the 1563–65 epidemic was one of the worst of the century.[12]

The Canterbury census was apparently taken after the dearth of 1563 had abated, but before the plague bacillus had gained a firm grip on the city. The document itself is undated and the council minutes give no clue to when or why the survey was taken. However, by comparing names in the census with parish registers we can establish that the listing took place in the last week of October 1563. The reason for the enumeration remains unclear: perhaps an attempt to take stock of the city's population in a year of crisis, or plausibly a precautionary measure against the looming epidemic – a move to assess the number of inhabitants likely to require

8. P. Clark, 'Reformation and Radicalism in Kentish Towns c. 1500–1553' in W.J. Mommsen et al. (eds.), *The Urban Classes, the Nobility and the Reformation,* Stuttgart, 1979, 108–10; A.A. Arnold, 'Rochester Bridge in A.D. 1561', *Arch. Cant.,* xvii (1887), 228.

9. CCL: AC 2, fol. 138; F /A 16, fol. 198v–9; AC 2 fol. 146v.

10. J. Thirsk (ed.), *Agrarian History of England and Wales: IV,* 1967, 853; BL, Lansdowne MS.6, fol. 154; CCL:F/A 16, fol. 251v; Dean and Chapter Misc. Accounts 40 (unfol.). At Michaelmas 1563 the Kentish justices were still complaining of the 'scarcity and dearth of corn, grain, victuals and other necessaries' in the shire (C.E. Woodruff, 'Wages Paid at Maidstone in Queen Elizabeth's Reign', *Arch. Cant.,* xxii (1897), 319). At this time there was also said to be 'great plague and dearth . . . throughout all these parts . . . about London' (Public Record Office [hereafter PRO], C 3/30/106).

11. KAO, Sa/ZB 6; P. Slack, 'Mortality Crises and Epidemic Disease in England 1485–1610' in C. Webster (ed.), *Health, Medicine and Mortality in the Sixteenth Century,* 1979, 13–4, 43, 49. For the high summer mortality at Milton near Gravesend: Kent Archives Office [hereafter KAO], TR 1303/6. CCL: AC2, fol. 163v–5, 167, 172; F/A 16, fol. 282. Archbishop Parker wrote in late September that the county was 'wonderfully afeared of all such as come from London' (BL, Lansdowne MS.6, fol. 178).

12. CCL, Bishop's Transcripts, St. Mary Northgate; Cowper, *St. Dunstan's Register*; CCL, St Mildred's Parish Register 1; Cowper, *St George's Register*; Slack, 'Mortality Crises', 13 *passim.*

relief should their houses become infected.[13] This idea is supported by the careful numbering of dogs and pigs in households. Canterbury magistrates, like those elsewhere, were concerned at the danger of animals spreading the disease. In December 1563 they ordered people having dogs (other than hunting dogs) to pay 2*d.* a week to the poor; the next year swine and dogs were destroyed for running the streets.[14]

The document which survives almost certainly comprises only part of the original survey. Of the 8 folios, fol. 2 and the last are blank and most are heavily damaged at the top; they may also be out of the original sequence. The first folio has column headings and is in a formal court hand; the later folios appear to be drafts. All parts of the listing seem to have been written by one man, possibly one of the assistants in the town clerk's office.[15] When he took the census, he probably went from house to house down the street, one side at a time. There is no suggestion of any kind of selectivity in the listing.

Only one or two references are given in the document itself to precise locations, but with the help of other sources we can establish that the extant survey of 173 households broadly covers parts of the adjoining parishes of St. Mildred's, St. Paul's, St. Martin's, and St. Mary Northgate.[16] All these were outer parishes stretching beyond the city walls to embrace the suburbs of Northgate, Longport and Wincheap, mainly on the south side. During the late sixteenth century St. Mildred's, St. Mary Northgate, St. Paul's and St. Martin's were ranked (usually in that order) as the poorest parishes of the city.[17] How complete is the survey? Comparison can be made here with the totals of households given for each parish in the 1563 and 1569 diocesan returns. Taking an average of the diocesan figures, we find that the census listed most of the households in St. Mary Northgate and about half of those in the remaining parishes. The 594 inhabitants recorded probably comprised about a sixth of the city's total population.[18] The Canterbury document is the earliest detailed town survey so far discovered in England. Standard information includes the name of the householder (and frequently occupation); an indication of spouse (albeit without her name); the names and ages of resident children and servants; details about lodgers and animals in the house. Where the survey information can be verified, the degree of accuracy seems high.

The survey data allows us to reconstruct the demographic anatomy of the parishes, to calculate the average household size, sex ratios, the types of household head, the incidence of children and other resident groups. Exploiting material from city, diocesan and governmental records we can flesh out this demographic skeleton and present a picture of the occupational structure of the area, the strength of neighbourhood ties, the pattern of mobility, and the character of life at the sharp end of urban society.[19] In other words, the survey offers us a key

13. We are very grateful to Paul Slack for his advice here. A similar precautionary survey seems to have been taken at Cambridge in 1630 (Goose, 'Household size', 355).

14. CCL, AC 2, fol. 167v, 176v, 179v; for similar orders against animals during plague at Lynn in 1585 see *Historical Manuscripts Commission,* 11th Report, App. III, 176.

15. It is possible though that the column headings on fol. 1 were prepared in advance and may be in a different hand from the listing itself (Charles Phythian-Adams kindly advised us here).

16. Fol. 1 cover parts of St. Mildred; fol. 4–5v, 7v St. Paul and St. Martin; and fol. 3v, 6v, 7r St. Mary Northgate

17. CCL: Dean and Chapter New Foundation – Treasurer's Accounts, 2; Misc. Accounts 41, fol. 172v; JQ 1630s.

18. BL, Harleian MS. 594, fol. 64–65v; CCL: Visitation Returns 1569, fol. 33–4v; Z.3.8, fol. 136.

19. The additional sources used here were principally for the period 1550–1575 and included: the city Burghmote or council minutes, chamberlain accounts, sessions papers, city rentals and 1563 subsidy roll; St. Mildred's

to trying to understand the social economy of the outer, suburban areas of the provincial town.

When our anonymous Canterbury official took to the streets to make his survey, he listed everyone by household. In the early section of the document the households are clearly differentiated; later the divisions are sometimes blurred. Nonetheless, with the aid of external sources it is possible to define the household groups quite precisely. In certain cases houses are being shared with newcomers. Where the latter seem to form a discrete family they have been counted as a separate unit. Otherwise they have been classed as lodgers, as additional members of the resident household.

The mean household size from the Canterbury listing was 3.4. There was some variation between the different areas surveyed, with the figure somewhat higher in St. Paul's (3.9) and lowest in St. Mary Northgate (3.2) (see Table 1). But these differences should not be over-

TABLE 1
Percentage distribution of Households by Size

Household Size	Parish 1	Parish 2	Parish 3	Parish 4	Overall
1	5.7	0.0	12.8	16.6	12.1
2	23.0	46.7	20.5	23.8	24.9
3	37.1	13.3	17.9	25.0	24.9
4	5.7	13.3	15.4	15.5	13.3
5	17.1	13.3	12.8	9.5	12.1
6	8.6	6.7	7.7	3.6	5.8
7	0.0	0.0	5.1	3.6	2.8
8	2.8	0.0	2.6	1.2	1.7
9	0.0	6.7	2.6	0.0	1.2
10	0.0	0.0	0.0	0.0	0.0
11	0.0	0.0	0.0	0.0	0.0
12	0.0	0.0	2.6	1.2	1.2
n	35	15	39	84	173
mean size	3.5	3.5	3.9	3.2	3.4

Parish 1 – St. Mildred's
Parish 2 – St. Martin's
Parish 3 – St. Paul's
Parish 4 – St. Mary Northgate

parish register 1; Bishop's Transcripts for St. Mary Northgate; diocesan court visitation and deposition registers (all at CCL); will registers and probate inventories (at KAO); Christchurch rental 1564 (Lambeth Palace Library, MS.814); 1571 subsidy roll (PRO, E 179/126/426); J.M. Cowper, *The Roll of the Freemen of the City of Canterbury*, 1903; *idem, Intrantes . . . within the City of Canterbury*, 1904; *idem, St. Paul's Register.*

stated. The samples are small and the topographical attributions of some households may not be wholly accurate (with tenements standing on the boundary between parishes). What is evident is the general bias towards a limited household size. Relatively small households (more or less coterminous with the nuclear family) seem to have been the general demographic rule in early modern England. But the Canterbury figure is at the bottom end of the range. Richard Wall's 45 mainly rural communities 1650–1749 had a mean household size of 4.75.[20] The Canterbury average is also lower than the figures derived from listings for other English towns in the late sixteenth and seventeenth centuries, mainly because these usually covered a wide swathe of better-off areas. However, when we confine our comparison to the suburban parishes of towns there is a greater degree of convergence. At Cambridge in the 1620s, for example, the outer parishes of Barnwell and St. Giles recorded mean household sizes of 3.95 and 3.89. Equally interesting, the Canterbury picture has affinities with the household pattern found among the poor in Tudor and Stuart towns: thus the mean household size for the Norwich poor listed in 1570 was 3.0; at Warwick in 1587 3.3; and at Salisbury in 1635 2.3.[21]

Turning to the broad composition of the population surveyed we find a sex ratio (males to 100 females) of 95.6. A surplus of women over men was a fairly common feature of towns in the sixteenth and seventeenth centuries, even allowing for a tendency to under-record the presence of women. Here, however, the imbalance was not due, as was usually the case, to a large number of female servants but primarily to a high proportion of widows in the population (inmates formed only a fraction of the total).[22]

TABLE 2
Sex ratio (m to 100 f)

Adults	82.0
Children	112.0
Servants	134.3
Inmates	55.0

The point is underlined when we analyse the status of household heads.

TABLE 3
Status of Household Heads (n = 173)

Married men	80.9
Widowed men	0.6
Widows	17.9
Single women	0.6

20.　R. Wall, 'Regional and Temporal Variations in English Household Structure from 1650' in J. Hobcraft and P. Rees, (eds.), *Regional Demographic Development*, 1977, 94. Peter Laslett's somewhat wider group of 100 communities 1574–1821 had a similar mean household size of 4.75 (P. Laslett and R. Wall (eds.), *Household and Family in Past Time*, 1972, 126).

21.　Goose, 'Household size', 363; C. Phythian-Adams *et al.*, *The Traditional Community under Stress*, 1977, 85; A.L. Beier, 'The Social Problems of an Elizabethan County Town: Warwick 1580–90' in P. Clark (ed.), *Country Towns in Pre-Industrial England*, 1981, 60.

22.　C. Phythian-Adams, *Desolation of a City: Coventry and the Urban Crisis of the late Middle Ages*, 1979, 119–201; Souden, 'Migrants'.

Though the great majority of households were presided over by married couples, nearly a fifth were run by single adults (virtually all widows). This is rather higher than the level found by Wall for his settlements 1650–1749. It is more typical, however, of poorer urban parishes, while listings of urban poor in the sixteenth and seventeenth centuries show similar high proportions.[23] The explanation is partly to be found in the greater mortality rates in less affluent areas. Another factor may be the way that the widows of craftsmen and lesser workers were forced by economic circumstances to move from their larger houses in the more central districts to the smaller, cheaper accommodation of the outer parishes. It is also possible that some of the 'widows' were in fact women whose husbands had left them – desertion was common among the poorer classes.[24] The census provides little evidence of widows taking up residence with their adult children, though there are signs of a number living not far from their children's houses. Finally, how do we explain the paucity of widowers as household heads? Apart from the biological fact that generally women live longer than men, differential mortality rates may have taken their toll with men suffering more from diseases. In addition, the widower ensconced in the family home with its fittings and furnishings was in a stronger position in the marriage market than his female counterpart, and was often able to pick and choose a new partner.[25]

The large contingent of widows played a significant part in depressing the average household size in Canterbury's outer parishes. The lower than normal proportions of children and servants had a similar effect. Less than a third of the inhabitants were children (including step-children) resident with their parents. This compares with the 37.6 per cent counted by Wall for his communities and is more in line with the incidence of children at Coventry in the 1520s (26.8 per cent), at a time when that city was ravaged by high mortality. Again only 52.6 per cent of the Canterbury households had children living with them, as against 71.1 per cent in Wall's communities.[26] Of 91 households with resident offspring, 40 had a single child. As well as the number of children being affected by high suburban mortality rates, the social economy of the urban periphery also discouraged the presence of older offspring. Poor families, numerous in such areas, were unable to provide employment and sustenance for their children at home: they had to be sent out to service. In general, only established craftsmen or traders could afford to keep their children with them to learn and help with their trade. James Lent, the blacksmith, had his son Sampson, aged 32, as a servant; John Patenson, an alehousekeeper, kept his two daughters Constance, 22, and Joan, 18, to serve drinkers and attract male customers. Other parents failing to send their teenage children out to service came under pressure from parish officers: the census recorded against Katherine Johnson, aged 15 and the daughter of a labourer, 'to be put in service'. Only one of the children listed in 1563 was said to be going to school.[27]

23. Wall, 'Household Structure', 93–4; Goose, 'Household size', 378; P. Slack, 'Poverty and Politics in Salisbury 1597–1666' in Clark and Slack, *Crisis and Order,* 174–6.

24. S.J. Wright, 'Women and Society in Tudor Salisbury: The Plight of the Widow', (paper to the Urban History Conference, Loughborough, 1981); Beier, 'Warwick', 60–1.

25. Phythian-Adams, *Coventry,* 93.

26. Children have been defined here to include single adult offspring residing with their parents (though the number of these was very small). Wall, 'Household Structure', 94; Phythian-Adams, *Coventry,* 221.

27. Census, fol. 1v, 6v. It was customary for the children of alehousekeepers to serve in the house. Census, fol. 7v (J. Johnson I); fol. 4r (Robert son of W. Selby).

TABLE 4
Principal Categories of Inhabitants

		%
Adults	311	52.4
Children	183	30.8
Servants	82	13.8
Lodgers:		
Adults	8	1.3
Children	7	1.2
Uncertain	3	0.5
Total	594	100.0

The age distribution of children, servants and lodger children is outlined in Table 5.

TABLE 5
Age Distribution of Children, Servants and Lodger Children

	children %	servants %	lodger children %
Under 1	11.2	0.0	0.0
1–2	20.6	0.0	0.0
3–4	14.7	0.0	0.0
5–6	4.7	2.5	60.0
7–9	18.2	0.0	40.0
10–12	14.7	26.8	0.0
13–15	10.0	29.3	0.0
16–18	4.1	26.8	0.0
19 and above	1.8	14.6	0.0
sample (ages known)	170	41	5
ages unknown	13	41	2

The age pattern was inevitably affected by heavy infant and child mortality. Particularly striking is the low representation of children aged 5–6, those born in the late 1550s. Almost certainly this age group suffered from the presumed influenza epidemic sweeping the country at that time, decimating both babies and prospective parents. The growing exodus of children into service after the age of 10 is obvious. By the time they were in their mid teens only a minority of children were still living at home.[28]

At the same time, the survey does not show what proportion of teenage children took up service in the area. The impression is, however, that whereas boys and girls in their early teens might work for a neighbour, older children moved further afield to larger households in the

28.   Slack, 'Mortality Crises', 27–32; Phythian-Adams, *Coventry*, 229–30.

inner city, where there were better prospects. Not only were suburban parishes unsuccessful at retaining their own children, but they were probably unable to attract any substantial inflow of young servants from other city parishes or the countryside. Only 26.6 per cent of the households listed in 1563 had a servant and the number in service comprised no more than 13.8 per cent of the population. At Coventry by contrast, almost a quarter of the recorded inhabitants in the 1520s were servants and nearly 40 per cent of households had one or more. The proportion of households with servants was also higher in the wealthy central parishes of Cambridge during the 1620s (over 54 per cent in St. Michael's), although the position was more akin to that at Canterbury in the suburban parish of St. Giles' (23.1 per cent). The reasons for the low density of servants in the Canterbury suburbs are fairly obvious. Servants were expensive to keep: the cost of board and lodging was escalating throughout the sixteenth century as a result of price inflation; this in fact may have contributed to a general fall in the number of living-in servants in both town and countryside.[29] Moreover, there was only a limited need for servants in suburban households. As we shall see, a significant proportion of householders left home to work and their houses were too small and rudimentary to require the services of maids.

What about the servants themselves? According to the survey, over a half were men (57.3 per cent), although it is possible there was some under-registration of female servants. Of the male servants 20 were listed as apprentices and only one as a journeyman; 14 were described as servants in covenant and another 12 just as servants. The census-taker may have failed to distinguish all the apprentices, and the servants doubtless include some journeymen. But there was clearly a substantial number of young, general servants around. A few perhaps were apprentices on probation, waiting to have their indentures enrolled (this was often several years after the start of service). A larger group probably came from homes too poor to pay the apprenticeship premium and were kept by their masters as cheap labour until they became bigger and less malleable and were then sent packing. The number of unapprenticed servants may also reflect the fact that only a minority of craftsmen and traders were freemen, a point we must return to shortly. There is little to suggest that any were servants in husbandry. Of the women half were called covenant servants, the rest servants. Some came from the countryside like Mildred Rugg from Ashford, who worked in John Wade's alehouse; others were from nearby families. Virtually all undertook household drudgery as maid-servants.[30]

The attenuated household size in these outer parishes was thus closely linked to the high number of single-headed families and the low incidence of both children and servants in the population. Nor was the suburban household bolstered by any significant presence of kinsfolk (other than members of the nuclear family). There are no identifiable multi-generational households in the listing. Occasionally we discover kin, a grandson or cousin, working as servants. But of our 173 households no more than 2.3 per cent are known to have contained kinsfolk outside the nuclear family. We have little evidence of the important extended households recently found at Ryton in County Durham. Rather, the Canterbury picture is more typical of the situation in other towns and communities in pre-industrial England, where the

29.   Phythian-Adams, *Coventry,* 204; Goose, 'Household size', 374 (for Cambridge we have aggregated households with servants and apprentices); A. Kussmaul, *Servants in Husbandry in Early Modern England,* 1981, 97 ff.
30.   P. Clark, 'Migration in England during the late 17th and early 18th centuries', *Past and Present,* no. 83 (1979), 61–2. Census, fol. 7v.

nuclear family grouping was the overwhelming rule.[31] This is not to say that *ad hoc* extended households could not be formed in exceptional circumstances. The year before the census Stephen Mathewe was living with his married brother and mother in a small house in St. Mildred's, all of them sharing one bed. Charged with incest, Mathewe declared that 'being but very poor folk [they sought] to spend that which they get with their travail to the common relief as well of themselves as of their poor and needy mother, aged, not able to gain anything for her own sustenation'. But the arrangement was temporary. The other brother kept up his own house where his wife and children lived and may have stayed with his mother when he was out working with Stephen (both were paviours). Stephen himself had only just got back from serving with the English expedition to Newhaven. By the time of the census Stephen was married, and living in his own house, and his mother and brother had apparently disappeared from the locality.[32] As for kin living in the same neighbourhood, the census reveals that this was reasonably common, as one might anticipate. Robert Binge of St. Mildred's dwelt 24 houses away from his cousin Stephen Holman; Bennett Grovehurst was 11 houses apart from her father James Lent; fathers and sons might live next door to each other. In all up to 16 of our households (9.2 per cent) may have had kin residing in neighbouring houses or streets, though in half of these cases the relationship is conjectural. In the suburbs at least kinship probably made only a modest contribution to social linkages.[33]

More surprising and puzzling perhaps than the low number of non-nuclear kinsfolk in our households, was the absence of any large tribe of lodgers and sojourners such as one might have expected from magisterial complaints about the influx of poor outsiders during this period. Only 2.7 per cent of our inhabitants can be classed as lodgers, and roughly half these were kept off alms, mostly orphans being fostered at parish expense. Even when we include in this category self-contained inmate families sharing houses, the proportion rises to no more than 4.7 per cent. This contrasts with the situation at Warwick in the 1580s when nearly a quarter of pauper households had inmates and at Cambridge in the 1620s where over a tenth of the suburban inhabitants of Barnwell can be broadly defined as inmates.[34] One possible explanation is that the great surge of outsiders into towns took place in the last decades of the sixteenth century and at the start of the seventeenth; that the earlier inflows were smaller. There may be something in this interpretation. Also crucial at Canterbury, however, was the timing of the census. It was taken when there was a growing panic that the city was infected with plague, and news of the outbreak was starting to circulate in the neighbouring country-side, scaring away possible incomers. No less important, during this period the city authorities were issuing strict injunctions against the lodging of suspected plague carriers. Even when migrants had braved the epidemic to become inmates, householders may have been loath to admit their presence. Here it is likely that the demographic profile of our parishes has been in

---

31. M. Chaytor, 'Household and Kinship: Ryton in the late 16th and early 17th centuries', *History Workshop*, no. 10 (1980), 36–51; but see the criticism of this paper by K. Wrightson, 'Household and kinship in sixteenth-century England', *op. cit.*, no. 12 (1981), 151–7. Goose, 'Household size', 376–7, 381–3; Wall, 'Household Structure', 89, 93–4.

32. CCL: X.10.8, fol. 173–4; Z.1.5, fol. 92–v; Census, fol. 1v; Lambeth Palace Library, MS.814, fol. 8v.

33. Census, fol. 1v (Binge), fol. 1r (Holman); fol. 1r (Grovehurst), fol. 1v (Lent). See also the limited importance of kin ties at the village of Terling, Essex: K. Wrightson and D. Levine, *Poverty and Piety in an English Village: Terling 1525–1700*, 1979, 82 ff.

34. Beier, 'Warwick', 61; Goose, 'Household size', 379–80.

some measure distorted by the special crisis conditions of late 1563.

Overall, however, the picture is clear, if hardly startling: the urban periphery at Canterbury was dominated by small, attenuated, nuclear households displaying a low commitment to the demographic future (having relatively few servants or children) and a high risk of disintegration (in a subtantial number of cases headed by single adults). We have contended that many features of this demographic structure were umbilically tied to the known poverty of the area. It is time now to examine the economic and social context in more detail.

From the census and other sources we can identify the principal occupations of 109 male householders. Ranking these by occupational or status groupings, it is evident that by far and away the largest category were labourers (see Table 6). At the opposite end of the economic pyramid there was only a sprinkling of prosperous gentlemen and distributive traders.

TABLE 6
Occupational and Status Groupings

		survey householders (suburbs) %	freemen 1560–1599 (whole city) %
1	gentry	0.9	4.8
2	professions	0.0	1.4
3	clothing trades	11.9	19.9
4	leather trades	8.3	12.3
5	food and drink	10.1	13.7
6	textile industry	8.3	6.5
7	household goods	1.8	4.4
8	distributive	0.9	18.7
9	building trades	11.0	5.9
10	yeomen	6.4	2.8
11	husbandmen	0.0	0.2
12	labourers	22.0	0.2
13	agric. misc.	4.6	1.6
14	service industries	6.4	7.0
15	misc.	7.4	0.6
	samples	109	642

Craftsmen tended to belong to lesser trades like leather or textile working. In order to compare the occupational order of our parishes with that for the wider city we have to rely on the freemen lists, biased though these are towards the more respectable classes of the urban community.[35] Nonetheless, the exercise is instructive (see Table 6). In late-sixteenth-century

---

35. Most householders probably had secondary employments but it has proved possible to identify only a few of these. City freemen lists are indexed in Cowper, *Freemen.* Cowper's coverage is not exhaustive and additional entries were culled from the city Burghmote Books. For the problems in using freemen lists for this kind of analysis see J. Patten, 'Urban occupations in pre-industrial England', *Trans. of the Institute of Historical Geographers,* New Series, ii (1977), 298–9.

Canterbury one of the leading groups comprised mercers, grocers and similar distributive merchants largely absent from the census. Other élite groups such as gentlemen and professional men were also more heavily represented in the freemen lists. Clothing workers, especially the ubiquitous tailors, and food and drink traders were found in both the outer parishes and the city as a whole. But the urban periphery had substantial contingents of building craftsmen, yeomen, miscellaneous agricultural workers, as well as labourers, all of whom figure much less prominently in the freeman economy. While the freemen lists may well understate the incidence of poorer trades in the main city, the broad picture would suggest that the occupational order of the suburbs complemented rather than competed with that of the established civic economy.

Though our samples are often small, if we correlate these occupational groupings with the household data from the 1563 census a rudimentary ranking becomes apparent. For comparative purposes Table 7 also includes information on our 32 male householders for whom we have no occupation, and also on our 32 female householders (widows and single).

TABLE 7

Household Data by Occupational or Status Groupings

		Mean household size	Mean no. children	Mean no. servants
1	gentry	9.0	5.0	2.0
2	professions	–	–	–
3	clothing trades	4.3	1.4	0.8
4	leather trades	4.0	1.4	0.6
5	food and drink	5.4	1.8	1.4
6	textile industry	4.6	2.2	0.4
7	household goods	3.0	1.0	0.0
8	distributive	3.0	1.0	0.0
9	building trades	5.1	1.8	1.2
10	yeomen	3.6	0.9	0.6
11	husbandmen	–	–	–
12	labourers	3.2	1.1	0.0
13	agric. misc.	4.8	1.4	1.2
14	service industries	3.9	1.0	0.2
15	misc.	3.1	0.5	0.5
	unspecified male householders	3.2	0.6	0.4
	female householders:			
	widows	1.5	0.4	0.0
	single	1.0	0.0	0.0

After our solitary minor gentleman with his large family, the food and drink traders came next in household size, among them a number of brewers and victuallers. The building craftsmen belonged to the same category of larger households with an average of nearly two children and more than one servant per family. But the household groups for most other craftsmen and traders were below the accepted national average: even the urban yeomen presided over small-scale families with few servants or children, confirming that they were only a pale reflection of their affluent country cousins. Further down the order were the labourers having diminutive families with an average of just one child and no servants. These families were on the margin of viability, likely to be shipwrecked any time by personal or economic misfortune. The figures for male householders without known occupation indicate that many were probably labourers as well. But it was the widows who diverged most from the household norm, frequently living by themselves or with a single child or possibly a lodger.

Broadly speaking, the evidence from probate inventories, rentals and other sources tends to support this picture of the different layers of suburban society. The only gentleman listed in the 1563 census, Gilbert Hyde of St. Martin's, not only presided over a large household: he was a landowner both in and out of the city. In 1564 he rented property from Christchurch Cathedral in St. Martin's and soon after he leased the rectory at Littlebourne, a village a few miles away. A man with some legal training, he acted as auditor for the cathedral; he was probably the father of the Elizabethan clerk of the peace for the county, Ralph Hyde.[36]

Among the food and drink traders John Cosby, also of St. Martin's, was the most prosperous, with interests linking both town and countryside. According to his inventory in 1568, his beer brewery was a fairly large establishment with equipment and raw materials valued at over £50. He had a side-line in corn dealing (his stock was valued at £234), probably trading through Sandwich, the principal grain port in east Kent. His debtors included city magistrates, neighbours from the outer parishes, county gentry, and villagers in the hinterland up to 7 or 8 miles away from Canterbury. His home had at least ten rooms and his personal wealth exceeded £400; his wife, Anne, was a smart lady with a lot of fine clothes.[37]

Other food and drink traders were minnows by comparison, but some of them were not insubstantial figures for the area. William Ansted, an established victualler, rented a house in St. Mildred's from Christchurch with at least five rooms; had as a by-employment a small-holding or market garden of 3 or 4 acres, apparently growing and selling vegetables for city markets; and died in 1566 leaving personal goods worth just over £16. Most of the other victuallers were smaller men – more typical of the trade. John Patenson, for instance, coupled his alehouse business with being a 'horse-rider', probably a hackneyman. Of the remaining food and drink traders several were better-off, renting property from the city. The widow of William Nashe, a brewer who died in 1565, had personal assets at her death a few years later worth £29 9s. including plate and jewellery.[38] One final point. Over half of this occupational group are known to have kept animals, dogs and pigs. The pigs were doubtless fed on the mash from the brewers' tuns (Cosby had ten hogs). But the possession of animals was also a sign of the modest affluence of at least some of these traders.

The building craftsmen likewise enjoyed some limited prosperity. A number were assessed to pay towards the parliamentary subsidy (an increasingly selective tax); 7 out of the 12 leased property from the city or cathedral; and a quarter held some form of civic or local office in the

36. Census, fol. 4v; Lambeth Palace Library, MS.814, fol. 8; CCL: Register, V, 3, fol. 127v; New Foundation-Treasurer's Accounts, 4; Dean and Chapter Act Book, II, fol. 64, 95, 107v.
37. Census, fol. 5v; KAO, PRC 28/2/57; 10/3/154; CCL, JQ 1565.
38. Census, fol. 1r; KAO, PRC 10/2/12; Lambeth Palace Library, MS.814, fol. 9 (Ansted). Census, fol. 6v (Patenson). Census, fol. 1r; KAO, PRC 10/6/175, 330 (Nashe).

early part of Elizabeth's reign. Robert Bettes, for instance, a high-class painter with three male servants, occupied property in Northgate ward; at his death in 1571 he left personal goods valued at nearly £16. Another resident of St. Mary Northgate was the plumber Stephen Redbourne, a freeman since 1543, who had a household of 12. Redbourne appears to have supplemented the income from his trade by sub-letting property in the area, doubtless to poorer inhabitants. A number of these skilled craftsmen, including Bettes and Redbourne, may have prospered working in the cathedral close (adjacent to Northgate).[39] Moreover, there was a buoyant demand for their services from prosperous merchants in the inner city parishes such as St. Andrew's or St. Mary Magdalen, busy now rebuilding and refurbishing their homes. But it is also evident that the suburban craftsmen answered rural needs as well. One tiler, Roger Nicolaus, had a master at the village of Denton, 8 miles from Canterbury. Stephen Mathewe, the paviour, claimed that he 'worked very often out of the parish where he dwells', apparently in the countryside. Not all the building craftsmen were prosperous. Mathewe, as we know, was accused in 1562 of sharing a bed with his mother and grown-up brother, and pleaded dire poverty. But the situation here was not quite so desperate as it appeared. A year later Mathewe had a wife and was renting his own house; eventually in 1569 at the age of 31 he obtained the freedom by right of patrimony (his father had been a freeman paviour). Mathewe was one of the marginal poor, never plunging into the depths of destitution.[40]

Among the superior crafts and trades such as building work, roughly a third of our sample were freemen. In the case of minor crafts and trades the incidence of freemen was somewhat lower with no more than one in seven in the service industries. At the same time, it is clear that at Canterbury the suburbs were not just the haunt of unenfranchised traders seeking to evade guild controls and under-cut recognised city traders, as the complaints of magistrates frequently implied. Those failing to take up the freedom were mainly deterred by the high cost of fines (if they were not the sons or apprentices of freemen), and guild insistence on formal training in their trades. Lesser craftsmen tended to be short both on money and formal qualifications.

The economic position of the lesser craft groups in the Canterbury suburbs was often precarious. Take firstly the textile workers. Only one in a sample of 9 householders was a tolerably substantial figure, assessed at having £1 in goods in the subsidy, and leaving inventorial wealth in 1576 of £7 6s. 8d.[41] Two of the others were classed as poor in the census and for the remainder little is known: none held any form of local office. The leather workers were hardly any better off. One or two leased gardens or tenements from Christchurch and another was a ward auditor, but the rest have left little trace of their presence.

Even so, the lesser craftsmen were a cut above the labourers. A fifth of these were listed in 1563 as poor. Only two (out of 24) may have leased city or Christchurch property. Many of the others probably rented small tenements on a weekly basis or lived in shacks up against the city walls. Their field of social interaction was limited. Not one occupied an official post, however lowly, in the early part of Elizabeth's reign or was well enough off for an inventory of his goods to be made after his death. The near destitution implied by their small household size

39. Census, fol. 3r; KAO, PRC 10/6/89; CCL, F/A 16, fol. 148v; 17, fol. 17v (Bettes). Census, fol. 6v; CCL, F/A 16, fol. 150v; KAO, PRC 17/39/6 (Redbourne).

40. CCL: X.1.7, fol. 73; X.1.11, fol. 107; Lambeth Palace Library, MS.814, fol. 8v; Cowper, *Freemen*.

41. For the substantial weaver William Newton: Census, fol. 4r; KAO, PRC 10/8/62; PRO, E 179/126/426.

and lack of servants in the census is echoed time and again by other sources. Quite a few no doubt were recent arrivals from the countryside, like William Symson who came to Canterbury in the spring of 1563 from Chilham, 6 miles away. Some sought work in the main city; others went to labour in the fields stretching out from St. Martin's or St. Mary Northgate. With limited family commitments they frequently moved on, passing quickly out of view. Nothing for instance is known of the Symson family after the death of one of their children in St. Mildred's in 1565.[42] While the possession of animals was fairly widespread among the craftsmen and tradesmen, even in the lesser occupations, it was noticeably less common in the case of labourers (only a fifth had a pig or dog), presumably because they could not afford to feed them. As we noted earlier, a major portion of our householders without identified occupation were probably labourers as well: over one in five were recorded in the census as poor.

Nonetheless, there can be little question who came last in the poverty stakes: the widow. More than half of those enumerated in the 1563 census were classed as poor or impotent in some way – aged or lame. A handful held leases of tenements from Christchurch or the city (probably succeeding their husbands as tenants). One woman recently widowed still paid the subsidy and lived in a more substantial house in St. Mary Northgate. But most probably occupied cheap cottages, so-called penny rents, in back-lanes: Ivy Lane in St. Paul's had a cluster of poor widows living next door to each other. On occasion widows may have divided a cottage between them. Some younger and more respectable widows like Margaret Agers, lately the wife of a prosperous shoemaker, managed to re-marry fairly soon and return to a recognized social position. But most of the others had to eke out a living taking in lodgers or parish orphans, spinning, working in the fields, especially at harvest time, selling ale or beer, and sometimes by acting the whore. Frequently, however, they might be forced to go from door to door asking neighbours for relief, like Mother Bassock from St. Alphege's (next to St. Mary Northgate), 'begging with her pot in her hand for drink with also a basket for her meat': other times they would have to fall back on parish doles. Little wonder that virtually none of our widows could afford dogs or pigs to keep them company – even the few scraps necessary to feed them were beyond their means. (This may help to explain why widows were notorious as witches for casting spells on animals.)[43]

Poverty then pervaded Canterbury's outer parishes. On the other hand, as we have seen, the suburbs were not a formless economic and social wilderness. Despite magisterial complaints the suburbs of provincial towns never posed a serious threat to the respectable economic world of the city. Rather they exercised a dual economic function, servicing the main city and rural hinterland. They sent servants and labourers to work in inner city houses and work-shops; their established craftsmen (quite often freemen) sold goods and skills to city inhabitants who could afford them; their smallholdings and nascent market gardens supplied vegetables, fruit and other produce to city markets. At the same time, the outer parishes sent labourers to hedge and hoe on neighbouring farms and to work further afield in harvest time, while their small craftsmen travelled from village to village offering specialist skills. When husbandmen and other country folk came to Canterbury to do business they would often take their refresh-

---

42. CCL: AC 3, fol. 188. Census. fol. 1r; St. Mildred's Parish Register 1. X.11.1, fol. 115v.
43. CCL: X.10.7, fol. 110v–112v; Census, fol. 3v; PRC 39/11, fol. 253v–4v; JQ 1560s; X.10.8, fol. 181v, 186. A. Macfarlane, *Witchcraft in Tudor and Stuart England,* 1970, 153–4 (pigs comprised the largest category of animals bewitched by witches indicted at Essex assizes 1560–1680).

ment at the small victualling houses on the outskirts of town.[44] Socially, too, the outer parishes had their own order, articulated by the pattern of households, housing and personal wealth: a pyramid-shaped hierarchy of better-off inhabitants and superior craftsmen and traders; lesser craft workers; labourers; and widows.

Further coherence was given to these poorer areas of the city by a network of neighbourhood ties and connections. The street was a cardinal unit of social communication in the pre-industrial town. Neighbours acted for each other as sureties or compurgators in litigation; as witnesses of wills or appraisers of inventories. They lent to or borrowed money from each other; periodically, they participated in street rituals or celebrations; routinely, they gossiped and worked together. Magdalena Lewis, of St. Pauls' described in 1560 how she sat 'spinning at her door situate in Ivy Lane with her other poor neighbours, sitting by and spinning as Goodwife Ward, Goodwife Morleyn, Margaret Golding, Goodwife Miller, Goodwife Valyar and one Ham's wife' – most of them listed three years later in the census. On that day in 1560 they chatted about how Margaret Richardson, another neighbour, had seen a couple making love together. Female neighbours attended at the delivery of children, with the local ale-wife sometimes acting as midwife, and perhaps dispensing some of her special strong beer to the mother. Better-off inhabitants took in the children of people in the street as servants; they might also bestow neighbourly relief on the aged and impotent.[45]

Trying to analyse the scale of neighbourly interaction is a difficult task. Because of the fragmentary nature of the census we never have a comprehensive picture of the potential social network. Identifying linkages between neighbours depends on the random survival of documentation. In these circumstances it is clearly not possible to ask many of the probing and subtle questions raised by social anthropologists and others working on networks in present day developing or modernised societies.[46] Here the most we can do is to establish the broad pattern of direct or so-called primary order linkages between neighbours listed in the census, defining those relationships according to certain rules.[47] We can say little about the durability, density or content of relationships. Again no attempt could be made to plot secondary or intermediate relationships because of the serious technical problems involved. However, a wide spread of sources has been exploited to make our survey of relationships as complete and representative as possible: not only testamentary documents biased towards more substantial people but deposition registers, sessions papers and city council minutes with their coverage of ordinary inhabitants. The period scanned for linkages was 1550 to 1575, though with a concentration on the early 1560s. Because of the problem of establishing the precise topography of the suburbs covered by the census, the area has been treated as a single neighbourhood. The

44.   Eg., CCL, JQ 1570s, 1606.
45.   For street bonfires in the early 1560s: CCL, Misc. Sessions Papers (Burrows case). X.10.7, fol. 110v–112v; X.1.5, fol. 90v, 91; X.10.8, fol. 181v.
46.   J.C. Mitchell (ed.), *Social Networks in Urban Situations*, 1969, chs. 1, 3; J.A. Barnes, *Social Networks*, Reading, Mass., 1972; for some of the problems in the historical analysis of social networks see R.M. Smith, 'A Note on Network Analysis . . .' in P. Laslett *et al.* (eds.), *Bastardy and its Comparative History*, 1979, 240–6.
47.   Neighbourly relationships are defined for our purposes to include: acting as a witness, executor or overseer of someone's will; appraisor of an inventory; compurgator for someone in a church court case; surety for a bond; taking a nearby child into service; acting jointly with someone in business matters or social activities (including gossiping); women slandering each other. Relationships are assumed to be two-way. Kinship ties have been ignored in this analysis.

drawbacks of this approach are obvious, not least the danger of ignoring or discounting parochial loyalties. On the other hand, the whole district included in the census was small (a person could walk through it in a few minutes) and certain streets criss-crossed several parish boundaries anyway.

Because of the problems of this kind of analysis attention has been focused on two particular issues: firstly, the proportion of households with one or more known linkages with other households – to show the *incidence* of relationships; secondly in the case of households with linkages, the mean number of links per household – to indicate the *range* of relationships. In Table 8 we have tried to correlate the incidence and range of neighbourly ties with the economic and social groupings in the area making use of our earlier occupational and status categories. Linkages cannot always be proven. Thus the table includes two series of figures: the first where the ties are definite *(minima)*; the second where they are less certain *(maxima)*.

TABLE 8

The Pattern of Neighbourly Ties between Households
According to Occupational or Status Groupings

		minima		maxima	
		incidence (% of sample groupings)	range	incidence (% of sample groupings)	range
1	gentry	100.0	1.0	100.0	1.0
2	professions	–	–	–	–
3	clothing trades	38.5	1.4	53.9	2.0
4	leather trades	55.5	2.4	55.5	4.0
5	food and drink	36.4	3.8	63.6	5.1
6	textile industry	11.1	2.0	55.6	1.2
7	household goods	50.0	3.0	50.0	3.0
8	distributive	100.0	2.0	100.0	3.0
9	building trades	41.7	3.2	83.3	3.3
10	yeomen	57.1	3.0	71.4	3.4
11	husbandmen	–	–	–	–
12	labourers	8.3	2.0	33.3	1.6
13	agric. misc.	20.0	1.0	40.0	5.0
14	service industries	28.6	3.0	28.6	6.0
15	misc.	37.5	2.0	50.0	2.5
unspecified male-headed households		9.4	1.7	43.8	1.6
female-headed households:					
widows		16.1	2.8	19.4	2.8
single		0.0	0.0	0.0	0.0

Even allowing that we have only scratched the surface of the neighbourhood network and that some of the samples are small, the picture presented in Table 8 is a reasonably coherent one. We can identify a relatively high incidence of neighbourhood contacts among most categories of craftsmen and above, particularly if we accept the *maxima* figures. Even some minor trades like leather-working display a significant level of commitment to the neighbourhood network, though it has to be pointed out that the linkages appear much weaker in the case of the textile trade. Further down the economic scale, only a minority of our large contingent of labourers and their families are known to have been involved in neighbourly interaction and even among these the 'density' of contacts – the number per household was relatively low. The experience of male householders without known occupation and their families was once again fairly similar to that of the labouring group. Widows stood apart from the local network most of all, though where their households were involved in the neighbourhood the links might be quite complex.

Neighbourhood ties were not only horizontal, linking households of similar social status, but up to a point they were vertical, crossing economic and social boundaries. At the same time, however, while the neighbourhood network regularly brought together some better-off inhabitants and lesser craftsmen, such links rarely seem to have extended down to the level of labourers and widows. Widows tended to maintain neighbourly ties, if they had any, with other widows – implying they may have been pushed into some kind of marginal ghetto.

One last comment about Table 8. The occupational group which exhibited the strongest commitment to neighbourly linkages was the food and drink trades, among them as we know several victuallers. This is no coincidence. For the alehouse and victualling house emerged as a vital hub of the neighbourhood and popular community in the sixteenth century. It was here that local people came to booze and drown their sorrows when times were bad, or drink, dance and celebrate if they had a little money, and take part in neighbourhood games.[48]

Neighbourly relations had their vicissitudes, of course. Margaret Lane, a widow from St. Mary Northgate, was accused in the church courts in 1560 of 'being a common eavesdropper and a bearer of tales from one to another'. Elizabeth Harrison, the wife of the tiler John Harrison, was charged in the year of the census with slandering her neighbours, while Agnes, married to Richard Martyman, was alleged to be 'a scold and a slanderer of her neighbours'.[49] But such conflict should not be over-emphasised. 'Offences' against neighbourly norms, mostly confined to women, served as the exceptions to underline the ruling value of supportive relationships, the most important of which were generally between male householders.

As we might expect, neighbourly contacts sometimes overlapped with occupational links. They may also have overlain geographical ties, with people having originated from the same village or part of the country. Significant, too, in the neighbourhood context were god-parentage ties, which in turn might confirm more distant kin relationships.[50] In certain

48. P. Clark, *The English Alehouse: A Social History 1200–1830*, 1983, especially ch. 7.
49. CCL: X.1.2, fol. 2v; X.1.5, fol. 90v, 91v.
50. E.g., the painters Bettes and Burnley lived next door to each other in St. Mary Northgate (Census, fol. 3r). Though there is no direct evidence from the census, godparentage ties (usually between less immediate kinsfolk) retained their significance into the late sixteenth century, with godparents sometimes taking in and bringing up their godchildren, looking after their property, as well as leaving them bequests (e.g., PRO, C 24/18 Clifford in mem; KAO: NR/JQ f 1/10; NR/JB 10, fol. 227v; PRC 17/22, fol. 204). Several householders in St. Mary Northgate had Thanet connections; see also P. Clark, 'The Reception of Migrants in English Towns in the Early Modern Period' (paper to conference on Migrants and the City, Göttingen, 1982).

instances when analysing the Canterbury network one has the uneasy sense that lurking underneath an apparent neighbourly connection was an extended kin relationship. But as we have seen there is little evidence that extended kinship provided the sinews of neighbourhood interaction in our period. Rather, neighbourly ties functioned as a major substitute for active kin relationships, in a context where the immediate family circle was narrow and other relatives often out of touch.

The neighbourhood network, for all its limitations, gave a degree of shape and coherence to the Canterbury suburbs, despite all the social pressures. It is hardly surprising that neighbourly ties failed to embrace the poor labourers in our survey, for a sizeable proportion of these were doubtless newcomers to the area. Labourers, widows and lodgers tended to travel from increasingly long distances. Elizabeth Richmond, a widow listed in 1563, had come with her small baby daughter from Lancashire; later in the century a stream of poor migrants arrived in the city from the distressed North. Not infrequently the newcomers stopped over at the alehouse, which thus served as a bridge between the floating, labouring poor and the local neighbourhood.[51]

As is well known, however, physical mobility was not confined to the poor in Tudor and Stuart towns. Approximately 90 per cent of Canterbury men testifying in the diocesan courts 1580–1640 had moved at least once in their lives, and the situation was probably fairly similar a generation earlier. The pattern of migration was somewhat different among craftsmen and tradesmen, as the census evidence shows. Whereas the majority of labourers were probably transients moving on rapidly to new destinations, often outside the city, respectable immigrant householders, usually coming from shorter distances, would put more roots down in the community. At Canterbury they quite often paid the intrantes (or strangers') tax to secure official permission for trading; in some cases they would go on to buy the freedom. When they moved the chances are they would not go far away. If their economic position improved they might take their family to live in one of the more central parishes like St. Andrew's (just as some widows moved in the opposite direction). Even the handful of aliens (mostly French) listed in the suburbs appear to have integrated well (the separate and large communities of Walloon and Dutch refugees only settled in the city in the 1570s).[52]

More substantial migrants meshed in fairly easily with the neighbourhood network described earlier. But the late sixteenth century witnessed a growing volume of poor subsistence immigration by labourers and the like. Canterbury magistrates issued a spate of instructions against the lodging of poor incomers, and appointed special officials to turn them away from the city gates (with many consequently ending up in the suburbs).[53] By the late Tudor period the pressures and tensions of life in the urban periphery – the precarious and probably deteriorating living standards of most lesser craftsmen and traders, the plight of numerous widows, and the high mobility and desperation of labourers – served to create a shadowy sub-culture of poverty and deprivation. One manifestation was a widespread reluctance or

51. Census, fol. 4v; Clark and Slack, *Crisis and Order*, 126–8, 138–9; Census, fol. 7v; CCL, X.1.8, fol. 141; Clark, *Alehouse*, 123–31, 135–7.
52. Clark and Slack, *Crisis and Order*, 122, 128–30, 133; Cowper, *Intrantes*, 214 ff. Several aliens worked in our suburban households; others like William Newton were established craftsmen employing native apprentices. For the later Stranger communities: F.W. Cross, *History of the Walloon and Huguenot Church at Canterbury* (Publications of the Huguenot Soc., xv, 1898), 27 ff.
53. CCL, AC 2, fol. 197v–8, 218v, 258v passim.

failure to attend church, especially among small craftsmen and labourers. Thomas Gill of St. Paul's, a petty householder in 1563, was repeatedly presented during that decade for being absent from service; the vicar noted in 1562 that Gill and his brother 'be poor men and seek their living abroad'. Stephen Mathewe, the paviour, was accused in 1563 of not receiving communion for two years and claimed 'he comes to the church when as he is at home', having to tramp abroad in search of work at other times; he and his wife continued to be presented for non-attendance for a couple of decades. Roughly one in twelve of the census households had at least one member charged with absenteeism during the early years of Elizabeth's reign: given the ineffectiveness of the church courts for part of this time, the real incidence of non-attendance was doubtless much higher. Some absentees may have been religious conservatives hostile to the return of Protestantism after 1558. Some years after the census Robert Binge, one of our yeomen, was forced to protest: 'I have been blinded in times past by the mass, but now mine eyes be opened, thank God.' During the 1560s the Canterbury magistracy was riven by religious controversy. But most absentees were too busy trying to scrape a living, or too poor to pay the necessary church fees; a number were excommunicated.[54]

That important popular centre, the alehouse, was frequently associated with religious non-attendance. John Patenson, the St. Mildred's ale-seller, was presented for not going to church; two more of our victuallers, William Ansted and John Kevell, kept people drinking in their houses at service time, playing at games. Alehouses provided other facilities for the lower orders as well. Agnes Conny, who retailed drink in Northgate, was accused of bawdry with a Londoner; another victualler, Thompson in St. Paul's, kept 'a harlot in his house', probably this was 'Jane, a Calais woman'. Not that commercial sex was confined to the alehouse. Michael Rowse's wife, a poor woman, was presented for acting as a bawd, keeping a woman in her house who became pregnant. Approximately 5 per cent of the householders or their wives listed in the census were charged during the period 1560–1575 with being involved in a variety of illicit sexual activities ranging from adultery to prostitution. It can be argued that liaisons of this type had their roots in a traditionally more permissive and open attitude towards sex and marriage among the lower orders. But there can be little doubt that at least some of the sexual encounters involving our census inhabitants were a result of social distress, with poor women drifting into casual prostitution to make a little money to keep them going, selling their favours to labourers and others on the tramp away from home.[55]

Whether crime was another strand in the sub-culture of social deprivation in early Elizabethan Canterbury is more problematical. A number of persons listed in 1563 were implicated in petty offences including theft, receiving, and disorder, during the decade. Robert Bettes was arrested for foraging in the fields in search of buried treasure foretold by a country

54. For Gill: CCL: X.1.3, fol. 4v; X.1.4, fol. 6v, 7; X.1.9, fol. 176. For Mathewe: CCL: X.1.5, fol. 92v–3; X.1.11, fol. 107; 1586. For Binge: CCL, JQ, 1578; P. Clark, 'Josias Nicholls and Religious Radicalism 1553–1639', *Journal of Ecclesiastical History,* xxviii (1977), 134–7. CCL: X.1.5, fol. 91; X.1.9, fol. 95. Absenteeism was encouraged by the structural difficulties of the urban church: Canterbury's suburban parishes had roughly twice as many households per church as the inner city parishes; St. Mary Northgate had only a curate in the 1560s and St. Paul's a negligent, pluralist vicar (CCL: Visitation Returns 1569, fol. 34v; X.1.5, fol. 89v; X.1.9, fol. 97).

55. CCL: X.1.9, fol. 177; JQ 1561–2; X.1.2, fol. 2v; X.1.5, fol. 90v; X.1.4, fol. 6v; X.1.7, fol. 71v–2. C. Hill, 'Sex, Marriage and the Family in England', *Economic History Review,* 2nd Series, xxxi (1978), 457–60.

56. CCL, JQ, 1563, 1568; J.S. Cockburn (ed.), *Crime in England 1550–1800,* 1977, 53, 63, 67–9.

woman in a dream. William Holman, the son of Stephen Holman, went out poaching rabbits in 1568 at Harbledown on the other side of the city, and ate some of the spoils with friends at a local alehouse. Both Bettes and Holman came from more substantial households in the suburbs, as did several other offenders; by contrast there is little evidence of our labourers being charged with criminal activities. But it would be wrong to conclude that crime was mainly a pursuit of those above the lowest ranks of society. Most craftsmen and traders, as we have suggested stayed longer in the locality and so there was a greater statistical probability of their committing – and being charged with – offences; labourers perpetrating crimes frequently moved on before they were caught. As economic conditions deteriorated for the urban lower classes in the late sixteenth century, there was almost certainly an increased resort to petty crime as one of the strategies for survival.

By the last years of Elizabeth's reign the social climate in Canterbury's outer parishes was bleak. The city's trade was in serious difficulty, while the economy of the hinterland was depressed by harvest failure: both developments squeezed economic activity in the suburbs. At the same time, pauper immigration, as we know, was high. All this inflicted serious strain on the world of the suburb. During the 1590s there were recurrent outbreaks of fighting, brawling and gang conflict in the southern districts of Canterbury. Early in 1596 the northern suburbs were the scene of a determined attempt by small craftsmen and labourers at their wits' end to seize grain carts leaving the city to take food to London. The following year Margaret Richardson of St. Mildred's, in 1563 the wife of a craftsman but now an elderly widow, surveyed the last four decades and declared seditiously it was 'a pity that ever she [Elizabeth] came unto the crown, because that since she came unto the crown there was no good order'. And in more pungent tones: 'it was pity that ever her Majesty had pissed any more clowts than one, it was a pity she ever wore the crown.' Here was the bitter cry of the suburban destitute.[57]

Poverty and social difficulty were not confined to the suburbs in Tudor and early Stuart towns. They seeped into the heartland of the community. Even the richest parishes had their quota of indigent, and slum areas are sometimes found well within the walls. But the complaints of magistrates indicated that the suburbs were generally regarded as worst affected – flooded with the poor and vagrant. As we have seen, however, the outer parishes at Canterbury were not just disorderly excrescences of the city community. They had their own distinct demographic, economic and social structures. Though cross-cultural comparisons are always difficult, there are parallels between the patterns of social and neighbourly organization found at Canterbury and those identified in some of the slum districts of cities in present-day developing countries.[58] On the other hand, the Canterbury evidence has shown how fragile many of the structures were in the late-sixteenth-century suburb. The social economy was unbalanced. The household units were frequently too small for viability and persistence; the work force was dominated by floating labourers and small craftsmen on the margin of subsistence. There was almost a structural propensity to attract large numbers of poor outsiders. As social pressures accelerated in the late sixteenth century, with the continuing economic instability of towns like Canterbury, and the multiplying numbers of subsistence

57. Clark, *English Provincial Society*, 229–30, 246–7; *idem*, 'Popular Protest and Disturbance in Kent, 1558–1640', *Economic History Review*, 2nd Series, xxix (1976), 368, 374; CCL, JQ 1597.
58. Beier, 'Warwick', 62, 64; J.F. Pound (ed.), *The Norwich Census of the Poor 1570* (Norfolk Record Soc., xl, 1971), 107; Phythian-Adams, *Coventry*, 166. O. Lewis, *The Children of Sanchez*, New York, 1969, xxiv *passim*; R. Piddington, (ed.), *Kinship and Geographical Mobility*, Leiden, 1965, 50 ff.

migrants tramping the kingdom, the social coherence of the urban periphery came under intense strain. No wonder that some city leaders at the close of the century felt themselves besieged by suburban disorder. But the 1590s probably marked the turning point. At Canterbury and elsewhere the local élites began to strengthen their control over the outer parishes in the seventeenth century: through wealthier parishes having to contribute to the relief of the suburban poor under the 1598 Poor Law Act; through an expanded parochial bureaucracy, tight settlement controls, and closer liaison with county justices. Eventually, even economic and other pressures began to abate.[59] After the Restoration the suburbs of English provincial towns were on the high-road to gentrification and embourgeoisement.

59.   E.M. Leonard, *The Early History of English Poor Relief,* 1900, 76–7; CCL, JQ 1600 ff.; Clark and Slack, *Crisis and Order*, 151; Clark, 'Migration', 73 ff.

FRANCIS AND FRANCIS MOTLEY AUSTEN, CLERKS OF THE PEACE FOR KENT

BRYAN KEITH-LUCAS

I.   The Office of Clerk of the Peace

An aspect of the eighteenth-century government which has been unduly ignored by historians is the role of the Clerks of the Peace. It is accepted that the real governing body of provincial England was the magistrates in Quarter Sessions. The Webbs have shown how they played a triple role as judges, administrators and legislators, and how the Quarter Sessions developed into 'an inchoate provincial Legislature'. The magistrates were laymen, and amateurs. The one professional man involved was the Clerk of the Peace. He was usually an attorney, and was appointed by the Lord Lieutenant in his capacity of *Custos Rotulorum*. In many cases the Lord Lieutenant appointed his own family attorney, and, when he died or retired, his successor in the attorney's firm, who had probably helped in the county business, would commonly be appointed to succeed him. This meant that in many cases a father was succeeded by his son, and perhaps by his grandson. Some of these dynasties held office in their counties for a century or more; the family of Hodgson held the office in Cumberland from 1809 until 1942, the Fooks family in Dorset from 1826 until 1925.

Commonly the Clerkship of the Peace was not the only office they held; they might be clerks of several turnpike trusts, Town Clerk (and perhaps Mayor) of the county town, clerk to the Lieutenancy, County Treasurer, and even, in some instances, Member of Parliament for the county. William Hodgson, the first of his family in Cumberland, was also Town Clerk of Carlisle, and five times Mayor. He was Clerk of the Peace and of Indictments at the City Sessions, Clerk of the City Court, Clerk to the City Magistrates, Deputy Lieutenant of the County, Clerk to the Coroners, Clerk of the Recognizances and Steward of the Court Leet. He was also legal agent to Lord Lonsdale, the Lord Lieutenant. His predecessor, John Baynes, was also M.P. for Cockermouth. Theed Pearse, Clerk of the Peace for Bedfordshire from 1798 to 1843, was also Town Clerk of the borough of Bedford, Clerk of the Bedford Improvement Commissioners, and Clerk of the Bedford and Newport Pagnell Turnpike Trust. He was succeeded by his son who held the offices from 1843 to 1857, and by his grandson, Theed William Pearse, who held office until 1890. John Story of Hertfordshire was Clerk of the Peace for the county, and for the Liberty of St. Albans, Clerk of two important turnpike trusts, receiver of the bridge moneys in the Liberty, twice Mayor of St. Albans, a partner in a local bank, Registrar of the archdeaconry, and steward of the manors and man of business for Lord Verulam, the Lord Lieutenant.

II.   The Austen Family

In Kent the clerks of the peace in the late seventeenth and early eighteenth centuries were a peculiar group. Francis Twisden, the younger son of Sir Thomas Twisden of Bradbourne in Kent held office from 1673 to 1680. His father was a High Court judge, who tried the Regicides and John Bunyan. His successors, Robert Saunders (1681–87 and 1690–1702), John

PLATE I

Francis Austen, Clerk of the Peace for Kent, 1753–73, by Ozias Humphry, R.A. (Reproduced by kind permission of the City of Sheffield Art Galleries).

Kennett (1688) and Philip Owen (1689–90) were alternately in and out of office as the political winds blew towards the Catholics or the anti-Catholics.[1] David Fuller, a Maidstone attorney, held the office from 1702 to 1753, when he was succeeded by Francis Austen, a Sevenoaks attorney.

Though the social standing of attornies was in general not high, some of the clerks of the peace were members of cadet branches of substantial county families, and many of them prospered in the office, and ended up as wealthy country gentlemen.

Such a man was Francis Austen. The Austen family had owned land in Kent for several centuries, having risen to affluence in the cloth trade. Two of them served as sheriffs of the county, and one branch of the family, at Tenterden, prospered sufficiently for its head to be made a baronet by Charles II.[2] Another branch was established at Horsmonden, where they owned two estates – Broadford and Grovehurst. It was from this branch that Francis Austen came.

The heir to the family estates at Horsmonden in the time of Queen Anne was John Austen, a young man of an improvident nature. He died in 1704, leaving a widow with seven children and large debts. His father, the owner of the estates, refused to help the widow, except in so far as he paid for the education of his eldest grandson, who was now his heir. So his daughter-in-law had to fend for herself and for the other children, none of whom was more than ten years old. She moved to Sevenoaks, selling such property as she possessed to pay her husband's debts, and there she took in as lodgers masters and boys of Sevenoaks School, where her own boys were educated. One of them grew up to become a surgeon at Tonbridge, but, dying young soon after his wife's death, he left three orphan children. One of these was George Austen, who in due course became Rector of Steventon in Hampshire and father of Jane Austen, the novelist.

Francis, the fifth son, was articled to an attorney in Clifford's Inn, and practised there and at Sevenoaks, near the school where his mother worked. He prospered, and was appointed agent for the Knole estate of the Duke of Dorset, Lord Lieutenant of the county, and one of the greatest Whig magnificos. Francis was then able to assist his orphan nephew, George, paying for his education at Tonbridge School, and purchasing for him the living of Deane in Hampshire. His wife later served as godmother to George's daughter, Jane.

We do not know how often the attorney of Sevenoaks met his wife's goddaughter, though she was often to come to Kent in later years when her brother Edward inherited the property of the Knights at Godmersham; but it is certain that she went with her parents and her sister Cassandra to stay with him at Sevenoaks in 1788 when she was 12 years old and he was nearly 90. Her cousin, Philadelphia Walter, met her there at dinner and reported that she was 'very like her brother Henry, not at all pretty and very prim, unlike a girl of twelve; but it is a hasty judgement which you will scold me for . . . Jane is whimsical and affected'.[3] Whether she visited him in Sevenoaks again is not established, but her knowledge of Chevening suggests that she did stay either with his son, Francis Motley Austen, at his big house at Kippington, or with his grandson, John, who became Rector of Chevening. Sir David Smithers has shown that

1. See Sir Edgar Stephens, *The Clerks of the Counties, 1360–1960*, 109–10.
2. The title became extinct in 1772 and the last Lady Austen moved to Olney, where she was the friend of William Cowper, the poet, and Thomas Scott, the Commentator.
3. Letter from Philadelphia Walter to James Walter, 23rd July, 1788, dated from Seale, *Austen Papers*, 131.

Chevening is undoubtedly the original and model of Rosings in *Pride and Prejudice*.[4]

Francis Austen had been born in 1698, and lived until 1791. He was described in later years by Henry, Jane Austen's brother, in a letter to his nephew, James Edward Austen Leigh:

> There (at Sevenoaks) my Father's Uncle, old Francis Austen set out in life with £800 and a bundle of pens, as an Attorney, and contrived to amass a very large fortune, living most hospitably, and yet buying up all the valuable land round the Town – marrying two wealthy wives and persuading the Godmother of his eldest son, Motley Austen, to leave to her said Godson a small legacy of £100,000 – He was a kind uncle too, for he bought the presentations of Ashe and Deane, that your Grandfather might have which ever fell vacant first – it chanced to be Deane. He left your Grandfather a legacy of £500, though at that time he had 3 sons married and at least a dozen grandchildren. All that I remember of him is that he wore a wig like a Bishop, and a suit of light gray ditto, coat, vest and hose. In his picture over the chimney the coat and vest had a narrow gold lace edging, about half an inch broad, but in my day he had laid aside the gold edging, though he retained a perfect identity of colour, texture and make to his life's end – I think he was born in Anne's reign, and was of course a smart man of George the First's. It is a sort of privilege to have seen and conversed with such a model of a hundred years since.[5]

III. Francis Austen and County Elections

The Duke of Dorset, as was expected of a man of his consequence, played a major part in the electioneering for the two county seats for Kent, and his agent was naturally involved. In the election of 1734 he was engaged in organising the campaign in the county for the duke's son, Lord Middlesex, and Sir George Oxenden, an east Kent squire and an unreliable placeman who later changed sides and became MP for Sandwich, as a protégé of Walpole's.[6] Middlesex was rarely in the county, and Oxenden resented being left to do most of the work.

The duke was in Ireland as Lord Lieutenant, and Austen reported regularly through the duke's secretary, Sackville Bale,[7] explaining the difficulties he was having in getting the candidates to work together, urging that Lord Middlesex should come and do his share of the canvassing and entertaining, and assessing in detail the support that could be expected from the freeholders of each parish, for they alone enjoyed the franchise in the county elections.[8]

Austen's principal colleague was Thomas Curteis, Rector of Wrotham and Sevenoaks, who was also writing regular and lengthy reports to the duke and to Sackville Bale.

4.   Article in *Country Life,* 30th October, 1980, 'Where was Jane Austen's Rosings?', and *Jane Austen in Kent* (1981), 37–56.

5.   *Austen Papers*, 16–7. The portrait referred to is by Ozias Humphry, R.A. There are two copies, one at the Graves Art Gallery at Sheffield, and one at the house in which Francis Austen lived in Sevenoaks, now the office of the firm of solicitors which he founded, now known as Knocker and Foskett. Ozias Humphry painted a number of portraits and other pictures for the Duke of Dorset at Knole. The duke gave the living of Seale and Kemsing (adjoining Knole Park) to his brother, William. Ozias Humphry fell out of favour with the duke on account of an alleged discourtesy to the duchess. (Victoria Sackville West, *Knole and the Sackvilles* (1922), 194). He also worked for the duke in Italy, and painted a portrait of the Young Pretender in Florence in 1770. See also *History of the Woodgates of Stonewall Park and Summerhill* by the Revd. G. Woodgate and G.M.G. Woodgate, and *Life and Works of Ozias Humphry* by George C. Williamson (1918).

6.   Oxenden was described by Lord Egmont as 'a proud, conceited, lewd man.' (*Diary of the Earl of Egmont,* Vol. 1, 213.)

7.   The Revd. Sackville Spencer Bale was given the living of Withyham by the duke in 1749, but appears to have continued as the duke's secretary, putting a curate in to do the work of the parish. In 1778 he was succeeded by his son, the Revd. Sackville Stevens Bale, as rector of Withyham.

8.   Kent Archives U148 Z52, 53.

As Lord Middlesex was rarely in the county, local agents were appointed to maintain his interest. For this the resources of the Whig squirearchy and of the Austen family were mobilised. Francis Austen's cousin, Sir Robert Austen, was to look after Erith, Crayford, Bexley and Foot's Cray (but he was unwell, and spent the whole summer in Tunbridge Wells).[9] Edward Austen was in charge at Tenterden and Francis' nephew, John, at Horsmonden. Sir Wyndham Knatchbull was responsible for Wye, Lord Romney's friends for Maidstone and Julius Deedes for Hythe.[10] The Bishop of Rochester was helping, and other clergymen were lending their support. But despite this help, and the regular detailed reports being sent across to Dublin Castle, and the distribution by Francis Austen of £2353 2s. 8d. on behalf of the duke's candidates,[11] they were beaten by the Tories – Lord Vane and Sir Edward Dering.

The next contested election was not until 1754. Again Francis Austen was heavily involved in the electioneering on behalf of the duke's candidates, the honourable Robert Fairfax of Leeds Castle (later Lord Fairfax) and the honourable Lewis Watson (later Lord Sondes) nephew by marriage of the Duke of Newcastle, two men of straw who had to be financed by the Dukes of Dorset and Newcastle. Austen was working closely with his neighbour, Thomas Curteis, the son of the old Rector of Wrotham and Sevenoaks, who had succeeded him in the Sevenoaks living. The Duke of Dorset was once more in Ireland as Lord Lieutenant, and a regular flow of letters went out from Sevenoaks, some of them about estate matters – leases of farms, damage to the park paling by badgers, the holding of courts baron, the condition of both hares and beagles, and the other business proper to the agent of a great estate. But Curteis and Austen were not always in accord, and Curteis hinted at distrust of his motives, particularly in relation to allegations that friends and relations of his were trespassing on the duke's estate in pursuit of hares, and that he was doing little to stop them – 'a very pretty farce, and just as much as we might expect from such an agent'.[12]

Most of the correspondence, however, related to the prospects of the election, in which Sir Edward Dering was now fighting alone on the Tory side, and so, as each elector had two votes, the distribution of their second votes was of great importance; on this matter also Curteis and Austen fell out, Curteis accusing Austen of soliciting these second votes for Fairfax but not for Watson. Austen, on the other hand, was apprehensive that, as Dering was advising his supporters to give their second votes to Watson, Fairfax would be left behind, and might be defeated.[13]

Dering's principal supporter was the Earl of Westmorland, of Mereworth Castle, who was entertaining the Tory freeholders from as far away as Maidstone, Rochester and Farningham, closely watched by Curteis and Austen. Westmorland was not only a Tory, but an active Jacobite. It was here, at Mereworth that, apparently, a year later (1755), Prince Charles Edward held the last of the great Jacobite councils in England.[14]

---

9. Sir Robert Austen of Boxley married Rachel, sister of Sir Francis Dashwood (Lord le Despencer) Chancellor of the Exchequer. After her brother's death Lady Austen unlawfully assumed the title of Baroness le Despencer.
10. Kent Archives U269 O106–7.
11. Kent Archives U269 O109, 110.
12. Kent Archives U269 C149/11, 15, 16.
13. Kent Archives U269 C149/16 (Curteis to Bale); U269 C149/17 (Austen to Bale).
14. A. Shield and Andrew Lang, *The King over the Water* (1902), 461, but the evidence on this point is not conclusive.

Both Curteis and Austen rode round the western part of the county, visiting the principal landowners, urging them to use their influence over the freeholders in accordance with the duke's wishes, and reporting in great detail to Sackville Bale, telling who was present at the meetings, and who had made promises of how they, or their dependents, would vote.

IV.   Francis Austen as Clerk of the Peace

In 1733 Francis Austen served as under-sheriff, and in 1753, on the death of David Fuller, the Clerk of the Peace, the duke appointed him to that office, not apparently without some murmurs of criticism. Writing to Sackville Bale in Dublin on the 29th January, 1754,[15] about his appointment, Austen expressed the hope that he would prove himself to be a just and faithful servant 'notwithstanding the illnatured insinuations to the contrary'.

As Clerk of the Peace, Austen did some of the administrative work himself, but his office at Sevenoaks was eighteen miles from Maidstone, where the West Kent Sessions were held, and forty-five miles from Canterbury,[16] where the East Kent magistrates met. Furthermore, he was still practising in Clifford's Inn, in London, for some of his time. Inevitably, therefore, much of the work was left to his deputy in Maidstone, and to his clerks. There are, however, many documents bearing his signature, signed, as was then the custom for clerks of the peace and some town clerks, with his surname only.[17] He appears to have attended the sessions regularly, swearing in some members of the grand jury himself, while others were sworn in by his clerks.

He apparently drew no salary, but received fees for most of his services, in some cases from the county rate, in others from the magistrates taking out their *dedimus*, or from the parties appearing before the court; for issuing certificates, precepts or warrants, for swearing witnesses, for the appointment of constables, registering the appointment of gamekeepers, sending returns to the Government, or for his many other duties. It is not possible to assess what his income was, nor what his outgoings were, but there was clearly a substantial profit to be made. The minutes of the Sessions, for example, disclose a number of payments 'for business done' (for example, £306 14s. 10d. at the Epiphany Sessions in 1765; £98 17s. 6d. in January 1767, from the West Kent Sessions, and similar payments from time to time from the East Kent Sessions). No complete record survives of the fees paid by the parties for preparing affidavits, swearing oaths and other such routine business. The costs involved in his legal work were, however, considerable. Among the commonest items were the disputes about the law of settlement – to which parish did some pauper belong? – to which parish could he or she be sent back, to be relieved out of the parochial rate? In a typical case of this sort[18] the bill of costs prepared by Austen's firm was for £5 18s. 0d., and much of this was for the routine business of the court procedure. Many other items occur, including, to take another example, in 1765, a payment to Mr. Austen of £29 15s. 3d. 'for money laid out and expended and for his trouble in printing and dispensing notices of the Distemper appearing and ceasing amongst the Horned Cattle in this County'.

Much of this work would have been done by his clerks, and there survives in the Kent

15.   Kent Archives U269 C149/9.
16.   The Sessions were not always held in Maidstone and Canterbury. For example, in 1809 General Sessions were held also at the Crown Inn, Sevenoaks, the Ship Inn, Faversham, and the Half-Way House, Challock.
17.   This convention continued in some cases until 1972. The Clerk of the Crown in Chancery also signs in this way.
18.   1770, Detling *v.* Gillingham on the removal of Mary Durham.

Archives Office a detailed diary kept by one of them showing how busy they were, riding to London, to Canterbury and to Maidstone; visiting clients to make their wills, instructing counsel, conducting petty sessional courts or meetings of turnpike trusts, and sometimes, on minor business, sending Bill (presumably the office boy) on a hired horse, to deliver documents, serve summonses, or take orders to a parish constable.[19]

In addition to his duties as Clerk of the Peace, Francis Austen carried out many other public functions; he served as under-sheriff, as Clerk of the Petty Sessional Court of Bearsted, as Clerk of the Lieutenancy, and as Clerk to the Commissioners of Assessed Taxes; he conducted the county court on behalf of the Sheriff, and he was a trustee of the Mereworth–Wrotham Heath, the Bromley–Beggar's Bush, the Cranbrook–Rolvenden, the Goudhurst, the Wadhurst–West Farley, the Wrotham Heath–Godstone, the Tonbridge–Maidstone, the Tunbridge Wells–Maresfield, the Mereworth–Seal, the Sevenoaks–Kipping's Cross, and the Wilsley Green–Kipping's Cross Turnpike Trusts. For this last trust he had promoted the parliamentary bill which gave the trust its powers. He attended the first meeting of the trustees, when a resolution was passed to pay him his professional fees for this, amounting to £78 12s. 4d., but thereafter there is no mention in the minutes of his presence. The chairman of the trust was his nephew, John, of Horsmonden, who served also as treasurer, and lent the trust the sum of £1,000 on mortgage, which he assigned soon afterwards.

The papers in the Kent Archives Office show him active through his long life in many ways, in addition to these official appointments.[20] He was a busy attorney in Sevenoaks, carrying out the normal duties of a country solicitor – drafting wills, buying or selling land, conducting litigation, and advising his clients. He was an 'Assistant' (i.e. Governor) of Sevenoaks School, where he had once been a pupil; he was agent for the Knole Estate, and parliamentary agent for the duke. Among the many letters preserved at the Kent Archives Office are several asking his kinsman, David Papillon of Acrise, to appoint a protégé of his to the office of Hop Assistant for the collection of the Land Tax; a letter of Sackville Bale begging a place in Sackville College at East Grinstead for Elizabeth Hoath, a poor widow; a letter to David Papillon on behalf of the duke, as *Custos Rotulorum*, authorising the setting up of the 'Press Gang' for taking up all 'Straggling Seamen', in accordance with orders from the Privy Council; letters to newly-appointed magistrates, telling them of their appointment, and letters dealing with the day-to-day routine of a busy attorney and agent of a large estate.

V. *Francis Motley Austen*

In due course, when he was 75, Francis Austen retired from the office of Clerk of the Peace, and was succeeded by his eldest son, Francis Motley Austen, who was also a member of the Sevenoaks solicitors' firm. He held the office for the next 35 years, until he was succeeded in 1808 by John Fellows Claridge, who had been his deputy for the previous sixteen years, and was also a partner in the Sevenoaks firm.[21]

Francis Motley Austen succeeded to many of his father's offices, as well as that of Clerk of

19. Kent Archives Q/CZ 3, 4, 5.
20. The *Law List* in 1790 and 1792 shows him as Town Clerk of Sevenoaks. This must be a mistake, as Sevenoaks was not a borough, so had no town clerk. By 1792 Austen was dead.
21. There is a portrait of John Fellows Claridge in the Red House, now the office of the firm founded by Francis Austen, known today as Knocker and Foskett. Jane Edwards, in her MS. Diary, describes him as 'a very clever man, but he was haughty and reserved'.

PLATE II

Francis Motley Austen (From a miniature in the possession of Francis Austen, Esq., by whose permission it is reproduced. Artist unknown).

the Peace; he became clerk to the commissioners of assessed taxes, an assistant at Sevenoaks School, and a trustee of half a dozen turnpike trusts.[22] He did not, however, have the same need to make his way in his profession as his father had; he was already a rich man, who could allow others to undertake the drudgery of the law on his behalf. The Quarter Sessions papers at Maidstone suggest that at first he did much of the work himself; one finds him travelling to London on Quarter Sessions business, prosecuting in court himself, and signing documents. But it would seem that, after a bit, he left more and more of the work to his deputies. Robert Parker, who was appointed Deputy Clerk of the Peace in 1776, was also Clerk to the Lieutenancy, and joint County Treasurer for the Western Division. He was in practice as an attorney at Maidstone, and it may be assumed that he did much of the routine work as Francis Motley Austen became increasingly involved in other business, as a country gentleman, in connection with the Militia, and in his property dealings. Moreover, until 1796, when he moved to Kippington, Austen lived at Lamberhurst, some distance from the office at Sevenoaks and from the meeting places of the Sessions – Canterbury and Maidstone.

In 1791 John Fellows Claridge was appointed Deputy Clerk of the Peace in place of Robert Parker. He was a partner in the Sevenoaks firm, and succeeded as Clerk of the Peace when Austen retired in 1808. By this time Austen's name no longer appeared in the *Law List* as a practising attorney – but the lists of that time are notoriously unreliable.[23] Official documents were commonly signed 'J.F. Claridge, Deputy Clerk of the Peace', instead of in the name of the Clerk of the Peace himself.[24]

The view that the work was mainly carried out by the deputy is further supported by the statement, a few years later, of Sir William Cosway, a Kentish magistrate, to the Select Committee of the House of Lords on the County Rates in 1834. He said of the office of Clerk of the Peace, 'In our County, and I believe in most others, it is a Patronage in the hands of the Lord Lieutenant, and he usually gives it to his own Solicitor, who rarely acts himself, but appoints a Deputy.'[25]

One particularly difficult problem which faced the Clerk of the Peace at this time was the relation of the two courts of Quarter Sessions for east and west Kent. Austen was Clerk of the Peace for both east and west Kent, but there were separate treasurers for the two divisions; in east Kent Thomas Smith and, later, William Bristow held the office in Austen's time. They were both booksellers in Canterbury and in their time mayors of the city. In the western division Robert Parker, Deputy Clerk of the Peace was also joint treasurer with Thomas Punnett, the Town Clerk of Maidstone.

Separate county rates were levied for the two divisions of the county, as instructed by the respective Courts of Quarter Sessions. A few magistrates sat in both courts, but this was rare, and, as in the case of Austen's neighbour and colleague in the election campaigns, Thomas

22. Unfortunately, the minutes of many of the turnpike trusts have been lost, so one cannot tell how many he served on. In the *Abstract of the General Statements* of the Turnpike Trusts 1835, the firm, then known as Austen and Claridge, was recorded as acting as clerks of the Sevenoaks, the Westerham and Edenbridge, and the Wrotham Heath Trusts.

23. See footnote 20 above.

24. e.g. Deputations of Gamekeepers, in 1806 (Kent Archives U269 0 26); Notice of Presentment of Gaol by the Grand Jury, 24th December, 1805, (Kent Archives Q/AG).

25. *Report of the Select Committee of the House of Lords appointed to inquire into the Charges of the County Rates in England and Wales*, 1834, 56. It is clear that John Claridge acted by deputy.

Curteis, was probably on account of territorial qualifications in both areas. In essence, the question was whether Kent was one county, or two. Were the two courts of Quarter Sessions technically distinct bodies, or were they meetings of the same body, each with power and authority over the whole county?

The matter came to a head in the time of Francis Motley Austen. The county gaol at Maidstone had been built in 1746, under an Act of 1736. It had no provision for the separation of hardened criminals, first offenders and other categories of prisoners. In 1765, a riot occurred as the prisoners were being escorted to the weekly service, to be conducted by the chaplain, Mr. Denne. The gaoler was overpowered and the prisoners escaped; troops were turned out from the barracks, and engaged the prisoners near Plaxtol, killing several of them. The chaplain never fully recovered his faculties. As a result of this episode, and of the agitation of John Howard and Sir Onesiphorus Paul for prison reform, the west Kent magistrates decided to build a new county gaol. After many delays, they proceeded with the scheme, and called upon the magistrates of the eastern division to pay their share.

There would seem to have been some lack of confidence in the Clerk of the Peace as legal adviser to the magistrates of the eastern division, for they took legal advice not from Mr. Austen, but from Charles Robinson, the Recorder of Canterbury,[26] and appointed a local solicitor, Mr. Forster, to act on their behalf.

The magistrates of west Kent issued an order to William Bristow, the treasurer for the eastern division, calling upon him to pay the share of the cost of building and maintaining the new gaol, which they claimed was due from the eastern division. The east Kent Magistrates then ordered him to disobey the order. Ultimately, the case was tried in the King's Bench before Lord Chief Justice Kenyon and a Middlesex jury, in December 1797. Judgement was given for the magistrates of west Kent, upholding the view that Kent was one county, and that the two courts of Quarter Sessions were in law the same body. This, however, was not the end of the ill-feeling between the two divisions. Ten years later the rival Quarter Sessions were still passing resolutions of hostile criticism of each other.[27]

It appears that in this matter the business was conducted for the western division not by the Clerk of the Peace himself, but by the deputy, John Claridge.[28]

At about this time there was a growing criticism up and down the country of the high fees charged by clerks of the peace. In 1817, this led to the passing of an Act (57 Geo. III, cap. 91) authorising the magistrates in Quarter Sessions to settle a table of fees, subject to confirmation by the judge of assize. The Kent magistrates appear to have ignored this Act,[29] but a list of the fees actually charged was prepared, and sent to the Secretary of State. This, though dated ten years after Francis Motley Austen retired from the office of Clerk of the Peace, may be taken as indicating approximately the level of fees in his time. There is not likely to have been much change in those years.

26. Charles Robinson was MP for Canterbury and also Recorder for the City and the Cinque Ports. He was brother of Mrs. Montagu, the 'Blue Stocking', and of Matthew Robinson-Morris, Baron Rokeby, the eccentric amphibian peer.
27. Kent Archives Q/SMa e.g. pp. 6–10. See also petition to Parliament from E. and W. Kent, about the gaol, 1813.
28. Kent Archives Q/CA 8; Memorandum on the Division of east and west Kent. There were also separate Quarter Sessions for Romney Marsh and for each of the boroughs.
29. Report of the House of Lords Select Committee on Charges on the County Rates, 1835, 56.

This list suggests that the fees charged by the Clerk of the Peace were high, allowing for the purchasing power of the pound at that time. The table includes, among many other charges, the following:

For every Prisoner convicted or acquitted of Felony . . .	9s. 4d.
For every order of Transportation . . .	13s. 4d.
Indictment for disobeying an Order of the Justices in a case of Bastardy . . .	10s. 6d.
Order of Filiation . . .	10s. 0d.
Every Conviction of Trespass . . .	10s. 0d.
Withdrawing every Plea of Not Guilty . . .	10s. 0d.
Submission and Plea of Guilty in Trespass and recording same including Discharge of Recognizance or Process . . .	£1 17s. 10d.
Appointment of Constable or Borsholder . . .	4s. 0d.
Licence for Performance of Plays . . .	£1 1s. 0d.
For every Bench Warrant . . .	2s. 0d.

A few years later, in 1826, an 'account of Receipts and Payment in the Business of the Clerkship of the Peace'[30] shows the Clerk of the Peace receiving £2009 4s. 7d. from the two divisions of the county. There were, however, substantial outgoings to be met from this.

In the years 1830 to 1833 the Clerk of the Peace for Kent reported[31] an average annual remuneration of £2,055 8s. 10¼d. – the highest in England except for the anomalous case of Lancashire, where the office was a sinecure in the gift of the Crown.

How much profit Francis Motley Austen made from his office of Clerk of the Peace cannot be calculated, but it is clear that it gave him a substantial income, though probably modest when compared with the rent roll of the property which he had inherited and bought.

VI. A Man of Property

Francis Austen and his son between them served the county for 55 years as clerks of the peace. They held also a number of other public offices, and played a considerable part in the life of Sevenoaks and its neighbourhood. Judging from Ozias Humphry's portrait of him, the father must have been a determined, even dogmatic, character, who knew well how to look after himself; this impression fits well with what we know of him from written sources. The son seems a more shadowy figure, less involved in his profession, more concerned with social activities. Family letters refer to his entertaining his cousins at Lamberhurst, or giving dinner to all the magistrates at Kippington after the proclamation of George IV, or in the decorative role of a captain of Volunteers, rather than to his professional functions.[32]

Francis Austen, the father, had prospered considerably since the days when he set up his practice 'with £800 and a bundle of pens'. His first wife, Anne Motley, was a rich heiress, only daughter of Thomas Motley of Beckenham. Through her he acquired a substantial estate at Wilmington, near Dartford. He then added to this the adjoining property of Shere Hall. According to Henry Thomas Austen he also 'bought up all the valuable land round the town' (Sevenoaks), and sold some of this, bordering on the Knole Estate, to his client and employer, the Duke of Dorset.[33] Among the other properties he bought were Trigg, in Goudhurst,

30. Kent Archives Q/CZ1.
31. *House of Lords Select Committee on the Charges on the County Rates*, 1835, 355.
32. *Austen Papers*, 125: *History of the Woodgates*, 180, 201.
33. C.J. Phillips, *History of the Sackville Family*, ii, 203.

Boxley Abbey (which he quickly sold to his cousin, Edward Austen), and the manors of East and West Yaldham (promptly re-sold to William Evelyn of St. Clere's).[34]

Francis Austen was undoubtedly generous to his nephew in his lifetime, though there was some disappointment when his will left nearly everything to his eldest son, Francis Motley Austen, ignoring his more needy nephews and nieces.[35] Jane's brother, Henry Thomas Austen, in the letter quoted above, referred to Francis Austen as 'a kind uncle', and he was certainly generous to his nephew, Jane's father. One recent writer refers to him as 'a sort of fairy godfather to Jane's father, as well as actual godfather to herself'.[36] But yet, on the other hand, there is an undercurrent of suspicion about his activities. He himself referred to 'illnatured insinuations' when he was appointed as Clerk of the Peace. Jane, apparently, also had her doubts; writing in 1807 to her sister Cassandra, about Francis Austen's grandson, John, when he inherited the Horsmonden estates from his cousin, she remarked that 'such ill-gotten wealth can never prosper!' This would seem to refer ironically to the rapidly acquired wealth of Francis and Francis Motley Austen, rather than to the Horsmonden property.[37] Another member of the family, Tysoe Hancock, writing in 1773 to his wife Philadelphia (Jane Austen's aunt), from India, said 'I am perfectly resolved to take my affairs out of your uncle's hands by the next dispatch; it would be cruelty to you not to do it, for by his management I may be a fourth time ruined'.[38]

His clients may or may not have been ruined, but Francis Austen was not. He married first a rich heiress, Anne Motley, by whom he had one son, Francis Motley Austen, his successor as Clerk of the Peace. After her death he married again, in circumstances described by Henry Austen in a letter to James Austen Leigh,[39]

> Wickham estate and advowson was the property of a Mr. Lennard some ninety years ago. He left it to his widow for life, and afterwards to his and her only child, a Miss (Mary) Lennard. The widow was legally attacked by the nearest male relation of the defunct – she flung her cause into the hands of my Great Uncle, old Frank Austen: he won the cause and the wealthy widow's heart and hand.

The Mr. Lennard in question was the illegitimate son of Sir Samuel Lennard, Bart., of West Wickham. By his will in 1726 Sir Samuel Lennard had left his very considerable estate between his two illegitimate sons, appointing Sir Robert Austen, a cousin of Francis Austen, as trustee of the estate. The younger son died unmarried and the whole property passed to the elder, Samuel. His will in fact did not leave it all to his widow for life, but divided it equally between the widow (who became Mrs. Francis Austen) and the daughter, Mary. There was, however, a hope expressed in the will that they would 'have some compassion on those unhappy Infants I had before Marriage which I have raised and named Stephen and Elizabeth Langford'.[40]

The property thus brought into Francis Austen's hands including the manors of Baston, Keston and West Wickham, with the mansion of Wickham Court, Coney Hall Farm and land

---

34. Hasted, v, 18.
35. *Austen Papers,* 142. He left £500 in his will to George Austen, Jane's father.
36. S.M. Andrews, *Jane Austen: Some Aspects of her Work, together with her Tonbridge Connections.*
37. *Jane Austen's Letters,* 182. The sentence is ambiguous, but there is no apparent reason why she should refer to the Horsmonden property as 'ill-gotten'; it had been passed down in the family since the reign of James I.
38. *Austen Papers,* 74. Tysoe Hancock was himself not entirely reliable in financial matters.
39. *Austen Papers,* 18.
40. Francis Austen obtained probate of the will in 1756.

in Hayes, Beckenham, Orpington, Bindbury, Thurnham and Detling, as well as shares in the Chelsea Water Company and the advowson of West Wickham.[41]

Francis Austen acted as trustee, and receiver of the rents and profits of his step-daughter's estate, and as steward of her manors. He regularly and scrupulously drew up accounts, which show, for her half of the estate, an annual rent roll of about £2,000, on which he charged her 5 per cent for his professional services, in addition to £100 a year for her board and lodging, and his fees as steward of the manors.

As trustee of the estate at West Wickham Francis Austen was in control of the advowson, and also, it would appear, of that of Chevening. He intended the West Wickham living for his second son, Sackville Austen,[42] but as it fell vacant before Sackville was of age to take it, he gave it temporarily to a nephew, Henry. But Henry was a Unitarian, and never resided there, nor did the duty. In 1784, he resigned to make way for Sackville Austen. Later, a grandson, the Revd. John Thomas Austen, held the living from 1848 until 1876. In Chevening another grandson, John, was later instituted as rector.[43] So the family benefited substantially from the Lennard connection.

Mary Lennard, the step-daughter, later married John Farnaby, the younger brother of Sir Charles Farnaby, Bart., of Kippington, near Sevenoaks. Sir Charles was Member of Parliament for Kent, and had rebuilt the mansion of Kippington. His expenses exceeded his income, and he mortgaged the estate to Francis Austen. He became bankrupt in 1788, and Francis Austen entered into possession under the terms of the mortgage. When Sir Charles died his brother John succeeded him in the title and property, but lived at his wife's house, West Wickham Court. Francis Austen's son (Francis Motley Austen) bought out the remainder of the Farnaby interest in Kippington, thus becoming absolute owner of the property, which included the mansion (now an old people's home), the Crown Inn, and nearly a thousand acres of land.[44] He sold the house his father had lived in[45] for many years, and moved into the much more imposing Kippington.

Altogether, Francis Austen, the father, amassed a very considerable fortune and when he died was said to be worth £6,000[46] a year which all went to Francis Motley Austen, 'Who was immensely rich before, his younger brother Captain John Austen, I understand, has only £12,000 left him.'[47]

The younger brother here referred to was John, who was regarded as a rather wild young

41. Marriage settlement of Mary Lennard and John Farnaby, dated 28th April, 1784. Some of the property was mortgaged to Francis Austen for £10,000.
42. Many of the families who depended on the Knole estate named their children Sackville; Sackville Bale, Thomas Sackville Curteis, Sackville Austen, Sackville Amherst.
43. Francis Motley Austen acquired also the livings of Crayford and Horsted Keynes in Sussex. In the former his grandson, Henry Morland Austen was instituted; in the latter his son John Austen.
44. I am indebted to Mr. T.E. Chester Barratt for lending me a number of abstracts of title relating to the Kippington and Chevening properties.
45. Francis Austen lived in the Red House, now the office of Messrs. Knocker and Foskett, the firm which he founded.
46. This may be compared with the expenditure of the Duke of Dorset of Knole. Victoria Sackville-West states, in *Knole and the Sackvilles* that the third duke, when he went as ambassador to Louis XVI 'was princely and lavish; he was spending money, as he himself owned, at the rate of £11,000 a year'. Later, when he retired to Knole, 'his expenses were reported to be reduced to four or five thousand a year.'
47. *Austen Papers*, 143, letter from Eliza de Feuillade to Philadelphia Walter.

man; he had quarrelled with his father and went out to India in the army, but came back in time to be forgiven and welcomed home.[48] He died in 1831.

The elder brother, Francis Motley, who inherited the great bulk of his father's wealth, had, in 1772, married one of the two daughters and co-heiresses of Sir Thomas Wilson of West Wickham. Under the marriage settlement his father had transferred to him properties in Goudhurst, Woodchurch, Minster-in-Thanet, Luddesdown, Burlington, Westerham, Edenbridge, Wilmington, Dartford, Birchington, Limpsfield, Brasted, Stangrave and Sutton-at-Hone. His father-in-law gave £9,000 as a dowry, as well as leaving his daughter half his considerable estate when he died in 1777.

Among his various legal appointments, Francis Austen acted as steward of the Manor of Billingham, conducting the Court Baron there in 1742 and 1745 on behalf of the Lady of the Manor, Sarah Inwen, a very wealthy widow.[49] Thirty years later he was still conducting the business of the court, but now described himself not as steward but as 'Lord of the said Manor', sometimes adding in his own hand 'in trust for Sarah Viscountess Falkland'. Lady Falkland was heiress to the considerable wealth of her father, Thomas Inwen, and had married first Henry Howard, tenth Earl of Suffolk and secondly the penniless Lord Falkland, whom she had loved since childhood. She agreed to act as godmother for her lawyer's infant son, Francis Motley, and in due course, in 1776, she made her will, no doubt advised by her lawyer, Francis Austen.

This will,[50] of which Francis Austen and Francis Motley Austen were appointed executors, with two others, bequeathed 'all and every my Manors, Messuages, Farms, Rents and Real Estates . . . lying in the County of Kent, Essex, Middlesex, Bedfordshire, Cambridgeshire, Lincolnshire or elsewhere in the Kingdom of England unto Francis Motley Austen Esquire grandson to the late Thomas Motley Esquire of Beckenham' on trust for sale after the death of her husband, Viscount Falkland, to pay the legacies, and then to Francis Motley Austen. He was also the residuary legatee for the whole estate.

The specific legacies were extensive, amounting to £43,000 (including £500 each to Francis Motley Austen, his two half-brothers, Sackville and John, and his father, Francis Austen), but none-the-less he seems to have done very well out of these provisions. The total value of the real estate is not known, but in Kent alone there were properties in Billingham,[51] Crouch, Hadlow, Lee and Benenden.[52] In these he quickly bought out Lord Falkland's life interest and became absolute owner of the fee simple. His cousin, Henry Austen, referred to the property

48. *Ibid.*, 131, letter from Philadelphia Walter to James Walter.
49. Widow of Thomas Inwen, who bought the estate in 1724. He was a rich hop merchant, and MP for Southwark with the brewer Ralph Thrale, father of Dr. Johnson's friend, Henry Thrale. Southwark was known as the 'Brewers' Borough', being usually represented in Parliament by brewers.
50. The copy of the will in the Public Record Office has a marginal note recording an application to the Master of the Rolls on 22nd November, 1850, for administration of the remainder of the estate, Francis Austen having failed to complete the administration of the assets.
51. The Lewisham Enclosure Act of 1810 refers in its preamble to Francis Motley Austen as one of the principal landowners. He was awarded over 37 acres on account of his ownership of 291 acres in Lewisham.
52. Recorded in Hasted, *passim*. Hasted consulted Francis Austen on this matter; MS. correspondence in Canterbury Cathedral Archives, letters dated 25th March and 10th September, 1779. Francis Motley Austen inherited from Lady Falkland some land at Southend and Russell's Grove in Beckenham, which he later exchanged for other land of John Cator, a rich timber merchant, Lord of the Manor of Beckenham, a friend of Samuel Johnson, and with him executor of Henry Thrale's will. Mrs. Thrale later accused Cator of dishonesty.

being worth £100,000, a sum which in modern money would be equivalent to several million pounds.[53]

In addition to all these properties he inherited from his father the legal practice in Sevenoaks, with its appendant offices, including the clerkship of the peace with its fees and profits. He was thus in a position to buy the Kippington estate from Sir John Farnaby, who had married his father's ward, Mary Lennard.

There he lived in considerable style with his family. He had eleven children, the eldest of whom was Francis Lucius Austen, named Francis after his father and grandfather, and Lucius after Lucius Cary, Viscount Falkland. He unfortunately went mad, and died in 1815, the same year as his father. The next son was Thomas, commonly referred to as Colonel Austen, who became MP for west Kent, and married, as his second wife, the sister of Cardinal Manning.[54] John, the third son, took Holy Orders, was rector of Chevening, and inherited the Broadford estate at Horsmonden, and ultimately the Kippington estate. The eldest daughter was Jane, who married William Campion, a special Act of Parliament being needed to deal with the trusteeship of her estate, when her brother Francis Lucius became insane and had to be replaced as a trustee by her brother, the Revd. John Austen. The marriage settlement brought in, on her husband's side, properties in Cranbrook, Hawkhurst, Frittenden, Biddenden and Hurstpierpoint and 'divers other places'. A portrait by Zoffany of Jane Austen is probably of this Jane, but some authorities maintain that it is of Jane the novelist.[55] The youngest daughter, Frances, married William Holcroft, a partner in the solicitors' firm at Sevenoaks.

As a wealthy landowner, Francis Motley Austen played his part in the county affairs, and in particular in the Militia movement at the time of the Napoleonic threat of invasion. In 1792 when the Kent Association was formed to support the Militia, meetings were held up and down the county to raise funds and stimulate enthusiasm. At the Sevenoaks meeting Francis Motley Austen was present, with all the other important people of the neighbourhood, and with him was his son, Francis Lucius Austen, his half-brother, John (who had a house on the Kippington estate), his nephew John, and the Vicar of Sevenoaks, Thomas Sackville Curteis, whose father had worked with Francis Austen in the election of 1754. A committee was formed, including Sir Charles Farnaby, Francis Motley Austen, Mr. Curteis and John Austen, to raise money for the Militia; John Claridge, the Deputy Clerk of the Peace and Austen's partner, was appointed as one of the treasurers. Austen subscribed £50 to the fund.

A Militia Regiment was formed, under the command of Lord Whitworth, who, having married the widowed Duchess of Dorset, was now master of Knole.[56] Francis Motley Austen

---

(Records of the Court Leet and Court Baron of Lee; Mrs. Piozzi, *Thraliana*, ii, 707, 799, 808, 812). Cator's nephew, General Sir John Cator, married Penelope, the daughter of Sir John Farnaby and Mary Lennard. Their son, John Farnaby Cator, inherited West Wickham Court. He changed his name to Lennard and became a baronet in 1880.

53. Calculating from the price of gold in 1776 and today (1981) it would be four or five million pounds.
54. Colonel Austen married first Margaret Morland, whose sister, Elizabeth, was married to Sir Charles Farnaby, the Rector of West Wickham, the son of Francis Austen's ward, Mary Lennard.
55. On the question of this picture, see articles in the *Annual Report of the Jane Austen Society*, 1973 and 1974. There are miniatures of the Sevenoaks Jane in the possession of Alwin Austen, of Wye, but the only unquestioned portrait of the novelist is a rough and amateurish sketch by her sister Cassandra.
56. When Earl Whitworth was sent to Ireland as Lord Lieutenant in 1813 he took with him, as A.D.C., Francis Motley Austen's son Thomas (Colonel Austen).

was given command of a company with the rank of captain in the Sevenoaks Volunteer Infantry, later known as the Sevenoaks and Bromley Regiment of Local Militia. The regiment was never called upon for active service, and involved but little hardship for its officers.

He gave his time also to church matters, serving on the committee for rebuilding St. Nicholas Church, Sevenoaks, for which a special Act of Parliament was obtained in 1811, and as a trustee of Tunbridge Chapel (at Tunbridge Wells), together with his half-brother John Austen of Broadford, and Lords Camden, Neville, Marsham, Abergavenny and Romney. Like his father before him, and his son Thomas after him, he served also as an 'assistant' or governor of Sevenoaks School.

It would be vain to try to assess the characters of these two men; they were essentially products of their age, not to be judged by the standards of today. The father was an example of an important group in the administration and government of the time; the powerful attorney who, holding the clerkship of the peace, added to it a number of other local offices in turnpikes and other bodies, becoming thereby not only influential, but also rich. The son rose into the ranks of the wealthy landowners, and became a member of the county society. Both were typical of their generations.

ACKNOWLEDGMENTS

I am grateful to many people for advice and help in preparing this article; some have lent me documents, some have criticized and improved my literary style or my grammar; some have answered my tiresome questions, either orally or by letter. I would particularly mention Mr. Alwyn Austen, a collateral descendant of Francis Austen, the subject of this essay; Mr. T. Chester Barratt, Mr. K.W. Best (Librarian of the Supreme Court), Josephine Birchenough of Lee, Major Gregory Blaxland, Mr. K.R. Cox (Chief Librarian of Lewisham), Mr. D.C. Gibson of the Kent Archives Office, Mr. David Gilson of Oxford, Anne Goodchild (Assistant Keeper of the Sheffield Art Galleries), Mrs. Margaret Dawes of Oxford, Mr. K.A. Doughty (Chief Librarian of Southwark), Dr. Bruce Lenman (University of St. Andrews), Jane Langton (Registrar of the Royal Archives), Hilary Magnus, Q.C., Professor L.S. Pressnell of the University of Kent at Canterbury, Mr. F.P. Richardson (Librarian of the Law Society), Col. J.H. Smart, M.B.E., M.C. (Sevenoaks School), Professor Sir David Smithers, Miss M.V. Stokes (of Coutts & Co.), Janet Taylor (of the Brewers Company) and Nigel Yates, County Archivist of Kent.

IMPROPER IMPROPRIATORS AND 'AUTIEL PETIT CHOSES'

FREDERICK LANSBERRY

Before 1836, when a tithe rent charge was substituted for tithe in kind,[1] tithes and their collection were one of the greatest causes of friction between clergy and laity. Although John Selden declared in the preface to *A Historie of Tithes* that his book had not been written to prove that tithes are not due by the law of God and that the laity may detain them, it provided one of the focal points in the persistent agitation against tithes in this country after the Reformation. Even in the great ages of faith there had been some reluctance to pay the tenth, and one may doubt the enthusiasm of the 'thankful acknowledgement' which the Kentish men sent to King Athelstan in 927 on the promulgation of the first general law in England for the payment of praedial and mixed tithes.[2] Certainly by the eighteenth century there were many who would have agreed with Selden in regarding tithes as a 'cabalistique operation in numbers' by which the tithes and first fruits offered by Abel had been given a mystical identity.[3]

Tithes were one tenth part of the increase of the produce of the soil and were of three kinds; praedial, mixed and personal. Praedial were those things which arose immediately from the ground, such as corn, hay, wood and fruit. Mixed were the increase from those things which received nourishment from the soil, and they included calves, lambs, chickens, milk and eggs. Personal tithes were 'such as do arise by the honest labour and industry of man . . . being the tenth part of the clear gain after charges deducted.'[4]

Tithes were the principal contribution made by the laity to the upkeep of the church; the other emoluments of a living were offerings, augmented by the profits of glebe land – the temporalities. Originally voluntary, the payment of tithes had become obligatory with excommunication for the recalcitrant. Statutes of Henry VIII's and Edward VI's reigns made tithes recoverable in the ecclesiastical courts,[5] but if the right to tithe was in dispute between clergy and laity the common law courts, especially the Exchequer of Pleas, took cognizance. The industry of these courts is some indication of the complexity of the law relating to tithes and of the readiness of parties, both clerical and lay, to resort to litigation. By 1783, John Rayner could fill three large volumes with cases concerning tithes and these were but a fraction of the cases heard.[6]

In the early church the rector had received all the tithes from his parish. But the practice of appropriation in the twelfth and thirteenth centuries, whereby patrons attached the revenues of their livings to a monastic order which provided the services of a priest or vicar, introduced the division of tithes into great and small. The great tithes, usually of corn, hay and wood, went to the rector and the small tithes comprising the remaining tithable commodities went to

1. 6 and 7 Will. IV c. 71.
2. H.W. Clarke, *A history of tithes from Abraham to Queen Victoria*, (1887), 75.
3. John Selden, *A historie of tithes*, (1618), ch. 1, sect. iv.
4. Richard Burn, *The justice of the peace and parish officer*, (1780), iv, 297–8.
5. 27 Hen. VIII c. 20; 32 Hen. VIII c. 7; 2 & 3 Ed. VI c. 13.
6. John Rayner, *Cases at large concerning tithes*, (1783).

the vicar. After the dissolution of the monasteries many rectories came into lay hands and they were known as impropriate rectories and their lay owners as impropriators.

The failure of both clergy and laity to keep adequate records led to many disputes; as few records of vicarial endowments survived, the vicar frequently claimed his tithe by prescription or constant usage. The grievances sustained by Francis Worrall, vicar of East Peckham, at the hands of the impropriator of the rectory, were typical of the plight of the lesser clergy in the late seventeenth century.[7]

Worrall complained to the Archbishop and to the Dean and Chapter of Canterbury that the parsonage at East Peckham had been bought by John Tucker from Sir Anthony Weldon and that the parsonage had all the land, which was improved every year by ploughing and liming, whereas the vicarage had not enough land on which to keep a cow. The parsonage took all the tithe corn and hay but the vicar could not get his tithe pig. Yet, the vicarage was charged with all taxations, tenths, subsidies and the 'cessing to the shipps'. Worrall claimed that he had spent between £40 and £50 repairing the vicarage house. After years of fruitless requests for tithe from the tenant of the impropriator the vicar had taken him to court. Much to Worrall's chagrin the tenant had died while the suit was in progress and it was at this point that Worrall had appealed to the Archbishop.[8]

The relations between vicars and impropriators were exacerbated in Kent owing to the value of some of the tithable commodities which the vicars claimed. Francis Fawkes, vicar of Orpington from 1755 to 1774, is alleged to have been parodied in the poem 'The Country Vicar', who whilst out shooting

> Surveying with a look most blithe,
> The growing riches of his tithe,
> Minds not the game for which he's beating;
> But to prevent his flock from cheating,
> Looks in each yard with jealous eye,
> With care examines every stye,
> Numbers the cows, observes their udders
> And at the dread of losing shudders . . .
> He counts the poultry, large and fine,
> 'Forty and five, then four are mine.'[9]

These mixed tithes were typically the lot of the vicar, but at Orpington, where there was an endowed vicarage as well as an endowed rectory, the vicars claimed tithes which elsewhere would have belonged to the rector. Also, in Kent, some small tithes were of greater value than the great tithes.

Hops were the most valuable crop grown in Kent. Usually the surveyors for the tithe commissioners made a separate assessment for hop grounds when apportioning the rent charge to be made consequent upon the Tithe Redemption Act of 1836. For instance, at Orpington the fruit plantations were assessed at seven shillings an acre; the hops at nine shillings an acre.[10]

7. G.F.A. Best, *Temporal pillars,* (1964), 13–21; C.E. Woodruff, 'Letters relating to the condition of the church in Kent during the primacy of Archbishop Sancroft', *Arch. Cant.,* xxi (1895), 186.
8. British Library, Add. Mss., 34178, *Tithe book of Francis Worrall, Vicar of East Peckham, 1632–1644.*
9. J.H.L. Vaynes, ed., *Kentish Garland,* (1882), ii, 758.
10. Public Record Office, IR. 29. 17/279.

Much depended upon whether hops grew in gardens or in fields. Judges differed in their opinions, and hops, 'minutae vel majores decimae' was a 'vexata questio'.[11] Some judges made the quantity and others the place in which hops were grown the deciding factor in their award. If they were grown in fields then they might be great tithes and belonged to the rector; but if they grew in gardens then they were a small tithe and as such due to the vicar. But how does a field differ from a garden? Certainly it was not simply by size. William Marshall, writing at the end of the eighteenth century, believed that, 'Lands which are kept continually in a state of hop ground as in the Maidstone quarter of this district cannot with strict propriety be classed among farm lands; as they are properly Garden Grounds. But where, as in the Tonbridge quarter of the Weald, and on all the weaker non-calcareous lands, their duration is limited where eight, ten or twelve years make up the full age of a hop ground, and where they are succeeded by ordinary farm produce, they become in reality and strictly, a Crop in Husbandry.'[12] Other judges seem to have believed that it was the manner in which the crops were sown which was the deciding factor. Seeds and grains were broadcast in a field but set in rows in gardens. Thus it was ruled that potatoes, normally planted in gardens, and therefore small tithes, even when planted in fields did not change their nature, and that peas and beans, set, drilled, sowed or planted in rows in a garden-like manner were small tithes, and the use of a plough instead of a spade made no difference.[13]

Another view was that hops were small tithe for, like hemp, saffron and tobacco, they were an article of late introduction to this country. When Thomas Risden, vicar of Ashford from 1667 to 1673, attempted to recover some of the tithes which had lapsed during the Commonwealth, John Crouch, the tenant of the impropriator, applied to the court of King's Bench for a prohibition which would have stopped Risden proceeding with his case against Crouch in the Exchequer of Pleas. But King's Bench refused the prohibition

> sur ceo suggestion quia le Court dit que ils voent prender notice que Hopps ne fuer cy ancient sed fuer use in Beer forsque de tardiffe temps nient obstant les Records cite per Seignior Co. al contra. Mes fuit dit que si le suggestion pur le Prohibicion ad eé a payer tant in lieu de touts small Tythes Prohibicion vaer quia Hopps, Oade & autiel petit choses de novel invention sont minutae decimae & pur ceo que le Suggestion ne fuit issint Prohibicion fuit deny.[14]

A case on the equity side of the Exchequer of Pleas was initiated by a written bill of complaint to which the defendant gave a written answer. The bill and answer were read by the Chief Baron or Barons of the Exchequer and, if they thought fit, local commissioners were appointed to order witnesses to appear before them and for depositions to be taken. This evidence was sent back to the Chief Baron and after all the submissions had been considered an order might be made for a hearing, followed by a decree.[15] Possibly, the most interesting class of material for family, local and agrarian historians is the interrogatories or questions prepared by the plaintiff's and defendant's counsels, which were put to the witnesses at the

11. Rayner, op. cit., i, xxvi.
12. W. Marshall, The rural economy of the southern counties, (1798), i. 288.
13. Rayner, op. cit., ii, 615.
14. T. Siderfin, Les reports des divers special cases argue & adjudge en le Court de Bank le Roy et auxy en le Co. Bank & L'Exchequer en les premier dix ans apres le restauration de son tres-excellent majesty le roy Charles le II, (1683), 443.
15. The bills and answers are in PRO, E. 112, the depositions in E. 134 and the decrees and orders in E. 128 to E. 131.

local enquiry, and the answers or depositions of the deponents. There were usually several questions aimed at establishing certain basic facts about the parties involved, the nature of the parish and aspects of its agriculture, as well as more specific questions about tithe customs and practices.

In 1705, Thomas Wardroper, vicar of Knockholt, complained that Richard Gee, the impropriator of the rectory of Orpington, had prevented him from taking his proper tithes. Witnesses for Wardroper maintained that the vicar had had all the tithes except that of wood for over seventy years. But, it was said, when Wardroper attempted to take his tenth sheaf of corn one of Gee's men shoved him on the ground, kicked the sheaf about the field and said he would have it. Timothy Stevens, a yeoman of Knockholt, said that Gee and his man came into his fields before the wheat had been bound up and threw it over hedges and hid other parcels in hedges so that the vicar should not find it. Another witness alleged that Gee's man came into his fields, took the vicar's tithe sheaf 'by little and littles' and scattered it about the field.[16]

Of equal interest with the antics of Gee and his bully boy is the incidental information which the deponents gave. Two yeomen, both aged over eighty, said that they knew the parsonage and vicarage house well because they went to school there and were taught by the curate, Mr. Flood. A Brasted blacksmith said that he knew the parsonage and vicarage when it was old and ready to drop down and that the vicar pulled it down and rebuilt it at his own expense. Another yeoman said that he had known about fifty acres of woodland in the parish of Knockholt to be grubbed up and converted into tillage and that the curate received the tithe of corn growing on the land so converted.[17]

Gee's mother[18] had been the plaintiff in an earlier case in the Exchequer of Pleas in which it had been decreed that the custom or modus of paying a sum of money for tithe hops was void. The defendant, Perch, had occupied a large arable farm in Orpington on which he grew grain of all sorts and hops. He alleged that it was the custom to pay ten shillings an acre for tithe hops and that the tithes were payable to the vicar. But the court confirmed that hops could not be converted into a modus, which was an ancient practice, and that they must be paid in kind.

Just how tithe hops were to be delivered had been a matter of much dispute. It had been noted '*per Twisden Justice (que vive in Kent) est un question a ceo jour coment Hopps serront Tythe, scil. si per le Hill, ou per le Poll, ou per le Bushel.*'[19] As hops had been planted in rows it had sometimes been the practice to offer every tenth row as tithe, but if the rows were uneven in length every tenth hill was offered. However, as the grower set out his own tithes it was said that he might not pay so much attention to those rows or hills which he knew would go for tithe, therefore the fairest method was to give the tenth bushel of picked hops. Chandler, a hop grower near Maidstone, attempted a compromise and paid the tithe of his early hops by the bushel and stripped the bines of every tenth hill of his later hops, which he left on the ground to be picked up. But this was rejected by the court.[20] An attempt to prove that the tithe gatherer was entitled to and should collect the bines as well as the hops was also unsuccessful. For it was said 'The flower of the hop is the sole object of cultivating the plant,

16. PRO, E. 134, 4 Anne, Easter 2, Kent. The enquiry was held at the Bull's Head, Chelsfield, 20th April, 1705.
17. *Ibid.*
18. Kent Archives Office, U. 36. T1, 299, leases of Orpington Rectory.
19. Siderfin, *loc. cit.*
20. Rayner, *op. cit.*, ii, 625.

of which it must be considered as the fruit, and it must be picked and gathered on the spot to preserve its quality and value.'[21] Robert Dodd of Boughton Aluph, who had planted and tended hops for forty-five years in the Ashford area said in 1671 that hops from bines which were cut by the ground before they were picked were not worth more than half a penny a pound.[22]

The manner of tithing hops eventually became the subject of an appeal to the House of Lords in 1753. Mr. Tyers, a Surrey hop-grower, had offered to pay £20 an acre in lieu of tithe but this had been refused by Mr. Walton, the incumbent of Mickleham and Dorking, Surrey. Tyers then proceeded to set out every tenth hill with the bines severed from the ground. Walton left the hops on the poles and after several months Tyers brought an action for damages against Walton for hindering the cultivation of his plantation. Walton then filed a bill in Exchequer Bench alleging incorrect setting out of tithe and won his case. Tyers appealed to the House of Lords claiming that he picked his hops according to fineness and colour into 'fine' and 'brown' and that this way of picking cost £5 an acre and that it was unfair that the person claiming tithe should profit by this expensive process of hop manufacture. But the Exchequer decree was confirmed by the Lords.[23]

Fine points arose over other tithable crops used in hop-growing. It was found that hop-poles and the bark from the poles were not tithable because the tithe owner had their contributory value in the hops, but the fuel used in drying hops should be tithed because the tithe of hops had been paid before the drying process.[24] The tithe of wood frequently caused dispute. Like hops it should have been presented in collectable lots – by the cord, or if underwood, by the bavin and faggot – and not left on the ground where it was felled.[25] Its value fluctuated according to time and place. In the case of the Earl of Clanricard v. Lady Denton, the defendant alleged an exemption from the tithe of wood in the Weald of Kent.[26] It was noted by the rector of Biddenden that 'by a kind construction of some lawyers the Weald is of a greater comprehension than in former times.'[27] In earlier times there had been so much wood in the Weald that the tithe was not worth collecting. Also, the process of cutting down trees and converting the land to tillage increased the value of the rectories. But by 1619, when the earl brought the case, it was said that wood was in short supply and therefore of value to tithe. The use of the wood could be crucial in deciding tithe. The Barons of the Exchequer found that fallen ash of above twenty years' growth used to make a plough or cart which were conducive to profit was tithable, but wood used in the construction of buildings was not.[28]

The changing profitability of the soil was of perennial interest to rectors and vicars alike. The introduction of a different sort of food for cattle might start a claim for an agistment tithe, one of the most contentious forms of tithe, for it was based on the profit gained from the value of the food consumed by the animal. In 1719, the impropriator of the tithes in the hamlet of

---

21. S. Toller, *A treatise of the law of tithes*, (1816), 113.
22. PRO, E. 134, 23 Chas. II Easter 10. Kent. Risden v. Crouch. Depositions of witnesses taken at the Saracens Head, Ashford 27th April, 1671.
23. R. Burn, *Ecclesiastical Law,* (1763), ii, 419–421.
24. Rayner, *op. cit.,* ii, 562.
25. PRO, E. 134, 2 Anne Easter, Kent. Gee *v.* Perch.
26. Rayner, *op. cit.,* i, 360–362.
27. Woodruff, *op. cit.,* 184.
28. PRO, E. 134, 2 Anne Easter, Kent. Gee *v.* Perch.

Mottingham in the parish of Chislehurst claimed against a farmer who had fed turnips to his cattle. The Court of Exchequer declared that the tithe was due even though the turnips had been sown after corn – and it was not usual to get tithe more than once a year from the same piece of land – and it was urged that the turnips had been fed to unprofitable cattle and that their manure would be an improvement to the land from which the parson would benefit the following year.[29] Agistment was probably the basis for some of the calculations of 'the pretended customs of Biddenden for small tithes' which so incensed the rector, Dr. Giles Hinton.[30]

for every sheep and wool	1*d.*	
for the tenth lamb	2*s.* 0*d.*	
for a cow and calf	3*d.*	
for a bullock of a year old	1*d.*	
for a bullock of 2 years old	1*d.*	ob.
for a fat oxe (though worth 10£)	4*d.*	
for a fat cow	3*d.*	
for piggs each	0*d.*	ob.
for 12 geese	4*d.*	
for an acre of meadow bearing often 2 loads of hay	1*d.*	ob.
for the tenth bushel of apples and pears	1*d.*	ob.
for a garden	2*d.*	
for a gallon of honey	4*d.*	

Tithe was paid on honey but not on bees, although they certainly increased every year; presumably taking one tenth of a swarm of bees would have made too painful an extraction, even for the clergy. Surprisingly, not only fruit and vegetables were taken from gardens. Margaret Bingham, the wife of a Goudhurst yeoman, said that the vicar sometimes sent his tithe gatherer for her roses and peonies, which she set out for him.[31]

Daniel Horsmonden, the vicar of Goudhurst at this time, was very vigilant and claimed a tithe of the produce of the malt and oatmeal hand querns used by some of the villagers. Some of his flock employed simple dodges. One yeoman, Thomas Burroughes, had twenty-two ewes and three kine which for most of the year were kept in Goudhurst but before shearing time they were removed into Lamberhurst parish where they were shorn and the wool carried away, and the cows were kept by a husbandman in Lamberhurst until after they had calved.[32]

There can be little doubt that the collection of tithes in kind could be vexatious and, as has been shown for Staffordshire and Warwickshire, complex in their assessment.[33] Also, by the early nineteenth century John Boys thought that tithes seriously deterred agrarian improvements in Kent.

There are immense quantities of poor land in East Kent, which experience has proved might be made to produce good crops of turnips and clover, that never yet have produced either; but the expense is so great to the occupier, with the idea before him that another may reap the greatest benefit, that hardly any person is willing to set about improving his lands on such terms.'[34]

29. PRO, E. 134, 6 Geo. I Mich. Crow *v.* Stoddart.
30. Woodruff, *op. cit.,* 186.
31. PRO, E. 134, 7 Chas. I Mich. 36. Horsmondon *v.* Burroughes.
32. PRO, E. 134, 7/8 Chas. I Hil. 2. Horsmondon *v.* Burroughes.
33. E.J. Evans, 'Tithing customs and disputes: the evidence of glebe terriers, 1698–1850', *Agricultural History Review,* xviii (1970), 20–25.
34. John Boys, *General view of the agriculture of the county of Kent,* (1805), 39–43.

An examination of the tithe cases for Kent in the Exchequer of Pleas might support Boys' contention; on the other hand, some agricultural improvements were made and an agreeable composition arrived at for both parties. At Iwade in 1632 a yeoman claimed that within the last twenty-three years he had witnessed between four and five hundred acres of land inned from the salts and made into fresh marsh. These lands when let were worth from five shillings to six shillings and eight pence an acre and that the occupiers had agreed to pay eight pence and twelve pence an acre as a composition for their tithes.[35] And no doubt there were many vicars, like Daniel Drayton of Little Chart, who were either uncontentious or perhaps too poor to go to law, who noted in June 1684,

> I did compound with Francis Nettlefold for all his tithes for three years paying for the same 40 shillings a year every year at or about Xmas the first year. I am to allow his wife a payer of gloves of 18 pence price because his corn is but mean this year and to this we set our hands.'[36]

35. PRO, E. 134, 8 Chas. I Mich. 30. Kingsley *v.* Lake.
36. Kent Archives Office, U. 386 Q5. Notebook of Daniel Drayton of Little Chart.

RICHARD BESELEY, RECTOR OF STAPLEHURST AND SANDHURST, SIX PREACHER AND MARIAN EXILE, c. 1511–85

ANNE OAKLEY

The exact date and place of Richard Beseley's birth are unknown. There is an extensive pedigree for a Beseley family living at Newington in Oxfordshire, but neither Richard nor his father Thomas are mentioned as part of that family despite the fact that it traces the family back to 1518.[1] There were other Beseleys in London, and it is more than probable that this was his birthplace.

Very little is known about Richard Beseley's early years although some of his father's career can be traced. Thomas Beseley was a member of the College of Arms and Rougedragon pursuivant at arms; he was promoted to Bluemantle pursuivant by patent on 5th November, 1522, at a salary of £10 a year;[2] and on 12th February, 1527/8, was appointed York Herald at an increased salary of £13 6s. 8d. in succession to Nicholas Toke.[3] When he died at midsummer 1530 Richard was not unprovided for. Thomas Cromwell, Cardinal Wolsey's chief administrative agent and chief architect of the Protestant Reformation in England was both friend and patron to the young man, at first for his father's sake but later for his own undoubted merits. It is a little difficult to understand exactly why Thomas Cromwell should have befriended a herald and very minor member of the court; all that is known is that he did so and that Richard gladly acknowledged the fact. It can only be a matter of speculation: perhaps there was some remote family connection or perhaps the herald had once helped Cromwell in his early years. Cromwell's loyalty to such persons was well known.[4]

The first open indication of the relationship between Thomas Cromwell and Richard Beseley is shown in a letter written by Robert Wodward, priest and Warden of All Souls College, Oxford to Cromwell on 29th July, 1529:

> Whereas you desire that this bearer, Richard Biseley, your scholar, should be chosen one of our fellows, I am very glad of your command; but what you desire is not in me alone but in the more part of the fellows. I shall endeavour to bring them over to your and my wish. If they will not consent, I will not agree to any person they shall choose, and then it will fall into the hands of my lord's grace of Canterbury, our founder, to elect anyone he pleases. Please, therefore, write to him and beg him to write me and my company at this time, and then you will be sure to have your scholar elected.[5]

The tone of his letter suggests that he will make certain that the patron's wishes will be carried out in any event. He speaks of Richard as Cromwell's scholar which in itself suggests that

---

1. Pedigree of Byseley, Bisley or Beazley of Newington and Warborough, Co. Oxon.; Ryde and Alverstoke, Co. Southampton; and Oxton, Co. Chester compiled by F.C. Beazley, in *Miscellanea Genealogica et Heraldica* 1929. The name is spelled in a great variety of ways. To avoid confusion Richard Beseley's most frequently used version has been used throughout.
2. *Letters and Papers Henry VIII*, 1522, 2654.
3. *Ibid.* 1528, 3991 (12) and 5130 where there appears to have been some intention to appoint him Lancaster Herald.
4. A.G. Dickens, *Thomas Cromwell and the English Reformation*, London 1959, 38.
5. *Letters and Papers Henry VIII*, 1529, 29th July.

Cromwell may have paid for some of Richard's education, or that Richard spent some years as a student in his household. Richard's letter of 1535 goes some way to confirming that this was so.

His enemies said that Cromwell was the leader of a country-wide conspiracy of heretics, a kind of feudal retinue. Cromwell himself denied this. He had, he said, only members of his household who were youths sent by their parents for an upbringing, as was indeed the case in many a Tudor household. Yet, parents who sent their children there can have had few illusions about the direction of the teaching in such a household where young men like Bartholomew Traheron, who had visited Calvin and Zwingli and had brought back books from Bullinger for Cromwell, were accepted into service. Richard Beseley's subsequent actions show that he was sympathetic to his patron's Protestant views, and that he absorbed and supported them, but neither he nor any of the others could be used by Cromwell to advance the English Church along true Protestant lines at this early stage because both his and their loyalty were to the king. And Henry VIII was no Protestant rather a nationalist who was essentially Catholic in all things. Cromwell was no fool. He used patronage as a means of securing loyalty; he promoted men of humble birth to ensure their dependence on him, and such men were, like himself, career men. Intellectuals like Beseley were loyal to Cromwell out of gratitude and because they were committed to his philosophy.[6]

With such assistance the young academic obtained his B.A. degree on 20th February, 1531/ 2. Three years later on 21st April, 1535, he gained his M.A. degree.[7] Seven months later, on 15th November Thomas Cromwell presented him to the rectory of Staplehurst in Kent in succession to another Nicholas Toke, exercising his patronage for this turn only.[8] Beseley's future was secure. He had an income from his rectory of £20 a year and his gratitude to his patron was unbounded. The letter he wrote on this occasion to Cromwell gives a clear picture of the young man and his relationship to Cromwell.

> To the Right honorable and my singuler good Master, Master Crumwell, chieffe Secretarie unto the kinges Highnes.
> When I consyder with my selfe, and revolve in my mynde (as eftsons I doo) Right Honorable and my singuler good Master, your manyfolde benefites doon, partlye unto Yorke the harrolde my father decessed, but especciallye to me his son: I am then forthewith greved with dolour and sorowe, not (as who saythe) repentinge your goodnes, for that were follie, but lamentinge and sorowinge, that my serviable mynde cannot excogitate somme meane and way, wherebie I myght somewhat declare and express my due office and service unto you, which alewais have ben and ar my onlye Patron and sautor towarde studye of good lerninge, as apperethe in your deades by evidente demonstration. Firste ye appoynted me student in Oxforde in the nue Colledg, which nue transposede afterwarde, ye promotede me to the feloweshipe of Alsolne Colledge, and now have preferred me to a benefice for suere contynuaunce of lerninge, so that all my bringinge up in studye hathe depended oonlye un your liberalitie. O so great beneficence, who is so dulle that perceavethe hit not; who so unkinde, that recordethe not so great beneficence; forsothe no Christien creature, for this is the deade more of a parent, then a patrone, even as the wise man saithe, the better parte of a father is not to begette a sone, but the childe borne, to see him instructe, as his age encreacethe, in Humanitie and other kinde of good Condition. And the proverbe, better a childe ungotten then untought, for he that lyvethe unlerned, is

6. See B.W. Beckingsale, *Thomas Cromwell, Tudor Minister*, London 1978.
7. *Alumni Oxonienses*, ed. Foster.
8. T.S. Frampton's notes from the Canterbury Archiepiscopal Registers in the Canterbury Cathedral Archives. He is also said to have been instituted to Cumnor, Berks., but I can find no real evidence for this.

as dedde lyvinge, and when he is dedde in deade, yet lyvethe his name in disdainfull reproche, for that he shewde no parte of his lyvelye lerninge, when he was a lyve. Whiche better parte, your goodnes hathe doon for me, then to my naturall father, if he were agayne in this worlde lyvinge, therfor now if I agayne for my parte, have in any kinde of doctrine, anythinge at all profitede, as I truste I have somwhat: Whollye that I owe unto you, my speciall master, and so reverentlye, with all humble thankes, I refer hit unto you, offering in moost lowlye wise, that if therbe any thinge in me, that may be acceptable and pleasaunt to you: ye shall have all, my hert, service, prayay, and brieflye my selfe, even assurdlye faithfull, diligent, and secrete always, as any of your howsolde servandes, as knowthe Almightie god, who have you still in his blessed tuition. From Oxforde the xxth day of Januarie, by thande of your Scoler and servande Richard Besiley.[9]

He had been provided with the means and opportunity to study and this debt he remembered all his life.[10]

Sometime between 1535 and 1538 Richard Beseley was appointed one of Henry VIII's chaplains with the title *sacellanus* which was peculiar to that office. He may have been licensed on 21st April, 1535. Holders of this office were not in fact chaplains only, but persons around the king who could keep their eyes and ears open and report to him, and presumably Cromwell, what they saw and heard.[11] At about this time also he was appointed to a prebendal stall in the cathedral church of Christ and St. Mary in Oxford. There is no information as to when the appointment was made, but it would have given him further income and a base in Oxford from which to continue his studies.

It seemed that a brilliant future lay ahead of Richard Beseley. He was launched on his clerical career and doubtless had the English Church continued in its traditional pattern, he might have become one of the clerico-legal administrators of the church, much as Cromwell himself. His work as a *sacellanus* confirms that his mind was already looking in this direction and his later work in the Canterbury church courts suggests that this may have been so.

He continued his academic studies but appears to have spent some time in Staplehurst. The newly introduced parish register is written in his own fine Secretary hand.[12] He progressed to his B.D. degree on 24th March, 1539/40, but Thomas Cromwell's fall from power and execution on 29th July, 1540, proved a severe blow to his career. In 1546 he was ejected from his prebendal stall at Christ Church and St. Mary in Oxford along with all the other prebendaries and the dean (though with a useful pension of £20 a year), and it was not until

9.   *Letters and Papers Henry VIII,* 1535 no. 68; and state Papers SP1/89.

10. In his wife's will there is a mention of his 'scollers gown and hoode' of black cloth faced with tawny taffetas which he had kept and which she had bequeathed to their son Basil. The All Souls gown is distinctive and longer than other Oxford College gowns.

11. B. Ficaro, *Nicholas Wotton: Dean and Diplomat,* University of Kent Thesis 1981. Nicholas Wotton was appointed a *sacellanus* in 1538 to help with the reorganisation of the judicial and economic functions within the church. See pp. 37, 38. While Beseley was a *sacellanus* he appears to have taken part in the trial of Lancelot Thorneton, priest in 1539. Speaking in his confession of Robert Holgate, Bishop of Llandaff, Lord President of the North, Thorneton said 'When one Mr. Beselay, as it is said, did or would complain upon my Lord President that now is to my Lord of Hampton, I wished heartily in my heart that my lord might be president there, if it were the king's pleasure and his desire'.

12. Original register in the church. See also *Arch. Cant.,* Chamberlain, J.S. FF. Staplehurst Register pp. 283–299. There were also at least two sons of the marriage, Basil and Bartholomew. They were born either in Canterbury or in exile. The Cathedral register is unfortunately incomplete. Bartholomew was abroad at the time of his parents' death.

1547/8 that he became a Doctory of Divinity.[13] Left with few friends in Oxford or London, and certainly fewer at court, he appears to have become almost permanently resident in his parish in the final years of the reign of Henry VIII. He does, however, appear to have retained his royal chaplaincy even if only in name, for this was a personal post.

The accession of the young king Edward VI and the innovations in clerical life which resulted brought a political climate which suited Beseley. His actions are those of a man totally committed to the reforming zeal enveloping and changing the English Church. The entries in the Staplehurst parish register illustrate his more than prompt response to the opportunities for clerical marriage and family life, the introduction of the new Book of Common Prayer and the clearing away of all popish superstitions. He employed Robert Stockton as his curate at Staplehurst. The two men were friends and held similar opinions.

In March 1547/8 Richard Beseley married. In the Staplehrust parish register he recorded the event.

> on March 24. Master Richard Beseley, teacher of Holy Scripture, chaplain to the late high and mighty prince King Henry VIII of blessed memory and Rector of this church accepted in marriage and married Jane Lenarde, an orphan, a virgin and a poor, modest and honest young girl.

He had lost no time in availing himself of the Act of Convocation asserting the right of the clergy to marry, even though the Bill legalising such marriage had not been passed in Parliament and did not become law until 1549. Yet, for all his apparent confidence, there always seems to have been a lingering doubt in his mind that he had been over hasty. In the baptism entry for his first child he included the words 'his lawful wif' as if to emphasise the fact that the marriage was legal and the child legitimate.

This particular entry is also interesting because it records his early use of the new Book of Common Prayer in his parish.

> The ninthe day of June [1549]. This day being whitsonday (wherein the booke of the Common prayer and Administration of the Sacramentes and other rites and Cereminies of the Churche, after the use of the Churche of Englonde, begon to be executed) there was first baptised Marie the dawghter of Richard beseley parsone of this Churche borne the last thursday (at 5 a.m.) of his lawfull wif Jane. Who were maried the yere before and in the firste day that the holly communion in the Englishe tonge (after thorder that now is) was here mynystered thei bothe, with others most humblye and devoutlie communicating the same. The parsone Christined his owne childe.

The 24th March, 1547/8, was the Saturday before Palm Sunday. The service of Holy Communion in English was published early in March and the bishops ordered that it should be used for the first time on Easter Day 1st April. Richard Beseley anticipated that order: he and his friends had communicated at the marriage service as the 1549 Prayer Book rubric was to direct. 'The newe married persones (the same daye of their marriage) must receive the holy communion'.

Their second child, another daughter, was born in 1550. Again in the register entry he stresses the lawfulness of his marriage. 'The seconde of November There was baptised Benet the dawghter of Richard beseley parson of this parishe by his lawfull wif Jane. Born 1 November at 8 p.m.' Another daughter was baptised in 1552. Their elder daughter may have died at about this time because their third child was christened Mary. The register entry was

---

13. *Alumni Oxonienses*, ed. Foster.

made by Robert Stockton, the curate. 'On the 10th day of July Ther was Baptysyd Mary beseley the dawghter of Mr. Richard beseley parson of staplehurst – whose godfather I am – borne the 8th day of the same at 5 a.m.'

This is the last reference in the parish register to Richard Beseley. In 1552 he was appointed a Six Preacher in Canterbury Cathedral, left the parish in the charge of Robert Stockton and moved to Canterbury.[14] According to Anthony Wood, Beseley was a learned and excellent preacher well known to Archbishop Thomas Cranmer.[15] Cranmer was the architect of the new foundation at Canterbury which replaced the former priory, and because he set great emphasis on learning and teaching, had created a group or college of six special preachers to do this work in the cathedral church. Many famous preachers were appointed often from obscure parishes when their gifts became known to the archbishop. Beseley had been diligent in transforming his church: plate had been sold, vestments disposed of and saints' lights abolished.[16] He was a man of scholarship and learning well suited to the task Cranmer had in mind. For two years the future seemed secure once more, but then in 1554 the blow fell. On 15th March he was deprived of his Six Preachership.[17] On 6th May he was deprived of his living also, on both counts because he was a married priest.[18]

Perhaps he foresaw the difficulties and dangers to come after the death of Edward VI. The king was a sick man and unlikely to have children. His successor was his elder sister Mary, a Roman Catholic who made no secret of her intentions to sweep away her father's and her brother's innovations. Through his association with Cromwell and Cranmer, Beseley was now a firm supporter of the Church of England as by law established. He was a relatively young man and perhaps for this reason chose exile with some of his Canterbury contemporaries in the hope of better times in the near future rather than face the fires of Smithfield and the inevitable hunting out of heretics. With John Bale, later a prebendary at Canterbury, and Robert Pownall, a fellow Six Preacher, he fled to Frankfurt and for some time lived on the Mentzer Gasse with his wife and two children.[19]

Strype in *Annals of the Reformation* says that Beseley lived obscurely in Frankfurst and did not enter so far or bitterly in the contention for reform as did many of the others. He was reckoned among the learned sort.[20] When the news of Elizabeth's accession reached Geneva, that church considered more good would result from a united front. With this mind, a circular letter was sent to other exiles at Frankfurt in Germany and Arrow in Switzerland on 15th December, 1558, seeking their acquiescence to Geneva's declared desire 'to cut off all occasions from papists, and other cavillers' that they might all teach and practise unanimously that knowledge of god's word which they had learned in exile, and seen in the best reformed churches.[21] Robert Pownall at Arrow fully agreed with the Geneva sentiments, but Beseley at Frankfurt and his colleagues there were more accommodating. He and ten others subscribed their names to the following letter on 3rd January, 1558/9:

14. See note 12 above.
15. Anthony Wood, *Athenae Oxonienses,* London 1721, i, 73.
16. *Testamenta Cantiana* and Archdeacon Harpsfield's Visitations of 1555, 1556, Z.3.32 printed in *Catholic Record Society*, 183–185.
17. Dean and Chapter of Canterbury Register N f. 152.
18. *Ibid.,* f. 67.
19. Christine Garrett, *The Marian Exiles,* Cambridge, 1938 and 1966.
20. J. Strype, *Annals of the Reformation and Establishment of Religion,* I(i), 491.

That it would not lie in either of their hands to appoint what ceremonies should be, but in such men's wisdoms as should be appointed to the devising of the same; and which should be received by common consent of parliament: and therefore it would be to small purpose to contend about them. . . . And that whereas all reformed churches differed among themselves in divers ceremonies, and yet agreed in the unity of doctrine, they saw no inconvenience, if they used some ceremonies diverse from them; so that they agreed in the chief points of their religion. Notwithstanding, that if any should be intruded that should be offensive, they, upon just conference and deliberation upon the same at their meeting with them in England (which they trusted by God's grace would be shortly), would brotherly join with them to be suitors for the reforming and abolishing of the same.

In other words Beseley and his colleagues at Frankfurt were fully prepared to temporise and accept whatever Parliament might devise, and here one can recognise the influence of the Frankfurt Pastor John Cox under whose influence they had come in exile. Some time after Queen Mary's death, and probably in 1559, Beseley returned to England. His Six Preachership was restored in 1559 and the living of Staplehurst by May 1560.[22] He returned to live in Canterbury and though he visited his parish, he did not live there but maintained a curate. On 27th August, 1560, he was instituted to the rectory of Sandhurst in Kent on the resignation of Richard Symonds, and held it in plurality with Staplehurst.[23] There is no evidence that his pension of £20 as a former prebendary of Christ Church and St. Mary, Oxford was continued or discontinued after the death of Edward VI. He almost certainly suffered financially in exile. The living of Sandhurst brought him a further £19 12s. 6d. and, if his pension had been discontinued, this would have restored his finances to their former value.[24]

His relationship with his two parishes was not good and seems to have deteriorated steadily after 1561. At Staplehurst in 1561 the churchwardens complained at the Visitation 'that their parson ys not Resydent but our Curat ys' and added that 'their parson should fynd them a clarke which hath been accustomed and now we have none'.[25] Beseley denied the accusation and the court found in his favour.[26] When the churchwardens made a similar complaint in 1562, the answer was written in the book 'in Christ Church' and was evidently deemed sufficient. In the 1569 archiepiscopal visitation Beseley was described as married, one of the Six Preachers at Christ Church, Canterbury, where he lives and is hospitable; his curate John Stephens was married but had no benefice, no licence to preach and was not a graduate.[27] This last was in direct contravention of the archbishop's injunctions, but John Stephens continued in office for a further ten years. He had already served the parish since 1561.[28] The churchwardens tried once more in 1569, and complained of Beseley's non-residence and added that he was 'behinde for the fortye parte of his benefice' which he was obliged to pay out of his stipend towards the relief of the poor. Nothing came of their complaints and the parson was still in debt to the parish in 1585. Nor did he ever pay the sum at Sandhurst. He was not a poor man. Perhaps he had a miserly streak.[29]

21. *Ibid.*, 153, 263.
22. Canterbury Diocesan records, Z.3.5 f. 180.
23. T.S. Frampton's notes.
24. *Valor Ecclesiasticus*, 65.
25. Canterbury Diocesan records, X.1.3 ff. 52, 53.
26. *Ibid.*
27. Archbishop Parker's Visitation 1569. *Ibid.*
28. See *Ibid.*, Z.3.7 ff. 14, 15, 63, 204, 236; X.1.5 ff. 2, 9; Z.3.9 ff. 2, 32, 61, 88, 114, 130, 178, 210, 236.
29. *Ibid.*, Z.3.10 f. 60; X.2.2 f. 7.

His care of the parish church and parsonage fabric in Staplehurst appears to have been equally negligent. In 1562 it was presented that the church and steeple lacked repair and in 1564 'that our churche and steple are somewhat decayed so that twentie Nobles will scarslie repaire the same sufficientlie. And further that our chauncell and parsonage howses also have neade of reparations and whatt will doo it we can not tell for our parson saith he entendeth to alter and transpose the Dwellinge howse of his parsonage Adding also therto the reparations of the chauncell shalbe perfectlie repaired in the forme they stand in at theis present we thinke 20 li. will scarclie do it'. They added 'that the place where the highe Aulter stoode is paved and decent but the place where the alter was in the syde yle is not paved nor decent'.[30] Two years later the parsonage house was fully repaired, but the chancel paving needed repair. 'As for the glasse wyndowes they be with ymages as they were.[31] In 1569 both these last were still a problem.[32]

He fared no better as rector of Sandhurst than at Staplehurst and possibly worse. He does not appear to have visited the place very often. In 1560 the churchwardens presented at the Visitation 'that we heer whe have a parson whiche hathe taken noo possession nor ys not Resident'.[33] Twice in 1561 they presented him for non-residence complaining that he took the 'frutes by Sequestracion' and gave them nothing.[34] The archiepiscopal visitation of 1569 stated that he lived in Canterbury and was not hospitable in Sandhurst. His curate Thomas Ryder was unmarried, had no benefice, did not preach and was not a graduate.[35] The curate was replaced first by Lawrence Smyth, vicar of Newenden close by, and after two years by Stephen Gray. A later curate, Oulton, was dismissed in 1576 for immoral behaviour and replaced by Robert Twysden 'that hath no lycence'. He was ordered to appear before the archdeacon of Canterbury at Lambeth. What happened there is unknown, except that Beseley transferred him as curate to Staplehurst in 1580.[36]

For five years the churchwardens complained that he had allowed the parsonage house to decay to such an extent that in 1564 'the Bakehouse and kytchen with other chambers perteyninge to the mansion howse for lacke of tymber worke walling tylinge and other thinges' that it would cost £5 to repair it. He does not appear to have done anything about the house although ordered to do so.[37] When he took over the church it still had its rood loft in place and old high altar and he did nothing about removing them until 1561. The church chancel for which he was responsible as rector was in great disrepair. There are continual presentments from 1561 about this. 'It ys further presented that our chauncell ys in decay and lacketh glassing and other reparacion'. In the same year they presented 'that the communion table standeth with owt the quere door whear ys Lyttle Romme by cause the chauncell ys anoyed with pidgons donge for save of glassing Mr. Byslye Receiving the proffytes'.[38] Again in 1564 they reported the chancel 'is in decaie for that the Leade of the church was stollen awaie'.[39]

30. *Ibid.*, X.1.7 f. 38.
31. *Ibid.*, X.1.10.
32. *Ibid.*, Z.3.10 f. 60.
33. *Ibid.*, X.1.2 f. 59.
34. *Ibid.*, X.1.3 ff. 57, 58.
35. *Ibid.*, Archbishop Parker's Visitation 1569.
36. *Ibid.*, Z.3.8 ff. 129, 209, 243; X. 1.13; X.2.2 f. 7.
37. *Ibid.*, X.1.7 f.18; X.1.4 f. 87.
38. *Ibid.*, X.1.3 f. 58.
39. *Ibid.*, X.1.7 f. 17.

The churchwardens were ordered to repair the church but no order was made for the chancel despite the fact that they said it would cost six pounds to repair. Beseley evidently did nothing for later in the year they presented 'that the wyndowes Lacke glasing so that the Curate neyther the communicantes are hable to sytt about the table for the vehemencie of the wynde. And for the fylthe of the doves and owles. And also the stone worke greatlie in decaie of the East windowe. Also it rayneth upon the Communion table for lacke of coveringe upon the ridging of the chauncell'.[40] Two years later rain was still falling on the communion table but still he did nothing to repair the roof and the windows. After 1576 no more is heard of the matter when it was apparently repaired. Sandhurst also lacked other things. There was no *Paraphrase of Erasmus* and no surplice; and in 1571 the churchwardens complained 'that the communion book is not as it ought to be because it lacketh in somme places parte of the servyce and also the byble is faultye in lyke maner for yt lacketh certen leaves in certen places'.[41] In 1576 they further complained 'that on Wednesdayes and fridayes sometyme they have had no servyce' and 'that they lack a cover for their communion cupp'.[42] These few defects were remedied, and although one might expect a certain amount of decay and defect, the problems in Staplehurst and Sandhurst do reflect a neglect of parish affairs in general.

Soon after his return as rector to Staplehurst there is a curious case in the Canterbury church court Act Book. In court John Bathurst of Frittenden was accused of uttering scandalous words against him at Le Starr in London saying 'Mr. Bisley parson of Stapleherst was an honest man after his comying from Geneva for the space of a year But syns that tyme a very varlet in suffering Hornden to be committed in his parishe unponished saying there was children borne and buryed in divers Hilles. And the matters so cloakid up by the parson that the law would take no place to punysshe them'.[43] He was obviously not interested in prosecuting persons for living together unmarried. Perhaps he remembered his own early doubts. Perhaps he considered it all unimportant after the greater trials of exile. A later case in 1577 of two persons living together unmarried in his parish had also gone unpunished. Robert Doggett and Maria Burrage confessed in court 'that they have been suer together these 12 monethes and have mynded longe agoe to marry, and were with holden from it, because they can not say the new cathecisme'. Despite the judge's order that they should learn it and marry, they were still unmarried in 1578. He and his curate had only themselves to blame for the cause. Neither had bothered to see that the parties could recite the new catechism and had neglected teaching in the parish.

If Richard Beseley took little part in the life of either of his parishes, he was certainly occupied elsewhere. As a proxy in the Lower House of Convocation he signed the Declaration of the 39 Articles in his own hand on 5th February, 1562, and eight days later was one of the 43 clergy who signed the acceptance of the Six Articles. These were of great importance to the exiles since they were all anti-papist measures and fundamental to Protestant principles. The Six Articles were that all Sundays should be holy days and no other days; that the minister should turn towards the people when he prays; that he omit making the sign of the cross on a child's forehead in baptism; that kneeling be left to the discretion of the communicant; that the minister wear a surplice and should not conduct divine service except 'in comely garb or habit';

40. *Ibid.*, f. 18; *Ibid.*, X.1.8 ff. 3, 125.
41. *Ibid.*, X.1.3 f. 58; X.1.11 f. 60.
42. *Ibid.*, X.1.13 f.
43. *Ibid.*, Y.2.24 f. 54, 2nd May, 1561 at Hackington; X.1.13 f. 125, 25th November, 1577.

and that organs should not be used. At the same Convocation he was also one of 64 priests who signed the 21 requests and petitions concerning the articles of religion and the liturgy. These requests ranged over catechism, baptism, confession, communion, removal of images and roods, discipline and dogma.[44] Beseley had signed his name to the *New Discipline* of Geneva while in exile in 1557, but under the influence of John Cox had evidently changed his mind about his attitude in the following two years. The Frankfurt Congregation had adhered to the specifically English system as set out in the second Edwardian Prayer Book of 1552 after their break with John Knox and his return to Geneva. Both the Frankfurt and Genevan Congregations were to have considerable influence in the new Church of England. Both supported a religion purified of all the works of Rome and therefore acquired the name of Puritans, but the Genevans wanted the complete Calvinist system with the *New Discipline* or order of Church Government and service which put power over the laity in the hands of the ministers. The Frankfurt exiles were among some of the first to return to England and clearly found a much more receptive ear to their demands than the men from Geneva and John Knox. Yet, even despite their reception, even they were unwilling to accept the restoration of the Henrician church. For this reason Elizabeth I was forced to accept some of the Frankfurt men both as bishops and teachers. Beseley returned to Canterbury as a Six Preacher and may have hoped for promotion under Matthew Parker, Elizabeth's first Archbishop. Perhaps his now obvious ambivalence made others distrust his motives.

During his early years in Staplehurst before the exile, Beseley had interested himself in the work of the local Probate courts; he was by then also a Notary Public, and as well as drawing up wills for parishioners, had appeared in court on their behalf and administered estates for them. This work he continued on his return and on several occasions sat in the Consistory Court of Canterbury as Substitute for the Official of the Archbishop to hear cases before the court. He was actually sitting as substitute for Vincent Denne in 1567 when his own Staplehurst churchwardens complained that 'as for the glasse wyndowes they be with ymages as they were', but as might be expected, all their other presentments suggested that most things in his parish were well.[45]

After his return he lived exclusively in Canterbury attending daily evensong in the Cathedral Church in surplice and hood, preaching on special preaching days: All Saints Day, Circumcision, Epiphany, Candlemas, Ash Wednesday, Good Friday, Rogation Days, Whit Tuesday and the Nativity of St. John the Baptist; and preaching his regulation twenty sermons a year; working in his study; discussing problems with his colleagues; and attending to his legal work. Occasionally, too, he reverted to his work of informing. In 1567 he wrote to Sir William Cecil observing 'that it is necessary to take warning for the future'; and in 1571/2 to Lord Burghley more specifically that he had heard from Peter Alexander, curate at Chartham who had been with him in exile, that Dr. Gyfford had lately arrived from Rome, and that the plans of the Duke of Norfolk had long been known there. He advised Burghley not to take any physic of Dr. Gyfford lest he might be 'Italionated'.[46]

44. J. Strype, *Annals* I (i), 502.
45. See Kent Archives Office Canterbury Probate Records 1549–1581 PRC17/27.17 (1549); PRC3/12.8 (1550); *Ibid.*, 12.74 (1551); *Ibid.*, 12.111 (1551): PRC3/15.194 (1558); *Ibid.*, 15.116 (1559); *Ibid.*, 15.202 (1560); PRC3/16.66 (1561); PRC3/20.156 (1580); *Ibid.*, 168 (1580); *Ibid.*, 188 (1581) and Canterbury Diocesan records X.1.10 (1567).
46. *Calendar of State Papers Domestic* 1547–1580, 287 4th February, 1566/7, and *Ibid.*, 435, 27th January, 1571/2.

Jane and Richard Beseley lived comfortably in Canterbury. He had a reasonable income: £20 a year from Staplehurst and almost as much from Sandhurst.[47] His salary as a Six Preacher was £25 a year which he received regularly from 1552–1554 and 1561 until his death; plus a free house in the Cathedral Precincts, stabling for his horse, and free wood for fuel.[48] Their house was not large but adequate with two large chambers, a parlour, hall, kitchen, a paved chamber and a study. The walls of the study were obviously lined with books in large numbers because his appraisers who were supposed to list them after his death, made no attempt to do so but made an estimated valuation of £7 for them as one lot. This was a large sum for books then and represents one-fifth of the total sum of all his goods. The chambers were well provided with beds and bedding; there was linen in plenty and pewter as well as six silver spoons. The walls of the chambers and hall were hung with painted linen hangings. Many of the furnishings, cushions and curtains were green. Others were in flower and tapestry work. In the parlour, most unusually, there was a pewter pot for flowers and a brasen ewer.[49]

Richard Beseley probably died in May 1585. It seems quite probable that both he and his wife were overtaken by some infection just before their deaths. He was not in the house when she made her will just before she died on or about 2nd May, 1585, but neither does she describe herself as a widow or relict. They may both have died of the plague as it was some weeks before the appraisers entered the house to make their inventory. His successor at Staplehurst was instituted on 19th May, 1585. He did not resign any of his other livings, not even Chislet to which he was instituted in 1583, but he did provide a preacher at Sandhurst who eventually took over the parish. By special permission of the Dean and Chapter of Canterbury he was buried in the cathedral near his two friends and companions in exile, John Bale and Richard Pownall. Pownall was buried there in June 1571, but there is no record of the burial of either Beseley or Bale because the Cathedral register is incomplete. Beseley does, however, mention the place of burial in his will:

> And my bodye I will to be buryed in the bodye of the said cathedrall churche of Christe in Canterbury with consent of the Deane and Chapter nere unto the bodyes of John Bale and Robart Pownall my companions in exile professors and preachers of the sacred word of our good god whose goodnes hath restored us into our natyve countrye to rest and slepe together after our travell. . . .

He was probably by then well over seventy years of age. He had been a priest and preacher all his working life and a true believer who had never deviated from his firm convictions either in his god or in the Church of England. In his will he sets out his confession of faith:

> 'I bequeathe my soule into the handes of the most holy blessed and glorious trynitye thre parsons and one god in unitye the Father the sonne and the holy ghoste to whome be eternall glorye amen.' And after his request to be buried near Bale and Pownall, he continues that they will rest and sleep together 'till the resurrection in the last day at what tyme all the deade shall rise againe and we with the rest of goods electe shall to our greate only and endeles comforte mete Christe Jesus to judge us who hath alredye redeemed [us] by his bitter passion with whome we shall possesse eternall lyfe and joy everlasting *hec spes mea reposita est in sinu meo*'.[50]

47. *Valor Ecclesiasticus*, 60, 65, 35.
48. Canterbury Cathedral Archives: Miscellaneous Accounts 40, 1541–1575 and 41, 1576–1642.
49. Kent Archives Office, Canterbury Probate Records: Inventory of Richard Beseley PRC21/7 f. 263 (1585).
50. *Ibid*. Will of Richard Beseley 23rd April, 1585, PRC 32/35 f. 167; proved 10th June, 1585, and will of Jane Beseley, his wife PRC32/35 f. 223. See also X.11.1 ff. 62, 78 about the making of her will.

Richard Beseley was a gifted, progressive and far-sighted man, a man of his own times willing to forward the Church of England along the path of his mentor Thomas Cromwell. He might have gone further along Protestant lines but exile tempered his judgement. He was above all a scholar with a legal bent who had little desire to carry out the responsibilities of a parochial ministry.

PURITANISM AND PATRIARCHY: THE CAREER AND SPIRITUAL WRITINGS OF THOMAS PAPILLON, 1623–1702*

DAVID ORMROD

In the pages of *Religion and the Rise of Capitalism,* Tawney addressed himself to that large question most conveniently described as the retreat of the Christian social tradition and the extent and manner in which issues of economic conduct became divorced from questions of religious morality;[1] and in more general terms in *The Acquisitive Society,* he outlined how 'God had been thrust into the frigid altitudes of infinite space' during the eighteenth century, when 'what was Christian in Christianity had largely disappeared', when 'religion, once the greatest social force, had become a thing as private and individual as . . . the working clothes of the labourer'.[2] In spite of the growing accumulation of literature devoted to puritanism and the history of dissent, the later seventeenth century still remains as something of a hiatus in these discussions, yet the years which separated Baxter's *Christian Directory* from Mandeville's *Fable of the Bees* saw not so much a decline in religious enthusiasm as a change in its direction.[3] Tawney realised this when he described the post-Restoration generation as one which held that 'the fact of most moment to mankind was not their external circumstances but their spiritual condition. It was the dangerous quest of infinity which embittered its controversies and ennobled its conflicts'.[4]

In the conservative puritanism of the post-Restoration period, however, we can perhaps see one of the most thoroughgoing of a series of attempts in the history of Christianity to reject Christian materialism in favour of an otherwordly spirituality and a prime concern with the realm of personal relations – a separation reflected in Thomas Papillon's habitual distinction between 'spiritualls' and 'temporals'. On the Continent and in Scotland, the all-important concern with predestination had turned the Reformed and the Presbyterian preachers towards a theocratic reform of society as a whole, whereas in England (according to Professor Haller), every move in the direction of theocratic ideas was frustrated from the early years of Elizabeth's reign onwards, so that the predominant effect of Calvinist teaching was to exploit the agony and anxiety for reassurance of personal salvation.[5] Hence the diary of experience and spiritual biography became accepted as modes for conducting a relentless self-examination which also served as aids to the religious life seen as an epic of the individual soul. It was precisely his Arminian tendencies which led Milton away from this obsession with personal salvation and towards an Old Testament emphasis on vocation to extra-personal service and

* I am grateful to Elizabeth Melling for first drawing my attention to the Papillon Collection, and to the staff of the Kent Archives Office for supplying copies of documents.

1. R.H. Tawney, *Religion and the Rise of Capitalism* (The Holland Memorial Lectures, 1922), 1926.
2. R.H. Tawney, *The Acquisitive Society,* 1921, 13.
3. R. Baxter, *A Christian Directory: a Summ of Practical Theologie and Cases of Conscience,* 1673; B. Mandeville, *The Fable of the Bees: or, Private Vices, Public Benefits,* 1714.
4. British Library of Political and Economic Science, Tawney Papers, Part I, 1/9, p. 1.
5. L.J. Trinterud, 'William Haller, Historian of Puritanism', *Journal of British Studies,* v (2), 1966, 38–39.

ministration to a covenanted people, an elect nation.[6] But the democratic and half-collectivist strands in puritanism which had come to the fore during the revolutionary decades soon fell apart, 'the metal cooled in the mould; and the puritan spirit, shorn of its splendours and its illusions, settled finally into its decent bed of equable respectability'.[7]

At the time of the Restoration, Thomas Papillon was thirty-seven, when he was placed on the Council of Trade and Foreign Plantations. Three years later, he joined the directorate of the East India Company and began to play a prominent and controversial role in public and commercial affairs within that circle of ultra-Protestant and Huguenot city merchants and financiers containing men such as Sir Patience Ward, Michael Godfrey, John Dubois, and the Houblons, who were to become leading opponents of the Court. His Victorian biographer found little difficulty in fitting the conservative puritanism, aggressive Whig politics, and extensive but interlocking commercial interests of his subject into a Smilesian paradigm:

> Integrity, industry, energy, and piety were the leading points of his character. As a merchant, he was active, intelligent, and successful; as a politician, sincere and loyal; as a financier, he was not in advance of his day; as a theologian, he was sound and earnest. Though of foreign descent, he was a true Englishman. Beginning life with small means, he rose to wealth and eminence'.

In recent years, the collection, analysis and publication of seventeenth-century confessional diaries and spiritual autobiographies has done much to illuminate the inner recesses of the puritan mind, and has provided more realistic evidence of attitudes and behaviour than that found in conduct books and sermons.[9] The justification for adding another example to this growing literature is perhaps twofold: in the first place, the reflections of merchants are considerably scarcer than those of clergymen and prophets. In the second the copiousness and range of Papillon's spiritual writings, unusual from one so deeply engaged in commercial and public affairs, provide added interest and are partly explained by the peculiar circumstances of Papillon's three-year exile in Holland from 1685–89, a period of acute personal anxiety when he was separated from his wife and family. The interweave of business, finance, estate management, politics, religion and family life which can be followed through the Papillon archives suggests that religious or theological considerations exercised little or no constraint upon Thomas Papillon's varied business activities, and illustrates the manner in which an inflated piety could be disengaged from business activity, applied to incessant self-examination and, more interestingly, discharged into an intensified form of patriarchy.[10] The encourage-

---

6. J.S. Hill, *John Milton: Poet, Priest and Prophet*, 1979, 5.

7. R.H. Tawney, *Religion and the Rise of Capitalism*, 212.

8. A.F.W. Papillon, *Memoirs of Thomas Papillon of London, Merchant, (1623–1702)*, Reading (privately printed), 1887, p. v. Smiles himself referred to the parliamentary careers of the Papillon family in *The Huguenots*, New York, 1868, 319.

9. See, for example, O.C. Watkins, *The Puritan Experience*, 1972; P. Delany, *British Autobiography in the Seventeenth Century*, 1969; M. Spufford, 'First steps in literacy: the reading and writing experiences of the humblest seventeenth-century spiritual autobiographers', *Social History*, iv (3), 1979.

10. Patriarchy has been understood in a variety of ways. In orthodox historical discussions by male historians, as a 'standard justifying category of political thought' (see G.J. Schochet, 'Patriarchalism, Politics and Mass Attitudes in Stuart England', *Historical Journal*, xii (1969), 441) or as a generalised description of certain 'social structures'. Amongst feminist writers, some regard patriarchy as an overarching concept central to understanding the subordination of women, both cross-culturally and transhistorically; whilst others adopt historically more specific terms, particularly in relation to the mode of production, see for example R. McDonough and R. Harrison, 'Patriarchy and relations of production' in A. Kuhn and A. Wolpe, *Feminism*

ment which puritanism provided towards patriarchy has frequently been commented upon, but the nature of that connection and the directions of change are by no means clear or agreed. Papillon's career and writings suggest that the relationship was conditioned by the dualistic character of puritanism which, in its rejection of materialistic Christianity and in its encouragement of possessive individualism, located the sphere of religious obedience firmly within the patriarchal nuclear family.

The Papillon family was in origin Huguenot, and had fled to England in 1588 to escape religious persecution.[11] Thomas' grandfather had been captain of the guard and valet-de-chambre to Henry IV of France, and his father David was brought to England as a small child by his mother. David Papillon became a successful architect and military engineer, built houses in the city and suburbs of London, and was elected a deacon of the French church in London. In 1646, he fortified Gloucester for Parliament and became Treasurer for Leicestershire. Thomas' mother was Anne-Marie Calandrini, grand-daughter of Guilliano Calandrini, a convert to the reformed faith who fled from Lucca to Lyons between 1557 and 1567 where he established himself as a merchant before settling in Paris. Following the massacre of St. Bartholomew of 1572, the Calandrini family dispersed, some to Geneva and some to Holland, and a relative wrote 'while banished from our earthly country, we became Citizens of Heaven'.[12] Carefully written copies of a narrative of these events in the Papillon archives suggest that they served as a reminder of the strength of the reformed tradition in the family for successive generations.[13]

Friday, 14th April, 1671 was, for Thomas Papillon, 'A day sett apart to seeke the Lord' since he understood that 'the Saints of God have on speciall providences, and also on their settlements in fixed places, in an especiall manner sought the Lord'.[14] He observed that there had so far been five periods in his life, '1st when I came to prentice, 2, when I removed from my masters to My Sister Fountaine, 3, my marriage, 4, when I layed out a good part of my estate in the country, And now 5ly Entring into Partnership with Mr Harrison and allso putting a part of my stock into a Brewhouse & a Steeleworks'. It was in 1637 that he was articled to Thomas Chamberlan, a London merchant, and in the following year apprenticed to the Mercers Company, of which he received the freedom in 1646. He had supported the 'riotous proceedings' of July 1647 by the London apprentices to force Parliament to restore the king, and when the Independents gained power was compelled to flee to France for three months.[15] Shortly afterwards he began business on his own account as a general merchant, and in 1651 married Jane, daughter of Thomas Broadnax of Canterbury. In 1666, he purchased Acrise Place, near Folkestone, for £5,000, described by Jane Papillon as 'a good bargain' if somewhat dilapidated,

---

and Materialism, 1978; and V. Beechey, 'On Patriarchy', *Feminist Review*, 3 (1979–80). This essay suggests that patriarchy may be understood in terms of the changing relationship between economic activity and social obligation, mediated through the family.

11. Family and biographical information is taken from Papillon, *Memoirs*, 1–32, and the *Dictionary of National Biography*.

12. 'Narrative of Pompeo Deodati' covering events from 1511–1598 in the history of the Calandrini family, reprinted in Papillon, *Memoirs*, 415.

13. Kent Archives Office, U1015 (Papillon MSS), F8.

14. KAO, U1015, F15/2.

15. Papillon, *Memoirs*, 16–17. He fled with Michael Godfrey who was then a fellow-apprentice, and later became a business associate.

and joined that small group of mercantile families whose wealth had been generated in the capital and who established landed estates in Kent following the Restoration, like Sir John Banks at Aylesford Friary and the Furnesses at Waldershare Park.[16] Although wealthy and influential, such families were few in number and Professor Everitt has suggested that the history of Kentish families between 1660 and 1688 contradicts the view that 'the land settlement at the Restoration was a triumph for the "new men" . . . businessmen who had thriven under the Commonwealth'.[17]

Unlike Sir John Banks who in 1671 possessed lands valued at £47,000, Thomas Papillon did not underpin his growing commercial and industrial interests with substantial land purchases.[18] In 1667, his trading capital was estimated at £8,600 excluding £500 of East India stocks, matched by lands valued at £8,080 and plate, jewels, and 'household stuffe' at £600, totalling £17,730.[19] The Acrise estate accounted for the bulk of his £8,080, valued at its purchase price of £5,000; his marriage settlement of 84 acres of meadowland at Lubenham, Leicestershire, for £1,600, and 69 acres of land in Romney Marsh purchased from his brother-in-law Sir William Broadnax for £1,480. Small additions were made to the 874-acre estate at Acrise which seventeen years later, in 1684, was valued at only £6,000, and two further small purchases of land in Romney Marsh were completed. Apart from a small estate in Ireland about which little is known, and which he may have acquired as a bad debt[20] his ambitions as landowner were confined to enjoying the 'comfort of a country seat, a rural retreat'.[21]

Nevertheless, surviving evidence leaves the impression of a small well-run estate: the compact Acrise properties produced annual rentals totalling a modest £282 in 1667, giving a 5½ per cent return, capitalised at eighteen years' purchase.[22] The estate was divided into three large farms of 165, 183 and 234 acres let on short leases of nine, seven and eleven years respectively, three small farms of 36, 65, and 72 acres, and two smallholdings. Substantial repairs were in hand at this time, and in April 1668, the part-time steward wondered whether to sow clover seed; by October, it was reported, 'we are now carrying out dung for the sainctfoyne'.[23] Papillon retained 91 acres for his own occupation, mostly woodland, and it seems that he wasted little time in exploiting its full commercial potential. A memorandum which probably dates from c. 1670 contains details of profits expected from an acre of woodland converted into barrel hoops for the London market, estimated by a cooper, together with a similar estimate of the cost, charges and profits from brickmaking, including the cost of 'removing clay, getting and burning of lime, digging and bringing of chalk, making of faggots'.[24] It is not clear whether brickmaking operations were actually undertaken on the

16. *Ibid.*, 97; D.C. Coleman, *Sir John Banks, Baronet and Businessman,* Oxford 1963, chapter 3.
17. A.M. Everitt, *The Community of Kent and the Great Rebellion,* Leicester 1966, 44–54, 324.
18. Coleman, *op. cit.,* 47.
19. KAO, U1015, E46 f. 16, 31st December, 1667.
20. Papillon, *Memoirs,* 103–106; his estate book records amongst 'bad and doubtfull debts', 'lands in Ireland & Edmund Leech owing on that account, £395.5.9', KAO, U1015, E46 f. 3.
21. Papillon, *Memoirs,* 98.
22. KAO, U1015, E46 f. 8–11.
23. KAO, U1015, C11/10, Jane Papillon–Thomas Papillon, 26th April, 1668; C11/24, Jane Papillon–Thomas Papillon, 8th September, 1668.
24. KAO, 1015, E49/5: 'Smart hoops for London market are bound up in bundles at lengths & not bent . . . and are made of the lesser sort of Ash & of oake, hazel, birch & willow; the general sorts & sizes follow, butt or pipe wch are 10 foot long, Hogshead 9½, barrels 8½, kelderken 7½, firken 6½'. Charges for brickmaking and

estate but an undated account of 'timber sent by brother Broadnax to the Key since my coming from Acris', consisting mainly coach timber, indicates that some exploitation of the woodlands took place.[25] By 1677, Papillon's financial situation was secure enough to allow him to engage an architect to draw up plans for a new house, though in the end, it seems that he settled for the rebuilding of a new eleven-bay south front.[26] It was trade rather than land, however, which provided the greater part of Papillon's income, and it was his reputation as a merchant which he was most anxious to enlarge. On receipt of a letter from Sir Joseph Ashe pointing out how little esteem merchants were in the opinion of some gentry because their estates were in money rather than land, Papillon wrote, 'I suppose all persons have not the like opinion of merchants, and that some will count it advantageous to have two strings to the bow, vizt. land and trade. I assure (and you know it) the latter affords more plenty and content though the other bee a good stake in the hedge'.[27]

Papillon's business papers have not survived in any quantity, but the Estate Book of 1667 shows that £22,321 passed through his trading and financial accounts for that year, and the indications are that his commercial interests expanded throughout the 1670s.[28] It was in 1671 that he put some of his capital into a brewery and a steelworks, and entered into partnership with Harrison, and whilst the progress of these ventures is not known, it is clear that ownership of the brewery remained in Papillon's hands until at least 1687.[29] In 1668, following a resurgence of complaints against the navy victualling contractors, Papillon together with Josiah Child and James Littleton 'attended the Treasury for many weeks, by request, to perfect a contract for the victualling of the navy, by which His Majesty is saved 10 per cent', but the syndicate was unsuccessful in dislodging Sir Denis Gawden, the chief contractor.[30] Four years later, however, an agreement was concluded with Gawden and his son, and an enlarged syndicate created so that during the Third Anglo-Dutch War, Papillon found himself party to a highly profitable arrangement, the morality of which his mother must have regarded as somewhat questionable, since she had pondered, a few years earlier, 'What would he (Papillon) do if the Navy were employed against the Church of God?'.[31] Papillon himself no doubt regarded the victualling contract merely as an extension of his earlier dealings with the navy, as he had been importing large and regular consignments of French and Flemish cable yarn for the Navy Commissioners since 1664, encouraged by a recommendation to Pepys that 'M. Papillon's yarn is the best ever had from France.'[32]

---

lime burning took account of the cost of providing for labourers' meat and drink, and 'there is little odds if all be considered between burning with wood & seacoale'.

25. KAO, U1015, E49/6.
26. J. Newman, *The Buildings of England: North East and East Kent,* 1969, 121; Papillon, *Memoirs,* 102–103.
27. KAO, U1015, C13/6 Thomas Papillon–Sir Joseph Ashe, 14th June, 1684.
28. KAO, U1015, E46 fs. 1–6.
29. KAO, U1015, C15/7 Samuel Rawstorn–Thomas Papillon, 17th June, 1687.
30. *Calendar of State Papers, Domestic,* 1668–9, 642.
31. Coleman, *op. cit.,* 32–33; Papillon, *Memoirs,* 100.
32. *Cal. S.P.D.* 1665–6, p. 23, Commander Thomas Middleton–Samuel Pepys, 21st October, 1665. Pepys seems to have held a low opinion of Papillon, however, when some years later, he wrote: 'Here I also heard Mr Papillon make his defence to the King, against some complaints of the Farmers of Excise; but it was so weak, and done only by his own seeking, that it was to his injury more than profit, and made his case the worse, being ill managed, and in a cause against the King', 23rd April, 1669, *Diary of Samuel Pepys* (ed. R. Braybrooke), iv, 157.

In spite of the enormous difficulties and incumbrances placed on Anglo-French trade during the 1660s and 70s, involving a 'stop-go' policy of treaties, prohibitions and tariff increases on both sides, Papillon's commodity trade was heavily concentrated in this branch of European commerce.[33] Indeed, he was one of the fourteen prominent London merchants trading to France who signed the well known 'Scheme of Trade' of 1674 which presented an exaggerated view of the unfavourable balance of trade with France, in an attempt to force the government to renew negotiations for an Anglo-French commercial treaty with a substantial reduction in Colbert's tariff.[34] The Estate Book shows that in 1667 (the year of Colbert's second major tariff increase against English imports), Papillon was mainly exporting English serges, draperies, and other cloths – often described according to their port of destination as 'Morlaix cloths' or 'St. Malo cloths' – on his own account for sale by agents and in large consignments of up to fifty bales worth from £500 to £1,300. In addition, less valuable consignments of tin, lead, coal, groceries and tobacco were sent out, in return for the usual assortment of French imports: Lockrams (canvas), cable yarn, silks, paper and brandy. On the French side, agents along the northern coast from Abbeville to Morlaix, including Rouen, Caen, and St. Malo, conducted this business; and on the west coast, at Nantes and La Rochelle. Agents are also named in Hamburg, Amsterdam, Bruges, Ostend, and in Cadiz and Tangiers, as well as Dublin and Limerick, but the composition of this trade is not indicated.[35]

We have already noticed that these extensive Anglo-French trading interests drew Papillon into what developed into one of the most controversial questions in post-Restoration politics, that of commercial rivalry with France. Throughout the 1660s and 70s in fact, he combined his trading activities with a series of public duties which greatly enhanced his reputation as a leading merchant in some circles, and continued to do so until the sharp vicissitudes of party politics in the late 70s and early 80s compelled him to withdraw. He served as MP for Dover from 1673 to 1681 and from 1689 to 1695, and for London from 1695 to 1700;[36] and remained on the Council for Trade and Plantations throughout the 1660s, giving evidence to the Committee appointed to consider the decay of trade of 1669–70 and recommending, amongst other things, the encouragement of foreign artisans.[37] As a director of the East India

33. See M. Priestley, 'Anglo-French Trade and the "Unfavourable Balance" Controversy', *Economic History Review*, Second Series, iv (1) 1951, 37–52; D.C. Coleman, 'Politics and Economics in the Age of Anne: the Case of the Anglo-French Trade Treaty of 1713', in D.C. Coleman and A.H. John, *Trade, Government and Economy in Pre-Industrial England; Essays presented to F.J. Fisher*, 1976, 187–211.

34. Priestley, *op. cit.*, 39, n. 4.

35. KAO, U1015, E46 fos. 1–6. Factors and houses named include Egbert Cappre (Rouen), Jean du Chesne, Nicolas Maurice (Abbeville), Musnier and Gobert, Roger Cole, Francis Guillottou (Morlaix), Henry Daniel (Caen), Van der Horst and de Bie (Nantes), Couveur and Hertner (Lyons), André Herbert (Paris), Daniel and Abraham Vanlinbergen (Amsterdam), Philip Cornelisen (Bruges), and Edward Ford (Cadiz). In 1669, Thomas Papillon led a group of importers of brandy in a suit against the Commissioners of Customs in their claim of double duty on brandy; and in 1671 drew up a paper headed 'Some brief Reasons against the Excise of foreign Commodities', which complained *inter alia* that 'additional duties will much injure the trade of the country, 1st by inducing other countries to retaliate, to the reduction of English exports; such a step is already mooted in Brittany where our drapery has been hitherto admitted duty free', Papillon, *Memoirs*, 58.

36. During the 1670s, he is described as a frequent and effective speaker, and sat on sixty-eight committees, (*D.N.B.*).

37. *Eighth Report of the Royal Commission on Historical Manuscripts*, House of Lords MSS, Calendar, sect. 133b/215, Committeee appointed to consider the causes and grounds of the fall of rents and decay of trade, 28th October, 1669–9th March, 1670. 'Mr Papillon says capital was much impaired by the fire (of London).

Company, he attended the negotiations between the English and the Dutch at Breda in 1667 on behalf of the Company, and became its Deputy Governor in 1681.[38] It was during the exclusion parliaments of 1679–81, however, that he became caught up in that nexus of emerging Whig politics and mercantile interests which marked the birth of the modern party system, and to which he was to fall victim. As opposition to Charles II's policies mounted during the 1670s, the East India Company became an important area of political struggle between the court and country parties and in 1682, Papillon was one of the first Whig members to be removed as a result of Sir Josiah Child's efforts to align the Company more closely with the court.[39] At the same time, the royal purges of the corporations swept through the city of London, and a political fine of £10,000 was imposed on Papillon as a result of proceedings which he had initiated following the disputed election of sheriffs in which he had been a candidate.[40] It seems that strong and pervasive anti-French feelings, which cut across party boundaries, also played a part in his victimisation. Mounting tension against France reached a climax in 1678 when the parliamentary opposition to Charles achieved a three-year prohibition of French imports. But this hostility was not confined to any one sphere of activity, and everything French became suspect.[41] As a deacon of the Huguenot Church in London where he 'generally received the sacrament' and where the Anglo-French business community gathered, Papillon rapidly became identified as an alien by his opponents.[42] Paradoxically, it was the 'Scheme of Trade' of 1674 which had provided the underlying economic arguments for increased discriminatory measures against France, and which Papillon himself had signed alongside John Dubois, a fellow deacon of the French Church and also a candidate for the shrievalty of London in the disputed elections.[43] During the crisis of city politics of 1683, their Tory opponents alleged that the pair 'were French or Walloon protestants that came into this nation for refuge and had got estates and would overthrow the government and cut our throats', to which the Lord Mayor replied 'I hope the King will take a course to send them back again to their own country'.[44] To avoid payment of the £10,000 fine, Papillon mortgaged his estates to his son-in-law and took up exile in Holland in 1685, returning after the revolution. Towards the end of his period of exile, he reflected on this affair: '. . . yet the Lord

being taken up in rebuilding. Some 100,000 people were lost by the Plague. Labour therefore scarcer. Money wasted in lawsuits. Foreign artisans should be encouraged. The Dutch have taken us out of the Irish Trade'.
38.   On Papillon's involvement with the East India Company and his relations with Sir Joseph Child, see W. Letwin, *The Origins of Scientific Economics, English Economic Thought, 1660–1776*, 1963, chapter 1, *passim*.
39.   Coleman, *Sir John Banks*, 85–9.
40.   November 6th, 1684. His trial was reported in *Cobbett's Complete Collection of State Trials*, x, 320–372. Papillon had in effect become the figurehead of the opposition after 1681, when, despite being elected Sheriff of London by an overwhelming majority, he was ousted at the Court's insistence in favour of its Tory nominees, see Letwin, *op. cit.*, 23–4; and D.R. Lacey, *Dissent and Parliamentary Politics in England, 1661–1689*, New Brunswick, 1969.
41.   Priestley, *op. cit.*, 37.
42.   KAO, U1015, C13/4 Thomas Papillon–Sir Joseph Ashe, 11th June, 1684. Little distinction seems to have been made between recent Huguenot arrivals and the Elizabethan immigrant families such as the Desbouveries, Houblons, Lethieulliers, Lordells and Papillons, described by P.G.M. Dickson as 'established city dynasties', *The Financial Revolution in England*, 1967, 259, n. 2.
43.   John Dubois was a friend and business associate of long standing; in 1657, the pair had been deputed by the French church in London to appeal to Cromwell and a Committee of the Privy Council over a dispute about the self-government of the French Churches in England, Papillon, *Memoirs*, 48–54.
44.   KAO, U1015, L1/11, 'Relation of what passed at my Lord Mayor's, 25th April, 1683.

hath done me good even thereby, for tho' I lost my trade and great outward advantage for getting an estate, yet I was preserved from the malice of men which possible might have designed to take away my life, and I hope my outward losses are abundantly made up in spirituall the Lord having given me time from wordly concerns to mind the better part, and weaned me in some measure from seeeking great things here (Utrecht)'.[45]

Compared with his extensive dealings in merchandise during the 1660s and 70s, Papillon's business activities during his period of exile were indeed modest but were mainly financial, involving exchange dealings and discounting of bills. 'My owne money', he said, 'I keep turning to and againe by Exchange wherein at present the hazards are great and little or noe profit, however I chuse it rather than to lett my mony ly in merchants hands'.[46] He maintained a regular financial correspondence with associates in Amsterdam, Rotterdam, Rouen, Paris, Morlaix, Bordeaux, Nantes and London, involving a different group of houses from those with whom he had engaged in commodity trade in the 1660s, with the exception of André Herbert of Paris.[47] There is no indication that Papillon drew any moral distinction between his own earlier commodity trading, 'the interchange of goods', and the purely financial dealings of his exile in the Low Countries, though he felt little sympathy for the business community of Amsterdam where, he said, 'there is noe good Christian society, getting of mony and saving of mony, is the businesse'.[48] A century later, Swedenborg was to observe that the Dutch had a 'spiritual love' of trading, 'for it serves the common good', to which the love of money was a mediate, subordinate love.[49] Papillon's assessment was less generous, but his objections were religious rather than social and arose from strong feelings of dissatisfaction with the reformed church of Amsterdam. 'The preaching here is not generally so spirituall as in England', he commented, and 'there is little of the life, power and spirituality of Religion'. He preferred the English and French churches in Amsterdam, 'in both which there was very honest and spirituall preaching'.[50]

Papillon's spiritual writings cover the period 1665–99 and as might be expected, his reflections were especially intense during his period of exile in Holland from 1685–89. From 1669–78, he kept a journal, a private confessional diary running to three large folio volumes containing mainly meditations on passages of scripture, and his extensive notes on sermons cover the years from 1655 to the end of his life.[51] Whilst in Holland, he composed a series of four discourses or extended meditations on the causes of his sufferings and the court proceedings against him, written in 1685; a discourse to his children, on the unchildlike theme of man's

45. KAO, U1015, F15/5, 6th September, 1688 (Considerations on Thomas Papillon's past life).
46. KAO, U1015, C27, Thomas Papillon–Sir James Oxenden, 27th August, 1685.
47. KAO, U1015, C27, copies of letters to various correspondents: Paul d'Aranda (Amsterdam), John Moore, Edward Browne, Daniel de Carbonel (Rotterdam), Abr. le Cordier (Rouen), André Herbert (Paris), Procter and Sedgewick (Morlaix), Pierre du Brevill, Henry Pick (Bordeaux), Madame Lee and Son (Nantes), and Robert Michell (London). On Huguenot involvement in financial activities, see A.M.C. Carter, *Getting, Spending and Investing in Early Modern Times: Essays on Dutch, English and Huguenot Economic History*, Assen 1975.
48. KAO, U1015, C29/9 Thomas Papillon–Jane Papillon, 27th February, 1685.
49. E. Swedenborg, *The True Christian Religion* (1771), The Swedenborg Society 1950, 859–60.
50. KAO, U1015, C29/9 *ibid.* See A.M.C. Carter, *The English Reformed Church In Amsterdam in the Seventeenth Century*, Amsterdam 1964, chapter 1.
51. KAO, U1015, F11/1–3 Journals of Thomas Papillon, 1669–70, 1673–74, 1674–78; F 13 Notes on sermons, 1665–99.

fallen state, dated 22nd August, 1686; a long essay on sabbath observance addressed to the Amsterdam merchant Paul d'Aranda, written in March 1686; and a series of considerations on his past life, dating from 1688.[52] The confessional element is strong in all of these pieces and especially so in his journal which displays in its daily entries a fervent and incessant search for the *summum bonum*, that goodness and confidence laboured after by many of the earlier puritans, tempered by a sense of personal inadequacy and sinfulness. On March 28th, 1669, he wrote: 'Last night I was made sensible of my inability and insufficiency to the service of God'; on May 2nd, 'I desire to engage against formality & slightnesse of spirit . . . in order here-abouts, I would get my heart more inflamed with love to Christ'; and, more seriously, on November 7th, 'Oh My God, I am ashamed and confounded before thee to consider how little improvement I have made of the last sacrament & my ingagmts then made to thee, how remiss and cold I am in duty, how wandring and distracted I am in the service of God'.[53] In Papillon's case, the journal served primarily as a confessional rather than the means for entering upon a spiritual pilgrimage. There was no prophetic task, no sense of mission, simply a striving for personal improvement, to 'walke more closely with the Lord, in all well pleasing'.[54] Papillon often wrote 'the spirit enlarging the heart' but describes no intense spiritual experiences of his own. Those of his wife and children however moved and impressed him. In a passage which strikes some resonance with Quaker language, he described how

> This morning when ready to goe to pray, my wife was taken wth a fainting that she forced to ly downe upon her bed and could not goe to Church. She came out of her closet in a very spirituall frame Enlarged after God, and breathing after that tyme when shee might serve God and enjoy him without any hindrance or Imperfection. I was much affected, and my heart went out to God. . . .'[55]

In his discourse to his children, he reminded them,

> Remember what one of you once said when young after some days workings of minde, how you should be sure you should goe to heaven, crying out one morning to your maide, I have found it, now I am sure, he hath said I will bee your God & ye shall be my people. Oh forget not this working of Gods spirit in your heart soe early'.[56]

By and large, however, Papillon's reflections suggest a controlled enthusiasm without any strong mystical leanings – the brooding melancholy of a Cromwell rather than the mysticism of Fox or Bunyan. His puritanism was austere, formal and rigorous, but he had little difficulty in combining his commitment to the Huguenot Church in London, with its strict moral discipline, with worship 'according to the liturgy and discipline of the Church of England' when away from the metropolis.[57] The Anglican church in east Kent had in any case existed for several generations alongside the reformed churches established by the French and Dutch refugee communities in Sandwich, Canterbury and Maidstone, and for a shorter period at Dover, and by the Restoration must have absorbed some of their influence.[58] Unlike the more prosperous

---

52. KAO, U1015, F15/3; F15/4; F16/6; F15/5.
53. KAO, U1015, F11/1 28th March, 1669, 7th November, 1669.
54. KAO, U1015, F15/5 6th September, 1688, f. 1.
55. KAO, U1015, F11/1 12th September, 1669.
56. KAO, U1015, F15/4 22nd August, 1686, f. 2.
57. KAO, U1015, C13/4 Thomas Papillon–Sir Joseph Ashe, 11th June, 1684.
58. J. Lindeboom, *Austin Friars, History of the Dutch Reformed Church in London*, The Hague, 1950, 104–108; F.W. Cross, *History of the Walloon and Huguenot Church at Canterbury* (Huguenot Society), 1898. See also G.F. Nuttall, 'Dissenting Churches in Kent before 1700', *Journal of Ecclesiastical History*, xiv (1963).

western parts of Kent which, in spite of its sprinkling of Presbyterians and Congregationalists, had 'shunned the more extreme and rigorous expressions of Protestant fervour', the eastern part of the county, especially Canterbury and the decaying Cinque Ports, inclined towards a more radical protestantism, including Quakers and Anabaptists.[59]

Papillon's theology was grounded in an orthodox and severe Calvinism, and his writings repeatedly stress the importance of justification by faith alone together with a firm belief in the doctrine of the elect – the two beliefs which underlay his rigid dualistic separation between temporal concerns and the life of the spirit. His journal entry for 17th June, 1670, reads, 'Wee are not to neglect the works of our calling but wee are mainly and principally to minde the things of our soules . . . work is our duty but it cannot merit'. Three days earlier, he had been considering, 'If all men were by Christ brought into a capacity of attaining salvation if they will, then all men are borne again. But all men are not borne againe, therefore that is not generall & universall redemption or grace as some speake. Their must bee a saving worke of the spirit'.[60] Towards the end of his life, in 1700, he grumbled and criticised the local incumbent at Acrise for looseness of doctrine in these critical areas (as well as for walking in the fields and lying in bed), since the latter had preached that Christ was a mediator, 'which implies conditions on our part to do, as well as favours on God's part to bestow'. Papillon thundered:

> I shall not take upon me the nice distinctions that possibly are used by Divines concerning conditions and qualifications. But I firmly believe that the Lord Jesus Christ hath purchased and merited Salvation for all the elect and that whatever any of God's children may be enabled to do in a way of duty, cannot merit any thing, and I think it would be sinful for any to join their own work with Christ's.[61]

The doctrine of justification by faith formed the basis of Papillon's discourse to his children of 1686, and his confessional statement of 1688 argued that the performance of works and duties caused 'this cursed self to creep in, and, jostle (as it were) Christ out of the throne' leading to 'pride, self love, unbelief, great ingratitude, and in a manner all sin'.[62] It was therefore idle to interfere with the external world, and by condemning it as unspiritual, the puritan, in Tawney's words, 'made it, and ultimately himself, less spiritual by reason of his contempt'.[63]

It is abundantly clear that Papillon's soul searchings did not derive in any sense from a need to find sanctification for his business activities. His conservative puritanism and more specifically, his dualistic Calvinist theology combined with a rational religious practice rooted in scriptural texts rather than mystical insights, shaped a personal religion which interfered only minimally with his everyday business and mercantile concerns.[64] He alludes to a kind of compensatory movement, a balance between his business accounts and his spiritual accounts –

59. Coleman, *Sir John Banks*, 143–4; P. Clark, *English Provincial Society from the Reformation to the Revolution: Religion, Politics and Society in Kent, 1500–1640*, Hassocks 1977, 401–3.
60. KAO, U1015, F11/2 17th June, 1674, 14th June, 1674.
61. Papillon, *Memoirs*, 110–11.
62. KAO, U1015, F15/5, 6th September, 1688, f. 1.
63. Tawney, *Religion and the Rise of Capitalism*, 229–30.
64. For an interesting comparison with the writings of the London artisan Nehemiah Wallington in the 1630s and 40s, see P. Seaver, 'The Puritan Work Ethic Revisited', *Journal of British Studies*, xix (2) 1980, which concludes 'Our mistake has been to assume that what the Puritan urban laity wanted was the sanctification of entrepreneurial energy and profits; it seems more likely that most Puritans sought assurance that a good conscience in hard times was blessing enough', (p. 53).

'I hope my outward losses are abundantly made up in spirituall' – and seems to have regarded God as a co-partner in his trading ventures:

> When I received a great losse by Webberly God was pleased soe to order it in his providence that in the end it turned to my advantage. When another losse befell mee and some thought by false insinuations and reports to make advantage to my prejudice, The Lord did frustrate their purpose and sustained me . . . When in publick employs in the East India Committee, in the Company of Mercers, in the Hospitall, in the Parliament, in the Citty; the Lord assisted & carried me thro all.[65]

In his career as a merchant and in the management of his landed property, in his accounting methods and his attention to a voluminous correspondence, Papillon was as rational and calculating as any of the commercial bourgeoisie of his day. His advice to his son, practical rather than pious, was not strikingly different from that doled out by the Tory Anglican, Sir John Banks, to a young relative:

> Pray bee very careful to avoide all idle company and to spend your tyme well to improve your selfe in knowledge. I could hartily wish that you did write better. Bee very exact in all your accounts and punctual in your correspondencies.[66]

Professor Waltzer's contention that among lay puritans, the weight of the diaries, letters and memoirs clearly suggests that the most significant expression of their faith was cultural and political rather than economic, certainly finds support in the career and spiritual writings of Thomas Papillon.[67] It seems that his public duties and political career derived less from religious imperatives demanding a social expression than from a politico-religious drive to struggle against Catholicism, and of course the decades following the disintegration of puritan political power and religious predominance provided ample opportunity to do so. To some extent, a violent anti-Catholic rhetoric served to obscure and protect Papillon's own questionable position as a dissenter possessing strong links with the French Church, especially in the late 1660s and 70s. But his hatred of papistry was real enough. Compromise and moderation was difficult in a political world which, in Papillon's view, was clearly divided between the godly and the ungodly, truth and error, between Protestantism and Papistry, Whig and Tory. The Papists, he considered,

> have made it their work to set these two parties one against the other, first by setting the Tories in power and countenancing them to persecute and oppress the Whigs, both Churchmen and Dissenters, that by these cruelties they might be the more willing to comply with the Papists, to obtain the ease and liberty which the Papists promised them, And then drawing such of them as were not aware of their designs to fall into countenance the practices of King James the Second's time.[68]

If the Tories were 'swearers, drunkards, or loose in their conversation', the Papists were guilty

---

65. KAO, U1015, F15/5 6th September, 1688, f. 4.

66. KAO, U1015, C27 Thomas Papillon–Phillip Papillon, 15th August, 1685; Sir John Banks wrote to a young relative in 1658, '. . . the Lord is most pleased with integrity, and it will be your glory. Keep your accounts punctual, be honest to all men', Coleman, op. cit., 146.

67. M. Waltzer, 'Puritanism as a Revolutionary Ideology', History & Theory, III(1) 1963, 71. Of his political obligations, Papillon wrote, 'In publick concernes I blesse the Lord, I have generally had a sincere desire to act according to the best of my understanding for the good and welfare of the Society, Citty, Country & State without respect to any private interest, yet I confesse Corruption hath many tymes beene rising & stirring', KAO, U1015, F15/5 f. 3.

68. Memorandum of the late 1690s, reprinted in Papillon, Memoirs, 375, from KAO, U1015, 051/55.

of 'more cruelties, massacres, dethroning, murdering and assassinating kings, and other public persons, than any other sort of men in the world'.[69] Of course, the sufferings of previous generations of his own family during the years of religious persecution underlay these deep feelings of hostility, and the weight of family tradition bore down heavily to perpetuate them.

In fact it was probably at the cultural and familial level that Papillon's religious beliefs found their strongest and most pervasive expression. With the 'contraction of the territory within which the spirit of religion was conceived to run',[70] Christian morality retreated from the worlds of commercial and business life and from the larger social environment into a smaller domestic province, that of the household. In Christopher Hill's words, the secularisation of the parish was accompanied by the spiritualisation of the household.[71] Certainly Papillon's world-denying theology stopped short at the boundaries of his own family: 'that which is contrary to the love of God and the love of one another is the love of the World', he wrote, '. . . my endeavours as to concerns in the affairs of the world being onely for my children'.[72] The encouragement which puritanism gave to patriarchal authority has long been recognised. There was need of a substitute for the shaken rule of priest and king,[73] and if society at large was beyond redemption, the duty of the husband and father was clear: to create a Godly society within the household. Some recent work on the history of the family, however, has suggested that this connection, plain enough for the later sixteenth and early seventeenth centuries, was sundered in the post-Restoration period. Professor Stone believes that the late seventeenth century saw an attack on patriarchy, philosophical and socio-legal, a weakening or even collapse of puritanism as a major religious and moral force in English life, and the growth of companionate marriage which is held to be incompatible with patriarchy.[74]

It is the last of these changes which carries the burden of Professor Stone's argument, that is, the growth of companionship in marriage and affective relations within the family which, it is suggested, undermined the strict subjection and obedience of wives and children. Yet, feminist historians have taken a different view. Sheila Rowbotham, for example, argues that patriarchy was once more secure after 1660 and the agitation of 'inferiors' was suppressed.[75] It is likely that the argument will only be resolved at the level of individual family histories. The experience of the Papillon family is especially illuminating, and it indicates a series of connections precisely the reverse of those outlined by Professor Stone, namely, that possessive individualism combined with a secularised puritanism created a fertile soil for the development of patriarchy as a residual growth, as a kind of reserved area within which spiritual obligations and the demands of a pious conscience could find expression. Above all, it seems that this was not in the least incompatible with mutuality and affection between spouses and their children, of which there is ample evidence in the Papillon correspondence. Whilst in Holland, Thomas wrote to his wife, Jane, 'I cannot live comfortably without thee; all the world is nothing to me in comparison', and 'I love thee as my own soule, and I hope God will bring us together in his

---

69. *Ibid.*, 375; KAO, U1015, F15/3 f. 4.
70. Tawney, *Religion and the Rise of Capitalism*, 278.
71. C. Hill, *Society and Puritanism in Pre-Revolutionary England*, 1964, chapter 13.
72. KAO, U1015, F15/4 22nd August, 1686, f. 4; F15/3 1685, f. 2.
73. S. Rowbotham, *Hidden From History*, 1973, 8.
74. L. Stone, *The Family, Sex and Marriage in England, 1500–1800* (1977), Penguin ed. 1979, chapter 6.
75. Rowbotham, *op. cit.*, 13.

due time with comfort that we may spend the rest of our days in a more spiritual and heavenly manner'.[76]

Relations between Thomas and Jane Papillon and their four surviving children (four had died in infancy) were likewise marked by strong bonds of affection and a somewhat critical recognition of the individuality of each child. In 1667, Jane Papillon wrote to her husband:

> Betty retains her wildness still, and Philly does not much advance for want of pronunciation; Sarah, I fear will be a dull girl, like the Mother; but yet I will not doubt but however God shall deal with me, thou wilt find some reason to continue thy tender love to every one of them: They all joy exceedingly in the kisses you send them; and 'Does Father remember me?' 'and me.' they all say. Ann Mary is well[77]

Elizabeth Papillon addressed her father as 'My honoured and dear Father' and ended her letters 'Your most affectionate and dutiful daughter'; yet the nineteen year old child was 'much troubled' as 'I am sure I am very wicked, for I am very neglectful of my duties both to God and man'.[78] As an orthodox Calvinist, her father adhered strictly to the doctrine of original sin and was clear that 'Parents derive corruption to their children, this should be a matter of humiliation to Us, and should engage us to earnest endeavours for their change and conversion'.[79] Papillon's Discourse to his children, of 1686, elaborates this point, together with the broader question of man's fallen condition and the means of redemption through the exercise of faith, but lays special emphasis on the duty of 'naturall parents' to 'Labour & use all meanes, that their children might be Regenerated & become the children of God'.[80] The Discourse begins with a reference to the lives of the Patriarchs and it would be difficult to find a clearer expression of the obligations of patriarchy and 'family government', though the rebelliousness of childhood is presented in rather less threatening terms than those of Cleaver and Dod, whose famous treatise of 1621 had warned 'The young child which lieth in the cradle (is) both wayward and full of affections . . . and is altogether inclined to evil'.[81] It is important to recognise throughout that Papillon's reflections were not merely abstract statements, but that patriarchy was constructed and reinforced through language, especially in its constant reference to scriptural authority, to recognised texts. The unique contribution of puritanism to patriarchal control was made at two interconnected levels, those of theology and a language possessed of divine authority – an authority which was itself patriarchal in origin through the male-dominated trinity. Only these kinds of considerations can adequately explain the powerful impact which Thomas Papillon's Discourse evidently made on subsequent generations of the family: several manuscript copies of different dates survive amongst the Papillon archives.[82]

In terms of religious practice, the primary means through which patriarchal authority was mediated were Sabbath observance and family worship, and it was on these matters that Papillon constructed his most thorough and elaborate theological reflections. In addition to his

76. Papillon, *Memoirs*, 259 (5th March, 1685); 268 (n.d.).
77. *Ibid.*, 387 (31st May, 1667) and 396, 'The children receive thy kisses and blessing with tears; Betty is very much affected with thy affection to her; Philly will have nothing but his love returned; the other little ones are well', (5th July, 1667).
78. *Ibid.*, 390 (31st May, 1667).
79. KAO, U1015, F15/4 22nd August, 1686, f. 1.
80. *loc. cit.*
81. Robert Cleaver and John Dod, *A Godly Form of Household Government*, 1621, quoted by Waltzer, *op. cit.*, 85.
82. KAO, U1015, F15/4; F16/7; F73.

daily responsibility for leading morning and evening prayers in his own household, he regarded his spiritual obligations as extending over the parish of Acrise, indicated in his correspondence with Dean Tillotson and his complaints to the local incumbent of 'looseness of doctrine'.[83] During his frequent absences from Acrise, however, Jane Papillon conducted family worship, though she worried about the responsibility, especially at harvest time when the reapers took their meals in the house and she was unable to induce them to attend morning prayers, although they came along in the evening.[84] Significantly, Elizabeth Papillon reported that on such occasions during her father's absences, 'Our dear Mother is as a Father and Mother both to us'.[85] Sabbath observance was regarded by Thomas Papillon as morally desirable although there were circumstances in which a dispensation might be allowed, whereas daily family prayers were accorded a position of paramount importance since daily repentance was essential for salvation. In his Treatise on the Sanctity of the Sabbath written in 1686 at the request of his friend Paul d'Aranda, an Amsterdam merchant, pride of place was given to those scriptural arguments which emphasised the obligations incumbent on the head of the household for the conduct of family worship. This important section is quoted in full:

This duty (of prayer) is not only personal to be performed by every one in secret, but I am fully persuaded that there lies a duty on me and every Master of a family and to pray with them, for as we stand in need of & daily receive not only blessings peculiar to our own persons singly considered, but also as we stand related to one another, and are in a family community, so certainly we should own and acknowledge God in that community by seeking to him and praising of him for family blessings. We read in 44 Ezel. that God, as a motive or encouragmt. to obedience proposeth family blessings, v. 30, that he may cause a blessing to rest in thine house. In 33 Jer. 1, God saith he will be the God of all the familys of the house of Israel. That God will not only be my God but the God of my family is a great mercy and deserves to be both desired & acknowledged. The blessings by & thro' Jesus Christ are extended to familys, 12 Gen. 3, in thee shall all the familys of the Earth be blessed. In the 3 Pro. 33, it is said the curse of the Lord is in the house of the wicked, but he blesseth the habitation of the just. And ought we not in prayer to deprocate the curse and beg the blessing. We find that the people of God have taken a special care of their familys. Abraham circumcised all the Males in his family as God required, 17 Gen. 13, 23, and he is commended for the care of his family, Gen 18, 19, I know that Abraham will comand his Children and his household after him &c. And we find Jacob going to worship God with his family, taking care of them that they might be prepared, 35 Gen. 2, 3.

Hence are those commands in 6 Deut. 7 & 11 Deut. 19, to teach God's statutes to our Children & to talk of them when we sit in our houses &c. We read in 2 Sam. 6, 20, after David had been worshipping God in publick that he returned to bless his household. And in the 101 (Psalm), he tells us what care he would take of his family & how to demean himself well in that relation, v. 2, I will walk within my house with a perfect heart; & there seems to me from the connexion of the last clause of the verse with the former part, to be an implication, that a Man cannot expect God's coming to him in favour & in a way of blessing without family, as well as personal worship.

When persons were converted to the faith, they took care of their familys. Hence we read that when Lydia was converted, she was baptised, and her household, Acts 16, 15; and the Jaylor in the same Chap. v. 33, he & all his were baptised; and Acts 18, 8, Crispus believed in the Lord with all his house, & were baptised. And in respect of the worship of God in familys, I suppose it may be the reason (or at least one reason) of those expressions, the Church in such a one's hour, 16 Rom. 5, 10, 11, 1 Cor. 16, 19, 4 Col. 15, Philemon 2. And it is said of Cornelius, in 10 Acts 2, that he feared God with all his

83. Papillon, *Memoirs*, 106–111.
84. *Ibid.*, 101. During August 1668 for example, seventeen men were employed in harvest work and were fed with five meals per day, KAO, U1015, C11/21.
85. Papillon, *Memoirs*, 390 (31st May, 1667).

house, & prayed to God always &, v. 30, that at the 9th hour he prayd in his house, which seems to be a set time for his family worship. There is a prophecy in the 12 Zech. that when God should deliver & restore his Church & destroy their enemies, a spirit of grace and supplication should be poured out upon every family, that they should repent & mourn apart. And as God extends mercy & grace to familys, so God threatens Judgmts. on familys in 20 Levit: I will set my face agst. that man and agst. his family. And Deut. 29, 18–20: lest there should be among you man or woman, or family or tribe, whose heart turneth this day from the Lord, & the Lord will not spare him &c. And in 10 Jer. there is a terrible imprecation on the familys that call not on God: pour out thy wrath on the heathen that know thee not, and upon the familys that call not on thy name.

Here I might further observe the practice of the serious and truly pious persons in all times, who have made conscience of family duties, and I never read or heard of any amongst Christians (who were not Atheistical or wickedly prophaned) that did not in their Judgmts approve, and in their speech acknowledge that the reading of God's word, and prayer, in familys, was religious and commendable. The author of The Whole Duty of Man saith, let no man that professes himself a Christian keep so heathenish a family as not to see God be daily worshipped in it.

Well then, if we would obtain the blessing of God on our familys and avoid his wrath & displeasure, surely it is our duty & concern to take care of our familys & to set up the worship of God there. And therefore I desire to resolve wth. Joshua, whatever others make their choice and practice, yet as for me and my house, we will serve the Lord, Josh., 25, 15.[86]

Papillon's piety was no doubt exceptional in the commercial world of post-Restoration England, but it was characteristic of an influential minority. As puritanism was transformed into dissent and dissenters were increasingly forced onto the defensive from 1661–1689, the influence of Calvinism turned more decisively towards supporting a liberal possessive individualism. As Tawney pointed out, both an intensive individualism and a rigorous Christian Socialism could be deduced from Calvin's doctrines, and the question of which predominated depended above all on whether Calvinists were, as at Geneva and in Scotland, a majority who could impress their ideals on the social order, or, as in England, a defensive minority.[87] If the route which these changes followed was an indirect one, as Tawney suggested, it is important to emphasise the enhanced role of patriarchy in this process. Thomas Papillon clearly saw his own family and household as a social world in miniature within which a range of residual spiritual obligations demanded fulfilment, and which he was more than willing to meet. The retreat of Christian social morality which this view represented was no doubt derived from an accommodation of commercial interests and political limitations, but it was religious nonetheless. Certainly, any attempt to understand the historical development of patriarchy solely in economic terms must remain incomplete.

86. KAO, U1015, F16/6 1686, 22–24. Papillon himself maintained a strict Sabbath observance and towards the end of his life excused himself from a meeting with the King and the Victualling Commissioners at the Secretary of State's Office on the grounds of Sabbath observance, 'I desire conscientiously to observe the Lord's Day in the Exercises of Religeous dutyes, both publick, private and with my family, and I beleeve that unless it bee in case of necessity I am bound by the word of God soe to doe', 051/13 Thomas Papillon–Sir John Trenchard, 10th November, 1693. On the persistence of Sabbatarianism in East Kent, see P. Clark, op. cit., 402–3.
87. Tawney, Religion and the Rise of Capitalism, 112–3.

THE KENTISH PORTION OF AN ANONYMOUS TOUR OF 1809[1]

JOHN WHYMAN

'In travelling thro' England, a luxurience of objects presents it self to our view: Where-ever we come, and which way soever we look, we see something new, something significant, something well worth the travellers stay, and the writer's care.'

Daniel Defoe, 1724.[2]

'I never Tour without taking short notes.'

The Hon. John Byng, 1790.[3]

These sentiments on pre-railway travelling might well have been shared by whoever undertook the tour of Kent during September 1809 which is reproduced below. The touring both of Kent and of Britain has a long history stretching back to at least the sixteenth century, involving travellers or diarists ranging from the most famous, such as John Leland (1503–1552),[4] John Evelyn (1620–1706),[5] Samuel Pepys (1633–1703),[6] Daniel Defoe (?1660–1731),[7] or Celia Fiennes (1662–1741),[8] to several who were less well known or even anonymous, but whose accounts and impressions are worth consulting. Moreover, even to this day, there are travel journals and diaries lying either unread or undiscovered in archives offices or private houses. Such is the case with this recent acquisition by the Kent Archives Office, the reproduction of which continues a tradition of scholarship associated both with Dr. Felix Hull and other editors of travel accounts in *Archaeologia Cantiana* over the past fifty years, as witnessed by

V.J.B. Torr, 'A Tour through Kent in 1735', xliii (1931);

F. Hull, 'A Tour into Kent, 1759', lxix (1955);

F. Hull, 'A Kentish Holiday, 1823', lxxxi, (1966);

and J. Whyman, 'A Three-Week Holiday in Ramsgate during July and August 1829', xcvi (1980).[9]

It comes as no great surprise to discover that Kent was a much visited county; however, when assessing travellers and their impressions of places or events it is pertinent to bear in mind the following questions about them.

---

1. Kent Archives Office, U 2402 F1.
2. Daniel Defoe, *Tour through the Whole Island of Great Britain,* i, (1724), Preface.
3. (Ed.) C. Bruyn Andrews, *The Torrington Diaries containing the Tours through England and Wales, of the Hon. John Byng,* iv, (1970), 149.
4. (Ed.) Lucy Toulmin Smith, *The Itinerary of John Leland in or about the Years 1535–1543,* iv, (1964).
5. (Ed.) E.S. de Beer, *The Diary of John Evelyn,* (O.U.P., 1959).
6. (Ed.) R. Latham and W. Matthews, *The Diary of Samuel Pepys,* 9 Volumes, (1970–6).
7. Defoe, *op. cit.,* as per above, n. 2.
8. (Ed.) C. Morris, *The Journeys of Celia Fiennes;* (1947). (Ed.) C. Morris *The illustrated Journeys of Celia Fiennes 1685–c. 1712,* (1982).
9. The first three articles appear also in (Ed.) M. Roake and J. Whyman, *Essays in Kentish History,* (1973).

1. What is known about them as people?
2. How were their interests and attitudes shaped by their background?
3. What interested them in particular and what was it they went out to see or to record?   and
4. If their visits to specific localities or places were confined to a day or a few hours did they really acquire much more than brief glimpses or first impressions?

The traveller in this particular case is absolutely anonymous, in the sense that his name, his normal place of residence and his vocation or situation in life are unknown. He travelled alone on public coaches, unaccompanied by a servant and presumably therefore with a minimum of personal luggage. He does not always state where he stayed, and his diary is silent on the costs involved.

He was in Kent over nine days between Monday, 4th September and Tuesday, 12th September, 1809, during which time his itinerary followed only partly the well-worn tracks of previous tourists. He zigzagged to places rarely visited by other people. Leaving London early in the morning his first day was spent travelling to Maidstone, via Eltham, Foot's Cray, Farningham, Wrotham Hill and West Malling. Two days were spent in Maidstone and its environs, partly in the company of some friends who accompanied him to Allington, Aylesford, Kit's Coty, Boxley, Penenden Heath, Leeds Castle and village and Mote Park. On Thursday, 7th September, he proceeded to Rochester, where he recalled previous and frequent passages through that city. He spent that day looking over Rochester Cathedral and the neighbouring town of Chatham before travelling on that evening to Sittingbourne. The morning of Friday, 8th September, was spent observing the nearby port of Milton before taking a coach on to Canterbury, where he occupied the remaining daylight hours in obtaining a general impression of the City. A long and tiring day was spent in exploring Canterbury in some detail on Saturday, 9th September, before proceeding via Barham Downs to Folkestone, where Sunday was agreeably spent. Setting out on foot, as he had done in the environs of Maidstone, he walked on Monday, 11th September, to Hythe, via Sandgate, Shorncliffe and Seabrook, observing much on the way. His final day on Tuesday, 12th September, took him by cart across Romney Marsh and along the Dymchurch Wall to New Romney, before proceeding into Sussex, where the diary suddenly terminates two days later at Hastings.

While economic, scenic, social, architectural and military details caught his eye, he had two overriding interests, antiquarian and military, in the sense of visiting or noticing churches and cathedrals, both externally and internally, castles, country houses, barracks and Martello towers. He was particularly and accurately observant of troop movements associated with the Napoleonic Wars, but was unable, unlike travellers today, to distinguish between Saxon and Norman architecture. He had an eye for good views and pleasant scenery and he recorded faithfully the size, importance and functions of several of the villages and towns which he visited or passed through.

He was well informed as to who owned particular properties, but the misuse of ancient buildings he rightly censured on at least three occasions in Canterbury. Neither did recent events or developments escape his notice, such as a fatal drowning in the moat of Leeds Castle, the laying out of the Dane John gardens in Canterbury or the newness of Sandgate as a coastal watering place. Observations relating to the famous engraver William Woollett (1735–85) at Maidstone, the water-colour painter and artist Thomas Hearne (1744–1817) at Allington

PLATE III

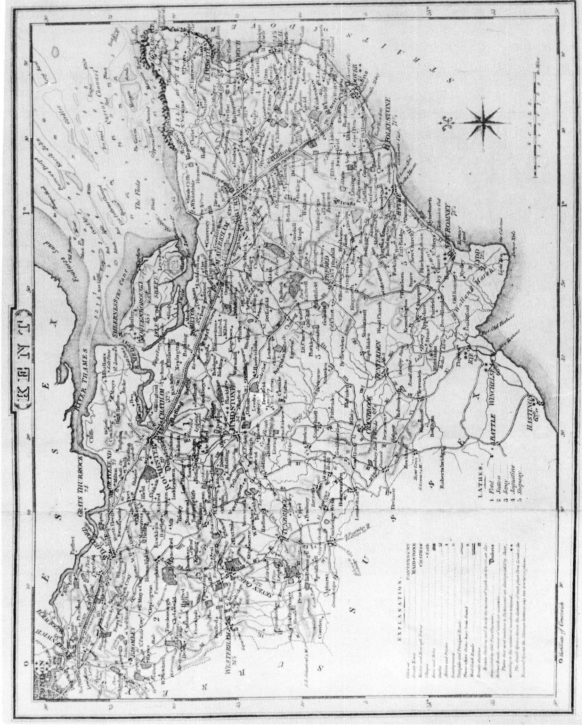

Map of Kent in 1818 (L. Fussell, *A Journey round the Coast of Kent*, 1818).

Castle, the historical painter Benjamin West (1738–1820) at the altar of Rochester Cathedral, and recent memorial monuments by J. Bacon Junior and Bacon Senior in Rochester Cathedral and in St. Mildred's Church in Canterbury respectively, testify to a cultured traveller, who had kept abreast of the latest creations of the artistic world.

The manuscript which follows, the handwriting of which was not easy to decipher, has been heavily footnoted, the effect of which is to underline to an amazing degree the accuracy of what was observed and recorded. Original modes of spelling have been retained, and only three minor alterations have been made to the original text. Every abbreviation of 'and' has been replaced by the word itself. The original text was punctuated by dashes, which have given way to fullstops. Additional punctuation and a few improvements to sentence construction have been effected, so as to produce more meaningful and flowing sentences where none existed originally.

Monday, *4 September* *1809*	I left London by the Maidstone Coach which goes alternately from the Blossoms Inn, Lawrence Lane, and the George, in the Borough, on this day from the latter at 7 a.m. in the morning.[10] The first stage is to Foots Cray on the way to which there is nothing particular to remark except the remains of the Palace at Eltham, which lay to the right and of which little can be seen from the road.[11] Foots Cray lies extremely low and is an insignificant small Place in a swampy disagreeable situation.[12] On leaving it on the left is the House built by Sir Bourchier Cleeve on the model of an Italian Villa from a Design of Palladio which, altho possessing a high degree of Architectural Elegance, has from its not being appropriate to our Climate lost a considerable degree of its Popularity, and is not likely to be imitated or adopted in its principles by those who in future are inclined to employ their superflous wealth in building Country Mansions.[13]

10. Regular coach services between the Blossoms Inn, Lawrence Lane, Cheapside, or the George Inn, Borough, and Maidstone are confirmed by *The Universal British Directory of Trade, Commerce and Manufacture*, iii, (1791), 873, at single fares of 8*s*. 6*d*. inside and 5*s*. outside, as well as by J. Cary in his *New Itinerary: or an Accurate Delineation of the Great Roads, Both Direct and Cross throughout England and Wales*, 4th Edn., (1810), in 'A List of all the Inns throughout the Metropolis from which the Mail and other Stage Coaches Depart', services 68, 69, 159 and 160. The particular service taken on this occasion was No. 159 'MAIDSTONE, MALLING, and WROTHAM, thro' Foots Cray and Farningham', departing daily at 7 in the morning and arriving at Green's Coach Office in Maidstone in 6 hours.
11. During the late eighteenth and early nineteenth centuries several artists and antiquarians visited the site and ruins of Eltham Palace and from their prints and accounts it is possible to visualize the state of the palace at that time, as noted by R. Brook, *The Story of Eltham Palace*, (1960), 53–7.
12. Foot's Cray had a population of 151 according to the first census of 1801, G.S. Minchin, 'Table of Population, 1801 to 1921', (Ed.) W. Page, *The Victoria History of the County of Kent*, iii, (1932), 368. Edward Hasted, writing a few years earlier, had drawn attention to 'a small street of houses' forming the village of Foot's Cray, part of which parish was 'very dreary and unpleasant', *The History and Topographical Survey of the County of Kent*, ii, 2nd Edn., (Canterbury, 1797), 135. In additional observations to the same volume he noted that 'the parish is small, containing only about seven hundred and fifty acres', in which 'the present *number of houses* . . . is only twenty-three', *id.*, 570.
13. The reference here is to Foot's Cray Place which, in 1797, stood as 'an elegant mansion of free-stone, built after the model, though with some few alterations, of the last earl of Westmoreland's seat at Mereworth . . . designed after one of Andrea Palladio, built for a Vincentine gentleman on the bank of the river

PLATE IV

Maidstone in 1820 (*Excursions in the County of Kent,* 1822).

From Foots Cray to Wrotham, which is the next stage, the road leads thro a country in an undulating uphill and down Hill way through Farningham, in a manner which furnishes nothing to admire. Near to Wrotham, however, on descending a high Hill a fertile and extensive Valley presents itself[14] and at the Close of its descent is a most comfortable House belonging to the rector of the

Bacchiglione, near the city of Venice', by Bourchier Cleve (amended to Cleeve on p. 571), a London pewterer, who possessed this seat until his death in 1760, Hasted, *op. cit.,* 138. According to J. Newman, *The Buildings of England: West Kent and the Weald,* (1969), 95–6, 276, Foot's Cray Place, burnt down in 1950, was built *c.* 1756 for Bourchier Cleeve, 'not so much in imitation of Palladio as to outdo his friend, Lord Westmorland, at Mereworth', as 'one of the major achievements of Palladianism', Mereworth Castle being Colen Campbell's 'most fulsome act of homage to Palladio', being 'a copy of the Villa Rotonda built on a knoll outside Vicenza'. Foot's Cray Place represented the latest of four English Villa rotondas, being the residence in 1810 of Benj. Harence, Esq., Cary, *op.cit.,* 13, or G.A. Cooke, *Topographical and Statistical Description of the County of Kent,* (*c.* 1810), 11.

14. The route taken so far comprised 'the high road which leads through the centre of this county from New Cross to Wrotham and thence to Maidstone', there being from Wrotham Hill 'a most beautiful prospect southward over a variety of country', Hasted, *op. cit.,* 135 and v, 2nd Edn., (Canterbury, 1798), 6. Early on his tour into Kent during September 1790 the Hon. John Byng had taken 'the Road hilly and stoney to Wrotham Hill; whence is a grand view of the Vale beneath – and of the country beyond; This Hill till lately – was dangerously steep – but now so cork-screw'd that a chaise may trot down it, with safety', Bruyn Andrews, *op. cit.,* 151. Farningham he described as being 'gloomy; and the surrounding country steep and stoney', *ibid.,* 151.

Parish, the income of which He has raised as I was informed from £600 to £1800 per Ann^m. The present Incumbent I believe is son of the late Archbishop of Canterbury.[15]

The road from Wrotham to Maidstone improves considerably and some miles short of the latter the Coach deviated to the right and passed thro Malling, a pretty little Town, adjoining to which is a beautifull small fragment of the Gate of its ancient Abbey.[16]

Tuesday,
5 September

Maidstone is the Town where the Assizes are held and is of a considerable Size[17] and altho not possessing the Advantage or Disadvantage of being a great Thoroughfare, enjoys a considerable degree of Activity and Employ from its having the Benefit of a navigable river, from its being the Place where the County Assizes are held and from the fertility of the Soil, which produces abundance of Fruit and Hops beyond all Calculation, and also from its

15. On entering Wrotham Hasted, *op. cit.*, v, 6, refers to 'the mansion of the rectory, a handsome house, well suited to the income of it', standing on the opposite side of the road to the church, this 'parsonage house' having been considerably improved into 'a handsome building' prior to 1770 by two previous rectors and vicars, Thomas Curteis and Dr. John Potter who, as the eldest son of John Potter, Archbishop of Canterbury (1737–47), 'was the principal benefactor to it, and expended a large sum of money upon this house and the offices belonging to it', *ibid.*, 31–2. Dr. John Potter was installed as Dean of Canterbury on 23rd December, 1766, and died at Wrotham less than four years later on 20th September, 1770, aged 57, having 'greatly improved the parsonage house there, at the expence of more than £2,000', *ibid.*, xii, 2nd Edn., (Canterbury, 1801), 46–7. Cary, *op. cit.*, 13, in drawing attention to 'the Noblemen and Gentlemen's Seats situate near the Roads', refers to '*Wrotham*, on r. the Rectory House, Rev. G. Moore', the son of Dr. John Moore (1730–1805), who, after having been appointed Dean of Canterbury in 1771 and Bishop of Bangor in 1775, was translated to the see of Canterbury on 26th April, 1783, (Ed.) Sir L. Stephen and Sir S. Lee, *The Dictionary of National Biography*, xiii, (O.U.P., 1959–60), 812, and H. Withers, *The Cathedral Church of Canterbury A Description of its Fabric and a brief History of the Archiepiscopal See*, (1917), 128, the patronage of the Wrotham living belonging to the Archbishop of Canterbury, Hasted, *op. cit.*, v, 31–2. It has been claimed of Archbishop Moore that while he was 'an amiable and worthy prelate, a competent administrator, and a promoter of the Sunday-school movement and of missionary enterprise, he appears to have dispensed his patronage with somewhat more than due regard to the interests of his own family', *Dictionary of National Biography*, *op. cit.*, 812, or, in the words of Withers, *op. cit.*, 128, 'he did not escape reproach for paying undue regard to the interests of his family'.

16. Meaning West Malling, 'now most commonly called Town Malling . . . is situated equally pleasant and healthy', being 'well built, having many genteel houses in it, the streets of a handsome width, and well paved', having at its eastern end the remains of an abbey, 'to which the approach is by a venerable antient gateway', with an 1801 population of 1,093, Hasted, *op. cit.*, iv, 2nd Edn., (Canterbury, 1798), 518, and Minchin, *op. cit.*, 361. Thomas Potts in his unpaginated *Gazetteer of England and Wales*, (1810), described West Malling as 'a pleasant neat little town, consisting of one long street: the houses are mostly ancient, but in good repair, . . . and the inhabitants are principally occupied in the cultivation of hops and fruit, which are here produced in great perfection', Malling 'in ancient times [being] chiefly noted for its abbey', of which 'the greater part of this building is still perfect, having been converted into a mansion by the proprietor of the land, Mr. Honeywood, the residence in 1810 of G.T.H. Foote, Esq., Cary, *op. cit.*, 13.

17. With an 1801 population of 8,027 which by 1811 had increased to 9,443, Minchin, *op. cit.*, 370. Potts, *op. cit.*, described Maidstone as containing 1,346 houses, consisting 'chiefly of four principal streets uniting at the market-place, the town is well built, paved and lighted [and] many of the houses are of modern erection'. *Holden's Triennial Directory*, ii, 4th Edn., (1808), 205, introduced Maidstone as 'the county town', which 'has been a considerable town in all ages . . . and is now pleasant, large and populous'.

PLATE V

Allington Castle in 1777 (*Antiquities of Great-Britain, illustrated in Views of Monasteries, Castles, and Churches, now existing: engraved from Drawings made by Thomas Hearne, 1786*). (Photo: *The British Library*.)

numerous Paper Mills.[18] [I] stayed at the Bell, [a] good [house].[19]

The Church is of an ancient Character and capacious but possesses not much worth notice. It is on an elevated situation on the banks of the Medway. Adjoining to it on the South are considerable remains of a religious Establishment, now called the College.[20] It is occupied by a Farmer and a principal part of the old Building is used as a Store House and drying Kiln for Hops.[21]

18. The economy of Maidstone in 1808 was centred to a considerable extent on hops, 'of which there are a great plenty of Plantations about the town, as well as orchards of cherries, . . . this [being] such a plentiful country, and the lands about it so rich, that London is supplied with more commodities from hence than from any market town in England', Holden, *op.cit.*, 205. Such a repetition of what was claimed in the 1720s by Daniel Defoe, *A Tour Through the Whole Island of Great Britain*, i, Everyman's Revised Edn., (1962), 113, is more than borne out by Potts, *op.cit.*, who observed that 'Maidstone is noted for its manufactures of geneva, paper, and thread, the paper-mills near the town [being] accounted the most extensive in the kingdom; and the Medway being navigable for small craft, and barges of 60 tons burthen, its manufactured articles, together with timber, wheat, and other corn, meal, malt, flour, hops, and fruit, find a ready market at an easy rate', while 'the neighbourhood of this town is rendered peculiarly beautiful, by the innumerable hop-gardens, and fruit orchards; the latter of which are cultivated solely for the supply of the metropolis'. Among the traders listed for 1808 were seven wharfingers and hoymen, some of whom were also coal merchants; six paper manufacturers; six corn and other mills; four timber merchants; three flax dressers, thread makers or linen weavers; three brewers; three corn factors or chandlers, and one hop merchant, one barge builder, an owner of a coal barge and one distiller, Holden, *op.cit.*, 206–8. Among the principal buildings noted by Potts, *op.cit.*, were 'the court-hall, in which the assizes for the county are holden, . . . and the county gaol, in which are combined strength, airiness, and neatness; the internal regulations doing honour to the county, and magistrates'.

19. Listed by Holden, *op.cit.*, 207, as being 'Friday John, Bell Inn, Week st.', being noted or recommended as a coaching inn by both *The Universal British Directory, op.cit.*, 873, and Cary, *op.cit.*, 12, with Potts, *op.cit.*, praising Maidstone's inns for offering 'excellent accommodation'.

20. Maidstone at the beginning of the nineteenth century possessed only one established church, that of All Saints, which had been erected on the site of an earlier church of St. Mary, once Archbishop Courtenay had received in 1395 the authority of Pope Boniface IX to make the parish church of Maidstone collegiate, whereupon not only was a college erected to house the master and clerks, but the church itself was completely rebuilt, Irene Hales, 'Maidstone's Churches', *Bygone Kent,* ii, (1981), 439, and Newman, *op.cit.*, 381. Hasted, *op.cit.*, iv, 2nd Edn., (Canterbury, 1798), 317, introduced the church as standing 'on the bank of the river Medway', being 'a large handsome building, consisting of a nave, great chancel, and two side isles', with a lofty roof, the body of the church having been 'neatly and regularly pewed' in 1700, with the addition of commodious galleries on each side. Hasted further noted that 'there were anciently in this church numbers of inscriptions on brass plates, as well on the monuments as grave stones, which are now almost torn away', *ibid.*, 318. According to Newman, *op.cit.*, 381, while Archbishop Courtenay in rebuilding Maidstone's parish church gave to Kent its grandest Perpendicular church, 'this spreading, plainly battlemented, ragstone building with its undersized SW tower cannot be called spectacular'. For Potts *op.cit.*, All Saints' church was 'supposed to be the largest in the county'. Overall 'on an eminence close to the Medway [stood] the church, the antient archiepiscopal palace, and the remains of the college, each forming conspicuous objects to the neighbouring country westward', Hasted, *op.cit.*, 265.

21. Following on from the previous footnote Hasted, *op.cit.*, 311, related that 'there are great remains left of this college, which appears to have been large and handsome; it is built of stone, and of gothic architecture; the entrance or gateway is almost entire; the whole is now made use of as a dwelling-house', while ten years later, according to Holden, *op.cit.*, 206, at 'a small distance south of the parish church stand the remains of St. Mary and All Saints Colleges, built by Archbishop Courtenay in the year 1396; the gate or entrance is still remaining with other parts of the building, sufficient to show it was once a handsome structure; it is now converted into a farm house'.

A little lower down the Stream is the Bridge in some degree venerable for its Antiquity, but the Super structure is modernised.[22] This town has a more than ordinary interest with me as being the Birth Place of Woollett, for whose admirable Productions I entertain the greatest Admiration and who it is universally admitted has carried the Art of Engraving to an Excellence which, in some respects, has never been equalled and which probably will never be excelled.[23] His father was a Manufacturer of Thread in a small way and being a Member of a Club who gained a Considerable Prize in the Lottery, his share of which amounted to Five hundred pounds, He engaged in a Public house the Non Success of which I believe proved that He like most others made no Advantage from such accidental and sudden Acquirement from property.[24]

On this day my friends took me a pleasant walk along the Banks of the Medway as far as a place of Recreation formerly known by the name of Porto Bello, but now called Gibraltar, at which place being punted across the River

22. In 1808, according to Holden, *op.cit.*, 205, Maidstone possessed 'a fine stone bridge', while two years later Potts, *op.cit.*, observed that over the Medway was 'a bridge of seven arches'. Hasted, *op.cit.*, 261, provided, however, a less flattering description in noting that 'over the river here there is an unsightly ancient stone bridge of seven arches, supposed to have been first erected by some of the archbishops, lords of the manor, [which] was repaired in king James I's reign by an assessment on the town and parish, but it still remains both narrow and inconvenient'.

23. William Woollett (1735–85), draughtsman and line engraver, established a reputation 'as the ablest landscape engraver who had yet appeared in England', being 'the first English engraver whose works were admired and purchased on the continent'. After becoming a member of the Incorporated Society of Artists in 1766, he produced ten years later his most celebrated engraving of Benjamin West's most successful painting of the 'Death of General Wolfe', which had been exhibited at the Royal Academy in 1771. Published in January 1776 this plate 'achieved extraordinary popularity both in England and abroad', and enjoyed 'the largest sale of any modern engraving'. George III was so impressed that he conferred upon Woollett the title of 'Historical Engraver to His Majesty'. During his lifetime he produced about a hundred plates, Ed. Sir L. Stephen and Sir S. Lee, *The Dictionary of National Biography*, xxi, (O.U.P., 1959–60), 901–2; also *ibid.*, xx, (O.U.P., 1959–60), 1237. In his chapter on 'Maidstone Worthies', J.M. Russell, *The History of Maidstone, with Illustrations*, (Maidstone, 1881), 394, concluded that William Woollett 'soon became known as the most accomplished of English engravers', when 'engraving in this country was at a low ebb, and those who practised the art in England were chiefly foreigners'.

24. *The Dictionary of National Biography, op.cit.*, xxi, 901, states that William Woollett was the son of Philip Woollett, who was a Maidstone flax-dresser. Shortly after his son's birth on 15th August, 1735, he won a share in a lottery prize and took the Turk's Head Inn at Maidstone, where 'young Woollett gave the first indication of his artistic talent by scratching the sign of the house on a pewter pot', following which he was sent to London, where he studied drawing in the St. Martin's Lane Academy. Russell, *op.cit.*, 392–3, relates how he was born in a house in East Lane, Maidstone, on 15th August, 1735, his family having originated from Holland and having been resident in the town for more than a century. His father, Philip, a foreman thread-maker, was one of twelve members of a small party or club, who met at the Ship public house on Gabriel's Hill. In 1753 they purchased a lottery ticket, and divided equally among them a prize of £5,000. Philip Woollett being asthmatic, and the dust from the flax being prejudicial to his health, 'this lucky acquisition enabled him to hire the Turk's Head public-house, in the Rose Yard, which was at that time frequented by many of the leading tradesmen and yeomen of the town and neighbourhood'. Maidstone's 'chief Trade or Business' during William Woollett's boyhood days was 'the making of Linnen *Thread*, and planting *Hops*', the former industry having been fostered by immigrant Walloon and Dutch settlers, W. Newton, *The History and Antiquities of Maidstone, The County-Town of Kent*, (1741), 100–2.

we arrived at the remains of Allington Castle,[25] which are more considerable than I expected to find them from the Subject given in Hearne's Antiquities which is merely the Gate shrouded by an old Inn and gives a very inadequate Idea of what appears on the otherside of the remains.[26]

25. The Gibraltar, Henry Pearce, was one of eight inns or taverns listed for the parish of Boxley in S. Bagshaw, *History, Gazetteer and Directory of the County of Kent*, i, (Sheffield, 1847), 295. Eight years previously it was pointed out that 'just below Sandling, and nearly opposite to Allington Castle, is pleasantly situated on the banks of the Medway, the Gibraltar Inn, a place of much resort during the summer', *Topography of Maidstone, and its Environs*, (Maidstone, 1839), 98. In the same source the Gibraltar is shown on a map standing on the opposite bank of the River Medway from Allington Castle, while an illustration of 'the ferry crossing from the Gibraltar public house to Allington Castle, drawn by W. Dampier in 1864', appears in H.R. Pratt Boorman, *Pictures of Maidstone the County Town of Kent*, (Maidstone, 1965), 167. John Evans, *The Juvenile Tourist: or, Excursions through Various Parts of the Island of Great-Britain*, (1804), 432, noted how from Allington

> 'on the opposite side of the Medway, in a romantic situation, stands Gibraltar house, an agreeable place of resort in the summer-time for the inhabitants of Maidstone. I once dined there with a respectable Book society, in the month of July. The rusticity of the scene was gratifying to the pensive mind. From the room in which we dined, the ruins of the dilapidated castle were visible; on each side the harmless sheep were cropping the herbage, and beneath us the Medway rolled along its silent waves'.

I am grateful to Miss P. Ward, Local History Librarian at Margate Public Library, for drawing my attention to this early reference to the Gibraltar as an inn or tavern, with a continuous history trading under that name from the 1800s at least to the 1860s.

26. The reference here is to Print XLIV of Allington Castle, the only Kentish print out of a total of 52 which appeared in *Antiquities of Great-Britain, Illustrated in Views of Monasteries, Castles, and Churches, now Existing: Engraved from Drawings made by Thomas Hearne*, Printed by James Phillips, in George-Yard, Lombard-Street, and Published by the Proprietors T. Hearne and W. Byrne, London, (1786). The text of this work was unpaginated, one side being printed in English and the other in French. Subscriptions for the work had been secured from the Dowager Countess of Aylesford and from Mr. William Woollett, 'the late Engraver to his Majesty'. As a single 'View of Allington Castle, Drawn by T. Hearne, Engrav'd by W. Byrne and T. Medland', Print XLIV was first published on 15th August, 1783, by W. Byrne and T. Hearne. The associated textual description was presented as follows:

> 'ALLINGTON CASTLE is situated close to the river Medway, upon its western bank, about a mile north of the town of Maidstone, and upon a spot where it is said there was a Fortress erected by the Saxons, called by them the Castle of the Medway, which was afterwards totally destroyed by the Danes. . . . The right honourable Robert Lord Romney is the present possessor.

> This Castle has long ceased to be the habitation of its owners, in consequence of which many parts of it having been neglected, are become ruinous, particularly some of the exterior Towers; yet the inside still affords a comfortable and convenient residence for the tenants of two adjoining farms. It was moated and defended by circular Towers on all sides, many of which remain. It is of a quadrangular form, divided by buildings within into two courts: and the arched gateway shewn in the Print, is the outermost entrance, through which is seen the Gate leading to the inner area of the Castle.

> The Drawing was made in the year 1777.'

Thomas Hearne (1744–1817) as a water-colour painter was awarded in 1763 a premium by the Society of Arts, two years before being apprenticed to William Woollett, the engraver, see above, n. 23, with whom he stayed for six years. In 1777, in conjunction with William Byrne, he commenced the most important under-

From hence we pursued our walk to Aylesford, a small Village,[27] where there is a venerable Bridge across the Medway, on which there is a Sun Dial of a handsome Construction which is a considerable Ornament to it, and adjoining is the Church most advantageously placed on a considerable Height rising abruptly from the river, the View from the Church Yard [being] very agreeable.[28]

In this parish at a short Distance is the Priory of which nothing remains but the Gate-way, behind which is an irregular built house which altho inhabited has a neglected Air. It belongs to Lord Aylesford who takes the name of his Title from this place.[29]

taking of his life, namely executing the 52 drawings in the *Antiquities of Great-Britain,* which occupied him until 1781. During his extensive tours throughout Great Britain which this work necessitated, 'Hearne studied nature with care, investing his topographical drawings with effects of light and atmosphere seldom attempted by previous draughtsmen in water-colour', and so 'he may thus be said to have done much to revive attention to Gothic architecture, and to have been one of the founders of the English school of water-colours'. Between 1781 and 1802 he exhibited drawings of landscape and antiquarian remains at the Royal Academy and he was elected a fellow of the Society of Antiquaries, Ed. Sir L. Stephen and Sir S. Lee, *The Dictionary of National Biography,* ix, (O.U.P., 1959–60), 338–9. F.W. Litchfield Stockdale, *Etchings from Original Drawings of Antiquities, in the County of Kent* (1810) was impressed by Allington Castle where

'some of the interior has been fitted up into two tenements; the rest is dismantled: but the remains are by no means so inconsiderable as Mr. Hasted, in his History of Kent, has represented them. The walls and towers are richly overgrown with ivy, and surrounded by a moat, which continues nearly in a perfect state. The entrance gateway, flanked by two circular towers, . . . is entire. . . . The rural beauties of the banks of the Medway, so often and so justly celebrated, are here eminently conspicuous . . . [The] eye is delighted with the ever varying scenery.'

Hasted, *op.cit.,* iv, 2nd Edn., (Canterbury, 1798), 448, had depicted Allington Castle as 'a venerable ruin, . . . now only used as a farm house', even though 'the remains are of considerable extent, and many of its external parts are in a good state of preservation'. Back in 1790 the Hon. John Byng had found Allington Castle 'as concealed a Spot and of as much Curiosity as can be found', yet 'it should be a survey of 3 Hours:– but all Tourists hurry', Bruyn Andrews, *op. cit.,* 154.

27. Aylesford, described by Litchfield Stockdale, *op.cit.,* as 'a small town upon the north east bank of the river Medway', had a population of 912 according to the first census of 1801, Minchin, *op.cit.,* 361.

28. Litchfield Stockdale, *op.cit.,* writing in 1810 noted how Aylesford's 'principal street [ran] nearly parallel with the stream of that river [the Medway]; over which there is a stone bridge of six pointed arches, built before the Reformation' and 'the ground rises suddenly between 80 and 100 feet, close at the back of the houses, on the eastern side of the street, and upon the eminence stands the CHURCH, an ancient edifice, dedicated to St. Peter. Hasted, *op.cit.,* iv, 2nd Edn., (Canterbury, 1798), 417–8, also observed how at the back of the village of Aylesford 'the ground rises suddenly very high, insomuch that the church and yard of it, close to which is the vicarage, stands higher even than the tops of the chimnies of the houses below it', while 'to that part of the parish on the opposite side of the Medway, there is a handsome stone bridge of six arches, built many years ago, and now supported by the public charge of the county'. Newman, *op.cit.,* 136, believes that the bridge dates probably from the fourteenth century, being the first of a series of medieval bridges over the Medway.

29. 'It [The Friary] is now the property of the Earl of Aylesford', Litchfield Stockdale, *op.cit.,* having been in 1798 'in the possession of the countess dowager of Aylesford, who makes it her chief residence in the country,' Hasted, *op.cit.,* iv, 2nd Edn., (Canterbury, 1798), 430. Hasted entered this property as 'THE PRIORY, now commonly called the Friars', *ibid.,* 427, 430. Contrary to the description of 1809 he felt that 'the greatest part of the ancient priory remains very fair, and by far the least demolished of any conventual

From hence ascending some lofty Chalk Hills on the right Bank of the river you arrive at an Antiquity called Kits Cotty House. Tradition says it was erected in memory of a Battle here fought between Hengist and Vortigern. It is a Cromlech and has more the Air of a Druidical Origin and what confirms it is that there are scattered about several other large Stones of the same kind to which the Country People attach something of a Magical Influence, for they believe that no person can count them twice alike and that from this Circumstance their number has never been ascertained exactly.[30]

We took our repast at a House commanding a most beautifull View. It is called the lower Bell but has as a sign Kits Cotty House[31] and returned in the evening by Boxley (where there are small remains of a Priory) and Pennenden Heath.

---

edifice in these parts', while 'the great gate from the road is yet entire', *ibid.*, 430. The earldom of Aylesford dated back to 1714, *ibid.*, 429. The Hon. John Byng in 1790 had enjoyed 'the beautiful walk towards the Friars where the Dowager Lady Aylesford Resides', Bruyn Andrews, *op.cit.*, 153.

30.   This particular antiquity attracted considerable notice and speculative comment. To Litchfield Stockdale, *op.cit.*, 'Kits Coty House, (or, as its etymology is usually explained, *Catigern's Coity House*, or house made of coits,)' represented in 1810 a 'celebrated British monument of antiquity', consisting of 'four immense stones, three of which are placed on end in the form of an H, and the fourth laid horizontally upon them', the tradition respecting this monument being 'that a fierce and bloody battle was fought on the spot, in the year 455, between Vortiger, the British King, and Horsa, the brother of Hengist, the Saxon general, in which the two chiefs, Horsa and Catigern, the brother of Vortiger, were both slain'. Hasted, *op.cit.*, iv, 2nd Edn., (Canterbury, 1798), 419–21, refers both to the battle and to 'that rude monument, somewhat in the manner of Stone Henge, though in minature, . . . composed of four large stones', in addition to 'numbers of large stones dispersed over the lands, some standing upright, and others thrown down by time', quite apart from another heap of stones nearer to Aylesford, 'some of which are partly upright, and others lying in a circle round them, in all to the number of nine or ten'. Here were monuments 'of such high antiquity as to be spoken of by our earliest historians as of things beyond tradition, the use of which could be even in their time but barely conjectured', *id.*, 421–2. Hasted was led to the belief that here were the burial places of Catigern, Horsa and other Saxons. More recent research distinguishes between Kit's Coty, as a 'megalithic burial chamber [consisting] of three uprights and a massive capstone', and Lower Kit's Coty as 'a jumbled and half-buried group of nineteen or twenty sarsen stones (the Countless Stones) which represent the remains of a megalithic tomb destroyed in the c 17', megalithic tombs being stone-built burial chambers of the New Stone Age, Newman, *op.cit.*, 137, 607.

31.   Kent Archives Office, Licensed Tradesmen Registers of Alehouse Keepers, Q/RLV 4/4, 1799–1813, lists William Finch at Kitts Cotty House, in 'A Register or Calendar of all the Recognizances' taken by the Justices of the Peace for the County of Kent, September, 1809, 'granting Licenses to Persons to keep Alehouses Inns Victualling Houses to sell Ale Beer or other Liquors by Retail'. More specifically in the Original Licensed Victuallers' Recognizances, Q/RLV2, on 4th September, 1809, William Finch of the parish of Aylesford 'victualler' and James Taylor 'of the same place Ffarmer', personally appeared before two Justices of the Peace paying the sumof £10 each, 'if the said William Finch shall make Default in the Condition underwritten', so that

'William Finch is this Day licensed to keep a common Alehouse or Victualing-house, for One Year, from the Twenty-ninth Day of *September* instant, at the Sign of the Kitts Cotty House in the Parish of Aylesford. . . . If the said William Finch shall keep and maintain good Order and Government, and shall suffer no Disorders or unlawful Games to be used in his said House, nor in any Out-house, Yard, Garden, or Backside thereunto belonging during the said Term, THEN this Recognizance to be void, or else to remain in full Force.'

PLATE VI

Aylesford in 1821 (*Excursions in the County of Kent,* 1822).

PLATE VII

Kit's Coty House in 1828 (W.H. Ireland, *A New and Complete History of the County of Kent,* 1828–30).

Wednesday,
6 September

We took a walk to see Leeds Castle which is about 4 Miles distant and belonged to the family of Lord Fairfax who took such an active part against an unfortunate King Chas. I. It has continued in the family till within these few years when the last of the name died. But I believe some person in America assumes for himself the extinct title of Lord Fairfax.[32]

It is at present enjoyed by General Martin[33] and two maiden Sisters, who mix but little with the world and, according to reports, these Ladies are not without considerable singularities of disposition, among which is their positive Aversion that any Strangers should be admitted to see the inhabited or uninhabited part of this magnificent and ancient Building which is situated in a Moat, or rather Lake, and is of so considerable a Size as almost to rival Warwick Castle. It has not only the Character of an old fortified Mansion but the inhabited part of it has an Air of the Grandeur of somewhat more modern Times. This part formerly communicated with the older part by a Draw Bridge under which the Water passing added much to the means of its Defence before the invention of Artillery.

The Entrance from the Park is also over another Bridge and thro a picturesque old Gate way which has the ancient Enrichments which are called Machicolations, from which you enter a spacious Court in which are many extensive Buildings now applied to the purpose of Stables and other domestic purposes, and is likewise filled with immense quantitys of Pigeons, Poultry and other domestic animals. The Park also abounds with Deer, Sheep, Cows and Rabbits by Thousands, so that the Owners of this noble place have the means of enjoying this disposition for Seclusion and have as little Occasion to mix with the World as possible.[34]

32. The Hon. John Byng and his travelling companion Col. Bertie were none too pleased at 'the Rudeness of Ld F. in refusing us admission to the castle' on Sunday, 19th September, 1790, after 'some few miles of good Road, in a charming country, brought us [from Maidstone] to Leeds Park, Ld Fairfax's', where 'the Col. was charmed with The Scenery; as everyone must be', and where 'for some time we sat us beneath a Grove at an hill Top, contemplating all these Beauties', Bruyn Andrews, *op.cit.*, 156. The reference here was to the seventh Lord Fairfax, who died in 1793, whereupon the castle and manor passed to an unmarried nephew, Dr. Fairfax, who was residing there in 1798, *ibid.*, 174, and Hasted, *op.cit.*, v, 2nd Edn., (Canterbury, 1798), 489–90. The suggestion that someone in America was assuming for himself the extinct title of Lord Fairfax derived perhaps from the decision of the unmarried sixth Lord Fairfax to quit England after having lived in Leeds Castle 'to reside on his great possessions in Virginia, where he continued to the time of his death', in 1782, Hasted, *op.cit.*, v, 2nd Edn., (Canterbury, 1798), 489.
33. Confirmed for 1810 by Cary, *op.cit.*, 14, and Cooke, *op.cit.*, 10.
34. For Hasted, *op.cit.*, v, 2nd Edn., (Canterbury, 1798), 490, Leeds Castle represented 'a magnificent pile of building, being built of stone, at several times, and of different architecture; not-with-standing which, it has altogether a fine effect, [being] pleasantly situated in the midst of a beautiful park, . . . incircled by a large moat of running water, in which there is great plenty of fish'. Litchfield Stockdale, *op.cit.*, in 1810 rated Leeds Castle as 'one of the most perfect baronial fortresses of the Gothic age, environed by a very broad moat', entered over 'a stone bridge of two arches, defended by a tower gateway, portcullised, in high preservation', added to which 'few of the parks in this county . . . surpass this of Leeds in the richness of its scenery, and fineness of its timber, [being] well stocked with deer: and the rabbits, owing to the needless care with which they are preserved by the present possessors, have multiplied to an astonishing number'. Planting and other estate improvements must have occurred over the previous twenty years, the Hon. John Byng

A fatal Accident happened here but a few days before. A young Man in a very respectable Situation had been dining with some friends at . . . [the village]. They had appointed him Chairman and it is supposed that in his exertions to promote Conviviality He found himself heated and unfortunately left the Company with intention to refresh himself by bathing in this extensive Water. He was an excellent Swimmer but is said to have been sitting under the Walls, having swam across, by a person who, thinking He appeared exhausted, hallowed to him not to come back and he would fetch the Boat for which purpose He was gone when this unfortunate Youth either not comprehending his Intentions or being confident in his own powers attempted to return but was drowned.[35]

We took a small repast in the village of Leeds and returned by a footpath thro a beautifull Succession of Hop Gardens, fields and Meadows and last thro Lord Romney's Park.[36] Part of our time these two days was employed in entering the little Parish Churches in search of specimens of Antiquity or Brass

---

having confronted in 1790 a stream 'capable of the greatest Improvement: The Park likewise wants much planting', with the castle standing 'safely, and awfully in a large Pool of Water'. However, having 'for its owners, during a course of years, a continuation of aged men, it has neither been Improved, nor demolish'd, but were a man of Taste and Fortune master, who would (keeping up the Antique) Repair, and refurnish the old Castle; Deepen and Clean out The Pool, (now sadly choaked up by Weeds), Plant the Hills, Enlarge the water in The Valley; It would be one of the first and most curious Places in this Kingdom', Bruyn Andrews, *op.cit.*, 156.

35. Certainly a fatal swimming accident had occurred not quite in the manner described, however, nor a few days before, but over a month earlier on Monday, 31st July, 1809, which subsequently attracted widespread press publicity, both locally and nationally. What had been a 'MELANCHOLY ACCIDENT' was first reported by *The Maidstone Journal and Kentish Advertiser*, on Tuesday, 1st August, 1809, 4c, followed a few days later by an almost identical report in *The Kentish Gazette*, 4th August, 1809, 4c. Apparently, according to the first report:

> 'Yesterday afternoon, during a Match of Cricket, in Leeds Park, Mr. George Edmeads, stationer, of London, went to bathe in the Moat, and after swimming across the widest part, returned, within a short distance of the shore, when he got entangled among the weeds, and unfortunately sunk. — His friends, whom he accompanied, were engaged in the game, at a distance, and no one was present except some boys whom he called to in his perilous situation. A boat was instantly sent off to the spot, and his body, after having been but a short time under water, was taken out, when every means that could be devised was made use of to restore animation, without effect, to the great regret of his numerous Relations and Friends in this Town.'

For 1808 Holden, *op.cit.*, 206, lists Edmeads and Pine, paper manufacturers, Ivey mill, Maidstone, suggesting thereby to whom he was related in that town. In its August list of 'Obituary, with Anecdotes, of remarkable Persons', *The Gentleman's Magazine*, lxxix, Part II, (1809), 787, while incorrectly locating the drowning in the Medway, at Maidstone, nevertheless noted that Mr. George Edmead 'had not exceeded his 23rd year', was a stationer in Leadenhall Street, 'was on a visit to his relatives and friends [and] had been playing at cricket, . . . when, being heated, it is supposed that on plunging into the water he became suddenly chilled, and sunk', following which 'his body was taken out almost immediately, and bled freely, but all means to restore animation proved ineffectual'.

36. Being listed in 1810 by Carey, *op.cit.*, 14, as 'The Mote, an elegant Mansion of the Earl of Romney', having also been noted back in 1790 by the Hon. John Byng as 'The Mote, the Seat of Ld Romney, a house and place of very habitable Description', Bruyn Andrews, *op.cit.*, 156.

Leeds Castle (E.W. Brayley, *The Beauties of England and Wales*, Volume VIII: *Kent*, 1808).

Plates or Monuments. Of these last, whenever they could be found, one of our party indulged his fondness for Subjects of that kind by rubbing off impressions.

Thursday, 7 September It had been my intention to have gone from Maidstone to Canterbury if possible without getting on the road from London to the latter place but no means presenting itself, except I went alone in a Post Chaise, I mounted a Vehicle which goes twice a day from Maidstone to Rochester 8 miles,[37] and my inducement to relinquish my first intention was that altho I had frequently passed thro had never stopped to see either its Cathedral or the works etc. at Chatham. The Cathedral is on but a small Scale and with respect to its Exterior the West front constitutes its chief Beauty. On the square tower in the Centre they have placed a squat wooden spire covered with lead, [of] which nothing can . . . be conceived more ugly. Within the Nave is what is commonly called Saxon, that is the Arches are round, but in the Choir and two Transepts the Arches and

37. *Paterson's British Itinerary Being A new and accurate Delineation and Description of the Direct and Principal Cross Roads of Great Britain*, i, 2nd Edn., (1807), 9–10, shows a principal cross road Rochester to Maidstone nine miles, or London to Maidstone and Cranbrook by Rochester.

PLATE IX

Rochester Cathedral in 1810 (Original print published January 1810, by John Buckler).

PLATE X

Monument in the Nave of Rochester Cathedral erected to the memory of the Rt. Hon. John, Lord Henniker in 1806 (By kind permission of the Dean and Chapter).

windows are pointed or Gothic.[38] At the Altar is a middling picture by West[39] and the Choir in performing the Afternoon Service consisted of One Priest, One Vicar Choral and eight Boys, but the Diocese I was informed is not by any

38. It was the opinion of one historian of Rochester Cathedral that 'in different parts of the fabric specimens can be seen of almost all the noteworty variations of style that appeared in English ecclesiastical architecture from the Early Norman to the Perpendicular period', G.H. Palmer, *The Cathedral Church of Rochester A Description of Its Fabric and a Brief History of the Episcopal See*, (1897), 63. While it was well known prior to 1809 that the Cathedral had Saxon origins dating back to 604, as mentioned for instance by Hasted, *op.cit.*, iv, 2nd Edn., (Canterbury, 1798), 86, its Saxon foundations were not excavated until the 1880's, Palmer, *op.cit.*, 7, or Newman, *op.cit.*,453–4. Considered both historically and architecturally the author was correct in drawing attention to a small cathedral, which possessed an imposing west front, having a central tower surmounted by a timber and lead spire and containing internal renewels or embellishments which were Gothic. However, most of the building dated from the twelfth century, including the west front and the nave, with the latter being Norman not Saxon, Palmer, *op.cit.*, 8–10, 15–16, 28–30, 38–40, 65 and 73; F. Underhill, *The Story of Rochester Cathedral*, (n.d.), 9, 10, 13 and 18–19; A.G.G.C. Pentreath, *The Pictorial History of Rochester Cathedral*, (1970), 6–7, 10, 12, and 15; and Newman, *op.cit.*, 453–62.

39. In 1788 a large oil painting by the historical painter Benjamin West (1738–1820) depicting 'The Angels appear[ing] to the Shepherds' was presented anonymously and inserted in place of the central panel of the altar-piece, Palmer, *op.cit.*, 94–5, and W.H. St. John Hope, *The Architectural History of the Cathedral Church and Monastery of St. Andrew at Rochester*, (1900), 114. Palmer, *op.cit.*, 95, claims that the name of the donor was revealed after his death as J. Wilcocks Esq., a son of Joseph Wilcocks, who was Bishop of Rochester from 1731 to 1756, Hasted, *op.cit.*, iv, 2nd Edn. (Canterbury, 1798), 148–9, who, according to Hasted, 'though the revenues of this bishopric were so small, yet he declined any higher promotion, though he was offered the archbishopric of York, frequently using the expression of his predecessor, bishop Fisher: *This church is my wife, and I will not part with her because she is poor'*, *ibid.*, 149. Before being appointed historical painter to the king in 1772, the 'Death of Wolfe' was exhibited at the Royal Academy in 1771 as 'the most successful and the best of all West's pictures', following which William Woollett's plate of this picture enjoyed 'the largest sale of any modern engraving', as noted above, n. 23, Stephen and Lee, *op.cit.*, xx, 1236–7. Three years later in 1774 West exhibited 'The Angels appear[ing] to the Shepherds' for the altar of a cathedral, proceeding thereafter to paint altar-pieces for St. Stephen's Walbrook, Trinity College Chapel, Cambridge, Greenwich Hospital Chapel, and other churches, thereby coming to be regarded as 'the greatest historical painter of the English school', *ibid.*, 1237. Regarded as 'the founder of historical painting in England', he was extremely industrious, producing over 400 works, including 64 pictures and other designs for George III between 1768 and 1801, and such was his prestige that he was appointed surveyor of the royal pictures in 1790 and in 1792, at the death of Sir Joshua Reynolds, he was elected president of the Royal Academy, a position which he occupied until his death on 11th March, 1820, whereupon 'his body lay in state at the Royal Academy, and was buried with great honour in St. Paul's Cathedral', *ibid.*, 1236–8. Palmer, *op.cit.*, 94–5, was incorrect in his reference to 'Sir' Benjamin West since he did not accept from the king an offer of knighthood, Stephen and Lee, *op.cit.*, 1237. To describe 'The Angels appear[ing] to the Shepherds' as 'a middling picture' was somewhat more generous than some subsequent assessments. To Canon Jelf, who was rector of St. Mary's church, Chatham, where it was hanging over the Communion Table in 1886 'he did not think it was suitable for the altar, [for] to him it was a most unpleasant picture, but of course it had its interest to some'; perhaps it would fetch £150, if it was sold, *The Rochester and Chatham Journal and Mid-Kent Advertiser*, 8th May, 1886, 2e. Palmer, *op.cit.*, 95, argued that 'it cannot be called a great work, and we can scarcely wonder that it was thought by many unworthy of its high place in the cathedral'. Beginning in 1825 Rochester Cathedral underwent a major restoration under the care of Mr. L.N. Cottingham, which involved the removal of the old Corinthian altar-piece, whereupon on 30th November, 1826, the Dean and Chapter decided to lend West's painting to St. Mary's Church, Chatham, 'on the understanding that when it was not required for the church the picture should be returned to them'. During 1886 Canon Jelf persuaded the Dean and Chapter 'to waive any right they might have to the picture', in the hope of selling it to raise money towards the General Restoration Fund, Palmer, *op.cit.*, 32, 95, and *The Rochester and Chatham*

means capable of supporting a good Establishment.[40]

This Cathedral contains no monument worth notice except one lately erected to the memory of Lord Henniker which consists of figures in Relievo nearly as large as Life, by Bacon Jun. but in its execution or Conception is nothing very extraordinary.[41]

I walked to Chatham by the upper road, which is at the back of the Town,[42] on the south side of which has been lately raised a considerable Fortification

---

Journal and Mid-Kent Advertiser, 8th May, 1886, 2e, and 24th July, 1886, 2g. As there is no trace of the painting today it was presumably sold, but when, how and to whom is not known, while according to Palmer, *op.cit.*, 95, in 1897 and in St. Mary's Church, Chatham, 'the picture is still to be seen hanging over the vestry door'.

40. It was, of course, a misconception to suppose that financing the cathedral establishment was a diocesan function. Then, as today, the diocese accepted no responsibility for supporting the cathedral foundation, which rested wholly on the Dean and Chapter, as an entirely independent and ecclesiastical corporate body. I am grateful to the present Vice-Dean and Librarian, Canon P.A. Welsby, for drawing my attention to this fact.

41. Noted by Newman, *op.cit.*, 466, as 'John Lord Henniker, [by] *J. Bacon Jun.*, 1806, and a pompous affair . . . of marble', while in 1897 Palmer, *op.cit.*, 76, argued that 'the nave and main transept possess none [monuments] that are very old or very remarkable'; however, among those deserving mention 'is the monument of John, Lord Henniker, who died in 1803', lying 'against the south wall, in the fourth bay from the west, . . . erected by J. Bacon, jun., in 1806, and is signed with his name', as

'The Remains of

The Right-Honourable JOHN, LORD HENNIKER, of an ancient Family in this County, are placed here by his Desire, in the same Vault with those of his beloved wife Dame ANN HENNIKER.

He succeeded to the Dignity of BARONET, by the original Patent, on the Decease of Sir JOHN MAJOR Bart. in February, 1781;
and was created by the BEST OF SOVEREIGNS, Baron HENNIKER, of STRATFORD-UPON-SLANEY, in the Kingdom of IRELAND, in July, 1800.

Humble to his GOD, loyal to his KING, kind to his Relatives, benevolent to All, at the Age of Seventy-nine, in stedfast Hope of Immortality, he completed a Life of unshaken Integrity, the 18. Day of April, 1803.

Piety was in him blessed with Prosperity,
Virtue crowned by Honour.

This Monument was erected to his Memory by his two surviving and affectionate Sons.

JOHN HENNIKER MAJOR, Lord HENNIKER, and the Honourable GENERAL BRYDGES TRECOTHICK HENNIKER.

J. Bacon, junior, Sculptor,
London, 1806.'

Here was a monument whose symbolism was Christian, incorporating honour, benevolence, a medallion of the deceased, a coronet, an unfolded patent of peerage and 'his coat of arms are seen against the base', Palmer, *op.cit.*, 76 and Newman, *op.cit.*, 466. The reference to 'figures in Relievo nearly as large as life', relate to 'a girl, holding a nest with a pelican in her piety, [leaning] on a sarcophagus, . . . about to be wreathed with olive by a substantial crowned female', Newman, *op.cit.*, 466.

42. Along what was 'an early example of a by-pass', 'The New Road' at the back of Chatham, from what is today Star Hill to Chatham Hill, 'over the chalk hill at about a quarter of a mile distance' from Chatham itself,

and is called Fort Pitt. It has Casemates, Bomb Proof and in the Centre a Martello Tower intended to prevent any Attack the Enemy might make from the South.[43]

The Dock[44] could not be seen by me as a Stranger without an order from a Commissioner[45] but I viewed the Barracks. Those for the Artillery are beautifull and the others very extensive.[46] During the whole of this day parties of Horse Artillery were returning from the Expedition[47] and the men seemed to have gained nothing in the appearance of their Cloathing but the poor Horses many of them were in a sad Condition. In the evening by a Return Chaise went to Sittingbourne.

---

completed in 1770 and resulting from a local paving and Improvement Act passed in 1769, viz: 9 Geo III c. 32, or 'An Act for paving, cleansing, lighting and watching, the High Streets and Lanes, in the Parish of *Saint Nicholas*, within the City of *Rochester*, and Parish of *Strood*, in the County of *Kent*; and for making a Road through *Star Lane*, across certain Fields adjoining thereto, to *Chatham Hill*, in the said County', *The History and Antiquities of Rochester And its Environs*, (Rochester, 1772), 259–60; Hasted, *op.cit.*, iv, 2nd Edn., (Canterbury, 1798), 58, 193; F.F. Smith, *A History of Rochester*, (1928), 424–7; and R. Marsh, *Rochester The Evolution of the City and Its Government*, (Rochester, 1974), 48–9, 51. In 1808 it was noted that 'since this has been executed, the old road, which lay through the town of Chatham, has been entirely deserted by travellers', E.W. Brayley, *The Beauties of England and Wales; or, Original Delineations, Topographical, Historical, and Descriptive, of Each County*, VIII: *Kent*, (1808), 665.

43. Partly in Rochester and partly in Chatham, Fort Pitt was erected in 1803, being originally intended as a military hospital, Smith, *op.cit.*, 484, described in 1847 as 'a strong fortress situated on the summit of the rising ground contiguous to the new road on the south', S. Bagshaw, *History, Gazetteer, and Directory of the County of Kent*, i, (Sheffield, 1847), 100.

44. According to Cooke, *op.cit.*, 197, 'the principal object of attention in Chatham is the Dock-yard'.

45. Contrary to the experience of Mr. and Mrs. Mount and their party on a tour of Kent in 1759, when despite 'the Seven Years War the writer and his friends could freely visit the dockyards at Chatham', so that on Tuesday, 15th May, 'went to Chatham about two Miles, Saw the Dock and yards, . . . [and] Was on Board the Valliant a Man of Warr then building, Had many things explained to Us in the Yards by Mr. Hughes, known to Mr. Mount', Ed. F. Hull, 'A Tour into Kent, 1759', *Arch. Cant.*, lxix (1955), 171, 173, or in Roake and Whyman, *op.cit.*, 185, 187. Subsequently Dockyard security was tightened up, for in 1790 the Hon. John Byng on Saturday, 25th September, obtained authorization 'at the Dockyard Gate', from where 'my name being ask'd and Permission Granted, I made the full survey of all the Cable Houses, Anchorage, Timber Yards, etc.', Bruyn Andrews, *op.cit.*, 170.

46. Chatham possessed extensive barracks by this time.

'Within this area, besides the naval establishments, are included the *Upper* and *Lower Barracks*, which have been built for the garrison . . . The Lower Barracks are spacious and uniform buildings of brick, inclosing a large quadrangular area. The Upper Barracks, which stand near Brompton, are also of brick, and extremely spacious and convenient. They rise one above the other on the acclivity of the hill, and having inclosed courts, occupy . . . a considerable tract of ground. The garrison consists of five companies of soldiers and a battalion of artillery.'

Brayley, *op.cit.*, 670.

47. A reference to the 1809 Expedition to Walcheren and elsewhere in the Scheldt in Holland and the Low Countries, a full account of which appears in The Hon. J.W. Fortescue, *A History of the British Army*, vii, (1912), chapters XXV and XXVI, 45–96, the failure of which, having involved 40,000 men, was reported from 'South Beveland, August 26' in a scathing criticism by *The Times*, 8th September, 1809, 2c.; also see below, n. 52. I am grateful to Professor N.C. Phillips and to Dr. G.M. Ditchfield for suggesting sources of information relating to this expedition.

Friday,
8 September
This was intended merely as a resting place in preference to Rochester, which is noisy in the extreme[48] and for which I entertained an unfavourable Prejudice. The Coaches not passing thro to Canterbury till one a clock, I walked to Milton which lies at about a mile distance on the left of the road from London. It is not a large Town but has the advantage of an Arm of the Medway which gives it a degree of Activity They seemed to be Employed in Shipping Bark and in the Commerce of Coke,[49] which is employed in the drying of Hops, the Produce of which is not favourable this Season. Last year the Duty on them amounted to Two hundred and fifty thousand Pounds and this year it is thought it will not amount to a fifth part.[50] There are also Paper and Corn Mills here and in the part of the River called the Swale are beds of Oysters so

48. As noted by Hasted, *op.cit.*, iv, 2nd Ed., (Canterbury, 1798), 58, for 'the high road from London to Dover leads through the High street, which has several large inns in it, for the accommodation of passengers, the traffic of the road here being extraordinary great'.

49. Milton-next-Sittingbourne had by 1811 a population of 1,746 compared to 1,622 in 1801, Minchin, *op.cit.*, 364, described as being 'principally situated on the acclivity of a hill, about half a mile from the high road, sloping down to a small creek, which falls into the Swale', where 'the streets are narrow, and badly paved', and 'the inhabitants are chiefly employed in maritime pursuits, or engaged in the oyster, and other fisheries', having 322 houses in 1808, according to Brayley, *op.cit.*, 699, 701. Potts, *op.cit.*, reckoned on there being only 259 houses in 1810; otherwise,

> '*Milton* . . . is situated on a small creek, running into the Swale. It consists of a number of little streets, intersecting each other at right angles, which are both paved and lighted. The houses are tolerably built . . . Its trade consists of a little coasting, and its oyster fishery . . . The imports are chiefly coals and groceries; the exports are corn and some fruit.'

Milton possessed four wharfs in 1808, from where 'considerable quantities of corn, and other produce of the neighbouring country, are annually shipped here for the London markets, goods of every kind being freighted in return', Brayley, *op.cit.*, 702. The references to 'other produce' and to 'Shipping Bark' were related to the fact that

> 'in the western part of this Parish are several hundred acres of coppice-wood, which adjoin to a much larger tract of the like sort, extending southward for the space of five miles. These woods, especially those in and near this Parish, are noted for the great plentry of *Chestnut* stubs interspersed promiscuously throughout them, and which, from the quick and straight growth of this kind of wood, is very valuable. These are so numerous as to occasion the woods to be usually called chestnut woods',

ibid., 702.

50. This information may have been derived from the 'Monthly (Agricultural) Report for August', which appeared in *The Times*, 1st September, 1809, 3c, pointing out that 'the Hop Plantations in Kent and Sussex, though cleansed by the heavy rains, are not expected to grow more than half a crop; the year's duty is not laid at more than £55,000'; also word for word in *The Maidstone Journal and Kentish Advertiser*, 5th September, 1809, 3c. A wet summer in that year produced a poor and deficient harvest, which was worse than in 1808, due to heavy rains beginning early in July and continuing till October, T.H. Baker, *Records of the Seasons, Prices of Agricultural Produce and Phenomena Observed in The British Isles*, (1883), 242–3; E.L. Jones, *Seasons and Prices: The Role of the Weather in English Agricultural History*, (1964), 158; J.M. Stratton and J. Houghton Brown, *Agricultural Records A.D. 220–1977*, Ed. R. Whitlock, 2nd Edn., (1978), 95. From Southwark early in October it was reported that 'the supply of New Hops in our Market comes very sparing — Prices in consequence higher', *The Maidstone Journal and Kentish Advertiser*, 3rd October, 1809, 4c.

esteemed by London Epicures under the name of native Miltons.[51]

About twelve a party of Hussars belonged to the 2. Legion of German Cavalry entered the place returning from the Expedition on their way to Ipswich, the Men well in appearance but the Horses had some of them suffered and it was insinuated that so long an immediate march as from Deal to Ipswich without a little time to recover themselves after the Voyage was not well judged. Before they could be billetted off a Deluge of Rain soaked them, and a part of them had to go forward in it to Milton and even to Rainham five Miles off.[52]

This weather made it impossible for me to proceed on the outside and I was therefore constrained to terminate my Pilgrimage to Canterbury in a manner I should not have chosen.

I was set down at the Kings Head,[53] a very good Inn, and amused myself till dusk in reconnoiting the Cathedral and in obtaining a general Idea of the Ichnography [Topography] of the City.[54]

Saturday, 9 September   I first visited the Castle which I had perceived on entering the Town by West Gate. It lays on the South, is a square remains not extensive when compared with Rochester, has nothing in its exterior picturesque[55] and the Area within is

51. 'For which it has been long celebrated', according to Potts, *op.cit.*, writing in 1810; while David Macpherson in his 'Commercial and Manufactural Gazetteer of the United Kingdom' included Milton for furnishing 'a great part of the oysters consumed in London, those of this place being noted for their goodness', *Annals of Commerce, Manufactures, Fisheries, and Navigation,* iv, (1805). Brayley, *op.cit.*, 701, maintained that Milton's oyster fishery provided 'the principal source of employment, . . . and has done so for many centuries, . . . [there being] a company of Free Dredgers, who are governed by their own particular rules, or bye-laws', added to which 'the oysters produced from the grounds within the limits of the Fishery are in great request, under the name of *Native Miltons*: their flavour is particularly rich'.

52. *The Maidstone Journal and Kentish Advertiser*, 5th September, 1809, 4c, reported that 'part of the troops from South Beveland have arrived and been debarked at Ramsgate; a part of which consist of the German Legion Cavalry, who were landed on Saturday, and marched to Canterbury immediately; the men and horses have a very healthy appearance. The sick have been landed at Yarmouth'. A week later it was noted that 'the 2d Light Cavalry of the German Legion, which had been landed at Ramsgate [on Saturday, 2nd September], has marched in two divisions from Canterbury, for the depot of the regiment at Ipswich', *ibid.*, 12th September, 1809, 4d. Fortescue, *op.cit.*, 81 refers to the involvement of the 'Second Hussars of the German Legion' in the 1809 Expedition who on 21st August had been 'cantoned towards the eastern end of South Beveland'. Subsequent evacuation from South Beveland was hastened and complicated by 'miasmatic fever' which 'finally decided the fate of the campaign', *ibid.*, 81, 87 ff., it being noted on 26th August how 'the army . . . begin to get very sickly', *The Times*, 8th September, 1809, 2c, *op.cit.*

53. Listed by Holden, *op.cit.*, 52, as 'Hacker James, King's Head Inn, High st.'. Also listed was 'Hacker James, builder, St. John's la.', *ibid.*, 52. The King's Head was listed for 1810 alongside two other Canterbury inns, the Fountain and the Red Lion (see below, n. 80) in Cary, *op.cit.*, 7.

54. Which he might well have done with the help of a town map of Canterbury, such as that 'Drawn and Engraved under the direction of E.W. Brayley', or more specifically 'Engraved by J. Roper, from a Drawing by G. Cole to accompany the Beauties of England and Wales', which was first published in London 'for the Proprietors, by Vernor, Hood & Sharpe, Poultry, Decr. 1st 1806'. Subsequently they included it in *The British Atlas; Comprising a Complete Set of County Maps, of England and Wales; . . . and Plans of Cities and Principal Towns,* (1810).

55. Perhaps he had access to *The Canterbury Guide; or, Travellers Pocket Companion,* By a Late Inhabitant, 5th Ed., (Canterbury, 1809), price 2s. 6d., printed and sold by Cowtan and Colegate, booksellers in Canterbury,

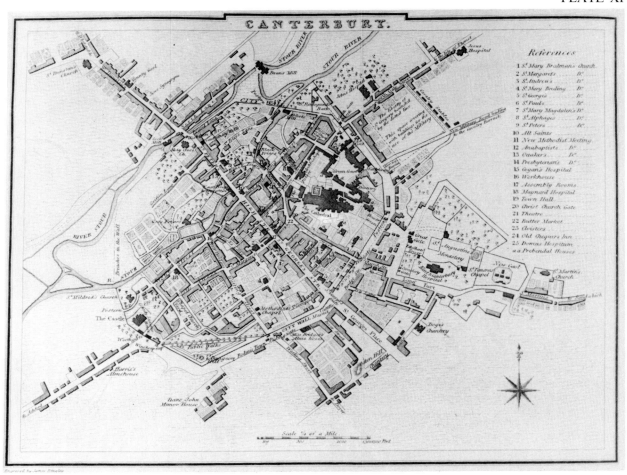

Map of Canterbury, published 1st April, 1822, which differs only marginally from the map of 1806 referred to in note 54 (*Excursions in the County of Kent,* 1822).

as a 'little Treatise . . . to accommodate the curious traveller with a true and concise description of whatever is worth his observation in and about Canterbury; . . . in a size neither to fatigue his memory nor incumber his pocket'. Of the castle this source noted that

> 'the remains of it at present are only the outward quadrangular walls, seemingly not near their former height, built with rubble stones, . . . of an extraordinary thickness . . . The Castle is in every respect similar to that at Rochester; it is eighty-eight feet long, and eighty wide; the walls are in general eleven feet thick', *ibid.,* 29−30.

At that time, according to Litchfield Stockdale, *op. cit*, 'little is known besides what may be collected from its appearance'; however, 'the *Keep* . . . much resembles those at Dover [or] Rochester', but 'it is presumed to have lost nearly half its height, being at present quite a ruin, and has a very heavy and ragged appearance'.

PLATE XII

St. Mildred's Church, Canterbury, in 1807 (E.W. Brayley, *The Beauties of England and Wales*, Volume VIII: *Kent*, 1808).

PLATE XIII

Dane John Hill, dedicated to Alderman Simmons (W?H? Ireland, *A New and Complete History of the County of Kent*, 1828–30).

occupied by paltry sheds used as warehouses by a Bricklayer for Lime, Bricks, etc.[56]

Near the Castle in a small Church called St. Mildreds is a small monument by Bacon Sen. It consists of a female figure in Relievo and an Urn by her side on which, within a circle of flowers, are the Initials of the person recorded to which She points. His name was Jackson.[57] At [the] bottom is a long fulsome

56. Completed as a fortification in 1174 the castle had decayed under private ownership since 1597, with the upper storey being demolished in 1817, leaving the wall passage open to the sky, S. Cantacuzino, etc., *Canterbury*, in the City Buildings Series, (1970), 10–11. According to *The Canterbury Guide, op.cit.*, 28, 'it had a bayle or yard, surrounded by a wall and ditch, both of which remained on the east side of it till very lately; but in 1792 the most considerable parts of the boundary wall were demolished, these outworks [being] not so well built as the tower itself, and were become rotten, and mouldered even to rubbish, whereas those of the castle remain firm, and solid'. By 1809 the ditch was 'mostly filled up, the only part now visible being that which was the city ditch, on the south side', *ibid.*, 28. It is well known that until 1928 the keep was used as a coal store, Cantacuzino, etc., *op.cit.*, 11, but who in 1809 had erected 'paltry sheds' for storing lime, bricks, etc? Holden, *op.cit.*, 51–4, listed two brickmakers and limeburners in 1808, Richard Petman in Best Lane and Joseph Simmonds at Cathedral Church Yard, while Mark Tiddeman was a bricklayer and plasterer in Longport. In addition there were two builders, operating from Castle Street, John Rumney and Alexander Spratt, jun. It was certainly polite not to record any names, even if they were known to a cursory traveller.

57. Namely William Jackson, the only son of Alderman John Jackson, who had died in the city in his 32nd year, following a short illness on 17th April, 1789, and whose death and qualities of character were reported at some length in *The Kentish Gazette*, 17th–21st April, 1789, 4c, and in *The Gentleman's Magazine*, lix, Part I, (1789), 377–8, under 'Obituary of considerable Persons; with Biographical Anecdotes'. *The Kentish Gazette* announced his death as follows:

'On Friday last died at the age of 32, after a short but severe illness, William Jackson, Esq., of this city. He met his fate with a manly fortitude and christian resignation. The sincerity of his friendship, the mildness of his disposition, his universal benevolence, and the many happy qualities which so particularly distinguished this excellent young man, have rendered him an irreparable loss to a very numerous and respectable acquaintance. On his grave the poor may shed many a tear, for they have lost a friend indeed. But what must be the heartfelt woe of his aged and much respected parents on the early death of their only son, the hopes of all their future happiness; their affection could only be equalled by his duty, who never gave them pain but when he died.

　　　"Go! fair example of untainted
　　　　　youth,

　　　Of modest wisdom, and pacific
　　　　　truth:

[etc]".'

In the words of *The Gentleman's Magazine*,

'he was of a disposition so amiable, that he was universally beloved, . . . a real friend to the afflicted . . . He read much, and well-chosen Authors; his studies were rewarded by a most retentive memory . . . There have been prodigies of Science, of Learning, of abilities which have blazed in every age, perhaps to shew the utmost extent of human faculties, but never was exhibited in domestic life a more excellent pattern: where, as a son we cannot sufficiently praise his unremitting attention to the infirmities of aged parents . . . [His] loss in early bloom is deplored by a whole mourning city; one universal face of woe pervades the neighbourhood: the rich, the poor, the old, the young, . . . all have some tale of his philanthropy to tell, some favours from his munificance or friendship [etc]'.

Following his death his parents erected a wall monument in his memory by Bacon, 'with his usual female

Panegyrick by which it should seem he was more than perfection.[58] Near the Castle, a little to the East, is a large space adjoining to the Walls which is called Dane John Fields, probably a Corruption of Dungeon fields, as there is a

leaning on an urn', having 'elegantly elongated proportions . . . to give room for the extensive catalogue of Mr. Jackson's virtues', J. Newman, *The Buildings of England: North East and East Kent*, (1969), 234–5.

58. Bearing in mind the previous footnote, this 'long fulsome Panegyrick, reads as follows.

'This Monument is erected by his afflicted Parents
To the Memory of their only Son.
    WILLIAM JACKSON Esq.[re]
Of this City, who died April the 17th 1789, aged 31 years.
Endowed with a clear apprehention, on accurate discernment
And with a memory uncommonly tenacious;
And having enriched the gifts of nature by continued application;
He was distinguished as a polite Scholar
        And a judicious Critic.
        By an exemplary uniformity of Conduct,
        He deserved and possessed the Character
Of a good man, a good Citizen and a good Christian:
Being, both in principle and practice, eminently just and sincere;
A most affectionate and dutiful Son;
A warm, steady and disinterested Friend;
A Promoter of every Useful Work,
And of every pious and humane institution:
A Patron of indigent merit;
An Adviser and Comforter of the distressed;
Benevolent in heart, and Charitable in practice;
To the Full extent of that affluence
With which Providence had blessed him;
A punctual, conscientious and unaffected Performer
        Of his religious duties.
And while, by the discharge of the many beneficent offices,
Which these various characters imposed upon him,
He commanded universal respect;
By the sweetness of his temper, the urbanity of his manners,
And the unclouded serenity of his mind,
The hearts and affections of all who knew him well
Were so imperceptibly engaged,
That he became the peculiar object of their love and veneration
And the constant theme of their praise,
The *general favourite* and the *general friend*
Of the society in which he lived.
Having passed, alas! a short life,
In the daily exercise of virtue;
He was translated, not prematurely, being "rich in good works",
To the full enjoyment, as we humbly believe, of that heavenly bliss,
To which Faith had taught him to aspire:
To which Hope had raised his dying thought;
And which his Charity, thro' the merits of his Redeemer,
Had rendered him worthy to obtain.

J.J./S.J.'

considerable Mount which has the Appearance of having been the Keep in which there was possibly a Dungeon. The Fields might probably be a place of Exercise for Troops on what is now called the Parade. This place had fallen into a state of great Neglect which induced W. Simmons[59] of this Town in the year 1790, at his own Expense of near £1500, to lay it out in Gravel Walks planted with Trees, to form a spiral Ascent to the Mount guarded by Quickset Hedges, and to make a great number of Seats within the Towers on the Ramparts and elsewhere, much to the Accommodation of his fellow Citizens and greatly adding to the Embellishments of the City. In 1802 the Corporation voted that £60 per Annum for ever should be applyed out of their funds for keeping these improvements in repair, and in 1803 an Obelisk was raised by Voluntary Subscription and placed on the summit of the Mount and under it on Tablets of Marble is inscribed that it was done to perpetuate the memory of this generous Transaction and as a mark of gratitude for his other publick Services.[60] I must here remark that in few of the fortified Towns in this County which have been dismantled the Walls are so entire as in Canterbury.

The approach to the Cathedral is thro a very elegant Gate of florid Gothic, apparently of the time of Henry VII and altho it has suffered by the hands of Barbarians and by the Corrosion of Time remains sufficiently entire by the assistance of a little Imagination to give a most favourable Idea of its pristine

59.   The reference here should really have been to Alderman James Simmons, from whom on Thursday, 23rd September, 1790, the Hon. John Byng 'borrowed money and Books', having 'walk'd to Mr. S[immons] (our Distributor of Stamps) a Stationer, and Mr. Somebody here', Bruyn Andrews, *op.cit.*, 164. It was James Simmons who edited and printed the first issue of *The Kentish Gazette*, 25th–28th May, 1768. In addition to being the official Distributor of Stamps for East Kent, Alderman James Simmons in partnership with Kirkby continued in 1790 to publish *The Kentish Gazette,* from their office in George Street, Canterbury, where stationery, books, patent medicines, etc. were sold, Bruyn Andrews, *op.cit.*, 176. Between 1778 and 1799 the First Edition of Edward Hasted's *History and Topographical Survey of the County of Kent* was published in four large folio one volume instalments by the Canterbury printers, Simmons and Kirkby. By 1790 James Simmons was also a banker and was playing a very active part in the municipal life of the city, Bruyn Andrews, *op.cit.*, 176. In 1804 James Simmons printed The Fifth Edition, with Additions of *A Walk in and about the City of Canterbury*, by W. Gostling, price 3s. 6d., in a convenient paperback size for visitors to the city. Alderman Simmons died on 22nd January, 1807.

60.   In 1810 Litchfield Stockdale, *op.cit.*, described 'DUNGEON or DANE JOHN HILL' as forming 'a high, artificial circular mount within the walls of the city', which

'within these few years . . . has been considerably improved, and ornamented, by having walks cut round its sides, and trees planted beside them in regular order, chiefly at the expense of the late alderman Simmons, who was for many years a respectable bookseller and printer in this city; and to whose memory the inhabitants erected by subscription, in 1803, a neat stone pillar on the summit of the mount. The prospect of the city, the surrounding villages, and gently rising hills in the distance, as seen from this eminence, form a most beautiful and pleasing panorama; and it is not therefore matter of wonder, that it should now have become the most fashionable promenade in Canterbury.'

The 1806 town map, as noted above, n. 54, highlights Dungeon Hill and its associated Public Walks. Back in September, 1790, the Hon. John Byng having decided to stay in Canterbury at The King's Head Inn, 'walk'd by the wall to Dungeons Hill', which he noted was 'now improving for the Town Parade', Bruyn Andrews, *op.cit.*, 164–5.

Beauty.[61] The South Porch is in a corresponding Stile,[62] but the whole of the western part of the Church as far as the first Nave including the noble Tower is considerably more modern than what is beyond it to the East.[63] This noble Building is of the largest Dimensions.[64] On the outside perhaps it is exceeded in ornamental parts but in no Cathedral whatever is it surpassed in the variety of its Beauties. The more ancient part to the Eastward is admirable for the rude simplicity of its component parts. The termination to the East is totally unlike all others which I have seen. The West Front is exceeded by some

61. The main entrance from the city to the Precincts of the Cathedral, as 'the chief curiosity and ornament of the city', Potts, *op.cit.*, was by Christ Church Gate, the construction of which had occurred between 1517 and 1521, the date of construction being wrongly inscribed as 1507, when the inscription was entirely recut during the 1931–35 stage of the gate's restoration, Newman, *North East and East Kent, op.cit.*, 220, and P.H. Blake, *Canterbury Cathedral Christ Church Gate*, (1965), ix, 7. Hasted, *op.cit.*, xi, 2nd Ed., (Canterbury, 1800), 506, described it as being 'a strong and beautiful building of elegant gothic architecture, built . . . in the year 1517, as appears by a legend along the whole front of it, though now scarcely legible, for that, as well as the rich ornamented carve work, which covers almost the whole of it: among which are the several coats of arms of the nobility and gentry of that time, . . . now in great measure decayed and mouldered away through length of time', the arms being 'those of the king . . . and ten others'. The illegibility of the dating by the 1800's was one of two reasons for supposing that the gate had been constructed in 1507, since according to Blake, *op.cit.*, ix, 'the date of construction has been bedevilled by the 17th century historian of Canterbury, William Somner, . . . who is, nevertheless, alone . . . in stating that the inscription on the front of the gate read 1507'; also W. Somner, *The Antiquities of Canterbury, or a Survey of that Ancient Citie*, (1640), 194. Had he been correct in supposing 1507, that was two years before Henry VII died on 22nd April, 1509, to be succeeded by Henry VIII, noting that over the arch is the red and white Tudor rose between the arms of Henry VIII and his first wife, Katherine of Aragon, Cantacuzino, etc., *op.cit.*, 28–9, or Canon J. Shirley, *The Pictorial History of Canterbury Cathedral*, (1966), 2, which also had probably weathered beyond recognition by 1809. Such is the complex history and architecture of Christ Church Gate that it is now believed to have been commemorative 'of Arthur Prince of Wales rather than of Henry VII', Blake, *op.cit.*, 38, Arthur having been heir to the throne when he died in 1502, as the first son of Henry VII and the elder brother of Henry VIII, and having visited Canterbury in 1500, Newman, *op.cit.*, 220. The reference to suffering 'by the hands of Barbarians', relates to 1642 when a statue of Christ formerly in the centra niche was mutilated by Parliamentary troops shooting at it, Blake, *op.cit.*, 1, or in the words of Hasted, *op.cit.*, 506, 'in the middle was a large statue of our Saviour, which, in derision, was shot to pieces by the parliamentary soldiers in the great rebellion of the last century'. In 1810, therefore, Christ Church Gate stood as 'a highly enriched piece of masonry of the latest Gothic era, . . . much defaced through wantonness', Litchfield Stockdale, *op.cit.*

62. The Chicheley tower, having 'formerly on the south side of it, over the porch, at the entrance into the church, the figures cut in stone, of four armed men; the niches in which they were placed still remaining, representing those who murdered archbishop Becket', while 'on the vaulting of the porch are carved a number of coats of arms in stone, on the ribwork of it', Hasted, *op.cit.*, xi, 2nd Ed., (Canterbury, 1800), 351–2.

63. As confirmed so well by Newman, *North East and East Kent, op.cit.*, 164–5 on a ground plan of the cathedral showing different dates of construction and rebuilding between 1070–7 and the mid-fifteenth century, with the central tower, or Bell Harry, having been built between circa 1494 and 1503', and with the nave having been 'lately new paved with white Portland stone, which is much admired for its simplicity and neatness', *The Canterbury Guide, op.cit.*, 72, in 1788, Potts, *op.cit.*

64. In 1809 *The Canterbury Guide* devoted thirty four of its 128 pages, or six chapters, to describing the cathedral as it then appeared, pointing out on page 70 that

'THE Cathedral of Canterbury is a noble and magnificent pile of building and notwithstanding the different ages in which the several parts of it have been built, and the various kinds of architecture singular to each, . . . the whole together has a most venerable and pleasing effect, . . . [a] great and magnificent edifice, the work of many ages, and of incredible labor and cost.'

others and unfortunately what there is in it to admire cannot be seen to Advantage. It is so much crowded on by Houses. On entering the Church[65] one is not immediately struck, but by its magnitude the Nave has the pointed Arch and Window but when you have approached to the first Transept the Advance to the choir is by a noble flight of Steps, adjoining to which in the North Transept[66] is a beautifull small Chapel, dedicated to the Virgin. On the right before you enter it there was formally an Altar and there they show a Stone which marks the place where Thomas Becket was so cruelly murdered. From this Transept you enter the Cloisters to the West which are of a square form and are very handsome and extensive, the Verger says only exceeded by those at Gloucester. On the East side of them is a fine proportioned room formerly a Chapel but now used as a Chapter House. On the same side of the Steps to the Choir is an Entrance to the Crypt, which extends the whole space of the more ancient part of the Building, viz from the entrance to the Choir to the extremity of the East End and is for its span and Beauty perhaps not exceeded by any thing of the kind in Europe. At the East End it terminates in a round form, which is separated from the more western part, and at this time One of the Prebends has applied it to the noble purpose of being a Depository for his Faggots,[67] a Degradation of its holy Establishment which almost makes him merit that they should be applied to put an End to his Existence for such a

---

One year later Litchfield Stockdale, *op.cit.*, suggested that 'the edifice, as it at present exists, is believed to exhibit the greatest variety of specimens of ancient architecture of any in the British empire'. Hasted, *op.cit.*, xi, 2nd Ed., (Canterbury, 1800), 383, presented as follows some of 'the MEASUREMENT of the whole building of this cathedral:

	Feet
Length from the east to west within side	514
Length of the choir	180
Breadth of the choir from pillar to pillar	40
Length of the nave to the foot of the steps	178
From thence to the skreen at the entrance of the choir	36
Breadth of the nave and side aisles	71
Height of it to the vaulted roof	80

etc.'; also compare Potts, *op.cit.*, or Newman, *North East and East Kent, op.cit.*, 166, confirming a total internal length of 515 feet and a nave vault 80 feet high, as well as a choir vault 69 feet high.

65. The tour of the cathedral which follows conforms to the Canterbury Cathedral ground plan of Newman, *North East and East Kent, op.cit.*, 165, cited above, n. 63, or according to the earlier 'Plans of Canterbury, At Different Periods', in Withers, *op.cit.*, 134–5.

66. And Martyrdom, as per the previous footnote.

67. In 1809 it was noted of the crypt or undercroft that 'the pavement here is almost entirely covered with dirt', *The Canterbury Guide,* op.cit., 100; while for 1800, according to Hasted, *op.cit.,* xi, 2nd Ed., (Canterbury, 1800), 415, the pavement of 'the cript or undercroft' was 'so entirely covered with a coating of dirt so thick, that whatever remains on the original pavement [gravestones, etc.], cannot be seen'. The offending prebend, the eighteenth-century equivalent of a canon today, as the nearest ecclesiastical precinct resident to the east end of the crypt, was Canon Robert Moore, who occupied the first stall of the cathedral from 1804 to 1862. For this information I am grateful to the Rev. Canon D. Ingram Hill. In *The Post Office Directory of the Six Home Counties,* (1851), 268, Canon Moore is listed under 'Gentry' as Moore Rev. Robert, M.A., Precincts, and Hunton, Maidstone.

Christ Church Gate in 1802 (G. Home, *Canterbury of our Grandfathers and of Today*, 1927).

sacriligious prostitution(?), add [ed] to which that from what is visible it appears to be the most admirable part of this beautifull Subterranean.

On the South of the Crypt a considerable part was enclosed and used by the French Protestants who quitted France and settled at Canterbury when the Edict of Nantes was repealed.[68] A few of their Descendants still remaining [a] French Service is still performed on Sundays when it can be done, but in winter it is sometimes under water. It being Saturday, a man was employed in sweeping and cleaning it for the next day.[69]

The Entrance to the Choir is thro a beautifull Gothic Screen of the florid kind under the Organ, which has in its Niche Statues of 8 Kings smaller than life, but the Saints and Angels which formerly enriched the Arch were demolished by the vile Puritans who hated Royalty but could not endure what they considered to be superstitious Images.[70] The Choir is very extensive and, on approaching the Altar, Steps are again ascended. The Altar piece as well as the Stalls are made of Oak and the Architecture is Corinthian and tho far from bad in its kind is very hetreogeneously blended with the more venerable and ancient early Norman.[71] Instead of a Picture usually seen over the

68. As noted much earlier in 1697 by Celia Fiennes, there being 'under the Cathedrall . . . a large Church just like St. Faiths under St. Pauls in London; this is given to the French protestants in the town for the worshipping God; it holds a vast number of people, its as full of seates as can thrust by each other, . . . [and] its so well arch'd that they cannot hear them in the Cathedrall when singing, at least no wayes to disturb them', Morris, *op.cit.*, 126. Defoe, *op.cit.*, 117–8, felt that 'the city will scarce bear being called populous, were it not for two or three thousand French Protestants, . . . including men, women and children', for whom 'under the· church is a large Protestant French church'.

69. The continued use of this church in the crypt is confirmed for 1808 by Holden, *op.cit.*, 50, there being 'under the cathedral . . . a large church for foreign Protestants'; or for 1809 by *The Canterbury Guide, op.cit.*, 100, whereby 'that part under the choir and the side isles has been, for a length of time, appropriated to the Walloons and French refugees, for their place of worship'.

70. This description of the entrance to the choir while being correct in substance is not entirely so in detail, as described in 1809 by *The Canterbury Guide, op.cit.*, 81.

'Let us ascend the noble flight of steps from the nave up to the stone screen at the west door of the choir, a beautiful piece of gothic carve work, built by Prior Hen. De Estrie [Eastry] in 1304; it is rich in . . . canopied nitches, in which stand six statues, crowned, five of which hold globes in their hands, and the sixth probably was meant for King Ethelbert, being an ancient man, with a long beard, holding a church in his hand; the figure next to him seems more delicately featured and feminine than the rest, and might perhaps be his queen, Bertha. Before the havoc made here by the Puritans there were thirteen figures, representing Christ and his Apostles, in the mitred nitches which are round the arched doorway, and twelve mitred saints aloft along the stone work';

compare Newman, *North East and East Kent, op.cit.*, 197, or C.J. Dudley, 'Canterbury Cathedral: the small Portrait Carvings of the Pulpitum, *Arch. Cant.*, xcvii (1981), 185–94.

71. For Potts, *op.cit.*, writing in 1810, 'the choir is reckoned the most spacious in the kingdom', having an altar-piece designed by Sir James Burrough, Master of Caius College, Cambridge, who had died in 1764. Hasted, *op.cit.*, xi, 2nd Ed., (Canterbury, 1800), 368, 370, described 'the present state of the choir', as follows.

'The stalls for the dean and prebendaries are at the west end of it, six on each side the entrance, and are said to have been carved by Gibbons. They are of wainscot, divided by neat pillars and

Communion Table there is a large square opening which is glazed and gives a view of the back Chapel to which you again ascend Steps and here was placed the Shrine of St. Thomas a Beckett and at the East it terminates with a round Chapel dedicated to the Holy Trinity.[72] I before observed that the Eastern part from the entrance to the choir is Saxon and early Norman.[73] but it is remarkable that the main pillars in it, the Shafts of which are alternately round and Octagonal, have Capitals which some of them much resemble the Grecian and all differ one from the Other. The part behind the Altar is particularly to be admired and, as well as in other parts of the Church, contains many Tombs worthy to be remarked.[74] There are also in different parts many flat Grain Stones which had Brass engraved Plates given in memory of Arch Bishops, etc. but here, as well as at Rochester, they are torn away without any exception.[75]

---

pilasters, fluted, with capitals of the Corinthian order, supporting arched canopies . . . This work was part of what was performed after the restoration, at a vast expence, among the repairs of those mischiefs done by the Puritans in the time of the preceding troubles.

The old monkish stalls, in two rows, on each side of the choir, remained till the year 1704, when the present new seats and wainscotting on each side, were put up in their room, being the design of Sir James Burrough and one of the Corinthian or composite order. This part was put up some years after the other, and though not so rich in ornaments, is intended to correspond in taste with them. . . .

The present altar-piece was erected soon after the year 1729, from a design of Sir James Burrough before mentioned: it is of the Corinthian order, very lofty and well executed, and makes a very grand and magnificent appearance. . . . At the same time, a handsome wainscotting was carried on from the altar-piece to the two side doors of the choir, in a taste designed to distinguish this part, being the *presbyterium*, or chancel, from the rest of the choir.'

A legacy of £500 had paid for the altar-piece, to which

'another of £200 was added in 1732, from which a new pavement of black and white marble, in a fancied pattern, was made, beginning at the altar-rail, . . . six or seven feet from which was . . . [a] noble flight of steps of veined white marble, reaching the whole breadth of the place', *ibid.*, 370–1.

72. 'Behind the altar is the beautiful chapel of the Holy Trinity, in the middle of which stood the shrine of Thomas a Becket', Potts, *op.cit.*, also Hasted, *op.cit.*, xi, 2nd Ed., (Canterbury, 1800), 407.

73. In 1070–77 Lanfranc, the first Norman archbishop 'rebuilt the cathedral church much larger', Newman, *North East and East Kent, op.cit.*, 164; also, compare a plan of the Saxon cathedral with the cathedral in 1174, Withers, *op.cit.*, 134. There were, however, no Saxon remains to be observed in 1809 for 'the Saxon Cathedral remains only in the words of Edmer, who wrote in the late eleventh century a detailed but puzzling description', added to which the choir was gutted by fire in 1174, leaving as a shell only the choir and east transepts as the work of Lanfranc's successor, Anselm, consecrated in 1130, Newman, *op.cit.*, 164. Thereafter the interior of the choir was rebuilt in 1175–8 under a French master mason, William of Sens, and extended eastwards under his successor William the Englishman, in 1179–84, to house the shrine of St. Thomas Becket, *ibid.*, 164.

74. Here being 'the monuments of Henry IV and his Queen, Edward the Black Prince, Cardinal Pole, etc.', Potts, *op.cit.*; also see Hasted. *op.cit.*, xi, 2nd Ed., (Canterbury, 1800), 407–14.

75. 'The Account of Monuments and Gravestones, throughout this church' runs to almost 34 pages in Hasted, *op.cit.*, xi, 2nd Ed., (Canterbury, 1800), 383–417, many of which, he notes, 'had been curiously and richly inlaid with ornaments and inscriptions on brass, but all of them have been long since defaced and the brasses purloined from them', *ibid.*, 383–4.

PLATE XV

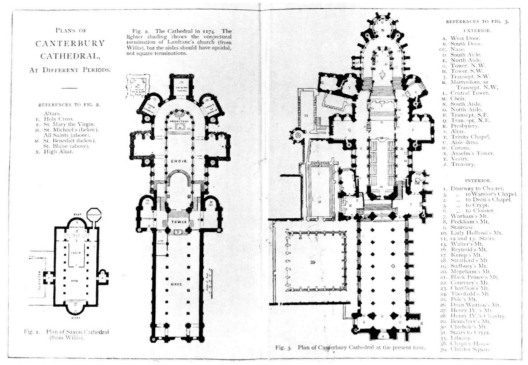

Plans of Canterbury Cathedral at different Periods (H. Withers, *The Cathedral Church of Canterbury*, 1917).

PLATE XVI

St. Augustine's Gate in 1828 (W.H. Ireland, *A New and Complete History of the County of Kent*, 1828–30).

Among others there is here a figure of Edward the Black Prince in Bronze, accompanied on the Base by a great many Coats of Arms in Enamel.[76] If the Beauty of this noble Building in its whole is exceeded by some others in the variety of matter for the Consideration of an Architect it is not excelled by any.[77]

On the north west side is a spacious Court, called Green Court, and in the North West corner of it is a beautifull Gate,[78] which leads into that part of the City adjoining to which is a Saxon Porch and Stone Stair Case, which leads to the Registry which most highly merits to be regarded.[79]

To the East of the Cathedral are what remains of the magnificent Monastery of the Augustins. It consists of two Gates of which that to the North is most beautifull and is now occupied by a Brewer which calls to my mind the many vile purposes to which I saw the religious Building had been applied by the abominable French Reformer.[80] The Entrance of South Gate is filled up and converted into a Dwelling House. Behind is a small remains of the Chapel and within its extensive Walls an Infirmary has been built by voluntary subscrip-

76. Hasted, *op.cit.,* xi, 2nd Ed., (Canterbury, 1800), devoted over three pages to 'the monument of Edward the black prince', 409–12, here being 'a noble monument, very entire and very beautiful: his figure, large as life, lies at length on it, . . . all in gilt brass', the sides and ends of the tomb being 'adorned with sculpture and shields of arms'.

77. Canterbury Cathedral, in the words of Litchfield Stockdale, *op.cit.,* writing in 1810, having, on account of its architecture, and the many ancient and curious tombs of persons of eminence contained within it, been long an object of diligent investigation with travellers'.

78. The 1806 town map, referred to above, n. 54, shows Green Court to the north west of the cathedral, having been called 'the Court of the Priory', which had been built around it, *The Canterbury Guide, op.cit.,* 109. According to *ibid.,* 109–10, 'at the north-west corner is a large high gate-way, formerly the outer gate of the priory, through which all sorts of provisions and necessaries were brought to it', which 'seems a very ancient structure, and probably built by Archbishop Lanfranc, for there is no mention of its having been at any time rebuilt', also see Newman, *North East and East Kent, op.cit.,* 205–8, 218–9, the construction being attributed to Prior Wibert after c. 1153.

79. As above and in the nave of Rochester cathedral, see above, n. 38 and 73, Saxon was incorrectly inferred for what was actually Norman so that here the reference is to the Norman staircase, built by Prior Wibert between 1151–67, when the priory was extensively reconstructed, which led up to a great guest hall and has been described as 'probably the finest example of Norman domestic architecture remaining in this country', Shirley, *op.cit.,* 23.

80. The Canterbury Guide, *op.cit.,* 115–21, described St. Augustine's monastery, as follows.

'In the eastern suburb of Longport are the ruins of the once magnificent Abbey of St. Augustine . . . for black monks of the Benedictine order. . . .

The front of this stately abbey extended towards the west 250 feet, having at each extremity two handsome gateways, which are still remaining; the northern one being the most superb. . . .

Besides the two gates . . . there is no more of it left than is sufficient for the use of a common ale-house, into which it has been for some years converted.

The present use the ruins of this monastery are put to, is as follows:
— The habitable part is turned into a common ale-house, the room over the principal gate-way into a cockpit, the gateway itself into a brewery, the church into a tennis and fives-court, with a skittle-ground adjoining, and the great court-yard into a bowling-green.'

tion, W^ch for neatness cannot be exceeded.[81]   Nearly adjoining they are erecting a new Prison and Sessions House. On the summit of the latter are two large female Figures, one representing Justice the other I apprehend Peace and under neath the Fasces and Staff with the Cap of Liberty in Relievo, the Architect W. Byfield.[82]

These desecratory uses are confirmed in other sources of the period, including W. Gostling, *A Walk in and about the City of Canterbury; with many Observations*, 5th Ed., (Canterbury, 1804), 45, the steam of the brewery having 'miserably defaced [a] fine ceiling', while in 1810 Litchfield Stockdale, *op.cit.*, lamented that 'so little regard is paid at this time to the remains of this once sacred edifice, that the principal apartments adjoining the gate are occupied as a public house; the gateway itself as a brewery; the great room over it is used for the cruel sport of cock-fighting; the great court yard as a bowling green; and the walls of the chapel on the north side enclose a fives court'. For 1808 Holden, *op.cit.*, 52, lists 'Giles Tho. and Jeremiah, brewers and maltsters, Long Port', while Gostling, *op.cit.*, 42–3, alleged that the monks' refectory had been 'pulled down to furnish materials for the Red Lion inn, in our High- Street, (which belongs to the owner of the monastery), for the wainscotting of the great parlour is said to have been brought from the hall of St. Augustine's, . . . having been painted with pieces of scripture history, as hanging up in frames; but some years ago an attempt to clean and recover one of these pictures having failed, the whole was battered to resemble pannel work, and painted over of one colour'.

81.   Shown on the 1806 town map, referred to above, n. 54, as the Kent and Canterbury Hospital, adjoining to Longport, the construction of which had been completed in 1793, 'through the benevolent exertions of the neighbouring gentry and clergy, after the example of other counties, the expence of it being defrayed by voluntary subscriptions, on which its future annual maintenance must in general depend', *The Canterbury Guide, op.cit.*, 44. Its wards were first opened for the reception of patients on 26th April, 1793, Dr. J. McDivitt, 'Statistics of the Kent and Canterbury Hospital', *The Maidstone Annual, or, British Medical Almanack*, Ed. W. Farr, (1839), 179. During the year falling between 31st December, 1807 and 31st December, 1808, £2,355 1s. 6d. had been collected in 'Annual Subscriptions, Benefactions, Collections, Legacies, etc'; 292 in-patients and 371 out-patients had been admitted; 415 patients had been 'inoculated with COW POCK at the Hospital, *gratis*'; while since the foundation of the Hospital 6,780 in- and out-patients had been admitted, with £5,295 19s. 1d. having been spent on the 'Purchase of Land, Building the Hospital, Furniture, Medicines, Housekeeping, etc. to December 31, 1793', *General Kent and Canterbury Hospital Report for the Year 1808.*

82.   Shown as the 'New Gaol' on the 1806 town map, occupying a site alongside St. Augustine's Monastery and the Kent and Canterbury Hospital, which *The Canterbury Guide, op.cit.*, 44–6, described thus.

> 'A little further, on the same scite, has been lately erected a very extensive building, the gaol and house of correction for the Eastern parts of the county of Kent; a structure, which . . . shews the consummate skill and taste of the architect, Mr. Byfield, and reflects the highest credit on the builder, Mr. Charles Hedge. The building has a very neat stone front, with appropriate devices over the entrance . . . The whole is enclosed by a strong brick wall of twenty feet high. The prison is capable of receiving and accommodating forty-one prisoners.'

Also, *ibid.*, 46–7,

> 'since the erection of the above gaol, the justices having found their sessions-house too small and inconvenient for the public business, a very fine building has been reared for that purpose, on the space of ground between the gaol and the Kent and Canterbury hospital. This sessions-house is equal if not superior to any other in the kingdom, having appropriate places for the transacting of all manner of county business; the court and offices, etc. belonging to it are fitted up in a style combining elegance and utility. The prisoners are conveyed from the gaol to the bar, through a subterranean passage, which prevents any apprehension for their escape, during their progress to trial. The whole has been built under the able management of the two gentlemen before alluded to.'

PLATE XVII

Folkestone viewed from the Beach in 1808 (E. W. Brayley. *The Beauties of England and Wales*. Volume VIII: *Kent*, 1808).

PLATE XVIII

Sandgate in 1817 (G.A. Cooke, *Walks through Kent*, 1819).

If to these be added the extensive Barracks in its neighbourhood,[83] few Cities are more justly entitled to Praise and few can more highly gratify its Visitors who are disposed to admire the Objects which I have endeavoured to here make a memorial of.

Sunday,
10 September

There being no communication by public Conveyance with Folkestone,[84] and the people of Canterbury requiring as much for a Man and Gig as a Post Chaise cost within a few shillings, I preferred the latter and left Canterbury on the road to Dover. Having past Barham Downs at near the 7 Mile Stone, turn[ed] off to the right, by the Park of Sir Oxenden.[85] The road affords nothing particular till you arrive near Folkestone, to which is a rapid descent from lofty Hills. Part of the Town lays on the Edge of the Sea, but other parts, together with the Church, are placed on high Cliffs. The Streets are by no means strait or regular and the Site of the Town being in parts so different it is perpetually up and down Hill.[86] After dinner[87] I first walked up to the Signal Tower which

83. Potts, *op.cit.*, was able to observe how by 1810 'the population of the city has greatly increased since the commencement of the late war, and the erection of permanent barracks for the military on the high road to Thanet', as shown also on the 1806 town map, noting the 'New Military Road leading to the Cavalry Barracks' and a 'space covering with buildings for the use of the Military'. Developments along these lines up to 1809 were recorded in *The Canterbury Guide, op.cit.*, 50–1.

> 'Since the commencement of the late war there have been erected for the military several ranges of barracks in and near the city. Near the northern suburbs on the Margate road, opposite to Barton mill, Royal Cavalry barracks were erected by [the] government in 1794, for a regiment; they are built of brick, elegant and spacious, forming three sides of a quadrangle, and are said to have cost £40,000. In 1798 barracks for 2,000 infantry were erected near the above, on the same side of the road, which have since been fitted up in an elegant and airy style, and are now made, by the board of ordance, a permanent station for detachments of the Royal Horse and Foot Artillery. In 1806, another extensive range of barracks was erected near the above [confirming thereby what is shown on the town map published that year] but far superior to them, both for neatness and accommodation, capable of containing 2,000 Infantry and 500 Cavalry. There are also temporary barracks in different parts of the city for Cavalry and Infantry.'

84. In 1791 there was from Folkestone 'a caravan [which] goes to Canterbury on Wednesday and Saturday, and returns the same evenings in summer . . . Fare 2s. 6d.', *The Universal British Directory, op.cit.*, 117. It is possible that this journey from Canterbury to Folkestone was undertaken on the Saturday evening after a full day touring the city.

85. Cary, *op.cit.*, 7, described how the London to Dover Road passed 'over Barham Downs, on which, at 4 M. beyond Bridge, on r. to Folkestone, 10¾'. Half a mile beyond 'the 62 Milestone' and on the right 'adjoining the Road, is Broome House, Sir Henry Oxenden, Bart', *ibid.*, 8, given as Broome House, Sir Henry Oxenden, in Cooke, *op.cit.*, 5.

86. 'Folkestone is a considerable fishing-town, of such a hilly situation, that it is hardly safe to ride in some of the streets of it'; such was the warning given to travellers in 1804 by Gostling, *op.cit.*, 303. 'A rapid descent from lofty Hills' formed in reverse 'an excursion from Folkestone into the interior of the county northward', towards Barham Downs, as recommended by L. Fussell, *A Journey round the Coast of Kent*, (1818), 179, for 'the difficulty of climbing up the lofty ridge of hills which rises abruptly as a boundary of the vale of Folkestone, will be amply compensated by the extensive prospect which it commends, both of sea and land', *ibid.*, 179. In 1810 Potts, *op.cit.*, described Folkestone as 'pleasantly situated on the circular ground near the sea', with 'the church, which occupies the most exalted spot, standing directly on the cliffs, while the other parts of the town are principally built on the acclivity of the hill', having 'three irregular and indifferently-paved streets', where 'the buildings are principally of bricks, and . . . many of the late-built ones [command] an extensive view over a fine country, and the French coast'.

87. Perhaps accommodation and dinner were taken at 'the principal inn' of 1791, namely 'the Folkestone Arms,

is on the summit of the lofty Hills which lead to Dover.[88] From thence returned to the Church[89] from whence there is a most beautifull walk along the Cliffs to Sandgate about 2 Miles[90] and from it being Sunday I was delighted with the appearance of the Inhabitants of Folkestone. The females were *all* cleanly and neatly dressed with a sufficient appearance of Fashion to show a variation from old costume, but there was not to be seen any wanton exposure of naked charms and no Hats or Bonnets cut or drawn aside with the mutinous Intentions so disgusting in London Ladies. But all had an appearance of Decorum and Modesty. I was since informed that the Women take their Afternoon Tea together in a very neighbourly manner but that the Sexes like Deer do not much associate, the Men making parties and taking this Amusement without the Admission of Females. The young ones are in general well looking and many of them handsome.[91] I did not look into the Church as the Windows in general resemble those of a House and consequently any thing worth seeing in the inside could not be expected.[92]

kept by George Janeway, where the traveller meets with good accommodation', *The Universal British Directory, op.cit.*, 117.

88. According to *A Guide to all the Watering and Sea-Bathing Places,* (1810), 245, 'about a mile and a half to the eastward on the road to Dover stands the Signal House, on a fine eminence, which commands a most enchanting prospect of the surrounding country, as well as the whole undulated French coast; in clear weather vessels passing into, or out of Boulogne harbour, the flag on the Pier Head, together with the encampment, may be distinctly seen from this place'. The reference here is to a flag station, situated on the cliffs at Wear Bay, approximately where the present Coast Guard Station is.

89. The parish church of St. Mary and St. Eanswythe; also see below, n. 92.

90. Along what is now 'The Leas' and described thus in 1810,

'the walk on the Cliffs to Sandgate is generally frequented, and certainly is one of the most delightful in the country. The bold and romantic scenery on the land side, the charming marine prospect, the view of the French coast, . . . with the stately fleets passing, . . . give particular animation to the scene',

A Guide to all the Watering and Sea-Bathing Places, op.cit., 245.

91. In 1818 Fussell, *op.cit.*, 166–7, commented as follows on

'the peculiar temper of the people of Folkestone. . . . They have not within their liberties a single chapel or meeting house, belonging to any other religious persuasion, besides that of the established church; . . . the missionaries and itinerant preachers, who have not been sparing of their lungs or their labours, have been hitherto unable to make any proselytes among them. It is nevertheless proper to observe that this indifference does not proceed from disregard for religion, for they are, generally speaking, very regular in their attendance upon the service of the church . . . No disputations engender animosities, or inflame the prejudices of the weak or the zealous: the inhabitants are even *proverbially friendly;* and the less polished perhaps the more sincere',

added to which 'Folkestone has been long known to valetudinarians as affording . . . salubrious air, tranquillity, and cheerful scenery', *ibid.*, 173.

92. Folkestone's parish church of St. Mary and St. Eanswythe was unimpressive in 1809, compared to what can be seen today, being described as 'a plain structure, with a square tower, having a beacon turret, a clock, and a peal of eight bells, . . . on the margin of the cliff, which overhangs the sea', *A Guide to all the Watering and Sea-Bathing Places, op.cit.*, 242. In 1818 it was said to be 'a plain unornamented structure, with a low roof, . . . irregular and low', Fussell, *op.cit.*, 163. The building was transformed during the incumbency of Canon

The Martello System of Defences here commences and continues all along the Coast between Folkestone and Romney. There are near thirty.[93]

Monday,
11 September I resumed the walk on the summit of the Cliffs to Sandgate and, having left Folkestone Church, on the right observed on one of the lofty Hills which I descended in coming from Canterbury (and which I then remarked) the appearance of a large Camp which on Enquiry I found was a right Conjecture as it is still called Castle Hill, probably therefore was Roman and Castrum is now become Castle.[94] When near Sandgate I descended into that small Place[95]

Matthew Woodward who, on becoming vicar in July, 1851, was 'appalled by what he saw and made extensive plans to restore . . . the church as a whole', whereupon the church was enlarged and decorated with furnishings and murals and every window was filled with stained glass, A. Reader-Moore, *St. Mary and St. Eanswythe, Folkestone*, (1973), 5–6; also Newman, *North East and East Kent, op.cit.,* 310.

93. Martello Towers, so named after a French tower at Mortella Point in Corsica, which had resisted an English attack in 1794, were planned and constructed during the 1800s to resist a possible Napoleonic invasion, Newman, *North East and East Kent, op.cit.,* 313–4, and P.A.L. Vine, *The Royal Military Canal*, (Newton Abbot, 1972), 24. Such was their novelty they attracted detailed descriptions and comment in publications of the period. Fussell, *op.cit.,* 185–8, devoted, for instance, a whole chapter to describing them as they existed in 1818, while in 1808 Brayley, *op.cit.,* 1114, pointed out how

'a long range of MARTELLO TOWERS has been built . . . at irregular distances, but generally within about half or three quarters of a mile from each other. They are all constructed of brick, and extend from the vicinity of East Were Bay to near Dymchurch. The largest, which is not yet finished, is at Burmarsh, near the commencement of Dymchurch wall, and is so contrived as to contain many others within it. Their form is circular, the walls being of vast thickness, and the roofs bomb proof. Two or more guns are mounted upon each, on a revolving frame, so as to enable them to be pointed every way, while the men who work them are completely secured from danger by a high parapet.'

Potts, *op.cit.,* offered the same description in 1810, adding that

'the entrance into each is by a narrow opening, at a considerable height from the ground, by means of a ladder, which is afterwards drawn up, and the aperture effectually closed from within. The lower part contains the ammunition and provisions, which are lodged in apartments that, like the roof, are bomb-proof; thus a small number of men may defend each for a very considerable time against any force, that may be brought to the attack.'

Confronted by those 'gun-posts', Newman, *North East and East Kent, op.cit.,* 313, William Cobbett gave 'full vent to what he felt was the squandering of public money', on 1st September, 1823, on one of his 'rural rides' through Sussex and Kent to Dover, Vine, *op.cit.,* 137–8. He reckoned to 'have counted along here upwards of thirty of these ridiculous things', William Cobbett, *Rural Rides,* i, (1934 Ed.), 236–7. In fact, thirty was an underestimation, since by 1810 seventy four Martello Towers had been constructed along the shore from Folkestone to Seaford, compared to only six towers having been completed by 1806, Vine, *op.cit.,* 74, 98. Vine's map of the 'Line of the Royal Military Canal and Road, 1810' shows 32 Martello Towers between Shorncliffe and Cliffe End in Sussex, *ibid.,* 55.

94. Hasted, *op.cit.,* viii, 2nd Ed., (Canterbury, 1799), 168, refers to a 'Roman fort, or watch tower, . . . built more than a mile and an half distant from the sea shore, on a very high hill, . . . surrounded with a strong entrenchment, . . . the remains of which are very visible at this day, . . . situated on the summit of that high eminence called *Castle-hill*'; compare Fussell, *op.cit.,* 184, 'the verge of the cliff [Folkestone to Sandgate] affords a delightful walk, overlooking the sea on the left, and embracing a fine prospect of the ancient works called Castle-Hill in the opposite direction'.

95. Most of Sandgate was situated in the parish of Cheriton, Hasted, *op.cit.,* viii, 2nd Ed., (Canterbury, 1799), 189, or Bagshaw, *op. cit.,* ii, 433, Cheriton having a population of 887 in 1811, as opposed to 727 in 1801, Minchin, *op.cit.,* 365.

which is situated on the Beach close to the Sea. Its shore is covered with Pebbles commonly called Shingles and seems well calculated for Bathing in fine weather. A Woman I met at Romney, who was not forty years of Age, told me She remembers when there was not more than two houses there. The whole of the Town therefore is quite new and has an Air of neatness which cannot be exceeded. There is a Circulating Library and Billiard Room and I think to those who are desirous of a Seaside Lounge scarcely any Place that I have seen I should so soon recommend.[96] Government have here constructed a beautifull

96. Lying about 1½ miles westwards from Folkestone, Sandgate had become well known as 'a small bathing-place, which has wholly grown up within the last sixteen or seventeen years, and is now much frequented by those who wish quiet and retirement', Potts, *op.cit.*, or Brayley, *op.cit.*, 1113. A more detailed description of 1810 introduced Sandgate as

> 'a pretty little village, exactly half way between Folkestone and Hythe, and which has suddenly started into notice. Here are six or eight bathing-machines, besides hot and cold baths. Lodgings may be obtained here on reasonable terms; and of late there have been erected some very good houses. Purday keeps a small circulating library, adjoining to which is a billiard-room. There is another billiard-table kept by Woore.

> The beach consists entirely of shingles, so that the water is very clear, and by shelving gently from the shore it presents any depth that may be desired. . . . The New Inn is the usual place of entertainment, but there is neither a ball nor assembly-room',

A Guide to all the Watering and Sea-Bathing Places, op.cit., 247. In 1818 Fussell, *op.cit.*, 190–2, looked upon Sandgate as 'a most desirable residence for those who visit the sea side in the summer months', being 'not the less fit for valetudinarians', while also 'a constant intercourse between Dover, Brighton, and Portsmouth, gives a considerable degree of animation to the road through this village, by the number of persons induced by business, or attracted by curiosity, to travel coastwise', quite apart from affording 'to the occasional visitor an opportunity, at comparatively a trivial expense, of seeing whatever is worthy of notice in this most interesting part of the country'.

Sandgate was the subject of a lengthy report in *The Kentish Gazette,* Tuesday, 12th September, 1809, 4d, which, contrary to the guidebook's description above, drew attention to the holding of fortnightly balls and also alluded to the poor summer weather of 1809, as noted above, n. 50.

> 'Sandgate, Sept. 8. This place (notwithstanding the hitherto unfavourable state of the weather) has been more fashionably and numerously attended this season than at any period since it became a watering place. The lodgings are all full, and in all probability will for some length of time continue so. Purday's Library recently fitted up with an elegant Reading-Room, has become a very fashionable *lounge*. The balls at Strood's Rooms (which are every fortnight) have been fully attended, and have greatly contributed to the amusements of the place. That of Tuesday evening [5th September, 1809] . . . boast [ed] a very large portion both of beauty and fashion. Besides the resident and neighbouring families, the rooms were honoured with the company of the Earl and Countess of Temple, Lords Cobham, Brook and Kinnoul, Sir George and Lady Nugent, Misses Oliver and Campbell, Major Ferris, etc . . . Upwards of ninety partook of an elegant cold collation. . . .

> The Sea Bathing here is in the greatest perfection, as the waters are *pure*. . . . With varied and pleasant walks and rides, cliffs of easy ascent (by the grand military roads) commanding a beautiful view of the British channel, bounded at a distance by the undulating line of the French coast, the whole of the luxuriant level of Romney Marsh, and a large portion of the neighbouring county of Sussex, with a diversity of interesting and romantic scenery in the background, . . . Sandgate can claim . . . at least an *equal* degree of admiration to any watering place in *England*.'

little Fort or Battery, built of Stone in the Centre of which is a Martello.[97] On resuming the Heights are Shorncliffe Barracks[98] where one of the York Reg^t. was partly confined and partly in a Camp adjoining. There was likewise a Battalion of the 95 which was busy in preparing for their Departure.[99] From

97. According to Potts, *op.cit.*, writing in 1810,

> 'a castle, in a similar style to those of Deal and Walmer, was erected here by Henry VIII about 1539. This castle has been greatly altered within the last two or three years, and a large Martello tower built up in the centre, to combine with other Martello towers erected on the neighbouring hills, to defend this part of the coast';

also Brayley, *op.cit.*, 1113–4, writing in 1808, and *A Guide to all the Watering and Sea-Bathing Places, op.cit.*, 247. Newman, *North East and East Kent, op.cit.*, 428–9, suggests that little of Henry VIII's original castle at Sandgate, constructed in 1539–40 for £5543 19s. 2¾d., remained by 1809, since 'in 1806 the central core was converted into a gun-fort, the intermediate ring of walls razed, and the outermost walls lowered drastically', so that 'it thus became in effect a Martello Tower'. For Fussell, *op.cit.*, 189, writing in 1818, Sandgate castle, 'converted into a Martellow tower, of larger size than usual, and built with stone instead of brick, [was] the first object which presents itself, [standing] on the beach, and so near the water's edge that its walls are frequently washed by the surf'; moreover, 'whether this building was originally more extensive than at present, may be doubted; for there are no vestiges of its ancient walls to be traced'.

98. Shorncliffe Camp or barracks were first built on the plateau above Sandgate as part of the Napoleonic defences in 1808, Newman, *North East and East Kent, op.cit.,* 429; or 'on the line of heights that edge the sea, a little beyond Sandgate, called Shorn Cliff are barracks for 1,000 men', and 'for several summers there has been an encampment on these heights', *A Guide to all the Watering and Sea-Bathing Places,* (1810), *op.cit.,* 246; or 'at SHORN CLIFFE, on the hill above Sandgate, . . . has been a summer *camp* for several successive years; and an extensive range of *Barracks* has been recently built there', Brayley (1808), *op.cit.,* 1114, and Potts, *op.cit.* In 1818 Fussell, *op.cit.,* 193, recalled how this site 'was occupied, during the war, by numerous regiments of infantry successively stationed in the barracks there', for

> 'few situations could have been found more airy and cheerful, and few buildings constructed more incommodious and uncomfortable. These were called *temporary* barracks by way of apology, it is presumed, for having been built of wood instead of stone. Why they were so built, and in a place where stone might have been obtained for the trouble of digging, or even without digging at all, surely none but those by whose order they were erected could satisfactorily explain. At the distance of half a mile from these noble barracks, the public were however presented with another specimen of architectural elegance, in a building of a similar nature for the use of the cavalry and artillery. These are built of stone.'

Perhaps the latter were the barracks 'recently built' in 1808, Newman, *op.cit.,* 429; also see the next footnote. The above references to temporary wooden barracks and to the failure to utilize the local stone for building are interesting for two reasons. N. Britton, 'Ragstone — A Lasting Appeal', *Bygone Kent*, iii, No 1, (January, 1982), 56, has located a disused ragstone quarry or pit half way between Folkestone and Hythe at Shorncliffe, while the Duke of York, in a letter of 28th August, 1804, addressed to the King, had 'the honor to report to your Majesty that I returned here [Horse Guards] the night before last from my tour through Kent and Sussex where I have reviewed the troops and examined the defenses of the coast, and have great satisfaction in acquainting your Majesty that I have found the troops in general in a very advanced state of discipline, and with very few exceptions perfectly fit for service, Major-General Moore's Brigade at Shornecliffe camp being certainly the prize in every respect', so that 'indeed I think I may safely say in no service I ever saw two Regiments so perfect as the King's Own, and the Fifty-Second', Ed: A. Aspinall, *The Later Correspondence of George III*, iv, (C.U.P., 1968), 226, Letter 2929. H.R.H. Frederick, Duke of York, was Commander-in-Chief between 1798 and 1809 and again from 1811 to 1827, Vine, *op.cit.,* 50.

99. A reference to the Rifle Brigade or the Old Ninety-fifth Foot Regiment, Fortescue, *op.cit.,* 652–3. According to Vine, *op.cit.,* 23, 'the training camp at Shorncliffe . . . not only created the light infantry division of the Peninsular War', but introduced also 'a new form of discipline, different altogether from that of the time'. Also see below, n. 108.

PLATE XIX

The Barracks and Town of Hythe, also showing some Martello Towers (W.H. Ireland, *A New and Complete History of the County of Kent,* 1828–30).

PLATE XX

New Romney Church in 1818 (G.A. Cooke, *Walks through Kent*, 1819).

hence I again descended to the Sea and at a small distance arrived at Seabrook where more than 300 men are employed in constructing a most extensive Battery.[100] Here also commences a Canal which goes to Rye.[101] At the distance of 5 miles from Folkestone is Hythe. In this Town there is not much to remark.[102] Its Church is situated on a steep Height and is of considerable Antiquity, especially the East End,[103] but in the interior there is nothing to observe except the prevailing practice of White Wash which is carried to such Excess that an Iron Helmet, etc. which are placed against the Wall in the North Transept are by this Process rendered of the same Appearance as other plastered Objects. In an under Croft at the East end is a vast Collection of Bones which they say were found near the place and are supposed to be those of Danes who having invaded this Country were on their Return overpowered and destroyed by the Britons near this Place.[104] In the N W part of the Church

100.   'At the head' of 'that great work of defence, THE MILITARY CANAL', constituting 'a large battery which occupies a ledge of the hill close to its eastern extremity', Fussell, *op.cit.*, 194–5. Vine, *op.cit.*, 46, refers to 'the Seabrook Mill stream near Shorncliffe', and also to how 'the draw-bridge over the Sea Brook at Shorncliffe was removed about 1840 and the unfinished defence work [presumably a reference to the above battery] blocking part of the Sandgate to Hythe road and the cause of frequent accidents to carriages and riders was removed in 1841', *ibid.*, 167.

101.   Namely the Royal Military Canal, the history of which has been fully recorded by Vine, *op.cit.* Contemporary sources noted how

'immediately under Shorncliffe, and within half a mile from Sandgate, commences the new Military Canal, which has recently been cut to impede the progress of an enemy, in the event of a landing being effected upon this shore. It extends . . . in nearly a straight direction along the coast, till it passes Hythe, when it crosses the Romney road, and following the course of the hills which skirt the extensive flat forming Romney and Walland marshes, terminates at Cliff End in Sussex, . . . with a raised bank to shelter the soldiery, and enable them to oppose the foe with better advantage',

Brayley, *op.cit.*, 1114, or Potts, *op.cit.* Vine, *op.cit.*, 55, has a map showing the 'Line of the Royal Military Canal and Road, 1810', from Shorncliffe to Cliff End, a distance of 28 miles in 1810, *ibid.*, 56, 225. Work on the canal had begun on 30th October, 1804, and by 'April 1809 . . . could be said to be completed for the purposes of navigation and defence', *ibid.*, 56, 97, having cost in excess of £234,000, *ibid.*, 99.

102.   Hythe, according to Litchfield Stockdale, *op.cit.*, writing in 1810, was 'anciently a considerable town, containing four parishes, and occupying a tract of ground on the margin of the ocean above two miles in length; but it is at present much reduced from its former consequence, owing to its having ceased to be a commodious haven for shipping through the recess of the sea', with an 1811 population for Hythe, St. Leonard (Cinque Port, Parish, and Borough) of 2,318, Minchin, *op.cit.*, 366.

103.   'The *Church* is dedicated to St. Leonard, and occupies a very elevated situation on the acclivity of the hill above the town, . . . the Church-yard [commanding] a fine view of the Sea, and coast of France', Brayley, *op.cit.*, 1117, 1119; standing 'on the side of the rocky hill above the town, about half-way up it', Litchfield Stockdale, *op.cit.*, of Norman origin, 'having the grandest chancel of any non-monastic church in the county', Newman, *North East and East Kent*, *op.cit.*, 344.

104.   In 1810 Litchfield Stockdale, *op.cit.*, described the church as follows.

'The building consists of three aisles, a north and south cross, or transept, and three chancels. . . . The crypt or vault . . . has long been famous as the depository of a very unusual quantity of human bones, which not only attract the notice of travellers, but have excited amongst antiquaries much speculation as to their origin, and the cause of their present appearance. The pile is curiously and closely stacked like billet wood, measuring in length twenty-eight feet, eight feet in

Yard there is a copious Spring of excellent water, which is a great Benefit to the town.[105]

In the afternoon I intended to have visited the Chain of Forts and Martellos but found walking on the loose Shingles so troublesome that I gave up that Project and ascended the Hill to the Barracks.[106] I had before seen the 95 which is a Rifle Reg^t come into Town,[107] and now was the moment when their Baggage Waggons arrived, the Bustle attending which, and the distribution afterwards of Bread and Straw for their Repose, gave me a View of Military Economy and Occupation to which I had not before been Witness. This Reg^t now consists of three Battalions – the 1st is in Spain, the 2^d with the Expedition to Holland.[108] When the last volunteering took Place a number sufficient to

---

height, and the same in breadth; but it has sunk considerably by the decay of such as lay next the earth. Many of the thigh bones are of large dimensions; and the skulls and others in proportion to men of between seven and eight feet in height. At present it is computed to contain not more than 1,500 skeletons of full-grown men, allowing one cubic foot to each skeleton; an estimate which, considering the magnitude of these bones, has been deemed a fair average by medical gentlemen of respectability and science.'

A Guide to all the Watering and Sea-Bathing Places, op.cit., 248, also noted how

'in a vault under the church is a remarkable pile of dry bones, which are kept in as good order as books in a library. Some of them are very gigantic, and appear, by an inscription, to be the remains of Danes and Britons killed in a battle near this place long before the Norman Conquest.'

'Hundreds of skulls in racks' remain to this day 'a macabre tourist attraction', Newman, *North East and East Kent, op.cit.,* 344. For accounts of the contemporary speculation surrounding the dating and circumstances of these bones, see Hasted, *op.cit.,* viii, 2nd Ed., (Canterbury, 1799), 251–2, or Fussell, *op.cit.,* 207–9.

105. 'A spring of good water rises in Hythe Church-yard', Brayley, *op.cit.,* 1119, being referred to as 'a spring of clear water', by Litchfield Stockdale, *op.cit.,* in 1810. According to Hasted, *op.cit.,* viii, 2nd Ed. (Canterbury, 1799), 249–50, the parish church of St. Leonard possessed 'a very large church-yard adjoining mostly on the west and north sides, in the middle of which is a large open well of water, under a cove of the quarry stone'.

106. 'On the heights immediately above Hythe are extensive ranges of *Barracks* for infantry, erected since the beginning of the present century; and near these are numerous mud-walled cottages, erected for the wives and families of the soldiers', while 'other Barracks, of a temporary kind, are within the town itself', Brayley, *op.cit.,* 1120.

107. See above, n. 99, and the footnote which follows.

108. A reference to two spheres of military operation in 1809 in the Scheldt and the Peninsular, which are fully described in Fortescue, *op.cit.,* 60–290. The evacuation of troops from South Beveland, on account of fever, occurred between 1st and 5th September, 1809, resulting in many sick soldiers arriving in the coastal towns of Kent and other counties, *ibid.,* 88, while subsequently 5,000 troops were moved to Kent 'to reinforce our coastal defences', D. Gray, *Spencer Perceval The Evangelical Prime Minister 1762–1812,* (Manchester University Press, 1963), 284. Two confirmatory reports of military activity concerning the 95th Rifle Brigade appeared in *The Kentish Gazette,* firstly on 8th September, 1809, 4d, when it was announced that 'the detachment of the 95th Rifle Corps, which arrived in the Hebe transport, has been debarked at Dover, and marched for the depôt of the battalion at Hythe barracks', but 'these men appeared very sickly'. A few days later the same source reported on 12th September, 1809, 4c, that

'our port letters announce the arrival of several ships from the Scheldt with the infantry of the Expedition, many of which have been landed, and have marched for their respective destinations in this district, [and] in general for the quarters they formerly occupied. . . . Sickness, more than

compleat the 2 Battalions offered and upwards of 400 Overplus, which occasioned Government to add this third Battalion, but the reason of this Preference is curious. It was because the Regimentals being throughout a dark Green they became exempt from the trouble of keeping the white front of Cloathing clean or, according to their Cant, they got rid of the Tobacco Pipe clay.

Tuesday, 12 September   I left Hythe by a Cart or Caravan not unlike the Waggons in Holland and at some distance there are the remains of an Old Castle on a Hill to the right, which I believe is called Lym Castle.[109] On the Shore nearly opposite commences Dymchurch Wall or Bank where they have built a large round Fort, called the eleven Gun Battery, which is supported by a continued line of Martellos.[110] The Road from hence to New Romney is amusing from its Novelty, on the right looking over an immense Tract of fertile Meadows and on the left over the expanded Ocean, the magnificent Music of whose rolling Billows form the most sublime Accompaniment.[111]

---

service, has made great inroads in their ranks. . . . The 3d battalion of the 95th has also proceeded from Shorncliffe to Hythe.'

Also compare above, n. 47, 52 and 99.

109.   In 1810, *A Guide to all the Watering and Sea-Bathing Places, op.cit.,* 246–7, felt that 'the situation of the [Lympne] castle, the church, and the various erections now standing at Limne, with the Signal-house on the hill, is truly romantic, and the prospects from every part of this charming eminence are of the most magnificent and beautiful description'. Litchfield Stockdale, *op.cit.,* also in 1810, had a somewhat different impression of this particular place.

'THE parish of Limne adjoins that of Hythe, and contains at present only a few low and mean houses, besides the church, and the manoral mansion called the castle; all situated on the brow of a hill . . . Close to the west end of the church stands Limne *Castle,* an ancient embattled manor house of the Archdeacon of Canterbury, not at all remarkable; but as a picturesque object, viewed from the side or bottom of the hill, will be found interesting.'

110.   Vine, *op. cit.,* 55, on his map showing the 'Line of the Royal Military Canal and Road, 1810' has a concentration of thirteen Martello Towers defending the Dymchurch Wall, the decision having been taken in December, 1804, that

'there were to be two kinds of tower, a large one mounting eleven guns and a smaller one mounting an 18-pounder and two carronades. Of the larger variety two only were to be built; one at the Seahouses, near Eastbourne, and one at the east end of Dymchurch Wall', *ibid.,* 33.

On 8th January, 1805, *The Kentish Gazette* reported that the Martello Towers near Dymchurch were to be 'placed immediately behind the wall' quoted in *ibid.,* 59, compare Fussell, *op.cit.,* 234, 'the Martello towers ranged along the coast here occupy a bank or islet of shingle close to the road', running in a line parallel with that 'steep mound or bank', Dymchurch Wall.

111.   This was in 1810 'the only highway for carriages . . . between Hithe and Romney', Potts, *op.cit.,* William Marshall, *The Rural Economy of the Southern Counties; comprising Kent, Surrey, Sussex,* i (1798), 357–8, 365–6, recalled how

'in 1795, during an excursion in EAST KENT, I examined the southeast, or sea side of the district, from Hithe to Romney and its environs, with some attention, . . . sufficient, to enable me, to give a general idea of the district, and an outline of its management. . . . On the sea side, the top of the embankment furnishes a firm road, at all seasons; and, in summer, a delightful one to travel, [but] in the dark stormy nights of winter, however, it must frequently be disagreeable, if not dangerous.'

New Romney is a small pretty Town,[112] but is said to be far from healthy.[113] It has one Church, the Tower of which is of the Ancient Saxon and of a grand square form.[114] In the interior are 2 Stones with Brass Plates, one of which I

112. By 1811 New Romney had a population of 841, as against 755 in 1801, Minchin, *op.cit.*, 366, the latter figure being quoted by Potts, *op.cit.*, in 1810, who described the town as containing '122 houses, . . . which are chiefly of brick, . . . ranged in a principal street, with a small one crossing it, in which stands the Hall, or Brotherhood-house: this has been recently re-built, together with the market-house', added to which 'the church is a spacious edifice'. The rising population between 1801 and 1811 resulted partly from 'extensive ranges of barracks, both for cavalry and infantry, which were built in 1805', *ibid*.

Marshall, *op.cit.*, 364, noted of Romney Marsh that

> 'the VILLAGES, everywhere, appear to be inconsiderable. And even Romney, its principal town, though neatly built, and respectably inhabited, is only a small place: ranking with the lower class of what are called country market towns.'

113. For centuries Romney Marsh and those marshes bordering the Thames, the Medway and the Stour, including Sheppey and the Hoo Peninsula, suffered from an illness known as ague, which as marsh fever or indigenous malaria continued in Romney Marsh to be 'a hazard into the early years of the present century' and, as such, 'was simply accepted', P. Macdougall, 'Malaria: Its Influence on a North Kent Community', *Arch. Cant.*, xcv (1979), 255–7. As far back as 1570 William Lambarde had noted of Romney Marsh that 'the place hath in it sundry villages, . . . not thicke set, nor much inhabited, bicause it is . . . Evill in Winter, grievous in Sommer, and never good', so that who 'should arrive and make his first step on land in Rumney Marshe, he shall rather finde good grass under foote, than wholesome Aire above the head', *A Perambulation of Kent*, (Chatham, 1826), 181. At the close of the eighteenth century, Hasted, *op. cit.*, viii, 2nd Ed., (Canterbury, 1799), 469–70, believed that some Romney Marsh villages were 'very mean', because 'the unwholesomeness of the air causes it to be very thinly inhabited', the village inhabitants being 'mostly such as are hired to look after the grounds and cattle, the owners and occupiers of which live in general in the neighbouring towns or upland country'. Based on personal observations made in 1795 and 1797, it was the view of Marshall, *op.cit.*, 357, 365, that

> 'with respect to the HEALTHINESS of this tract of low lands, reports speak differently. Its inhabitants do not acknowledge it to be particularly unhealthy: indeed, it has recently been advanced, that the soldiers, which have been quartered within it, have been found more healthy, here, than in many parts of the uplands of the county. . . . The inhabitants of the uplands [however] speak of it, as an aguish, unhealthy country: and, seeing the great quantity of stagnant water, which is, at present, pent up, within its area, reason inclines to the latter report.'

While he too noted 'inconsiderable' villages and the habit of graziers, living at a distance, committing the care of their stock to 'Marshmen, provincially "LOOKERS"; whose cabins and pens are seen scattered over the area of the Marsh', Romney housed 'several capital men', and 'the stagnant water having, of late years, been drawn off, in some degree from the town, [it] has thereby been rendered more healthy, than it was formerly', *ibid.*, 364, 366. Overall 'the thinness of inhabitants', he felt, 'may not be wholly attributed to the unhealthiness of climature; but, in some part, to the badness of the ROADS', *ibid.*, 365. Hasted, *op.cit.*, 449, also observed how New Romney 'stands rather higher than the neighbouring country, on a soil of gravel and sand'. Traditionally, whether in literature or by common hearsay, Romney Marsh was considered to be unhealthy, but equally 'of course, neither Lambarde nor Hasted knew the cause', Macdougall, *op.cit.*, 257.

114. Dedicated to St. Nicholas, 'with a large and curious tower at the west end', Potts, *op.cit.*, and certainly an ancient church of the Norman not the Saxon period dating from the twelfth century, *The Church of Saint Nicholas, New Romney, Kent*, (1981), 1. There is no known trace of a Saxon chapel, 'although one was built at the mouth of the river, or more precisely on the bank, of which nothing remains', according to Miss Anne Roper, M.B.E., F.S.A., J.P., to whom I am grateful for information contained in this and the following footnote. As at Rochester and Canterbury Saxon was mistaken for Norman, see above, n. 38, 73 and 79, for 'an ambitious Norman church was built c. 1160–70, aisled and richly arcaded on the west front', and 'immediately after, a proud tower was added to the west, blocking the arcading of the previous front', Newman, *West Kent and the Weald, op.cit.*, 415.

should have been glad to have had the means of rubbing off, as it is to the memory of one of the most early Topographers of Kent — Lambarde, Author of the Perambulations thro Kent.[115]

From Romney to Ryde [Rye] is a dead Flat, dull but not unprofitable, as it is across the Marshes which are said to contain 27,000 Acres of the most fertile Pasture in the Kingdom.[116]

115. Brayley, *op.cit.*, 1144, described these 'Brass Plates' as follows.

'On a tomb in what is called the north chancel are small *Brasses*, in the habits of the times, of THOMAS SMYTH, a Jurat of this town, who died in January, 1610, and *Mary*, his wife. On another slab is a Brass in memory of THOMAS LAMBERD, who died in August, 1510: his dress is a long gown, with very large sleeves; and a scrip hangs from his girdle.'

It has been assumed, rightly or wrongly, that Thomas Lamberd was a cousin of William Lambard(e) who in 1570 compiled *The Perambulation of Kent*, which in 1576 was published as 'the first county history, or more strictly "survey"', W.G. Hoskins, *Local History in England*, 2nd Ed., (1972), 18. While Miss Roper cannot substantiate this possible relationship, she has established that the former died in 1514 and not in 1510, as stated above, or as commonly presumed by Newman, *West Kent and the Weald, op.cit.*, 416, or *The Church of St. Nicholas, New Romney, Kent, op.cit.*, 3. The inscription on the Lamberd brass represents a 'rhyming epitaph', *ibid.*, 3.

'Of yo[r] charity pray for me
   Thomas Lamberd of Romeney
whiche dyed the xxiiij day of
   August
In lyke wyse so alle ye must
For dethe is c'me to Alle
   mankynde
Therefore have my soule in mynde
Which ended MVXIV yeres of
   hym y[t] dyed for alle men.'

The other brass on an altar tomb in the Sanctuary shows that Thomas Smyth died on '3 daye of January 1610'.

116. Marshall, *op.cit.*, 357–9, 372, 376, saw Romney Marsh as

'A DISTRICT, whose lands are nearly uniform, whose produce is principally herbage, and whose pasturing stock is similar throughout, . . . [which] wants much less time and application, to examine it, than one which is composed of various soils, resting on a variety of substrata, forming varied surfaces, and producing wood, corn, grass, and livestock of different descriptions. . . . The principal part is situated in the county of Kent: the south western quarter, however is aukwardly included within that of Sussex . . . The former goes by the name of ROMNEY MARSH, the latter by that of GUILFORD MARSH.

The EXTENT, if the mean length be estimated at eleven miles, and its mean width at seven, may be set down at seventy-five square miles; or fifty thousand acres . . . The SURFACE of ROMNEY MARSH . . . appears not only *level*, but remarkably *smooth*. . . . The PRESENT PRODUCE of the lands, which thus owe their immense value to the invention and industry of man, is principally GRASS, . . . [and] the main OBJECT of the Marsh farmer . . . is SHEEP; with, however, a certain proportion of CATTLE; some HORSES; and with [a] few ARABLE CROPS. . . .

In the neighbourhood of Romney, in the early part of September, . . . the whole was in a state of lawn; and, to the agricultural eye, the appearance was rich and beautiful.'

SIR STEPHEN GLYNNE AND KENTISH ECCLESIOLOGY

NIGEL YATES

Among the archive holdings of St. Deiniol's Library, Hawarden, now administered by the Clwyd Record Office, are 107 volumes containing notes made between 1824 and 1874 on some 5,150 churches in England, Wales, Scotland, Ireland, the Channel Islands and the Isle of Man.[1] The author of these notes was Sir Stephen Glynne (1807–74), who succeeded to the baronetcy in 1815. Sir Stephen was educated at Eton and Christ Church, Oxford. He sat as Liberal member of Parliament for the Flint boroughs from 1832 until 1837, and thereafter for Flintshire until his defeat in 1847, and he served as Lord Lieutenant of Flintshire for many years.[2] Sir Stephen never married. In 1839, his sister Catherine married the future Prime Minister, William Ewart Gladstone, with whom he had shared a close friendship since his schooldays, and they all lived together for part of each year at Hawarden. Sir Stephen's abiding passion was English church architecture and his notebooks are one of the principal, though surprisingly little used, sources for the appearance of British churches in the period immediately before, during and immediately after their Victorian restoration, refurbishing or, sometimes even, complete rebuilding. His sudden death, indeed, occurred during one of his ecclesiological expeditions.[3]

A number of Sir Stephen's notes – those for the whole of Wales and for twelve English counties – have already been published, including those for Kent. These were transcribed by his nephew, William Henry Gladstone (1840–91), and published by John Murray within three years of Sir Stephen's death,[4] though the originals have since vanished and cannot now be traced. Altogether the published volume contains descriptions of 312 churches in Kent with some notes, mostly on restorations since Sir Stephen had visited them, contributed by two local clergymen, Archdeacon Harrison and Canon Scott Robertson, the honorary secretary of the Kent Archaeological Society. The volume, however, because of its early publication date, contains no critical introduction or commentary, but merely a four page preface, extolling Sir Stephen's personal qualities, and his abilities as an antiquarian and ecclesiologist. The aim of this paper is to provide, despite the gap of a century, precisely that critical apparatus and to re-assess the usefulness of Sir Stephen's notes for the modern ecclesiologist.

*   *   *

Sir Stephen's visits to Kentish churches can be conveniently divided into two distinct periods:

1. *Guide to the Flintshire Record Office*, ed. A.G. Veysey, Mold 1974, 139.
2. *D.N.B.*
3. P. Magnus, *Gladstone*, rev. ed. London 1963, 234: 'Sir Stephen's personality had been completely submerged by that of "the great people", as he had always dubbed his sister and her famous husband, and Gladstone told his wife that Stephen's willingness to allow others to arrange his life for him had been positively feminine. Sir Stephen's bachelor life at Hawarden had been lived so modestly and quietly that it was not always easy to remember that he was the real owner of the place, and the Lord Lieutenant of his county'.
4. *Notes on the Churches of Kent*, London 1877.

those visited before the mid-1850s when little restoration had taken place anywhere, and those visited after the mid-1850s when there was a more even balance between restored and unrestored churches. Between 1829, the earliest dated visits, and 1854, he is known to have visited 82 churches, and the vast majority of the 144 undated visits probably also took place in this period.[5] The main concentration was in 1846–47 when at least 26 churches were visited, but there is also at least one dated visit for every year in this earlier period. Between 1855 and 1873 the visits were more heavily concentrated into a few years, with no visits at all recorded for eight years, and only two in 1857 and four in 1866. The years in which a sizeable number of churches were visited were 1859 (27 recorded visits), 1861–63 (16), 1868 (13) and 1870–73 (26).

There is another distinction to be made between the earlier and the later visits which to some extent marks a transition in Sir Stephen's outlook from the antiquarian to the ecclesiological. In the early period he was primarily interested in the fabric of churches, and frequently failed to make any comment whatsoever on their furnishings or their liturgical arrangements. In the later period he nearly always had something to say about how and whether the churches he visited had been restored, and he occasionally described the fittings in some detail. It is therefore probably fair to say that, overall, Sir Stephen's later notes are of more wide-ranging historical value than his earlier ones, though all provide information about church buildings rarely available in such detail elsewhere. The Kentish notes as published are not in any chronological order but presumably reflect the arrangement of the, now lost, notebooks. There is, however, a topographical index which makes the volume easily usable.

*   *   *

The historical value of Sir Stephen's notes lies in four specific areas. Firstly, they provide a detailed description of the fabric of churches in the nineteenth century. Secondly, they record the condition of churches as yet unaffected by Victorian restoration. Thirdly, they give the views of a contemporary on the early restorations carried out in some churches. Fourthly, they describe major furnishings, either medieval or post-Reformation, which were swept away in subsequent alterations to the building. It will be useful to look at each of these four aspects of Sir Stephen's notes in turn.

The descriptions of the fabric of churches contained in Sir Stephen's notes are primarily of interest to the architectural historian. A comparison of Sir Stephen's description with the present condition of the building provides valuable evidence of the changes made by the restorer, especially in the many cases for which other documentation in the form of plans, drawings, photographs or the minutes of building or restoration committees simply do not survive. Apart from those churches altered through restoration since Sir Stephen visited them, several churches in Kent were entirely rebuilt at a later date: these included Murston, Langley, Ripple, Swalecliffe, Brasted, Brenzett and St. Mary, Chatham. Unfortunately, Sir Stephen confined his notes, almost without exception, to churches of medieval foundation, so there are very few descriptions of new buildings, although he does record his impressions of Holy Trinity, Maidstone, visited in 1829. It would certainly have been interesting to have had his

5.   W.H. Gladstone alleged (*Ibid.*, p. iii) that all the undated notes referred to visits made prior to 1840, but this is not always borne out by the internal evidence of the notes themselves.

views on some other new buildings in the county, for example Christ Church, Kilndown, begun in 1839 and much embellished a few years later by A.J. Beresford-Hope. Both Beresford-Hope and Sir Stephen were 'high churchmen' and they later together formed the executive for supervising the building of All Saints, Margaret Street, London, intended to be a model for future church building designed for 'high church' worship.[6] Nevertheless, despite this limitation, Sir Stephen's notes do provide vital evidence for the architectural historian which has, despite their easy availability, been comparatively little used.

Sir Stephen's descriptions of unrestored churches are without parallel. For Kent he provides observations on the unrestored condition of about a hundred churches, sometimes in very considerable detail. These descriptions are contained in the appendix to this paper. Unlike some of his contemporaries, Sir Stephen did not condemn all pre-ecclesiological fittings as improper. He distinguished between what he considered the more and the less tasteful furnishings and liturgical arrangements. Many of the unrestored interiors noted by Sir Stephen were clearly extremely simple with deal pews and crude galleries, but some, such as those at Staplehurst, Whitstable, Lullingstone, Downe and North Cray, contained particularly good examples of pre-Restoration fittings, of which only those at Lullingstone and North Cray have survived virtually intact. Other, more simple, unrestored interiors noted by Sir Stephen, which have also been little altered since he wrote, were those at Brookland, Old Romney and Stelling. Although he visited two other still unrestored churches, Badlesmere and Fordwich, he does not record any impression of interiors that were then commonplace, though now exceptional. For some of the unrestored interiors recorded by Sir Stephen, the modern ecclesiologist will need to look for surviving parallels outside Kent. Northfleet, where only the eastern part of the church was fitted up for worship, must have resembled the larger country churches in Ireland, which are still treated in this way and the unused sections screened off.[7] The magnificent jumble of galleries and pews at Deal and Walmer must have been similar to the surviving interior at St. Mary's, Whitby, which was similarly enlarged and fitted up in the late eighteenth and nineteenth centuries. At Queenborough and Stone-next-Dartford, Sir Stephen noted interesting survivals from the 'high church' liturgical arrangements of the seventeenth century, the credence table and lectern at the former, and the vested altar with candlesticks at the latter. The daily services noted at Rolvenden were certainly an indication of Tractarian activity, even though the church was otherwise ecclesiologically unacceptable. At Cranbrook Sir Stephen noted, what is still a unique survival, 'on the south side of the nave . . . what is scarce to be found in any other church – a square baptistery of stone for the purpose of immersing such Baptists as desire to enter the communion of the church; it was erected in 1725 by the Revd. John Johnson, Vicar, and resembles a bath with a descent of several steps. It is said only to have been used twice'.[8] Considering the losses of important eighteenth-century fittings in other Kent churches, including many at Cranbrook, this survival is all the more remarkable.

Sir Stephen noted far fewer restored than unrestored churches, but these include important descriptions of the completed restorations at Egerton (1854), Pembury (1868), Woodchurch

6. B.F.L. Clarke, *Church Builders of the Nineteenth Century*, rev. ed. Newton Abbot 1969, 119. For Kilndown, see J.F. White, *The Cambridge Movement*, Cambridge 1962, 157–8.
7. e.g. the country cathedrals at Killaloe and Old Leighlin.
8. *Notes*, 79.

(1859) and Preston-by-Wingham (1863), and of restorations in progress at Sellindge (1861), Boxley and Swingfield (both 1866). He unfortunately visited Boughton Malherbe in 1847, shortly before an important ecclesiological restoration in 1848–50, though he adds in a footnote that 'this church has since been partly reconstructed, and much embellished, at great expense'.[9] All the descriptions of restorations, giving details of fittings and liturgical arrangements, have, like those of unrestored interiors, been included in the appendix to this paper. Known dates of restorations subsequent to those of Sir Stephen's recorded visits are appended in the appropriate footnotes to the appendix.

The fourth, and perhaps greatest, value of Sir Stephen's notes is that they do not just record fabrics that have been altered, or liturgical arrangements that have been discontinued, but they also record many important medieval and early post-Reformation fittings which were swept away by later restorers. The most serious casualties were rood screens, choir stalls and stained glass. Screens and/or stalls noted by Sir Stephen at Preston-next-Faversham, Herne, Alkham, Wootton, Adisham, West Wickham and Halling have been either completely destroyed or heavily mutilated. Important medieval glass at Meopham, Molash and Shadoxhurst has also disappeared. Sir Stephen also noted that several medieval fonts were, at the time of his visits, encased in wood, but all these casings seem to have been removed. At Borden he noted: 'the font is curious, from being a specimen of 1723. The bowl is octagonal, on a similar stem. The cover is of Gothic wood-work upon iron, with pulley and inscription giving the above date'.[10] This font was presumably destroyed when an earlier medieval font was 'replaced in the church only after 1918'.[11] The 1662 poor box at Wootton has also gone, as have the 'modern Gothic' rood screen and chancel roof 'ceiled in 1740' noted at Cowden in 1853.[12] There was a screen of similar design replacing a removed chancel arch at Guston.[13] One of the most serious losses has been at Wingham, where Sir Stephen noted that the chancel was 'approached from the nave by a wood screen of the style of the 17th century with twisted columns. In the chancel are all the original stalls in good preservation with misereres. . . . There are several texts inscribed on the walls; a seraphine in the chancel is played by the incumbent's lady'.[14] The screen seems to have been placed on a medieval base, and this alone has survived,[15] although Sir Stephen did note 'a bit of the rood screen in the vestry' and this could have been reinstated when the other screen was removed. At Chilham the magnificent *mausolea* on either side of the chancel were destroyed during a vigorous restoration by David Brandon in 1863.[16] They were described in some detail by Sir Stephen after his visit in 1846:[17]

> The original chapel on the north [of the chancel] is replaced by one of Italian character, of circular form, with a high dome and coloured glass, containing monumental tablets to the Colebrooke family. This domical chapel, built in 1755, under the direction of Sir Robert Taylor, as the mausoleum of the Colebrooke family, has been much admired for its gorgeous though incongruous character. . . . The

   9. *Ibid.*, 143.
  10. *Ibid.*, 165.
  11. J. Newman, *North East and East Kent*, Penguin Buildings of England, Harmondsworth 1969, 143.
  12. *Notes*, 179–80.
  13. *Ibid.*, 45.
  14. *Ibid.*, 109–10.
  15. J. Newman, *op. cit.*, 480.
  16. *Ibid.*, 259.
  17. *Notes*, 133.

north rotunda is of brick. On the south side is another monumental chapel of Italian design, built temp. James I by Sir Dudley Digges. This is highly enriched, and contains an elaborate tomb, full of urns, emblematic figures, &c., with a pompous inscription commemorating Sir D. Digges, and his lady, obt. 1638.

The monuments survived the demolition of the *mausolea*. Another significant curiosity which has fortunately survived is the medieval cope at East Langdon, which it has been alleged was cut down for use as an altar frontal.[18] Sir Stephen, however, noted its actual use:[19]

> The pulpit cloth is a remarkable feature in this church, it seems to be a part of the priests' vestments, and is of crimson velvet richly embroidered with a representation of the Annunciation of the Virgin Mary with the lily pot and scrolls, and other elegant devices and cyphers. The scrolls are inscribed: *Ave grā plena . . . Ecce ancilla dñi . . . fiat michi secundum,* &c. The colour of the velvet is well preserved considering its age.

But he also noted that 'the cushion of the pulpit is also of a similar material', and it would appear that this cushion was discarded when the cope ceased to be used as a pulpit hanging.

*   *   *

The church notes of Sir Stephen Glynne are therefore an important source for both the architectural and the ecclesiastical historian. They contain not merely descriptions of buildings and their fittings, but they are also, like the pages of the *Ecclesiologist,* a useful contemporary guide to the opinions of those most involved in the restoration of churches. In Sir Stephen's case, however, because he began his notes some two decades before ecclesiological opinions came to dominate the whole subject, his reflections are all the more interesting, and one can detect in the notes the gradual change in his attitudes, opinions and prejudices over the years. He began, as has been indicated, as a typical antiquary of the late eighteenth or early nineteenth century, with a largely romantic interest in medieval buildings. This approach was shared by many others including contemporary artists and lithographers, much of whose work survives in the topographical collections of libraries, museums and record offices.[20] This approach concentrated on accentuating the surviving medieval detail and ignoring later accretions; thus early nineteenth-century illustrations of the fine Norman church at Barfrestone concentrate on the elaborate carving and the interior furnishings are either noted only in outline or entirely blotted out, and Sir Stephen's description of the church, which he would appear to have visited in 1830 since a footnote records that the process of restoration began after that date, is limited to an enthusiastic appreciation of the fabric.[21] It was only after 1840 that Sir Stephen began to record in greater detail whether church interiors were restored or unrestored, and his comments on their aesthetic value. In a way therefore he seems to have been more a 'follower' of the ecclesiological movement than someone who had endeavoured to anticipate it. He also, in his efforts to be reasonably objective in his attitude to restoration and non-restoration, deliberately set himself apart from the more single-minded ecclesiologists,

18.   J. Newman, *op. cit.,* 292.
19.   *Notes*, 99.
20.   e.g. the two volumes of drawings of churches in the Charles Collection at Maidstone Museum, which date from the 1820s, and the fine series of Ubsdell water colours of Hampshire churches in the 1830s and 1840s in Portsmouth City Museum and Art Gallery.
21.   *Notes*, 42–4.

who were happy to praise virtually any restoration and condemn any fittings of post-Reformation date, and even some later medieval ones that they considered 'debased'. Indeed, it would have been interesting to know what he thought about some of the Kentish restorations in which medieval glass and woodwork were systematically destroyed to be replaced by imitations of earlier Gothic fittings.

Altogether then, although they do not always tell the architectural and ecclesiastical historian everything he or she would like to know about the fabric and fittings of the churches visited, the church notes of Sir Stephen Glynne are one of the most valuable available sources for the appearance and condition of British churches in the second and third quarters of the nineteenth century. In the case of Kent the fact that the original notebooks have disappeared makes one particularly grateful that they should have been published in their entirety, even if this has meant that the form of publication was so basic. The footnotes provided by Archdeacon Harrison and Canon Scott Robertson also throw valuable light on the restorations carried out after Sir Stephen's visits, and occasionally even, as in the case of Sittingbourne and Folkestone,[22] give details of previous fittings which Sir Stephen himself had not recorded. One can only hope that architectural and ecclesiastical historians will make more systematic use of them, and they should be compulsory reading for any person contemplating the compilation of a guide to or a history of their parish church.

APPENDIX

Liturgical and seating arrangements in Kentish churches, 1829–73

The churches are listed in the order printed in the notes. The page reference is given in square brackets, the date of visitation where stated in round brackets, place names have been modernised where necessary.

[p. 3] Maidstone (1829): A large new church (Holy Trinity) has been erected in the upper part of the town, of fine stone, in the plain Grecian style with a lofty spire. It is very capacious; contains an organ, galleries, &c.[23]

[p. 8] Milton-next-Sittingbourne: The whole interior is kept very neat, and the whitewash has been taken off some of the ornamental portions. There are no galleries.[24]

[p. 15] Faversham: The altar screen is of woodwork, and is a pretty good imitation of Gothic work; the altar itself is a marble slab supported on iron work.[25]

22. *Ibid.*, 9, 51. At Sittingbourne Harrison noted: 'the western gallery removed, . . . the square pews taken away, the nave fitted up with open seats, and the chancel arranged chorally, the organ being placed on the north side of the chancel'. At Folkestone: 'The church has been well restored, 1870, the nave extended two bays to the west, and all the wretched modern work replaced by some of appropriate character; the whole of the nave fitted with open seats, the chancel stalled for a surpliced choir, and a very fine organ placed on the south of the tower'.
23. Built 1826–28, now disused and awaiting conversion to an arts centre.
24. Main restoration 1889 by W.L. Grant, a local architect.
25. Canon Scott Robertson notes that the altar screen 'was replaced by a stone reredos, when the church was restored'. Restoration began in 1858, reaching its height in 1873–75.

[p. 26] Patrixbourne: The interior is newly and handsomely pewed.[26]

[p. 35] St. John-in-Thanet: The interior disfigured by shabby irregular pews and unsightly galleries.[27]

[p. 37] St. Peter-in-Thanet: The pews are neat and uniform, and the altar handsome.[28]

[p. 38] St. Lawrence-in-Thanet: The whole church is fitted up with pews and galleries painted with most glaring white.[29]

[p. 47] St. Margaret-at-Cliffe: The interior is wainscoted, and has a gaudy modern altar-piece. The pews are neat.[30]

[p. 49] Dover, St. Mary (1829): The interior is roomy and spacious, but not elegant, and much crowded by pews and galleries. At the west end is a large organ. The Corporation seat is situated behind the altar.[31]

[p. 50] Dover, St. James (1829): The interior is ugly enough, with flat ceilings, and encumbered with very high lumbering pews and a large west gallery in which is an organ.[32]

[p. 65] Lydd: The pews do not occupy the whole space in the nave, and there are no galleries.[33]

[p. 69] Tenterden: The pews and galleries are crowded, the altar-piece Grecian and Modern.[34]

[p. 71] Ashford: There are galleries along both aisles, and one at the west end.[35]

[p. 78] Cranbrook: The [chancel] ceiling is coved and painted in bad taste; there is much modern wainscoting, a neat Grecian altar and marble pavement within the communion rails. There are no galleries save one at the west end of the nave, in which is a fine organ.[36]

[p. 82] Hawkhurst: The appearance of the interior . . . is much injured by the insertion of numerous unsightly galleries.[37]

[p. 86] Marden: There are ugly deal high pews, and a west gallery with a barrel organ.[38]

[pp. 87–9] Staplehurst: The chancel arch has been removed, and is replaced by an ugly Italian one of wood. . . . The pews are highbacked. A west gallery contains an organ. . . . The altar is neat, the reredos and adjoining portions are of modern wainscot. . . . The altar picture

26. Presumably pewed when north aisle rebuilt c. 1824; the church was fully restored in 1857.
27. Galleries removed and church re-seated during restoration of 1875–6.
28. Restored 1852–59, pews replaced by open seats.
29. Restored 1858.
30. Restored in 1869 when whitewash taken off and altar-piece removed.
31. All these fittings were removed and the church re-seated during a vigorous early restoration in 1843–44.
32. Archdeacon Harrison noted that the church had been 'recently restored', but the building is now a ruin as a result of war damage.
33. Clearly the church was large enough to accommodate worshippers without them. No major Victorian restoration recorded but chancel rebuilt in 1958 and other parts restored in 1951–53 after war damage; see J. Newman, *West Kent and the Weald*, Penguin Buildings of England, Harmondsworth 1969, 375.
34. Fittings removed and church re-seated during restoration of c. 1864–66.
35. Galleries removed when nave lengthened in 1860.
36. Fittings removed and church re-seated during major restoration in 1863.
37. Galleries were removed when church was restored between 1849 and 1859.
38. Restored 1868.

represents the Descent from the Cross.[39]

[p. 94]   Lyminge: The tower . . . arch . . . much hidden by an ugly singing gallery. . . . The church is for the most part obstructed by high pews. (Revisited 1862): The interior has been cleared, the gallery taken down, and the pews replaced by open seats.

[p. 99]   East Langdon: There is a west gallery and hideous pews.[40]

[p. 100]   Ringwould: The pews are as usual high and ugly, and there is a west gallery with a barrel organ. . . . The walls are inscribed with several texts mostly in lozenge compartments.[41]

[p. 101]   Deal: Has undergone many injudicious and tasteless alterations . . . pillars are hideously painted in imitation of marble. . . . There are numerous galleries and a most horrible gallery pew erected between the nave and chancel.[42]

[p. 104]   Northbourne: The nave is fitted up with deal pews, but the avenue in the centre is tolerably wide. . . . The walls are inscribed with texts.[43]

[p. 107]   Staple: Many of the original open seats are perceptible, but on some of them modern pews have been exalted.[44]

[pp. 111–2]   Hawkinge: The interior is dirty and out of condition . . . There are hideous high pews in the chancel especially offensive in so small a church.[45]

[pp. 112–3]   Langley: The nave is short and confined, and still further impaired by the presence of high pews, and a hideous gallery at the west end. . . . The chancel is wainscoted within, so that the sedilia, &c., if any, are completely hidden.[46]

[pp. 117–8]   Walmer: This church in its present state is but an unsightly object . . . a mean bell-turret has been erected over the west end, and a huge brick excrescence added on the north, filled with pews and galleries, and making the church quite shapeless. . . . The pulpit fronts the north, in order to face the congregation, who occupy the north wing or excrescence.[47]

[p. 119]   Ripple: The interior is neat, but has high pews. In the chancel are quasi wooden stalls. The reredos of mediocre modern Gothic design.[48]

[p. 121]   Gillingham (1844): The east window is filled with poor modern stained glass. The sacrarium is paved with marble. . . . The south chapel is partly disfigured with high pews,

39.   Archdeacon Harrison notes: 'The church has been restored externally, and reseated throughout, the western gallery removed. . . . The organ has been placed on the north side of the church'. Canon Scott Robertson adds: 'This wooden arch, as well as the high pews, the west gallery, and the wainscot reredos, disappeared when the church was restored'. This work appears to have been carried out over a period of years between 1853 and 1876, see J. Newman, op. cit., 522.
40.   Restored 1892.
41.   Archdeacon Harrison notes that 'this church has been restored and reseated'.
42.   No complete restoration ever undertaken but only the west gallery, dated 1705, now survives; see J. Newman, North East and East Kent, 269.
43.   Restored 1865.
44.   All the seating was apparently renewed during G.E. Street's restoration in 1868–69.
45.   Restored and reseated in 1875.
46.   Entirely rebuilt in 1853–55 for the then rector, W.B. Pusey (1843–86), who was the brother of the Tractarian leader, E.B. Pusey. Subsequent alterations have made Langley a rather less good example of a typical Tractarian church than it was originally. The architect was William Butterfield, himself a Tractarian.
47.   North aisle demolished and interior refitted in 1898.
48.   Entirely rebuilt in the neo-Norman style in 1861.

partly in a wretched state of dirt and neglect.[49]

[p. 124] Wye (1845): There is a west gallery with an organ and a south gallery.

[p. 126] Boughton Aluph (1845): The pews are deal, and very ugly.

[pp. 135–6] Whitstable (1846): In rather a dilapidated state. . . . The pews are most unsightly, and many are coloured light blue; they are, however, about to be removed, and a general repair effected. . . . The pulpit is a sort of 'flying' one, apparently supported on air, and approached by a singularly ugly staircase and passage.[51]

[p. 139] Temple Ewell (1847): The north chapel is separated from the church and used as a school. . . . There are wretched blue communion rails, and pews in the chancel also painted blue. Those in the nave are of deal.[52]

[p. 142] Hougham (1847): Pews high and ugly.[53]

[pp. 144–5] Chislet (1848): There are north and west galleries. . . . The sedilia are partly hidden by wainscoting; and there is an ugly reredos and quasi stalls of modern work. The walls are whitewashed, and the floor of brick.[54]

[p. 146] Hadlow (1861): The chancel is stalled. The nave has low regular pews, and a gallery at the west end.[55]

[pp. 146–7] Lullingstone (1859): The interior is much modernised, but on the whole handsomely fitted up with oak pews, marble pavement and stuccoed ceiling. . . . Between the nave and chancel is . . . a rood screen which seems post-Reformation, with debased Gothic tracery and groining. . . . There is a kind of screen in stucco at the west end of the chapel with inscription commemorating Percival Hart, Esq., the repairer and beautifier of the church, who died in 1738. . . . The chancel is stalled, and the windows full of stained glass, some of late character with armorial shields, some representing saints.[56]

[p. 150] Bexley (1846): There are frightful pews, and a gallery at the west end with a good organ. It is written on a pew, 'these three pews were built at the charge of the Parish, 1765'.[57]

[pp. 152–3] Leigh (1847): This [south transept] chapel is pewed, and in its shed-like roof is a dormer window. There is an altar picture representing the Man of Sorrows. . . . There is a west gallery and barrel organ. Some part is pewed, some fitted with open benches. [Additional note]: Leigh church underwent a laudable restoration in 1861. . . . The new seats are all open, and the gallery has been removed. Several windows are filled with stained glass.

[p. 155] Leybourne (1847): The aisle of the nave is galleried.[58]

[pp. 155–6] Egerton (1854): This church has lately had the benefit of a careful restoration, by which the interior has been placed in a condition of much beauty. . . . The chancel roof is

49. Restored by A.W. Blomfield in 1868–69.
50. Presumably removed in 1878 when west window replaced, see J. Newman, *op. cit.*, 486.
51. Church largely rebuilt 1875–6.
52. North chapel rebuilt and incorporated in the church, and rest of interior re-arranged, in 1874.
53. Church largely rebuilt 1866.
54. Restored 1866.
55. Improvements carried out between 1847 and 1853.
56. This interior survives virtually as described, see J. Newman, *West Kent and the Weald*, 370–2.
57. Restored 1882–83.
58. Restored 1873–77.

richly coloured, of a deep blue with gilt stars, and divided into panelled compartments, the effect of which is very fine. Across it is a beam on which is inscribed: 'The Lord is in his holy temple'. There is a screen separating the aisle from the chancel, and a brazen altar rail. . . . The sacrarium is laid with tiles; the altar set on a pace. . . . The nave is fitted with very neat new oak benches, having flat-topped ends. The pulpit of similar character.[59]

[pp. 159–60] Hinxhill (1861): The Decalogue is between the nave and chancel, written on plaster and supported on a beam. . . . The reading-desk is constructed out of some pretty good ancient screen work. The pews are ugly and painted white.[50]

[p. 160] Loose (1850): An organ in a west gallery; also a north gallery. . . . The church is crowded with large pews.[61]

[p. 166] Tunstall (1850): The chancel is large and stalled in oak; the floor laid with tiles. . . . The east window is . . . filled with stained glass by Ward and Nixon.[62]

[p. 168] Littlebourne (1851): There are ugly pews, and an organ in the west gallery.[63]

[p. 169] Thanington (1851): The interior of the church has been recently much improved; the seats all open; the pulpit low, and a small organ in the south chapel.[64]

[pp. 176–7] Upchurch (1852): The interior is in good condition and has recently been much improved. . . . The south chapel is unfortunately used as a school, and a horrid brick chimney added. The floor of the nave has been laid with nice new tiles, red, black, and white in patterns, and a fine new font erected of Decorated character, with ball-flower ornament.[65]

[p. 179] Queenborough (1852): The interior is full of high pews. The altar rails are of iron, the sacrarium laid with marble, there is a credence table of wood, and a lectern within the sacrarium containing the Homilies and a book of sermons. A west gallery contains a seraphine.[66]

[p. 181] Canterbury (St. Mary Bredin, 1861): Recently restored and partially rebuilt, but it is to be lamented that the interior should have been treated with so little regard to ecclesiastical propriety . . . there is no distinction of chancel . . . the whole space is pewed, and there is a gallery with an organ at the west end.[67]

[p. 183] Canterbury (St. Alphege, 1861): There is a western gallery with an organ; the pews, old and ugly, are full of green baize.[68]

[p. 184] Milton-juxta-Canterbury (1861): Has been put in good condition and is kept very

59. J. Newman, op. cit., 264, describes the 1854 restoration as 'unsympathetic'.
60. Restored in 1881 but the reading-desk survives.
61. Nave rebuilt after fire damage in 1878.
62. Sir Stephen visited during a restoration begun in 1848 and completed in 1856.
63. Archdeacon Harrison notes that 'the church has been reseated'.
64. The improvements were carried out by Butterfield in 1846. The doubts expressed by J. Newman, *North East and East Kent*, 457, about whether Butterfield was responsible for the pulpit would seem to be cleared up by Sir Stephen's description.
65. The restoration of the church was completed by Blomfield in 1875–76. The tiles in the nave were followed by new tiles in the sanctuary in 1854, a contemporary description and illustration of which survives in the diary of the incumbent preserved in the Kent Archives Office, P377/28/34.
66. Restored 1885; the credence table and lectern appear not to have survived.
67. Entirely rebuilt in 1867–68.
68. Restored 1888.

neat . . . the nave has open seats; the chancel is stalled, and there is a good deal of stained glass.

[p. 185] Pembury (1868): The interior is in excellent condition, well restored, with nice new open seats, and the galleries are gone. The chancel is laid with new tiles, and fitted with seats stallwise. On the south are two new sedilia, and the reredos of alabaster is very elegant. The font is new.[69]

[p. 186] Capel (1863): The nave is filled with hideous pews. The altar and rails bear the date 1682.[70]

[p. 187] Chillenden (1870): The pews are high, and old-fashioned.[71]

[p. 189] Womenswold (1870): The nave has good new open benches.

[pp. 189–90] Sutton-next-Ripple (1870): Has undergone a recent restoration and partial rebuilding. . . . Encaustic tiles have been laid in the sacrarium, and at the back of the arcade is some ornament in terra-cotta. The chancel is stalled.

[p. 191] Bobbing (1871): The nave has open benches, and the whole church is neat.[72]

[p. 194] Oare (1871): The nave is neatly fitted with open seats.[73]

[p. 196] Luddenham (1871): The chancel is nicely arranged; fitted stall-wise; the sacrarium is laid with tiles, and has an ascent of three steps. The altar has a marble slab.

[p. 197] Tonge (1871): The chancel is neat; the altar space well paved; and the altar cloth good.[74]

[p. 199] Lynsted (1871): The nave is pewed and has a west gallery with organ.

[p. 202] Doddington (1871): The seats are mostly open.

[p. 203] Bidborough (1872): Much in want of internal improvement and re-arrangement. . . . The seats of the nave are very badly arranged, and the chancel much blocked.[75]

[p. 204] Speldhurst (1872): This church has been lately rebuilt (by G.G. Scott, junior) . . . and all the internal arrangements are satisfactory. Organ on the north of the chancel.[76]

[p. 205] Bilsington (1873): The church is pewed and unimproved. The walls are patched with brick work.[77]

[pp. 206–7] Newchurch (1873): The seats are all open, and the chancel has been much improved.[78]

69. Described as 'over-restored' by J. Newman, *West Kent and the Weald,* 432. His question about whether R. Wheeler of Brenchley, who carried out the restoration in 1867, was responsible for the 'alien' reredos, sedilia and font, would seem to be answered in the affirmative by Sir Stephen's description.
70. The altar rails survive, see J. Newman, *op. cit.*, 191, but Archdeacon Harrison noted that 'the pews have been removed, and open seats substituted'.
71. Restored 1871.
72. Restored 1863.
73. Restored 1868.
74. Largely unaltered by conservative restoration in 1873.
75. Reseated 1876.
76. J. Newman, *op. cit.*, 519–20, claims J.O. Scott as the architect, and describes the building as 'enjoyable'. Sir Stephen visited before most of the stained glass, which includes windows by Clayton and Bell, Kempe, Morris, and Burne-Jones, was installed.
77. Restored 1883.
78. An early restoration, *c.* 1845, extremely unusual for Romney Marsh.

[p. 209]   Wootton (1873): The church is as yet unrestored and has high pews.[79]

[p. 210]   Sellindge (1861): The interior has been lately improved in some respects, and further improvement is being carried on in the chancel. . . . All the seats are open. The chancel . . . is fitted with stalls.

[pp. 212–3]   Woodchurch (1859): The nave is fitted with open seats having square bench ends. . . . The sacrarium is raised on four steps, and is laid with rich glazed tiles. . . . The chancel has a coved roof, with ribs and bosses, painted blue; and it is fitted with stalls and an harmonium.[80]

[p. 217]   Kingsnorth (1859): The chancel is stalled: the nave has open seats.

[p. 218]   Rolvenden (1859): The nave is unfortunately galleried and pewed, though in a uniform style, and kept in good order. . . . There are daily services at a quarter past six a.m., and in the evening.[81]

[p. 220]   Sandhurst (1859): The interior is damp and ill-kept, with pews painted blue, and a west gallery containing a barrel organ. . . . The southern chapel is wholly modernised, and used for vestry and school.[82]

[p. 221]   Biddenden (1859): The nave has lately been fitted with open benches of pitch pine, and is in good condition.

[p. 224]   Bethersden (1859): The church has recently been put into very good condition; the nave fitted with low but rather too plain open benches: the chancel has a new reredos, and the sacrarium is laid with fine glazed tiles.[83]

[p. 225]   Chartham (1861): Still pewed and having a west gallery.[84]

[p. 231]   Leaveland (1859): The church is pewed.

[p. 233]   Eastwell (1859): The church was restored some years ago, but rather too soon to be entirely satisfactory. . . . The floors are laid with encaustic tiles, and the seats are open, with poppy heads. There is also a reredos; the font new.

[p. 234]   Brasted (1859): The seats are mostly open and the chancel fitted stallwise. . . . The chancel is laid with encaustic tiles, and has poor stalls and modern drapery at the east end.[85]

[p. 238]   Selling (1862): There is a modern reredos. . . . The interior is in a very neat and improved condition, yet the pews, though uniform, have doors. The pulpit is very fair.[86]

[p. 239]   Hernhill (1862): The nave has unimproved pews. . . . The interior is clogged with

79.   Restored 1878–81.
80.   Restored 1846–58.
81.   Restoration appears to have been gradual and incomplete, see J. Newman, *op. cit.*, 478.
82.   Restored 1875–86; Archdeacon Harrison notes that 'pews [have been] removed, and open seats substituted; windows restored, and the south chapel thrown into the church'.
83.   The reredos is described as 'early C19' by J. Newman, *op. cit.*, 149, but Sir Stephen clearly implies that it may be later than the style suggests.
84.   Archdeacon Harrison notes that 'this gallery and the high pews were removed when the church was restored'. This restoration was carried out by G.E. Street in 1873–75, and described as 'intelligent' by J. Newman, *North East and East Kent*, 255.
85.   Entirely rebuilt, except for the tower, in 1864–65.
86.   Restored 1841–46.

whitewash.[87]

[pp. 241–2] Dover Castle (1863): Has been lately restored. . . . Mr. G.G. Scott has done the restoration very judiciously. . . . The nave is fitted with open benches.[88]

[p. 242] Elmstone (1863): Some of the old benches remain, but with pews mounted upon them.[89]

[pp. 243–4] Preston-by-Wingham (1863): This church presents quite a model of successful restoration, in the true spirit of what should be applied to a village church, without unnecessary rebuilding or the application of unsuitable ornamentation, in contravention of the original character and prevailing style of the county. . . . Within [the chancel arch] is a nice new wood screen. . . . The chancel has at the east end a triple lancet, filled with very good stained glass by Lavers. . . . The nave is fitted with neat open benches; the chancel is stalled, and occupied by a surpliced choir. The north chapel contains a good organ.[90]

[p. 245] Adisham (1863): The nave is internally much disfigured by very ugly high pews of deal. . . . The north transept . . . had deal pews and fittings and an harmonium, it is used by the choir. The chapel on the west of this transept is partitioned off and occupied by rubbish and dirt.[91]

[p. 246] Eythorne (1863): The interior is fearfully disfigured with pews and galleries.[92]

[p. 249] Ridley (1863): The seats are open.

[p. 251] Hartley (1863): The interior has open seats, and seems to be well arranged.

[p. 252] Boxley (1866): The nave has neat open benches of pitch pine. . . . There is an organ in the chancel, the north side of which is stalled, the southern pewed.[93]

[p. 253] Brenzett (1868): The interior is clogged with whitewash, the west gallery painted blue, after the manner of the Marsh.[94]

[pp. 254–5] Snargate (1866): Through the laudable exertions of the present curate (who is endeavouring to place the whole church in a state of good repair and ecclesiastical propriety) the south chapel has been opened to the church and put into an improved condition, but is still without pavement. . . . The north chapel is still dilapidated, with holes in the roof, and boarded off. It was once, and not so very long ago, occupied for the purposes of smuggling! . . . The pews are painted white and the interior has a glaring whitewashed character. If nicely arranged and put into good repair, the interior would be really handsome and striking.[95]

[p. 256] Swingfield (1866): The nave has been lately fitted neatly with open benches. The chancel is damp and out of condition.[96]

87. Restored 1867–77.
88. Restored 1860–62; previously, according to Sir Stephen, 'long in a state of hopeless ruin'.
89. Only four bench-ends remain, see J. Newman, *op. cit.*, 299.
90. The restoration was by William White in *c.* 1857.
91. Restored 1869–70 when 'fitted with open seats', according to Archdeacon Harrison.
92. Archdeacon Harrison noted that 'this church has been thoroughly restored and refitted throughout'.
93. Restoration not completed until 1875–76.
94. Restored 1876.
95. Restoration completed 1870–72.
96. Chancel virtually rebuilt 1870.

[pp. 257–8]   Paddlesworth (1868): The nave is fitted with new open seats with heavy poppy ends.

[p. 258]   Waltham (1868): Now in good condition, has new open seats.

[p. 259]   Stelling (1868): There has been no attempt at restoration or improvement; the pews are ugly, and there is a gallery in the aisle.[97]

[pp. 261–2]   Stowting (1868): This church has been almost wholly rebuilt . . . the floor is laid with tiles, and the seats are all open. The whole in very nice condition. . . . There is a new piscina and a fine reredos of stone.[98]

[p. 263]   Ivychurch (1868): The interior is naked and forlorn, and very glaring, but the few scattered white painted pews, however ugly, do not block up the church, which is sadly too large for its scanty population.[99]

[p. 265]   Brookland (1868): The interior is glaring with whitewash, and the pews are painted white, and very high.[100]

[p. 266]   Dymchurch (1868): The nave and aisle are thrown into one by the removal of the arcade, but the seats are all open.

[p. 267]   Appledore (1868): The interior is still pewed, and has a western gallery. . . . The north chapel is now wholly excluded and used as a school.

[pp. 268–9]   Old Romney (1868): The nave is glaring with whitewash, and thoroughly unimproved in condition; the pews high and mostly painted white. . . . The chancel arch is wholly modernised, and masked in wainscoting, and the whole of the chancel has modern wainscoting. . . . The north aisle, now used as the vestry. . . . The south chapel, which is now occupied by rubbish.[101]

[p. 271]   Bromley (1829): In the interior the arches and piers have been removed, in order to facilitate the erection of galleries. . . . There are north, south and west galleries, the latter containing a fine organ.[102]

[p. 273]   Keston (1832): The interior is neatly pewed.[103]

[p. 273]   Downe (1832): The interior is neatly and even elegantly fitted up, the pews and pulpit are handsome, and there is a barrel organ. . . . The east window has modern stained glass; the altar rails and table are handsome, and the altar cloth is a curious ancient one of damask.[104]

[p. 274]   Eltham (1830): The interior is neat and well pewed; with galleries all round, and a double one at the west end with the organ.[105]

---

97.   This church remains unrestored, exactly as described by Sir Stephen; see J. Newman, *op. cit.*, 449–50.
98.   There were several bouts of restoration, beginning with the chancel in 1843–44, followed by a new north aisle and north-west tower in 1857–68, and further restoration between 1876 and 1890.
99.   Restored 1888–90, 'with kindness', see J. Newman, *West Kent and the Weald,* 334.
100.   Largely unaltered, *ibid.*, 186–88.
101.   The wainscoting has been removed from the chancel arch but many other fittings survive, *ibid.*, 423–24.
102.   Bombed 1941, but had been heavily restored after Sir Stephen's visit.
103.   Restored and extended 1878.
104.   Restored 1879.
105.   Entirely rebuilt 1875.

[p. 275]   Dartford (1829): the nave has crowded pews and galleries, and an organ at the west end.[106]

[p. 276]   Horton Kirby (1831): The whole interior is covered with glaring whitewash, but is very neatly pewed.[107]

[p. 277]   Meopham (1863): The seats are open.[108]

[p. 278]   East Farleigh: The nave is very neatly pewed.[109]

[p. 279]   Tonbridge (1833): There are galleries north and south, and one at the west end contains a fine organ.[110]

[p. 281]   Westerham: Has been fairly restored since 1850. The sacrarium is laid with fine new tiles. There is a new pulpit and some good wood-carving.[111]

[p. 288]   Goudhurst (1873): Has been nicely restored, fitted up with neat open benches (save the south aisle, where there are still high pews) and the chancel with stalls for surpliced choir, the organ being moved to the south aisle of the chancel. . . . The reredos is tiled.[112]

[p. 290]   Nettlestead: The interior is neat and well pewed. . . . The altar-piece is very neat, in the Corinthian style.[113]

[p. 295]   Snodland: The pews are modern and uniform.[114]

[p. 301]   Seal: The pews are very neat and uniform, and there is a double gallery at the west end.[115]

[p. 303]   Chevening (1859): The church was restored in 1858, and fitted with open seats.[116]

[pp. 311–12]   Northfleet: Consists of a spacious nave with side aisles, in two distinct divisions, a partition being placed between them and the western portion not used for service. The chancel and eastern portion of the nave are appropriated to the service, and pewed. . . . The western portion of the nave is left open without pews. . . . Between the western and eastern division of the nave is a pointed arch, and there are similar ones in the side aisles. Across the whole runs a screen and a singing gallery facing the east division, which is now fitted up for the service.[117]

[p. 313]   Chalk (1832): The interior is dark, but neatly pewed.

[pp. 314–5]   Shorne: Both the side aisles of the chancel are partitioned off from the chancel

---

106.   Restored 1862–63.
107.   Restored 1862–63.
108.   Restored 1859.
109.   Partly rebuilt 1891.
110.   Enlarged and restored 1877–79.
111.   The restoration referred to was that by Teulon in 1854; there was a further restoration in 1882.
112.   This restoration took place in *c.* 1865–70.
113.   Restored 1858.
114.   Restored 1870.
115.   Various alterations carried out between 1855 and 1879.
116.   Further restorations in 1869 and 1902.
117.   Restored 1862; Canon Scott Robertson noted that 'every part of it [the church] is now available for use at the frequent daily services', the parish being a centre of Tractarian activity in the last quarter of the nineteenth century.

and used as schools. . . . The church is neatly pewed.[118]

[p. 319] Rochester (St. Nicholas, 1831): The interior is neatly pewed.[119]

[p. 328] Milton-next-Gravesend: The interior is much modernised, with a flat ceiling, walls painted blue, a large west gallery, and smaller side galleries north and south, which, though not deep, are very unsightly in this narrow church. In the west gallery is a tolerable organ. The pews encroach very much on the altar.[120]

[p. 335] Stone-next-Dartford: There are three steps to the altar, which is adorned with velvet cloth and candlesticks. . . . The pews [are] hideously high and inconvenient, and there is a barrel organ in a west gallery.[121]

[p. 341] Luddesdown (1847): The pews are very hideous.[122]

[p. 344] North Cray (1849): The chancel . . . roof is coved, panelled with ribs and bosses, and lately painted blue with gilt stars, which is the best thing that has been done in the church. The Decalogue, &c., are written in illuminated characters, and there are scrolls with texts beneath the chancel roof. The stained glass is not of a very high order, though there is a good deal; the pulpit has some rich wood carving, and the reredos is of somewhat elaborate Flemish sculpture in wood, representing the flight into Egypt; but it does not harmonise well, or look as if it were in its proper place. The chancel is sadly encumbered with pews quite close to the altar, the nave also abounds with pews, some of which are embellished with rich carving.[123]

[p. 345] Erith (1849): There are high pews.[124]

[p. 346] Chatham (1852): The church is galleried.[125]

[p. 346] Sundridge (1854): The chancel has been laid with handsome new tiles, and those in the sacrarium are of still richer character than the rest.[126]

[p. 349] Cliffe-at-Hoo (1857): The interior is spacious and part of the nave is wholly clear of seats . . . but the existing pews are very ugly.[127]

[p. 351] Hoo St. Werburgh (1857): The church is pewed and has a barrel organ in the gallery.

118. Restored 1874–75; Canon Scott Robertson noted that 'no school is held in the church. The arches have been completely opened up'.
119. Restored 1860–62, now partially converted to office use for the diocese of Rochester.
120. North and west galleries survive, see J. Newman, *op. cit.*, 290.
121. Restored *c.* 1859–60 by G.E. Street who contributed a major architectural study of the church to *Arch. Cant.*, iii (1860), 97–134. Although the sanctuary arrangements described by Sir Stephen are more likely to be a survival than a revival, Frederick William Murray, rector of Stone-next-Dartford 1859–1906, was a prominent local ritualist. It was Murray who commissioned Street to restore the church.
122. Largely rebuilt 1866.
123. Rebuilt between 1850 and 1871, but retaining many of the fittings described by Sir Stephen, see J. Newman, *op. cit.*, 418.
124. Restored 1877.
125. Entirely rebuilt between 1884 and 1903, now redundant and awaiting conversion to a heritage centre.
126. Restored 1848–49.
127. Various restorations took place between 1853 and 1884.

WEALTH, TRADES AND AGRICULTURE IN THE ELIZABETHAN WEALD

The Weald in the sixteenth and seventeenth centuries is often portrayed as a wild and untamed region, peopled by a race of independent-minded forest dwellers living beyond the authority of state and church, England's natural rebels. The description may fit for the late fourteenth and fifteenth centuries, but it will hardly do for Tudor times. True it may be that travel along Wealden roads could be problematic during winter, but the Kentish Weald in the reign of Elizabeth I was anything but cut off from the rest of the kingdom. In fact the economic specialities of the Weald during the sixteenth century were drawing the region more closely into the national market for both agricultural produce and manufactures. The ties with London were especially important, but equally necessary were the trading links with north Kent (for corn) and the Highland zones of England and Wales (for livestock). The purpose of this essay is to illustrate the economic life of the Kent Weald via an analysis of the surviving probate inventories lodged in the Kent Archives Office. It can hardly claim to be a definitive study, but is rather an example of what can be done with a single, systematic source.[1]

Probate inventories have in recent decades come into their own as a major object of historical research. They are frequently the empirical backbone of studies of the economic life of towns, regions and counties, and transcripts of many have been printed.[2] Before proceeding to my analysis of the inventories, the limitations of the source must be pointed out. Probate inventories are by no means 'the perfect source'. For the sixteenth century, practically none survive for the more substantial gentry landowners or peers.[3] Coverage is uneven both in geographical and chronological terms. This is perhaps the greatest limitation of the present study, for there are no inventories before about 1565 for any part of Kent, and none at all for the diocese of Rochester or Shoreham deanery before the mid-seventeenth century. Thus this essay covers the central and eastern Weald only. In addition an unknown, but substantial, share of even the adult males is unrecorded in testamentary records of any kind. *Most* of the wealthier residents (except the aristocracy) and *some* of the poor are covered by extant inventories. It is untrue to claim that very small estates (under £5) were never the subject of

1. Probate inventories in the Kent Archives Office (hereafter *KAO*) PRC 10/1–29, PRC 21/1–16 and PRC 28/1–4. The research for this study was supported by a grant from the Social Science Research Council. The full findings will appear in due course as 'Kentish Wealden Society in the Sixteenth Century'.
2. A good example is M.A. Havinden (ed.), *Household and Farm Inventories in Oxfordshire, 1550–1590*, (1965). The classic studies using inventories are W.G. Hoskins, 'The Leicestershire Farmer in the Sixteenth Century' in *Essays in Leicestershire History* (1950), *idem., The Midland Peasant* (1957) and Joan Thirsk, *English Peasant Farming* (1957) (on Lincs.). A more recent and stunning example is Margaret Spufford, *Contrasting Communities: English Villagers in the Sixteenth and Seventeenth Centuries* (1974), and for urban subjects, Alan D. Dyer, *The City of Worcester in the Sixteenth Century* (1973), and *Victoria History of Leicestershire*, iv, *City of Leicester* (1958), 'Social and Economic History, 1509–1660' by Eric Kerridge.
3. Most landed gentry of any significance who left wills, had them proved in the Prerogative Court of Canterbury, as did many of the more prosperous clothiers and a few of the less well off. Almost no probate inventories survive (in the Public Record Office) from this period among the PCC records.

probate inventories, only that most of the very poor were not included. People who made wills are also represented by probate inventories, but many inventories also survive for intestates. A further limitation of inventories is that they record only contemporary money values of chattels and stock, and thus inflation must be taken into account. In addition the inventories may give an unreliable indication of the total wealth of individuals, because they record only cash, chattels and debts due; real property is ignored. Although they provide some idea of a man's farm, they give neither indication of land tenure nor of land owned – but not directly farmed – by the deceased. One final weakness of the inventories used in this study is that they only rarely give the occupational or social addition after the name of the deceased. Thus in many cases the trade or occupation followed by the deceased cannot be known, where it cannot be inferred from chattels owned by the person. This is particularly damaging in the case of inventories which show no trade goods or tools and no real agricultural activity (beyond a cow or two). In such cases the person may have been a labourer, a semi-skilled artisan, a retired person or occasionally a minor. A similar doubt arises from inventories which record what appear to be extremely small farms. Should such individuals be counted as 'farmers' (which would of course lower the average size and value of 'farmers' estates in the study) or should they be recorded as 'labourers' or 'cottagers'? Most of these smallholders could not have supported families by their farming activities alone, but some may have been skilled artisans, others agricultural labourers. I have chosen to call the former problem cases 'labourer or retired', and the second 'smallholder plus?', akin to what other historians have called cottagers. Thus the Wealden inventories are not a representative sample in any statistical sense, but they do present something of a cross-section of Wealden society with certain notable exceptions. The very poor, and the simpler agricultural and building trades, are not well represented, and women are under-represented throughout. Nevertheless, probate inventories provide a detailed and substantial portrait of large numbers of ordinary Englishmen and women which can be subjected to simple quantitative analysis.

i

The Kent Weald is represented in this study by about 1,500 inventories from the following fourteen parishes: Benenden, Bethersden, Biddenden, Cranbrook, Frittenden, Goudhurst, Halden, Hawkhurst, Marden, Rolvenden, Sandhurst, Smarden, Staplehurst, Tenterden.[4] The

4. Newenden has been excluded because of its tiny population. The estimated total population of the sample parishes, based on the 1557 returns of communicants (in *Harpsfield's Visitations,* Catholic Record Society, 1950–51) with communicants estimated as 65 per cent of the total:

Parish	Total	Density	Parish	Total	Density
Benenden	925	138/1000a.	Hawkhurst	1,230	189/1000a.
Bethersden	615	96/1000a.	Marden	770	99/1000a.
Biddenden	925	128/1000a.	Rolvenden	615	126/1000a.
Cranbrook	2,300	221/1000a.	(based on later survey)		
Frittenden	370	106/1000a.	Sandhurst	430	98/1000a.
Goudhurst	1,385	141/1000a.	Smarden	615	114/1000a.
Halden	400	107/1000a.	Staplehurst	615	104/1000a.
			Tenterden	1,075	126/1000a.

The 1557 returns have been preferred to those of 1563 as more accurate: in the latter there are even serious disagreements in household totals between the two manuscripts: British Library, Harleian MS. 594 f. 63 ff., and Corpus Christi College, Cambridge, MS. 122, 291 ff.

inventories come from both the archdeaconry and consistory court series, and all identifiable inventories from the sample parishes have been included. Table 1 offers a breakdown of the occupations and trades represented in the inventories from all the sample parishes besides Sandhurst (whose total number was very small). The very small parish of Frittenden has here been grouped with neighbouring Cranbrook. In all, just under 1,200 inventories can be assigned to a trade or occupational group. The remaining 230-odd inventories are mostly those of women who do not appear to have been engaged in either trade or farming, and 43 miscellaneous or uncertain male inventories. This initial breakdown, which classes persons under a single occupational or trade grouping, oversimplifies the nature of economic activity in the Weald. As will be shown, a significant share of those classified under a craft or trade were also engaged in agriculture. But for the moment, it is the wide variety of trades and manufacturing which demands attention.

A glance at the table shows immediately that even in the Weald farming was the most common occupation. In the non-manufacturing parishes in the east, Rolvenden and Halden produced absolute majorities of farmers and graziers, and even semi-urban Tenterden shows farming as the main occupation of more than 40 per cent of the classified inventories. In Rolvenden less than 20 per cent, and in Halden under 15 per cent of the inventories show an identifiable non-farming occupation (other than labourer or retired). Marden and Bethersden, further north, also seem to be more basically agrarian than the circle of parishes round Cranbrook, although both parishes had some clothmaking activity.

Compared to occupational surveys in champion districts of England, the wide variety of trades and the intensive cloth manufacturing taking place in these Wealden parishes stand out quite clearly. The inventories suggest that weaving was the most widespread non-agrarian pursuit in the Weald: even including the mainly agricultural parishes, more than ten per cent of inventories were those of weavers (and the number may well have been higher if many weavers did not own their own looms). In the sample as a whole, only in Halden was the woollen industry unimportant. At the other extreme, almost a quarter of inventories in Benenden, Cranbrook and Frittenden, about 30 per cent in Biddenden, and a fifth of inventories in Smarden, are of residents engaged in the three basic clothmaking trades. In Goudhurst and Hawkhurst those trades include 15 per cent or more of all inventories classified. The inventories also suggest even more precisely the institutional centre of Wealden clothmaking, in Cranbrook, Biddenden and Benenden, the parishes where the largest numbers of clothiers are to be found. In fact, these records underestimate Cranbrook's dominance because a number of Cranbrook clothiers' wills were proved by the Prerogative Court of Canterbury in London, and thus not included here. Smarden, the fourth most important clothmaking centre, according to the inventories, was not adjacent to Cranbrook like the other two, but its clothmaking role was already notable in the fifteenth century, perhaps before Cranbrook had grown to its sixteenth-century predominance.[5] The economic significance of clothmaking was certainly much greater than its role as the main occupation of more people than any other after farming (as shown in inventories). As a by-employment, spinning yarn for the Wealden looms was probably carried on in *most* households in the Kent Weald, especially among the relatively poor. Spinning wheels or trendles, and cards, appear in a majority of the inventories in the

5. See a long list of Smarden men pardoned in 1450, giving occupations. They include 5 clothmakers, 2 fullers and 6 weavers: *Calendar of Patent Rolls, 1446–52*, 363–4.

TABLE 1

Occupations in Wealden Probate Inventories, 1565–1599

Occupation	Benenden	Bethersden	Biddenden	Cranbrook & Frittenden	Goudhurst	Halden
Farmers, Graziers	38 (34.2%)	51 (50%)	28 (29.5%)	46 (28.6%)	26 (26.3%)	29 (61.7%)
Smallholder plus?	7 (6.3%)	15 (14.7%)	9 (9.5%)	15 (9.3%)	15 (15.2%)	4 (8.5%)
Labourer or retired	20 (18%)	15 (14.7%)	20 (21.1%)	33 (20.5%)	17 (17.2%)	8 (17%)
Weaver	17 (15.3%)	10 (9.8%)	13 (13.7%)	26 (16.2%)	13 (13.1%)	1 (2.1%)
Clothier	8 (7.2%)	1 (1%)	12 (12.6%)	12 (7.5%)	2 (2%)	–
Clothworker	1 (0.9%)	–	3 (3.2%)	2 (1.2%)	–	–
Smith	1 (0.9%)	2 (2%)	4 (4.2%)	3 (1.9%)	10 (10.1%)	–
Carpenter	3 (2.7%)	3 (2.9%)	2 (2.1%)	3 (1.9%)	4 (4%)	3 (6.4%)
Building trades	–	1 (1%)	–	–	2 (2%)	–
Shoemaker	1 (0.9%)	1 (1%)	3 (3.2%)	1 (0.6%)	–	–
Glover	–	–	–	1 (0.6%)	1 (1%)	1 (2.1%)
Tanner	2 (1.8%)	–	1 (1.1%)	2 (1.2%)	–	–
Tailor	2 (1.8%)	2 (2%)	–	2 (1.2%)	3 (3%)	–
Shopkeeper	6 (5.4%)	1 (1%)	–	8 (5%)	4 (4%)	1 (2.1%)
Miller/brewer	1 (0.9%)	–	–	5 (3.1%)	2 (2%)	–
Professional	4 (3.6%)	–	–	2 (1.2%)	–	–
Totals	*111*	*102*	*95*	*161*	*99*	*47*
Misc. and Non-farming wids:	19	29	23	38	17	7

Occupation	Hawkhurst	Marden	Rolvenden	Smarden	Staplehurst	Tenterden	Totals
Farmers, graziers	23 (27.1%)	40 (49.4%)	56 (56%)	38 (42.7%)	30 (43.5%)	62 (41.3%)	467 (39.3%)
Smallholder plus?	14 (16.5%)	11 (13.6%)	12 (12%)	13 (14.6%)	2 (2.9%)	16 (10.7%)	133 (11.2%)
Labourer or retired	22 (25.9%)	15 (18.5%)	15 (15%)	10 (11.2%)	17 (24.6%)	40 (26.7%)	232 (19.5%)
Weaver	11 (12.9%)	4 (4.9%)	8 (8%)	11 (12.4%)	5 (7.3%)	6 (4%)	125 (10.5%)
Clothier	2 (2.4%)	2 (2.5%)	–	6 (6.7%)	3 (4.4%)	1 (0.7%)	49 (4.1%)
Clothworker	1 (1.2%)	1 (1.2%)	–	1 (1.1%)	1 (1.5%)	1 (0.7%)	11 (0.9%)
Smith	2 (2.4%)	–	1 (1%)	1 (1.1%)	–	2 (1.3%)	26 (2.2%)
Carpenter	3 (3.5%)	2 (2.5%)	3 (3%)	4 (4.5%)	2 (2.9%)	2 (1.3%)	34 (2.9%)
Building trades	–	–	4 (4%)	–	–	1 (0.7%)	8 (0.7%)
Shoemaker	2 (2.4%)	–	–	1 (1.1%)	1 (1.5%)	1 (0.7%)	11 (0.9%)
Glover	2 (2.4%)	–	–	1 (1.1%)	–	–	6 (0.5%)
Tanner	2 (2.4%)	1 (1.2%)	–	–	2 (2.9%)	3 (2%)	13 (1.1%)
Tailor	–	3 (3.7%)	1 (1%)	–	2 (2.9%)	3 (2%)	18 (1.5%)
Shopkeeper	1 (1.2%)	2 (2.5%)	–	3 (3.4%)	3 (4.4%)	6 (4%)	35 (2.9%)
Miller/brewer	–	–	–	–	1 (1.5%)	4 (2.7%)	13 (1.1%)
Professional	–	–	–	–	–	2 (1.3%)	8 (0.7%)
Totals	*85*	*81*	*100*	*89*	*69*	*150*	*1189*
Misc. and Non-farming wids:	15	16	25	12	4	35	

sample parishes, be they of farmers or of craftsmen. Although spinning was probably in most cases a by-employment carried on by women and children, weaving in the Weald was both a by-employment and a main occupation. As a by-employment it appears in the inventories which show farming as well as the ownership of looms. It would not appear if the loom was owned by a clothier, or on loan from a kinsman or friend, and from these records alone it is difficult to estimate how widespread was the practice of weaving on clothiers' looms. One would suggest that it was not as common as some of the classical economic theories about the domestic system of manufacturing might imply. A kersey loom was worth well under £1 in the Elizabethan period, while a broad loom (which required two workmen) could be had for £2 or £3. The putting out system was indeed a reality in the Weald, but more in terms of raw materials than with respect to basic machinery like looms and spinning wheels. This suggestion is strengthened by the fact that the inventories of clothiers very rarely show more than a single loom, and usually none at all. In almost all cases of estates with two or more looms, the owners appear to have been master weavers rather than clothiers.

No other craft or trade besides clothmaking stands out from the rest in the Kent Weald. In the sample parishes as a whole, the range of occupations other than clothmaking trades mirrors what historians have come to expect in populous rural areas. The notable exception here is that building workers are less numerous than normal, but this is due to the deficiency of occupational additions on the manuscripts. Their prominence is hinted at by the large number of individuals we have been forced to classify as 'labourer' or 'smallholder plus?'. The less skilled tradesmen's inventories are not easily separable from the cottagers' and labourers' inventories because many of their tools were extremely common, and equally, because many labourers in agriculture and building did not own their own tools. The only other well-known Wealden industry of any size, ironworking, does not appear to be of much significance in the sample parishes. Although there were a few ironworks in the central Weald, most were in the west, and only at Goudhurst is there real evidence in these records of an ironworking industry. In Goudhurst alone is there a concentration of metal trades. Here was the residence of the only two colliers (charcoal burners)— identified in the whole sample, and here, too, was the only group of more than a handful of smiths. Goudhurst boasted the normal blacksmiths, but was also the home of several extremely wealthy whitesmiths and scythesmiths. No definite explanation springs to mind for the concentration of metal trades at Goudhurst. In the Elizabethan period there were, at least for part of the reign, active ironworks in neighbouring Brenchley, Cranbrook, Horsmonden and Lamberhurst. In Goudhurst itself, Chingley furnace was in operation during the latter decades of the sixteenth century. Its owner, Henry Darrell, had leased the furnace to the ironmaster Thomas Dyke, along with over 450 acres of woodland, in 1579.[6] Goudhurst's singularity may turn out to be an illusion, visible in the inventories alone, for after all there are no identifiable inventories for either Goudhurst or Cranbrook of the craftsmen of the basic ironfounding industry. It is just as likely that the secondary metal trades simply found a convenient base at Goudhurst. It was close to the forges and furnaces of the surrounding parishes, but not itself dominated by the cloth industry.

6.   For Wealden ironworks see D. and G. Matthew, 'Iron Furnaces in South-eastern England . . . 1578', *English Hist. Rev.*, xlviii (1933); J.J. Goring, 'Wealden Ironmasters in the Age of Elizabeth' in *Wealth and Power in Tudor England*, ed. E.W. Ives *et al.* (1978); Public Record Office, SP 12/117 no. 39. Thomas Dyke: East Sussex R.O., Dyke (Hutton) MSS. 602–607. For Horsmonden (Sherenden furnace): P.R.O. KB 9/610 no. 141; Lamberhurst: KAO U120/T99.

ii

The wealth of Wealden tradesmen and artisans, as depicted in their probate inventories, varied enormously. In part, of course, the variation is an illusion, because inventories were not prepared at a similar stage in each person's career, and thus are not strictly comparable one with another. But they do demonstrate the different degrees of economic success possible in the same trade. And, taken as a group, the sample probably has some validity as a picture of the distribution and of the relative wealth of different trades. Table 2 gives the distribution of the values of estates of the commonest Wealden trades and crafts, as well as the average total values of their estates in three successive periods of Elizabeth's reign. Most striking is the wide spread of values in most trades. That a quarter of all weavers had estates worth less than £20 is hardly surprising. More remarkable is the quarter of all weavers whose estates were valued at £50 or over. Most shoemakers' estates were valued within the lowest categories, and yet four of that trade possessed chattels worth at least £60. Both carpenters (which includes joiners and sawyers) and smiths also showed enormous differences in wealth. A few examples will illustrate the prosperity of some and the relative poverty of others better than all the statistics.

TABLE 2

Values of Estates of Wealden Tradesmen and Craftsmen, 1565–99

Total Value	Weavers	Clothiers	Shopkeepers	Smiths	Carpenters	Tailors	Tanners	Shoemakers	Millers/ Brewers
Under £10	8 (6.5%)	–	–	–	–	3 (13.6%)	–	2 (16.7%)	–
£10–20	24 (19.5%)	3 (6.4%)	2 (6.7%)	2 (8%)	3 (9.4%)	4 (18.2%)	–	3 (25%)	–
£20–30	31 (25.2%)	2 (4.3%)	1 (3.3%)	6 (24%)	11 (34.4%)	3 (13.6%)	1 (7.7%)	1 (8.3%)	–
£30–40	19 (15.5%)	2 (4.3%)	7 (23.3%)	–	5 (15.6%)	3 (13.6%)	1 (7.7%)	2 (16.7%)	3 (21.4%)
£40–50	8 (6.5%)	1 (2.1%)	3 (10%)	2 (8%)	2 (6.3%)	–	–	–	3 (21.4%)
£50–60	12 (9.8%)	1 (2.1%)	4 (13.3%)	3 (12%)	3 (9.4%)	3 (13.6%)	2 (15.4%)	–	1 (7.1%)
£60–80	9 (7.3%)	9 (19.2%)	6 (20%)	2 (8%)	3 (9.4%)	–	4 (30.8%)	3 (25%)	3 (21.4%)
£80–!00	4 (3.3%)	4 (8.5%)	3 (10%)	2 (8%)	1 (3.1%)	1 (4.6%)	1 (7.7%)	–	1 (7.1%)
Over £100	8 (6.5%)	25 (53.2%)	4 (13.3%)	8 (32%)	4 (12.5%)	5 (22.7%)	4 (30.8%)	1 (8.3%)	3 (21.4%)

Average Values of Wealden Tradesmen and Craftsmen's Inventories

Occupation	1565–1579		1580–89		1590–99	
	Median	Mean	Median	Mean	Median	Mean
Weavers (123)	£34	£40	£24	£40	£29	£39
Clothiers (47)	£116	£301	£112	£125	£74	£108
Clothworkers (12)	£30	£54		£43	£40	£48
Shopkeepers (30)	£45	£51	£65	£67	£54	£88
Smiths (25)	£58	£88	£30	£43	£148	£148
Carpenters (32)	£32	£42	£33	£42	£38	£62
Tailors (22)	£22	£35	£104	£112	£28	£37
Tanners (13)	£74	£83	£57	£141	£460	£355
Shoemakers (12)	£28	£26	£16	£46	£40	£63
Glovers (6)	£132	£113	£40 (1 only)		£31 (2 only)	
Miller/brewer (14)	£95	£109	£45	£50	£53	£54

John White, a carpenter of Smarden, died in early 1572 leaving goods worth under £25. He had wheat in the ground worth £4 (about two or three acres), two cows and some swine and poultry valued at £4 13s. 4d. and 13s. 4d. in stored corn. His carpenter's tools were rated at only 8s. and the rest of his goods, about £14 worth, was household stuff. White is as good an example as any of the artisan-smallholder, many of whose inventories survive, although the craft of a large number of them is unknown. About four years after White's death, John Sharpe of the same place died. He, too, was a carpenter – in this case a joiner – but his goods were worth four times as much as White's. His joinery tools ('with planes and chisels') and planks of timber were worth almost £7 alone. He had a plough and a wagon and farmed on a substantial scale by Wealden standards. His corn in the ground (in June) consisted of 7 acres of wheat and four acres of oats and peas (suggesting a total arable acreage of 15 or 16 acres). He had 6 kine, 2 oxen, 2 steers, 3 two-year heifers, a one-year bud and 2 calves, as well as 2 mares, all valued at over £30. There are no debts listed, and therefore Sharpe's household goods and clothes were worth more than £50, or twice John White's whole estate. John Sharpe's prosperity appears to have been due as much to his farming as his busy joinery business. In fact craftsmen at both ends of the continuum of wealth in Smarden and elsewhere in the Weald were often active farmers. One, John White, was a smallholder of six or eight acres, while John Sharpe was farming for the market on forty acres or more. In both cases agriculture and artisanal activity went hand in hand.[7]

Metal craftsmen, too, displayed great disparities in wealth. Two smiths who died in 1591 were Edward Waghorne of Hawkhurst and Thomas Brattle of Goudhurst.[8] Waghorne, whose total estate was worth just over £20, had no smallholding. In his shop were 2 anvils, 3 sledge-hammers, one rickhorn, four hammers, 15 pairs of tongs, an old pair of bellows and some coal and iron. In all it came to just over £3. Besides a pound and a half in cash and 5s. in wood, the rest was household stuff. At the opposite extreme was Thomas Brattle with an estate valued at £192 14s. His equipment and raw materials including iron and steel, and coal, came to £60 alone. He also had £10-worth of wood, debts amounting to £14, but most important, a sizeable farm. His summer crops in the ground were worth almost £10, and his farm was well-stocked. He had his own plough and wagon and 7 oxen. There were 18 other head of cattle, 20 sheep, swine, and 2 geldings, 2 mares and a colt. Brattle's crop acreage is not given but it was probably about 8 to 10 acres, plus fallow. His animals would have required at least 45 acres. Brattle was not only a substantial farmer but also manufactured tools in quantity. Since the inventory includes scythes in his shop, he was most probably a scythesmith, whereas Waghorne was a humble blacksmith. Both were householders, although Waghorne might still have been a young man. Having a sideline in farming was not necessary for survival, but in most cases the wealthy craftsmen in the sample parishes also actively farmed. In many cases the value of their livestock and corn was considerably higher than that of their trade goods. The inventories do not inform us about how much labour the larger farmers and craftsmen employed, but in cases like Thomas Brattle and that of John Sharpe mentioned above, hired labour would have been essential, even assuming that prosperous smiths and carpenters had apprentices at the same time. In the case of the wealthier master weavers, each with two or three broad looms, it

7. KAO PRC 10/5 f. 299; 10/8 f. 263.
8. KAO PRC 10/22 f. 30; 10/20 f. 79.

would be reasonable to assume a journeyman for every loom after the first, in addition to apprentices.

Comparing trade with trade, Wealden clothiers were undoubtedly the wealthiest occupational group, despite the handful of clothiers with estates valued at less than £50. The bulk of these apparently poor clothiers seem not to have been actively involved in business if their inventories are anything to go by, and one or two may well have been apprentices. The greater wealth of the clothiers is to some extent artificially depressed by the absence of inventories of many of the wealthiest clothiers whose wills were not proved locally. Standing behind the clothiers were a number of trades with many representatives among the wealthiest groups. Almost 70 per cent of tanners' inventories were worth over £60, while just about half of the estates of both smiths and millers and brewers were rated at that same amount or higher. The next highest group, shopkeepers, showed about 43 per cent of inventories in excess of £60. The wealth of both clothiers and tanners – and some smiths – is in part a reflection of the larger capital investment in those trades. At the same time, many of the wealthiest of all three groups had farming goods and livestock worth much more than their trade goods and debts. Thomas Glover of Benenden, clothier, died in 1578 leaving goods worth £194. His trade goods, including four broadcloths, were valued at £56. On the other hand, his livestock, corn and hay were worth over £113. Another example is John Netter of Cranbrook, a tanner who left an estate worth £220 in 1579. His stock in trade and equipment were valued at £46, while his farming goods came to £65. He also had debts due of £66.[9] In general, the more prosperous clothiers were less heavily involved in farming than other wealthy craftsmen. Many had substantial inventories of cloth in the process of manufacture, and large stores of wool, as well as extensive debts owed them at their death. More typical of the balance of goods in an estate of one of the successful clothiers – although few could match his enormous total – was the inventory of Peter Courthop of Cranbrook, valued late in 1567. His livestock and hay were worth less than two per cent of the total estate; debts made up about 46 per cent of the total, wool and yarn 31 per cent, finished cloths 10 per cent, dyestuffs and clothmaking equipment about 2.5 per cent. Peter Courthop was exceptionally rich, but other clothiers with estates valued at two to five hundred pounds had a large share of their wealth as circulating capital, either debts due or raw materials and cloths in the various stages of manufacture.[10] However, it is worth emphasizing that *most* Wealden clothiers were small operators, usually with less than half a dozen cloths in stock or being made. The Courthop clan, like the Allards, was quite exceptional.

Weavers and shoemakers were – among the common trades represented in this sample – the poorest occupations on average. Over the whole period 1565 to 1599 two-thirds of both groups died with estates valued at under £40. In between the richest and poorest trades came the tailors and the carpenters: almost 60 per cent of their number had inventories of less than £40. Also in the middle ranks were the twelve clothworkers (fullers or shearmen) identified in the inventories. Just about half of them died with chattels valued at under £40, while at the same time a third of their number had estates worth £60 or more.

Clothmaking was not the dominant non-agrarian industry in all parts of the Kent Weald.

9.   KAO PRC 10/9 f. 233; 10/10 f. 186.
10. KAO PRC 28/1 fs. 112–115: total was £1,783 plus £45 in bad debts. The inventory is calendared in *Kentish Sources*, iii, *Aspects of Agriculture and Industry*, ed. Elizabeth Melling (Maidstone, 1961) 110–112.

From the sparse evidence available about the western parishes of the Weald, there appears to have been no intensive clothmaking in this area. A few weavers turn up here and there, and there was at least one clothier established in Tonbridge in the late sixteenth and early seventeenth centuries. But from a variety of non-probate evidence it can be shown that the cloth-making region extended only as far west as Brenchley and Yalding.[11] There are no systematic sources for occupations in the western Weald. However, on the basis of fragmentary evidence it can be suggested that the leather industry was much more significant in the west than in the east. Simply from accusations brought by informers against tanners in the Court of Exchequer in Elizabeth's reign (usually for infractions of the penal statutes governing the preparation of leather or the statute of apprentices), the importance of tanning in the western Weald becomes clear. Certain names crop up again and again: the Amhersts of Tudeley; the Deanes of Brasted, Edenbridge and Sundridge; the Sones or Sownes of Edenbridge; and the Staceys of Westerham. Of all the Kentish tanners informed against, the majority come from the western Weald. The largest number came from Brasted, but most of the parishes in the south-west corner of Kent had some tanning industry. However, it would be overstating the case to suggest that the leather trades provided the equivalent manufacturing employment that cloth-making did in the central and eastern Weald. In general, the western parishes were more agricultural than those in Canterbury diocese, but the large number of cattle raised in both parts of the Weald may not have all gone to feed the metropolis. Some provided the raw material for an active leather industry in the Weald itself.[12]

Finally, a word must be said about labourers. From the inventories alone it is impossible to establish how many men were farm labourers plain and simple, how many cottagers who worked as wage labourers at certain seasons or part-time to supplement the produce of their smallholding, how many were artisans employed by a master craftsman or tradesman, and how many were simply retired. If most of those classified here as 'smallholders' and 'labourers or retired' were either full-time or part-time labourers – which is quite likely – then the part of the population which depended wholly or partly on wages for its sustenance was indeed large. The thirty per cent of the total represented by inventories is unlikely to be as large as the true share of the whole population of the region which was in that situation. The poorer labourers were most likely to be ignored by the testamentary courts. At the same time, it is arguable whether the bulk of labourers in the Weald were *farm* labourers. As will be shown below, the size of typical farms in the Weald was small, and most would have not required labourers beyond the family members themselves. Thus many of the labourers must have been 'servants' or employees or tradesmen and craftsmen, who – if more information were available – would have been added to their appropriate trade category. Whatever the classification, however, labourers and other landless men made up a considerable share of the Wealden population, all of whom would have been dependent on the market for all or part of their daily bread. Some of the cereals needed to feed the Weald's burgeoning population came from outside the region, but most of the necessary foodstuffs were produced by the Weald's numerous farmers.

11. In Rochester diocese the only parishes with a concentration of clothiers were Brenchley and Horsmonden, as shown by the residences of clothiers fined at Blackwell Hall in London: P.R.O. E159/329–380, *passim* under 'Recorda' section.
12. Some Wealden tanners can be identified from wills proved in Rochester consistory court (KAO DRb/Pwr). The concentration in west Weald parishes is shown in the penal informations: P.R.O. E 159/340 ff. *passim*.

iii

Farming remained the basic industry of the Weald, notwithstanding the concentration of cloth-making in the eight or nine parishes surrounding Cranbrook. It has already been noted that farmers and graziers comprised the largest single occupational group shown in the inventory sample. Taking all the inventories as a whole, a solid majority recorded some farming activity, and even among the identified tradesmen and craftsmen almost a half were farmers as well. This is not to postulate that a majority of adult males held a farm, for it is likely that most of the adults whose death went unnoticed by the courts were landless. It is, however, worth remarking just how numerous were the smallholders in the Weald, on the basis of inventories alone. In an age when in other parts of England the numbers of smallholders and husbandmen were allegedly declining, at least relatively, in the Weald they were thick on the ground. The reasons for their survival here are complex. First, there was the prevailing high level of population growth, which combined with gavelkind customs that specified partible inheritance and the free alienation of land, tended to produce an active market in small parcels of land. The fact that most land had always been held in severalty in the Weald – and usually in fenced closes of two to five acres – also encouraged a busy land market, and made possible the acquisition of a smallholding by quite poor families. In addition to the active market in freehold land, the larger landholders regularly leased a part of their estates – which in most cases were not consolidated around a single capital messuage. Not only were the gentry rentiers, but so too were most of the wealthier clothiers. The inventories of smallholders and husbandmen do not reveal if the deceased was a freeholder or a tenant farmer, but the wills of the relatively poor in the Weald usually show little or no freehold land to be devised, suggesting that a large proportion of the smallholders and part-time farmers at least were leaseholders rather than freeholders. Many farmers also leased additional pasture on top of a small freeholding. Most of what follows is based on the inventories of those we have classified as 'farmers and graziers', as well as those tradesmen who appear to have had a substantial farm as well. The category 'farmer' is susceptible of a dozen different definitions, but since the purpose here is to shed light on the type of farming which prevailed in the Weald, it is unnecessary to include everyone who practised any husbandry no matter how limited it was. Excluded are all those inventories which show only a cow or two, and all those with only an acre or two of arable, unless they also had more than a handful of cattle or sheep. The peasant farmers who are included all had enough arable and/or livestock to suggest a holding large enough to support a family.

The full range of Wealden farms is shown in Table 3, covering the twelve sample parishes with a reasonably large number of extant farming inventories. Not all inventories from each parish which show evidence of farming are included in the detailed figures in the table, since a number of them give no specific information on crop acreages. But a wide range of farmsteads are represented in this table, including a few with more than thirty acres in crop – exceptionally large farms by Wealden standards. These stand out by their very rarity. The more typical Wealden farm had no more than six to nine acres in cereals, representing perhaps eight to twelve acres of total arable. From one parish to another there is a good deal of variation in the average farmstead, with mean summer acreages from only six acres (Benenden) to fourteen acres (Sandhurst). The variation amongst farms in a single parish could be much greater. But when the few large farms are excluded – say those of more than sixteen acres in crop – then the average summer acreage in all the parishes falls between six and ten acres. From the few

TABLE 3
Wealden Farming Estates, 1565–1601

Parish	No. of inventories w/farming	Summer Inventories w/known acreage							Winter Inventories		
		No.	Wheat	Oats	Beans/Peas	Other	Total crop acreage (mean)	Livestock: Corn value	No.	Livestock: Corn value	Mean winter acreage
Benenden	49	16	47%	46%	1%	6%	6 a.	3.4:1	20	3.0:1	4 a. (1 farm w/12 a; mean of rest = 3.5 a.)
Bethersden	45	20	- 46%	53%	1%	–	11 a (1 farm w/31 a; mean of rest = 10a.)	3.0:1	10	4.2:1	3.5 a.
Biddenden	37	18	48%	52%	–	–	7.5 a.	2.5:1	16	3.2:1	4.5 a.
Cranbrook	41	12	43%	49%	2%	6%	11.5 a (4 farms of 19–21 a; mean of rest = 7a.)	3.7:1	13	3.2:1	6 a (1 farm w/20 a; mean of rest = 5a.)
Goudhurst	26	6	44%	39%	15%	2%	12a (1 farm w/33 a; mean of rest = 8.5a.)	2.1:1	9	3.0:1	5.3a.
Halden	30	13	42%	57%	–	1%	8a (1 farm w/36a; mean of rest = 6a.)	3.7:1	13	4.6:1	2.5a.
Hawkhurst	30	13	48%	41%	11%	–	8a (2 farms w/25 & 18a; mean of rest = 3.8a.)	2.1:1	12	3.9:1	3 a.
Marden	45	26	47%	48%	3%	2%	11.8a (2 farms w/29 & 33a; mean of rest = 10a.)	2.3:1	12	2.2:1	4.5a.
Rolvenden	65	20	47%	43%	4%	6%	7 a.	3.7:1	30	3.3:1	4 a.
Sandhurst	30	10	42%	54%	3.5%	.5%	14.5a (2 farms w/37 & 45a; mean of rest = 7.5 a.)	3.5:1	13	3.6:1	4.8a (2 farms w/10 & 12 a; mean of rest = 3.5 a.)
Staplehurst	35	12	47%	47.5%	4%	1.5%	10a (1 farm w/23a; mean of rest = 8.75a.)	2.7:1	13	2.3:1	6a (3 farms w/10a. each; mean of rest = 5a.)
Tenterden	58	16	48%	32%	14%	6%	8a (3 farms w/14–16a; mean of rest = 6.5a.)	5.3:1	18	4.4:1	3.5a.

Explanation: The first total shows the total number of inventories with significant husbandry activity; very small estates have been excluded (i.e. those with total estate under £20, except in a few cases where full crop acreages were included; also excluded were those larger estates which included only a handful of domestic livestock and no arable activity). Due to the nature of the source, very few gentry estates are included: the exceptionally large for this region estates (noted in parentheses) in most parishes are those of yeomen farmer/graziers, and the occasional wealthy clothier. The livestock to corn ratio is the ratio of the value of all livestock to the value of all corn (but not hay) in each estate; the ratios for each farm in a parish for either summer or winter inventories have been averaged: the figures on the table are the mean ratios.

inventories which record fallow acreage, it would appear that most Wealden farmers planted between 70 and 75 per cent of their arable each year.

Wealden farmers tended to stick to a fairly traditional choice of crops. By and large, about half of their sown acreage was devoted to a winter grain – usually wheat – and most of the other half was then sown with the most appropriate spring cereal for heavy clay soils, oats. In a few of the sample parishes oats actually accounted for more than 50 per cent of the crop acreage shown in the combined summer inventories. In none of the twelve parishes did wheat comprise as much as 50 per cent, but in five of them there was slighty more wheat than oats. Wheat and oats were the predominant cereals in all the parishes, with the exception of Tenterden, a parish that was also exceptional in the extent of marshland within its bounds. Peas and beans were the next most common crops with many farms showing up to an acre or two of these grains, planted presumably as fodder for livestock. Only in Goudhurst and Hawkhurst were peas and beans a significant part of the spring sown crops. Why these two should differ so much from neighbouring Benenden and Sandhurst is not clear. The other winter grain, rye, appears only occasionally in the inventories, usually planted in small quantities alongside wheat. Barley only very rarely occurs, and hops had not yet made a significant impact, at least in these central and eastern parishes of the Weald. The basic crop choices outlined here remained constant from the 1560s to the 1590s. The dominance of wheat and oats is the hallmark of the region's arable farming, as has been shown in studies of farming in the Sussex Weald.[13] Of necessity, malting barley would have had to be imported into the Weald from other parts of Kent.

Arable farming, however, was by no means the main business of the Wealden farmer. In this region of generally intractable clay soils the balance of the agrarian regime was tipped in the direction of livestock husbandry. We have attempted to measure this balance between cattle and corn in a number of ways, and these are shown in Tables 3 and 4. One method has been to compare the money value assigned in the inventories to livestock with that placed on all corn, whether in the barn or in the ground. The other method has been to estimate the amount of land devoted to crops as compared to the acreage necessary for the livestock listed on the same inventory. The virtue of the first method is that it avoids problems due to the changing value of money. The second method complements the first by showing the balance between arable and

TABLE 4

Medium-Sized and Large Farms in the Weald, 1565–1601

Parish	No.	Val. of Corn and Livestock: Median	Mean	All Cattle: Median	Mean	Median Pasture	Median Arable	Median Total	Mean Ratio of Livestock: Corn Values
High Weald:									
Benenden	14	£77	£92	21	26	43.5a.	17a.	60.5a.	4:1
Cranbrook	18	£67	£70	22	23	43a.	17a.	60a.	4.5:1
Hawkhurst	15	£43	£43	13	15	21a.	15.5a.	36.5a.	2.7:1
Low Weald:									
Bethersden	22	£42	£54	15	21	34a.	17a.	51a.	3.9:1
Biddenden	19	£50	£50	16	16	32a.	15a.	47a.	3.2:1
Marden	22	£49	£53	14	15	30a.	21a.	51a.	2.2:1
Staplehurst	18	£62	£65	16	21	41a.	18.5a.	59.5a.	3:1

Explanation: Values of corn and livestock combined taken from inventory total, which in some cases was very much greater, due to large debts or manufacturing activity; hay and farm equipment are excluded. 'All cattle' includes calves and weaners. Pasture acreage estimated on the basis of 1.5 acres per head of cattle (but excluding calves and weaners), 1.5 acres per horse and .5 acre per adult sheep or colt. Arable acreage estimated from total summer acreage in crop where given, or twice winter acreage. Fallow included as 30% of total acreage.

13.   On all aspects of agriculture in the Sussex Weald see C.E. Brent, 'Rural Employment and Population in Sussex between 1550 and 1640', *Sussex Arch. Collections*, cxiv (1976), esp. 38–48; G.H. Kenyon, 'Kirdford Inventories, 1611–1760' in *ibid.*, xciii (1955).

livestock in terms of acres rather than money values. Table 3 allows a comparison of the livestock to corn value ratios in both summer and winter inventories. It shows that both in the winter and in the months between spring sowing and harvest the value of Wealden farmers' livestock was at least twice that of their corn. The variation amongst the ratios in different parishes between winter and summer suggests a good deal of local variety in farming, as there was plenty of local variation in soils and topography. It also puts paid to the old chestnut that farmers regularly slaughtered and sold many of their cattle and sheep at the start of winter. In half of the parishes the mean livestock–corn ratio was higher in the summer than in the winter inventories; in the other half the situation was reversed. But in all parishes the mean ratio of livestock to corn was at least two to one. The mean ratio of all the *parochial* averages for the summer inventories was over three to one. If one includes the value of hay, which figures regularly in farmers' inventories, the margin between livestock and corn would be further increased. Wealden pasture and meadow land was regularly mown, and the resulting hay along with the cheaper grains sufficed to feed the livestock over the winter months.

Land use in Wealden agriculture equally demonstrates the bias towards livestock, which in these parishes means cattle rather than sheep. In both High Weald and Low Weald parishes, as shown in Table 4, the average arable acreage is less than half the land estimated as the minimum acreage needed for the livestock shown in the inventories. In fact the livestock–corn ratios correlate quite well with the equivalent ratio between arable and pasture in the sample parishes. Only Marden and Hawkhurst appear to be out of step. The reason for the relatively high proportion of arable among the farms in Marden is not yet clear, but the explanation in Hawkhurst seems to be the relatively high number of small farms there. The general rule appears to be, the greater the share of small family farms in the sample, the greater the likelihood that farmland will be more evenly divided between pasture and arable, and the livestock–corn ratio lower.

Wealden farmland was not ideal for corn. However, in this period agricultural specialization had not yet advanced to such a degree that farmers on claylands had given up arable farming altogether. For the small farmers, planting wheat at least insulated them from the vagaries of the market, for their bread, even if yields on most Wealden soils were lower than in other parts of the country. For many farmers, too, wheat was a useful cash crop, in a region with many landless families to be fed. Oats grew well in Wealden soils, could be fed to livestock and served as a bread grain for the local poor, at least in years of high wheat prices. Thus the Wealden farm remained a mixed enterprise, but with the livestock side of farming providing the lion's share of the farm's cash income. In general, as the size and value of Wealden farms extended upwards, so the ratio between livestock and corn becomes larger. Only a very few of the farmers with estates worth over £100 or £150 in all produce livestock–corn ratios below two to one. Much more commonly, the most prosperous farmers in the Weald were rich in livestock, while their crop acreage was only two or three times that of the typical small farmer. A few examples, chosen from the more informative inventories will illustrate the range of Wealden farms as well as the typical farming regime shown statistically in the tables.

Family farms abounded in the Weald. Typical of those small mixed farming units was the estate of Thomas Turner of Marden (June 1571), worth in all less than £25. His crops consisted of 3 acres of wheat, 4 acres of oats and peas and a half acre of barley, and he still had £1 12s. in corn on hand in June. His livestock included 2 kine, 2 heifers, 1 mare and 3 hogs, which were worth only slightly more than his corn. A different balance was struck by another typical peasant farmer, Richard Allen of Goudhurst (April 1573), whose goods were worth just over £25. His winter wheat crop was just two acres, but his livestock came to £14 10s.: 5 kine, 2 heifers, 2 buds, 2 bullocks, 1 calf, a mare and colt, 8 sheep and 3 hogs.[14] Neither of these family farmers possessed his own plough or team of oxen, nor did most small and medium-size Wealden farms. A representative intermediate size farm estate is that of Edmund Baker of Rolvenden (April 1572) whose goods totalled £68. His arable crop was 3 acres of wheat, 3 acres of oats and an acre of beans. He owned 11 kine and heifers, a bull, 3 buds, plus a mare, 6 sheep and 3 hogs – which would have required something like 25 acres of pasture.[15]

At the opposite end of the scale from these small and middling farms stood the much smaller number of large, commercial farms owned by gentry and wealthier yeomen. Only a very few of even these large Wealden farms can compare to the estates of many of the more prosperous east Kent yeomen and gentry, many of whom had agricultural goods worth three to five hundred pounds alone. Nevertheless, there were Wealden farmers who were as rich or richer than almost all of their neighbours other than the most successful clothiers or well-off gentlemen. Robert Willard of Rolvenden died late in 1572, leaving an estate valued at £161. His winter crop (wheat) extended to 13 acres, and he also had £14 worth of corn in store. But his livestock was worth almost half of his total estate: 4 oxen, 9 kine, 6 'young steers', 8 one year bullocks, 10 weaners and a bull, as well as 68 sheep, 3 mares and a colt. Wealthier still was Stephen Gibbon of the same parish, whose family would soon be recognized as gentlemen. His estate of February 1570 amounted to £339 including debts due totalling £85. He had 8 acres of wheat in the ground, and £13 in corn in his barn. But that was small beer compared to his livestock. He had 53 head of cattle and a large sheep flock by Wealden standards, 81 animals.[16]

Raising and fattening cattle for the market was the key-note of Wealden farming for those with access to substantial acreage. The inventories of most wealthy farmers show that store cattle had been purchased – probably in the metropolitan markets – for fattening. The favoured breeds seem to have been the 'Northern' and the Welsh. Stephen Gibbon, mentioned above, had 10 'Northern runts', and another wealthy grazier, Thomas Boone of Biddenden, had both Northern heifers and runts among his herd. The latter also owed £17 to 'the Welshman' for cattle.[17] Some of the big graziers not only occupied scores of acres of pasture in the Weald, but also hired summer grazing in Romney Marsh or in Tenterden parish.[18] But even at the level of the small family farm the emphasis was on beef. The peasant farmer – like the cottagers – usually had one or two dairy cattle, but what distinguished the farmer from the cottager was the presence of bullocks and steers. The extent to which the small farmer as well as the cottager were able to pasture their stock on commons or waste is uncertain. Several Wealden parishes still had open waste ground or commons, although generally not very large, in the seventeenth century. For other parishes in the region there is no record of any common land in the sixteenth or seventeenth centuries, and it is to be doubted that there was a great deal of open woodland available to all and sundry for grazing as late as the Elizabethan period.

14. KAO PRC 10/5 f. 240; 10/6 f. 308^V.
15. KAO PRC 10/6 f. 224^V.
16. KAO PRC 10/6 f. 311; 10/5 f. 55.
17. KAO PRC 10/7 f. 197 (Boone's total was £227).
18. e.g. Boone, note 17; also Peter Piers of Tenterden (April 1572) with three leases of marshland; much of his livestock, especially the sheep, were pastured in Romney and Guildford Marshes: KAO PRC 10/6 f. 151^V.

TABLE 5

Values of Estates of Full-Time Farmers and Graziers, 1565–1599

Total value	1565–79	1580–89	1590–99	1565–1599
£10–20	21 (10.1%)	6 (4.1%)	9 (5.4%)	36 (6.9%)
£20–30	45 (21.6%)	13 (9%)	19 (11.4%)	77 (14.8%)
£30–40	32 (15.4%)	23 (15.9%)	14 (8.4%)	69 (13.3%)
£40–50	19 (9.1%)	13 (9%)	19 (11.4%)	51 (9.8%)
£50–60	18 (8.7%)	13 (9%)	18 (10.8%)	49 (9.4%)
£60–80	22 (10.6%)	10 (6.9%)	23 (13.8%)	55 (10.6%)
£80–100	13 (6.3%)	19 (13.1%)	22 (13.2%)	54 (10.4%)
Over £100	38 (18.3%)	48 (33.1%)	43 (25.8%)	129 (24.8%)
Totals	*208*	*145*	*167*	*520*

TABLE 6

Total Wealth in Male Probate Inventories from Sample Parishes, 1565–1599

Total Value	1565–69	1570–74	1575–79	1580–84	1585–89	1590–94	1595–99
Under £15	22.5%	20%	18.2%	18.7%	16.3%	21.5%	17.7%
Under £20	32.8%	29.7%	24.1%	28%	25.6%	32%	26.3%
£20–30	17.2%	21.3%	16.8%	10.4%	13.4%	15.6%	13.2%
Under £30	50%	51%	40.9%	38.3%	38.9%	47.6%	39.4%
£30–60	25%	24.5%	27.7%	23.3%	26.8%	18.9%	28.8%
£60–100	15.2%	10.3%	14.6%	16.1%	15.1%	16%	16.7%
Over £100	9.8%	14.2%	16.8%	22.3%	19.2%	17.3%	15.2%
Median:	£30	£29 11s	£35 7s	£38	£40	£30 17s	£40 10s
Mean	£55 14s	£57 2s	£66 10s	£69 13s	£66 12s	£62 16s	£62 1s
No. in Sample:	209	158	137	193	172	237	198

On balance, it must be assumed that only smallholders might have had sufficient free grazing for their few animals on waste ground, and that most of the stock owned by farmers was pastured on their own land, be it freehold or leased.

The separation of craftsmen and tradesmen on the one hand and farmers on the other – as has been used here – remains an oversimplified picture of economic life in the Weald. The backbone of the economy was fundamentally agricultural, in the widest sense. Most of the most successful tradesmen and manufacturers financed their commercial enterprises in part by the profits of farming. In addition many of them were rentiers as well, as an examination of the wills of many of them will show. Lower down the social ladder, all types of craftsmen and tradesmen combined farming with a trade or handicraft. This last generalisation applies not only to artisans in the cloth industry, but to most crafts from the metal and leather trades to tailors and carpenters. More than half the identified craftsmen and tradesmen were also farmers. To ask, in fact, which activity was the main employment and which the by-employment is a *question mal posée*. Given the nature of landholding, inheritance customs and continuing demographic growth, only the combination of farming with manufacturing or a trade could guarantee economic survival for many Wealden families. The possibility of taking up a wide variety of non-farming employments encouraged population growth both through high fertility and immigration, while at the same time the dense population and competition for land rendered alternative employments a necessity. The material result of this complex Wealden economy was not only huge variations in wealth, between the poorest and the richest, but also a large number of men of middling levels of prosperity. Both these pheno-mena can be seen in the final table, which shows the distribution of wealth as set out in all the surviving inventories from the sample parishes. It suggests that the values of estates were growing steadily – with prices – up to the 1570s, but that from the 1580s onwards they remained most stable in money terms, and thus were falling in real terms. The share of inventories worth £100 or more rose to a peak in the early 1580s, at over one in five, but then declined to the level of the preceding decade. Median inventories, too, in the last fifteen or twenty years of the century, remained at about the level they had reached in the 1570s. The conclusion must be that unless a significantly poorer section of the population was becoming the subject of probate inventories in the 1580s and 1590s, a large number of the relatively better-off families of the early decades of Elizabeth's rein were less well off by the end of the century. As for the landless, labouring poor, who mostly did not leave inventories to enlighten us, their condition may also have been further depressed by the end of the period. Their only consolation might have been a recognition that their fellows in other parts of the realm – where local economies offered less variety of employment – were living in even more wretched conditions than they were.

GENERAL INDEX

Stonar, 37
Stone, Lawrence, 134
Stone-next-Dartford, 21, 189, 202
Story, John, 87
Stour, River, 35, 37, 45–6, 52
Stowting, 200
Street, G.E., 194n., 198n., 202n.
Strode, Sir George, 18–19
Style bridge, 52, 58, 61–2
Sundridge, 202, 211
Surrey, 59, 107
Sussex, 55, 60, 140, 214
Sutton-at-Hone, 63, 100
Sutton-next-Ripple, 197
Swale, The, 160
Swalecliffe, 188
Swanscombe, 21, 45
Swedenborg, E., 130
Swingfield, 190, 199
Symson, William, 79

Tangiers, 128
Tankerton, 42
Tawney, R.H., 123, 137
Taylor, Sir Robert, 190
Teise, River, 52
Temple Ewell, 195
Tenterden, 89, 193, 204–18 *passim*
Terling, 74n.
Ternbridge, 51
Teston bridge, 52, 56, 58, 61–2
Teulon, S.S., 201n.
Thames, River, 49, 59
Thanet, 33–4, 82n.
Thanet, Earl of, 13–14, 27
Thanington, 196
Thatcher, John, 11n., 21
Thorneton, Lancelot, 113n.
Thornhill, Joanna, 16n.
        Richard, 12, 15–16, 27
Thrale, Henry, 100n.
        Ralph, 100n.
Thurloe, John, 11
Thurnham, 99
Tillotson, Dean, 136
Toke, Nicholas, 111–12
Tonbridge, 15, 21, 51–3, 55–6, 58–60, 62, 89, 105, 201
Tonge, 197
Torr, V.J.B., 139
Town, Henry, 58
Tucker, John, 104
Tudeley, 211
Tunbridge Wells, 102

Tunstall, 13, 196
Turner, Thomas, 215
Twisden, Francis, 87
        Justice, 106
        Sir Roger, 15, 18–19, 27
        Sir Thomas, 87
Twyford bridge, 52, 58, 61–3
Twysden, Robert, 117
Tyers, Mr., 107

Upchurch, 196
Upper Hardres, 17
Urry, William, 66n.

Valyar, Goodwife, 80
Vane, William, Viscount, 91
Villiers, Col. Edward, 12n.
Vortigern, 150

Wade, John, 73
Wademarsh, 32–3, 35, 43, 45
Waghorne, Edward, 209
Waldershare Park, 126
Wall, Richard, 70–1
Waller, Edmund, 15, 27
Walmer, 17, 189, 194
Walter, Philadelphia, 89, 99
Waltham, 200
Walton, Mr., 107
Waltzer, M., 133
Wantsum, River, 35, 42
Ward, Goodwife, 80
        Sir Patience, 124
Wardroper, Thomas, 106
Ware, Capt. John, 21, 27
Warner, John, 27n.
Warwick, 70, 74, 152
Warwickshire, 108
Washlingstone hundred, 52
Watling Street, 52
Watson, Lewis, 91
Weldon, Sir Anthony, 18–19, 21, 104
        Col. Ralph, 18, 21–2
Wentworth, Sir George, 27n.
West, Benjamin, 142, 157
Westerham, 100, 201, 211
West Malling, 140, 144
Westmorland, Earl of, 91
West Wickham, 98–9, 101n., 190
Wheeler, R., 197n.
Whitby, 189
White, John, 209
        William, 199n.

LIST OF SUBSCRIBERS

Dr A.J. Allnutt
Dr A. Ashbee
Mr J.H. Ashdown

Mr R.A. Baldwin
Mrs. D. Beck
Rev. E.L.W. Bell
Mr L.W. Belton
Mr D.E. Bennett
Mr D.H. Bennett
Mr C.F. Burch
Mr J. Bynoe

Canterbury Archaeological Society
Christ Church College, Canterbury
Mr D.A.H. Cleggett
Mr M.G. Cook
Mrs. D. Coster
County Record Office, West Sussex
Mr D.S. Cousins
Mr R.S. Craig
Mr G.A. Cramp
Mr A. Cronk

Mr G.J. Davey
Dean and Chapter, Rochester Cathedral
Mr J. de Launay
Mr P.M. de Paris

Mrs N.R. Edwards
Dr F.G. Emmison

Mr W.E. Fairhead
Mr R.G. Finn-Kelcey
Mr R. Foster
Mr A.E. Furness

Mrs. I.P. Garrard
Mr H. Gough
Mr G.C.B. Gidley-Kitchin
Mr K.W.E. Gravett
Mrs. W.M. Griffiths
Mrs. W. Grimmette
Mr L.R.A. Grove

Mr D. Harrington
Mr H.A. Hanley
Mrs. D.L. Hartley
Mr R.H. Hiscock
Mr J.A. Hope
Dr N.P. Hudd
Dr T.P. Hudson
Mr R. Hutchings

Institute of Heraldic and Genealogical Studies

Mr D.A. Jeffery
Mr F.W. Jessup
Mrs. J. Jones

Mrs. J. Kelly
Mr E.G. Kemp
Mr D.H. Kennett
Kent County Library
Prof. L.A. Knafla
Mrs. P.E. Knowlden

Dr H.C.F. Lansberry
Mrs. M.T. Lawrence
Mr A. Lawton
Leeds Castle Foundation
Mr G. van Loo
Mr L.D. Lyle

Mr N.H. MacMichael
Mrs. D. McCall Smith
Miss K.M. McIntosh
Manchester Public Libraries
Miss E. Martin
Miss I.E. Morris
Mr P. Mussett

Mr J.A. Newman
Mr N. Nicolson

Miss A.M. Oakley
Mr P.E. Oldham
Mr and Mrs. A.E.B. Owen
Mr J. Owen

Mr A.J. Percival
Mr C. Powell-Cotton
Mrs. M. Priestley
Public Record Office

Mr B.C. Redwood
Miss K.M. Roome
Miss A. Roper
Mr A. Ruderman

Mr D.L. Sattin
Mr D.G. Scurrell
Mrs. J.L. Semple
Mrs. J.E. Sharp
Mr J.R.E. Sharp
Dr P.A. Slack
Mr A.D.W. Smith
Mr L.A. and Mrs. J. Smith
Mrs. M.J. Sparks

Mrs. E.A. Stazicker
Mrs. M. Stevens

Mr F.H.C. Tatham
Mr T.W.T. Tatton-Brown
Mrs. A. Thompson

University of Aberdeen, The Library
University of Birmingham, The Library
University of Leeds, Brotherton Library
University of London, Institute of Historical Research
University of Sussex, The Library

Mr D.E. Wickham
Canon B.J. Wigan
Dr J. Whyman
Miss Y. Williams
Sir John Winnifrith
Wye Historical Society